Best Wishes

C. Richard Gillespie

The James Adams Floating Theatre

Original Floating Theatre

26th ANNUAL TOUR

SHIP AHOY FOR JOY!

ANCHORS AWAY FOR HAPPINESS!

—BANK NITE—

$5.00 GIVEN AWAY

LAST NITE!

Ladies FREE Nite

ONE LADY ADMITTED FREE WITH 1 PAID ADULT TICKET

REMEMBER . . .
2 NIGHTS ONLY

25c AND 15c

DOORS OPEN 7:30
CURTAIN 8:15

LOOK—THE ONLY TRAVELING SHOW EQUIPPED WITH MODERN OIL HEATING — FORGET COLD WEATHER OUTSIDE — COME ABOARD FOR AN ENJOYABLE AND COMFORTABLE EVENING.

——OPENING PLAY——

She Knew What She Wanted

——AND——

Feature Concert and Marine Band!

—TOMORROW NIGHT FEATURING—

TEN NIGHTS IN A BAR ROOM

ALSO OUR BIG BANK NITE
$5.00 Absolutely Given Away
On Board The Old Show Boat
ONE PERSON MUST WIN
Don't Forget—We Carry 3 Tons of Special Scenery for TEN NIGHTS!

A SUPERB PRODUCTION OF T. S. ARTHUR'S IMMORTAL WORK

A portion of the herald for the 1939 season. Courtesy of the Curtis Showprint Company.

The James Adams Floating Theatre

By
C. Richard Gillespie

Tidewater Publishers

CENTREVILLE, MARYLAND

Library of Congress Cataloging-in-Publication Data

Gillespie, C. Richard
    The James Adams Floating Theatre / by C. Richard Gillespie. — 1st ed.
        p.   cm.
    Includes bibliographical references and index.
    ISBN 0-87033-416-6
      1. James Adams Floating Theatre—History. 2. Showboats—History.
  3. Theater—North Carolina—History—20th century. 4. Theater—
Chesapeake Bay Region (Md. and Va.)—History—20th century.
  5. Adams, James Even, 1873-1946.   I. Title.
PN2293.S4G5 1991
792'.022—dc20   91-11076
                                                             CIP

"The James Adams Floating Theatre: Edna Ferber's Showboat," by Michelle Francis (*Carolina Comments,* Vol. 28, No. 5), quoted with permission of North Carolina Division of Archives and History.

Charles M. Hunter's letters to Edna Ferber quoted with the permission of the State Historical Society of Wisconsin.

Numerous photographs, as captioned, courtesy of the Mariner's Museum, Newport News, Virginia; and the Chesapeake Bay Maritime Museum, St. Michaels, Maryland.

"Who's Who in This Issue," *Woman's Home Companion,* August 1926, quoted with the permission of the Edna Ferber Proprietors.

Manufactured in the United States of America
First edition

To Maravene, because our life together is rich in love,
joy, and the excitement of creative work

Contents

Foreword

Richard Gillespie has left no stone unturned in his pursuit of the history of the James Adams Floating Theatre, an enterprise that played a unique part in the world of American repertoire theatre. From James Adams's beginning career as a circus performer to the ignominious end of his showboat in a Georgia river in 1941, Dr. Gillespie takes us on a nostalgic cruise through the tidewaters of the East Coast in the days before movies and television jaded our appetites for the real thing: live drama. Maybe the sets weren't Hollywood, nor the performances Broadway, but to the patrons of the "Opry Barge" it was entertainment of the first water—no pun intended.

For the first time, the *real* story of the James Adams Floating Theatre is being told. When the novelist Edna Ferber spent a few days aboard in the early twenties to gain background for a book she wanted to write—the now-famous *Show Boat*—the Floating Theatre was little known outside of the Chesapeake Bay and coastal North Carolina. The sudden success of Ferber's novel, which soon became a movie and then a Jerome Kern musical, reflected some of its glory onto Adams's theatre, unfortunately in a distorted form. It obscured the real James Adams with publicity that was a parody of the book.

In the fifty years since it sank, many newspaper and magazine articles have been written about the Floating Theatre. The articles run the gamut from merely inaccurate to totally ludicrous. A recent gem that appeared in the Elizabeth City, North Carolina, newspaper during the city's annual Riverspree—a festival that is supposed to commemorate the Floating Theatre—stated that the audience hissed the villain and threw cabbages and tomatoes at the stage. In light of such reporting, Richard Gillespie's book is not only factual, but timely. With the zest of a real historian and uncommon insight, he has sifted through what must be tons of material to present this account of Adams's showboat, in its own right a far more interesting story than the one Ferber wrote.

This book is much more than its name implies. It is also a fascinating study of the repertoire movement in America in the early twentieth century; an exploration into the development of various character parts that make up a theatre troupe; and a touching, funny, poignant story of the Adams family. Their life and experiences in show business read like a movie scenario. It's all there: love and romance, success, fame, then hard times, lies and deception, revenge, and final defeat. Their years touring the Chesapeake Bay on the marvelous Floating Theatre were the happy ones, and it perhaps was the memory of these good times that sustained them through the rough seas that subsequently lay ahead.

I grew up in Elizabeth City, North Carolina, in the 1920s, with the Floating Theatre—then in its heyday—an exciting backdrop to my life. My father, Leslie Waldorf, was one of the early troupers. He joined in 1915, the theatre's second season, as pianist in the orchestra and trombone player in the band. He stayed for three years, but his friendship with the Adamses and other longtime members of the company was deep and lasting; they were an extension of my family. I was a stand-in child for these people who had none of their own, and the warm love they gave me made me feel very special. I loved them back with great devotion. I find it hard to tell about them without going overboard with lavish praise. I hope that's not another pun.

There was Beulah Adams, leading lady and my idol; her husband, Charlie Hunter, the troupe's creative force; Selba and Clara Adams, managers; and Carl "Pop" Neel, who stayed forever and was as much a part of the boat as its timbers. They were the constant around which the ever-changing cast revolved and the nucleus of my "family." They were dear friends, wonderful companions, and, despite criticism from those who looked askance at all show folk as riffraff, they were decent, moral people with great integrity who were generous to their detractors. They were proud of the high standard of entertainment they presented and took brickbats as well as bouquets with equal equanimity.

For many years Elizabeth City was the home of the Floating Theatre. I remember the excitement of seeing everyone when the company came in the spring for rehearsals. My family was considered "déclassé" by some in the community because we attended the shows, hobnobbed with the players, and had noisy parties at our house with the troupe late at night. On opening night I could hardly wait for the curtain to go up. When I was too young to stay up for the performance, Clara and Selba put me to bed in a drawer of their bureau in the apartment behind the balcony. When I was older I was allowed not only to stay up for the show but also for the party after the show. I never understood why people in the community thought the theatre people were immoral. My grandmother was a lady with strict Victorian principles who ruled us all and tried to shield me from what she called the "rough elements" of life. If there had been any shady doings on the showboat, she never would have allowed me to set foot on it. A few people even knew the actors drank beer at the parties—and during Prohibition yet! In actual fact it was a sort of "home brew" that my grandmother and Clara Adams made from an old German recipe. The noise was my Dad playing the piano while Beulah and some of the others sang, and the laughter following Charlie's outrageous stories. If music and laughter were sins, I guess we were the worst of it.

They all loved to tell stories. They had a wealth of inside jokes, running gags, stage bloopers, and traveling mishaps, not to mention one-liners that probably came from old skits. Charlie's stories of his adventures even had a ring of truth now and then. With new members of the company each year came new stories to join the flood of old stories we loved to hear over and over. With typical childish candor I even furnished them with a few. Once they referred to someone as being "related by marriage." I remarked that I was related to my mother and father by marriage, and everyone laughed hysterically. I didn't think it was funny. It made sense to me. But there was never any malice in their laughter; somehow I was made to feel that I had said something very witty. Charlie used to say I didn't know I was a kid; I just thought I was short. There was double-barreled humor in this. All of the Adamses were short; so were Pop Neel and Eddie Paull. By the time I was ten I was as tall as everyone but Charlie, who was nearly six feet if he stood up straight. He said he was stoop-shouldered from talking to his in-laws.

At the end of the season, when the boat returned to Elizabeth City for the winter, there was a big closing night party. Clara Adams and my grandmother would cook all day, usually Italian spaghetti or Clara's delicious Chinese chow mein. The company would gather for one last evening of music and story telling before going their separate ways for the winter. Living as they did on the water for most of the year, some of the stories involved boats on the Chesapeake Bay. There is one (true, by the way) that should be preserved. I remember it because it was always retold to new members of the company, and it concerned people I knew.

There was a man in Elizabeth City who owned a cargo vessel named for his wife. He was carrying a load of lumber up the lower Chesapeake to a town on the Piankatank River in Virginia. It was the custom of ships passing each other to call out and identify themselves. It was even more important on foggy nights to keep them a safe distance apart.

The skipper of the second vessel hailed the first: "Ahoy, who goes there?"

The answer: The *Annie Crank!*

Who's the skipper?

Thomas Crank!

Where's she from?
Pasquotank!
Where's she bound?
Piankatank!
What's her cargo?
Pine plank!

After a few seconds the skipper of the second vessel, convinced he was being kidded, shouted after the departing *Annie Crank,* "Go to hell!"

The actors loved this story. They acted it out, shouting across the room, cupped hands held like megaphones.

The old tales seem flat on paper, but they came alive with laughter when they were fleshed out by the talents of the show people. They made a vivid impression on me. Even today I see things on television that I first saw in those early years, and I realize that entertainment hasn't changed that much after all. Beulah and Charlie and the others are gone now, but their art is very much alive, although confined too often to a small box in our living rooms.

I am very honored and grateful to be part of this story. Contributing my happy childhood memories and impressions to this book has given me enormous pleasure. Perhaps the greatest satisfaction of all is knowing that Richard Gillespie, through many years of painstaking research, has found the real "Original Showboat"—the one Edna Ferber and subsequent writers lost.

As my friend Selb Adams would say as you crossed the gangplank: Welcome aboard!

Maisie Waldorf Comardo
November, 1989
Leicester, New York

Preface

*T*wo compulsions in my life are theatre and the Chesapeake Bay. This history of the James Adams Floating Theatre is a natural product of the two compulsions.

I was born and raised in the Baltimore, Maryland, area. As a young boy in the late 1930s I lived on the Severn River. I saw my first professional theatre production in Ford's Theatre in Baltimore when I was nine. I was ten when the Floating Theatre made its last visit to the Bay. Unfortunately, at the time I did not know that the Floating Theatre existed.

The only showboat I ever visited was Bill Menke's *Goldenrod*. The boat was moored permanently at the riverfront in St. Louis. I was in college nearby, studying to become an actor. I went several times, with a group of aspiring Thespians, to see performances there. We found it an irresistible challenge to our youthful cleverness to match wits with the performers. That was the point. The audience tried to top the actors with wisecracks. We always lost. They were too good for us.

The experiences were not good preparation for a study of an important and neglected period in American theatre. I had come too late to witness the essence of the period, which had, for the most part, dried up years before I boarded the *Goldenrod*.

But one performance I saw on the *Goldenrod* sticks in my memory even now, after seeing and participating in professional, university, and community theatre for forty years. That was Menke's version of *Hamlet*. At the time I saw the performance I was preparing to play Laertes in a college production of Shakespeare's play. I took my work seriously. I didn't want to surrender to the *Goldenrod*'s nonsense, but I could not help it.

The premise of Menke's version was that a social do-gooder decides to bring culture to the deprived inmates of a prison. She is surprised to discover that all the actors want to play the grave diggers. The fun of the play lies in the confusion of the rehearsals—great fun with the potential foolishness in Shakespeare's plot and characters—while the "grave diggers" dig an escape tunnel under the prison walls. I have since seen other productions of *Hamlet*, including Albert Finney's at the National Theatre in London; I have acted in the play and I have directed it. But the production that still stands paramount in my memory is the one I saw on the *Goldenrod*.

I have sailed on the Chesapeake since as a young boy I rigged a homemade sail and leeboards on a borrowed canoe. Over the years, I have explored most of the rivers and creeks that border that great estuary, from Cape Charles to the Chesapeake and Delaware Canal. Sometime early in my journeys I encountered tales of the showboat that played the Chesapeake. For understandable reasons, the stories fascinated me.

In 1970 I began seriously to research the subject. I wrote to Beulah Adams in Saginaw, Michigan. She was gracious in her reply, but suggested that she could not be of much help to me. At the time I did not know enough to ask her the right questions.

A growing theatre program at the university and other projects interfered, and I laid aside my research. I picked it up again in the fall of 1987 when I took a much-delayed sabbatical from teaching. Unfortunately, in the intervening seventeen years many people, including Beulah, who could have shone great light on the subject, were gone.

The two years (1987 to 1989) that I spent researching and writing this book were a time of great delight. I was amazed at the resources available. I traveled to fifteen states in search of the Floating Theatre. I met hundreds of people who helped me find my way through the scattered remains of information. I was excited and buoyed by the eagerness of their responses, and I was moved by the depth of good feeling that remains in the hearts of those who watched the entertainments on the Floating Theatre and waited each year for its return. I hope that in this history I have caught some of the mystique that surrounded the Floating Theatre and that I have done reasonable justice to a complex subject.

To acknowledge all the people who have helped me with this project is impossible. There are many whose names I do not know: librarians who helped me solve the mysteries of antique microfilm readers; courthouse clerks who interpreted filing systems that were incomprehensible to me; people on the street who directed me to destinations that were no longer where the map indicated I should find them; and good Samaritans who suggested people I should interview or sites I should visit, many taking the time to guide me in person to a potential source of information.

There are a few people to whom I owe a special debt of gratitude: Maisie Waldorf Comardo, who shared with me her love of the Adams family and the Floating Theatre, who helped me navigate many tricky narrows in interpreting information I uncovered, and who graciously wrote the introduction to this book; Robert H. Burgess, who shared with me his ency-clopedic knowledge of the tidewater area and prevented me from making some embarrassing errors; Rachel Seymoure Marsh, who shared her mem-ories of the last eight years of the Floating Theatre; members of the Adams and Struble families—Dr. James B. Adams, Mr. and Mrs. George B. Davies, Vivian O'Leary, Robert Struble, and Marguerite Young—who shared with me not only their memories of the showboat folks, but also pictures and family memorabilia; Caroline Schaffner and Dr. William L. Slout, who guided me into the fascinating world of repertoire theatre; Al Gough, Jr., who helped me un-cover the mystery of the Floating Theatre in Leonardtown; Gerald Bordman, who took time from his own writing to guide me through the intricacies of the secondary theatre of America; Nyle Stateler, who made available showboat posters from the Curtis Showprint Company; James Pickett, who drew the maps for the book; the reference and interlibrary loan librarians at the Cook Library at Towson State University—especially Robert Shouse, Susan Mower, Marcella Fultz, and Sharon Mollock—who responded efficiently and with good spirits to my many needs; and to my wife, Maravene S. Loeschke, who not only encouraged me but endured with good spirits my many long ab-sences from home while I was away sailing in the wake of the Floating Thea-tre.

I owe special thanks to Robert H. Burgess, Maisie Comardo, Mar-guerite Young, Caroline Schaffner, William Slout, Robert Struble, Al Gough, Jr., Gerald Bordman, Maravene Loeschke, Jacques Kelly, and Aumelia Sheppard for reading drafts of the manuscript. I thank them for their cor-rections and encouragement. Any remaining errors of fact are solely my responsibility.

I am most grateful, also, to the Faculty Research Committee of Tow-son State University for the grants which helped to finance the research on the Floating Theatre.

Space does not permit me to acknowledge the specific assistance of all the people who helped me with this project. In the list that follows, I am certain I have left out names that should be there. I apologize. It is not inten-tional. It is an oversight caused by an overloading of my memory circuits.

In alphabetical order, my thanks go to: Dewey Ambos, Alethia An-derson, Dr. Joseph Arnold, Eloise Baily, Sarah L. Barley, Mose Basnight, Trude Bazeman, John Beale, Irvin Beauchamp, JoAnn Becker, Doris Berry, Paul Berry, Ester Blanchard, Dr. William Bodenstein, David Bohaska, Don Bollman, Mrs. John Bond, Kathryn Braig, Helen Bridges, Laura Brown, Teresa Brummett, Sue Bunch, Ann Lewis Burrows, Gerald Butler, Marilyn Carlon, Catherine Carter, John Christian, Kevin Clark, Melissa Clark, Don-ald Cleaton, W. A. Cleaton, Harold Cline, Louis Collins Jr., Mr. and Mrs. Walter Cooling, Nancy Cooper, Paul Couch, Robert Couch, Tom Crew, Carolyn Crowder, Billy Culpepper, Carter G. Culpepper, Peter Curtis,

Segar Cofer Dashiell, Campbell Dawson, Kermit Deboard, Mr. And Mrs. Charles Deshazo, Fielding Lewis Dickinson, Lee Disharoon, Furman Dixon, Dr. Richard J. S. Dodds, Dr. Arno Drucker, Ruth Drucker, Geraldine Duclow, Elaine Ebo, Robert Ellis, Dr. Ralph Eshelman, Dr. Dean Esslinger, Clarence Evans, Marian Everett, Anna W. Ewalt, Muriel Ewing, Fred Fearing, Charles Fenwick, Ann Flanagan, Goeffrey M. Footner, Dr. Michael Framme, Kiki Freer-Parsons, Margaret K. Fresco, Shannon Gallagher, Dorothy Gardiner, Stuart Gardner, Gloria Gateway, Patricia C. Geeseon, Richard B. Gerrish, Mildred Gibbs, Julie Goldsmith Gilbert, Irvin Glazer, Dr. George D. Glenn, Carlista Golden, Don Green, George Grim, Toni Gutwein, Rick Hall, Harry Hamilton, Irene Hamlin, Evelyn Adams Hammlett, Dr. H. Joanne Harrar, Carl Harrell, Mrs. Bleeker Harrison, Mrs. Walter Hartridge, Florence Mayo Haynie, Miriam Haynie, Linda Higgins, Nancy Hughes, Doris Humphries, Phyllis Hurd, Robert Hurry, Eleanor Insolo, Paula Johnson, Willard Jones, Jacques Kelly, Elizabeth Killam, Peggy Langley, Pepper Langley, Heber Latham, Jean Lerche, Gillian Lewis, Russel Lewis, Arrington Littleton, Effie Lucas, Peggy Lugthart, Mrs. Mason Lumpkin, Becky Luton, Katherine Maloney, Leon Massey, Nelson H. McCall, Shirley McClellan, Dr. James McCullum, Donald McDaniel, Joseph C. Mcguire, Robert N. McKenney, Dawn Meisel, P. D. Midget, Harold L. Miller, Betty Moll, Charlie Moore, Margaret Morgan, Dorothy Mortensen, Carolyn Mulligan, Ed Newton, Donna Nichol, Paul Nichols, Scotti Oliver, Martha Tell Oyler, June Parker, Norris Parks, Tra Perry, Nelle Pitman, Margaret B. Reid, Vernon and Dorothy Reynolds, Robert L. Roberts, Jr., Rip Rouzie, Lisa Royse, Joan Scarlotto, Virmardel and Elizabeth Schriner, Billie Henderson Schuler, Raymond Sheely, Nelson S. Sherman, R. S. Spencer, Martha Spruill, Phil Sterling, Barbara E. Taylor, Maravene Taylor, Edwin Thomas, Jack Tucker, Billie Turley, Andrew Velcoff, Michael Voss, William Wall, Don Walls, Miller Warren, James Watson, John Watson, Jennette Westerfield, James Wharton, Dorothy Wheeler, Karen Wible, John Wilson, Thomas Wood.

The James Adams Floating Theatre

CHAPTER ONE

Here Comes the Showboat!

MONDAY, AUGUST 9, 1926

*T*here were two of them in a 1922 Ford. Both were thin. Both wore glasses, but one was tall and lanky and the other was short and wiry. The first place they stopped was at the office of the Northern Neck *News* in Warsaw, Virginia. As soon as they got out of the car, people greeted them.

"I hear you're in Bundicks this week," a man called after them. "Are you gonna play Mt. Holly this year?"

"Yep. Next week," the taller man answered.

"I'll catch 'er there," the local answered.

Everyone on the street recognized the tall visitor. He was Charlie Hunter, the director and character man from The James Adams Floating Theatre, and more importantly, Beulah's husband. Beulah Adams was the star of the showboat, and had been as long as most people could remember. Some claimed she had been the star since day one, but others claimed differently.

"Nope," one old-timer argued. "When they first came, back in 1914, she wasn't on the boat." Others argued she was, but the old-timer stuck to his guns. "They didn't play in these parts in those days," he corrected. "But they played down at Irvington, and I saw the show, and Beulah wasn't there. She came later."

"And she wasn't on the boat in 1920, either," argued a younger man. "That was the first time I saw the show in Mt. Holly, and I remember she wasn't there. The first time I saw her was in 1921."

People loved to argue about who was and who wasn't on the boat and when, but one thing was certain. Beulah, "the Mary Pickford of the Chesapeake," was the star.

While Charlie talked to the people congregating around him in front of the newspaper office, the shorter man went inside to place the ad for the next week. He was Eddie Paull, the blackface comedian and xylophonist on the boat. The people greeted him courteously. He was new with the theatre this year but anyone with the Floating Theatre was a celebrity. He wasn't greeted with the enthusiasm reserved for Charlie. After all, Charlie was married to Beulah.

"I'm glad you're not as late this year as you were last," someone remarked to Charlie. "Last year," he complained, "we had the dickens of a time getting the kids to school after the shows. It's better if you come while they're still on vacation."

"Didn't play so long in North Carolina this spring," Charlie explained.

"That's a good decision," the local responded. "It's better to get up here in Virginia where you're appreciated."

"Can't argue with that," Charlie agreed.

"I thought that book that woman wrote about showboats was about your boat," another complained. "You know, the one running in the *Women's Home Companion*?"

"Well, she wrote it on our boat, last year in North Carolina," Charlie answered.

"But her boat's out on the Mississippi."

"I know that," Charlie agreed. "But she wrote it in North Carolina. If you read it carefully, you can find some of us in it."

"Who is she, anyway?" somebody else asked. "I never heard of her."

"She won the Pulitzer Prize a couple of years back for a novel she wrote." When the listener just shook his head in confusion, Charlie explained further, "She wrote the Emma McChesney stories in the *American Magazine,* about the traveling saleslady."

When Eddie Paull returned from the newspaper office and they could politely get free of their well-wishers, Charlie and Eddie got back in the car and drove over to Montross, the county seat of Westmoreland County. They stopped by the post office to drop off a pile of heralds.

What show people call heralds other people might call handbills, flyers, or posters. For the Floating Theatre they were printed on lightweight colored stock about 8¾ by 11¾ inches. There were facts and pictures about the theatre on both sides. The heralds were printed before the season. For years the showboat had been using the Curtis Showprint Company in Continental, Ohio, to do the big printing. There was space on the heralds to print the date and place of the showboat's current stand. That was done locally. Selba Adams, Jim Adams's brother and the business manager of the Floating Theatre, got the dates and places for the Northern Neck added when they were playing in Tappahannock. Selb didn't like to get the local printing done too early, because he didn't like wasting heralds if the route was changed unexpectedly.

Charlie had been talking to Selb about using larger heralds in the future. Jim Adams didn't like putting a lot of money into advertising and Selb was tighter with a dollar than Jim, but Charlie felt that by using larger paper, doubling the size they were now using, they could get more pictures on the herald and list the bill for the full week. Charlie argued that more information would make the heralds worth more and would be a better bargain in the long run. Charlie felt Selb was listening to him and that there might be a change in 1927.

Charlie and Eddie talked a while with the postmaster and left a pile of heralds with him. The postmaster opened a stack and began to stick them in the mailboxes.

"No matinee?" he asked.

"Nope," Charlie answered. "Just evenings."

"Too bad," the clerk responded. "My kids used to always go to the matinee on Saturday when you had it."

"Bring 'em at night," Charlie answered. "We never do a show you can't bring your wife and kids to."

Next Charlie and Eddie stopped by the telephone office. The business that brought them there was arranging for the telephone next week for the box office on the boat, but when their business was done, they left a few heralds with the telephone operator and gave her a list of the bill for the week. They knew she would get the information out. In some of the small towns the operator would put out a line call and give out the bill when the people picked up their phones. That wouldn't happen here. Montross was too big a town and too far from where the boat docked. Mt. Holly, where the boat docked, really wasn't a town. It was just the closest the boat could get to Montross.

After a few more social stops, Charlie and Eddie drove over to the ferry dock at Mt. Holly to check on the docking for the next week, gave some passes to kids to post heralds, and then headed down the peninsula to Bundick on the Coan River.

As they drove from Mt. Holly to Bundick, Charlie and Eddie talked about how easy it was doing the advance work for the Floating Theatre. Charlie reminded Eddie it hadn't always been that way. As they drove they talked about the old times.

When Jim Adams started with his Floating Theatre he had had to work a lot harder to get the people out. He wanted audiences, but he didn't want to encourage other people to get into the business in competition. Jim's experience in carnivals and vaudeville had been that when you had an idea going that made for good business, you soon had rivals trying to take that business away from you. Jim was publicity shy. He looked for ways to publicize his showboat in as local a way as he could. Initially, he was reluctant to buy ads in the local papers, but he soon found that local ads, particularly in the weeklies, were essential. Jim preferred the weeklies over the dailies when there was a choice, because he got a bigger ad for his money and because people tended to let the weeklies lie around the house longer than they did the dailies.

Jim found early that the arrival of the boat itself was his best publicity. The circuses announced their arrival in town with a parade, and an important part of the parade was the band. Many of the traveling theatres did the same. In the early days Jim augmented his show orchestra—usually five or six pieces—with actors and crew members who could play, put them in fancy band uniforms, and had them playing on top of the Floating Theatre when it pulled into the wharf. When the theatre was docked in a town, he had the band play concerts in the town square, and when the theatre was docked in a rural area, such as Bundick or Mt. Holly, Jim put the band on a tug and toured the nearby rivers and creeks. But by 1926 they didn't have to do that any more. The people kept track of the boat now, as it worked its way up the Bay, and were expecting it when it arrived. The kids were always hanging around the wharf waiting for the theatre hours before it hove into sight. They fought to take the mooring lines from the deckhands.

Eddie recalled a manager of a tent theatre he had worked for who put every available body from the troupe in his band and pulled his band around the town in a wagon. If an actor couldn't play, he held an instrument and faked it. The manager wanted the townspeople to think his tent had the biggest band of any tent show they had ever seen. Jim never did that, Charlie explained. Jim was less worried about the size of the band than the quality. Always, as far back as Charlie remembered—and Charlie started with Jim as a musician back before Jim even had his vaudeville show, back when he ran a circus—Jim had good music. They don't know bad acting, Jim insisted, but they know bad music.

Jim had other tricks up his sleeve as well. In the early days he got a list of automobile owners from local garages and sent each owner a free ticket to the Floating Theatre. Jim figured, correctly, that the automobile owners would bring their family or friends—paying customers—with them. And they did.

When Charlie and Eddie got back to Bundick they saw Harry Delaney's car parked by the Floating Theatre. The car looked almost as good as new. The garage at Reedville did a pretty good job on it. Two weeks earlier, when the Delaneys and some other performers with the theatre were driving from Kilmarnock to Reedville, they banged into a car driven by Harry Covington of Burgess Store. Harry Delaney was driving pretty fast, for a dirt road, and Mr. Covington didn't stop to look before he came out of his lane. The folks from the theatre were only shaken, but Mr. Covington banged his head up pretty badly. Monday Beulah took him some flowers and Selb sent along one of Aggie's stuffed hams.

SUNDAY, AUGUST 15, 1926

The theatre played its last performance in Bundick on Saturday evening. Because the trip from the Coan River to the Nomini River was a relatively short one—about twenty-five miles—the boat didn't leave until the middle of Sunday afternoon. There was time for everyone to go to church on Sunday morning, and a number of the performers and crew took advantage of the opportunity. The troupe traveled so often on Sunday mornings that most had gotten out of the habit of church, and it was pleasant to go for a change.

Sunday morning through Monday night was the biggest break the cast and orchestra got between performances and as often as possible they would be out in their automobiles—which they drove from port to port—on sight-seeing trips. But most were saving their sight-seeing for an overnight trip to Washington, D.C., later when the theatre was at Leonardtown or Solomons, Maryland, the closest they would get to the Capital. That was the last chance of the season for the women. After Solomons the theatre crossed the Bay to the Eastern Shore where there would be hunting and fishing for the men, but no big city shopping for the women. At least not until they got to Chesapeake City, where Jim kept his yacht, and the women could get into Philadelphia. They all liked going to Philadelphia because that was where Jim and Gertie lived, and they always put on a good feed for visitors from the showboat.

On Sunday afternoon, while the James Adams Floating Theatre was being pulled by its tugs from Bundick to Mt. Holly, most of the performers drove to Kilmarnock, where the theatre had played two weeks earlier, and went swimming at Whitestone Beach. The week at Bundick had been terrible for the heat. One of the hottest spells in memory, the locals claimed. But by Sunday afternoon a cold front mercifully passed through the area and the showboat people drove from Kilmarnock to Nomini through heavy rain.

As they topped the hill at Mt. Holly and started down the slope to the ferry dock, they saw through the haze the big white form of the Floating Theatre, looking every bit like a long, flat-topped, floating barn, safely moored on the other side of the creek. As they got closer they could make out the forms of the usual gang of urchins going in and out of the theatre, carrying water to fill the big barrels in the galley and cleaning up in and around the auditorium. For these and other tasks Selb gave them passes to the concerts.

MONDAY, AUGUST 16, 1926

Joe and Aggie, the black cooks, got breakfast started Monday morning at nine, but most people didn't bother to get up until about ten. The bread man arrived at nine-thirty, lugged his twenty-five loaves of bread past the sleeping roustabouts scattered along the auditorium aisles. He passed through the orchestra pit in front of the stage, ducked through the low doorway, and stepped down into the galley under the stage. The leeward ports were open, but the humidity from the steady rain outside and the smoke from bacon, eggs, and pancakes frying on the big cookstove turned the low-ceilinged room into a steam bath.

"I got a beautiful pound cake today, Aggie," he claimed. "Put a little fruit and some cream on it, and you got a dessert fit for an opera singer."

"Get out of here with your store-bought baking," Aggie responded with mock seriousness. "Any cake's going to be baked around here, I'm doing the baking!"

"Where's Captain Selba?" he asked.

"Captain Selba ain't buying your cakes," Aggie responded vehemently. "He runs the boat, but he don't run my kitchen!"

Just then Beulah wandered in, her eyes still filled with sleep, her hair tied up in little rags.

"He's not trying to sell you cakes," Beulah, with a wink, explained to Aggie. "He's just making conversation until someone offers him a pass for tonight."

"If it's OK," he responded apologetically.

"Of course it's OK. You just sit down and have some breakfast, and when Charlie gets up he'll give you a pair."

One by one the other members of the cast and crew wandered in. Most were dressed still in their nightclothes, the women with their hair still up or in braids. Some of the women had taken time to throw on a light robe, but the heat of the galley argued against dressing. Some of the men had cut the pants legs off their pajamas just above the knee.

The milkman arrived. He rolled in his big cans of fresh milk and was rewarded for his efforts with breakfast and two passes.

By ten o'clock the theatre was alive with activity. The usual joking and teasing filled the galley and overflowed into the auditorium and out on the decks under the overhang where people took their food to escape the heat. Mary Delaney and Ann Keyes continued their feud. They sat at opposite ends of the dining table, neither speaking to the other. Their husbands went out on the deck where they could shake their heads in amazement at the women's stubbornness.

"Beats me," said Mary's husband, Harry. "She won't even tell me what started it."

"Who cares?" responded Lewis, who enjoyed Ann's occasional silences.

The rain put a damper on plans for the day. There definitely would be no wiener roast for lunch. Things had been hectic for the past few weeks, anyway. The towns on the Rappahannock—Urbanna, Tappahannock, Port Royal—were party towns. Everyone needed a little rest before Leonard-town and Solomons. At Solomons there was a dance every night at the pavilion, whereas the only thing that ever happened at Mt. Holly was the

Saturday night dance at Mt. Holly House. The boys in the band would be hired to play, if the neighborhood kids planning the dance could get the money together.

Around noon the iceman arrived and lugged four hundred pounds of ice to the galley icebox, a hundred pounds at a time in a canvas bag balanced on his thick shoulders. He was too late for breakfast but was rewarded for his efforts with the usual two passes.

During the rainy Monday the showboat people settled down to domesticity. Some did laundry. Others wrote letters. Some played cribbage or pinochle. It was safe to play pinochle because Jim Adams wasn't there, and there was a chance for someone else to win. At four o'clock they had lunch. Aggie and Joe served a light meal because of the heat: fried chicken, cold roast beef, fresh vegetables, and fresh applesauce.

Fewer customers stopped by the box office than usual, but by lunch, Selb was satisfied it would be a good opening despite the rain. The telephone had been ringing all day, they had sold a lot of season tickets the year before, and ladies' night always helped. On Mondays ladies got in free when accompanied by a paying customer.

All afternoon, boats of all sizes arrived in the creek. A few of the larger vessels, owned by old friends of Jim, Selb, and Charlie, tied up beside the theatre. Others anchored in the creek and at show time rowed their tenders through the rain to the wharf. Later in the afternoon, the smaller boats arrived: fishing boats pushed along by noisy one-lungers, the passengers huddled under small awnings; and runabouts with outboard motors, the passengers holding umbrellas. There were a few hardy souls dressed in oilskins who rowed dinghies, and one gentleman with a white beard paddled up to the showboat in a canoe.

The auditorium was hot. The electric fans didn't help much. Despite the rain, the outside temperature was still in the eighties. There was no breeze, and the humidity was oppressive. There didn't seem to be much chance that darkness would pull the temperature down, and the heat from the stage lighting would more than compensate for whatever drop there was. The orchestra decided not to wear their uniforms for the evening performance, and Selb didn't object. The actors were frustrated because their makeup kept melting and running.

There was a steady stream of customers in raincoats and umbrellas hurrying over the gangplank and past Selb's warm greeting from where he stood near the box office informally dressed in dark trousers and white shirt. The audience entered through the center doors and filed down the aisles to their seats. Children raced about the rows visiting long-lost friends they hadn't seen since the day before. A few blacks climbed the stairs to the balcony. A bunch of white teenagers went up with them. The whites sat in the front rows. They claimed they could see better from there than from the main floor. In some places Selb worried about mixing black and white in the balcony, but not at Mt. Holly. There were never any problems at Mt. Holly.

At seven-thirty the orchestra started the preshow concert. The only thing visible on the stage was the oleo, the painted picture curtain that served the Floating Theatre as its front curtain. On the oleo there was an oval picture of a huge urn filled with flowers with mountains in the background. Around the edges of the curtain were painted advertisements for local establishments. Some were for merchants in Elizabeth City or other regular stops for the showboat; some were for local merchants in Montross or the Nomini area. These had been painted that day by Jim Wilson, the scene painter who followed the Floating Theatre about in his own boat. Other local ads were tacked on the walls beside the stage.

Partway through the band concert the curtain rolled up to reveal a movie screen. One of the crew projected slides from the balcony onto the screen. The slides were pictures illustrating the songs the band played, not the words of the songs. There was no need to project the words—everyone knew them. During the slide presentation, Beulah Adams, already in costume for her role that evening, came on stage to the right of the screen. The audience greeted her with shouts of "Hi, Beulah," and rousing applause. Beulah waved back and blew the audience kisses. The orchestra, which had paused for her entrance, picked up the beat again, and Beulah led everyone in singing the songs they all knew.

As they enjoyed the music and the pictures, many of the audience crunched the peanuts and sipped the lemonade they had bought on the way in. By the time the band ended a medley of weather songs with the hopeful "Blue Skies," there wasn't a spot left on the parking lot that wasn't deep in mud.

Because of the problems the audience had faced with the weather, Charlie delayed the curtain, letting the band play longer than usual. No one in the auditorium complained.

At 8:07 the slides stopped and the heavy green act curtain slid shut from each side of the stage. Behind it, unseen by the audience, the movie screen rolled up. The stage lights came up and Charlie Hunter, dressed for his role in the play, stepped through the center break in the act curtain and, holding onto the edge of it to mark his exit, greeted his audience. He welcomed them all to the Floating Theatre's thirteenth season. In this case, he assured them, thirteen was a lucky number. He mentioned each of the actors in the company, reminding the audience of their favorites returning from the year before and assuring them that the new folks were the best there were in the business. He introduced the band, asking for a special hand for the cornet player, Pop Neel, who was in his twelfth year with the showboat. "Only Captain Jim himself has been with the Floating Theatre longer," Charlie explained. He described the plays the showboat was performing that week, urging people to get tickets during the intermissions to the ones they didn't already have. He invited everyone to the concert after the play. "It is a humdinger this year," he assured them. "It's only fifteen cents, and don't any of you kids hide under the seats trying to get in free," he warned, "because this year we have a magician on board who will turn you all into frogs if you do." Charlie concluded by asking the audience to thank the performers with their applause if they liked what they saw and heard. As he ducked back behind the curtain, the audience's appreciative applause followed him.

The curtain opened for the first act of *Judy O'Grady.*

Beulah and Charlie played the kind of parts everyone loved them in. Charlie was onstage when the curtain opened. He was "hard boiled Dennis O'Grady," a self-made, rich, cantankerous Irishman, who trusted no one and argued with his wife, Rosie, who didn't want him to forget their humble beginnings. Ten minutes into the act Beulah entered as the wisecracking younger daughter who had her father's gumption and her mother's unspoiled sweetness. The applause for Beulah's entrance stopped the play for a few moments while she modestly acknowledged her admirers' praise.

The play was a mystery-comedy. The older daughter, Margaret, was in love with a stuffy English nobleman, Reginald Wellington, and Judy was in love with the family chauffeur, Jimmy Maloney. The question was which suitor was the thief intent on stealing the jewels O'Grady lavished on his wife. By the end of the first act, matters were totally confusing. There were reasons to distrust both men.

The curtain closed for the intermission and opened again on the movie screen upon which now were projected advertisements for local merchants.

Charlie stepped in front of the screen and waved at the audience in appreciation for their response. As the applause died, he addressed them again.

"I thank you for all the actors," he said. "They most surely do appreciate your kindness. But what really brings me here," he continued, "is to warn you about some unscrupulous musicians. They are going to try to stick you with some bad bargains."

Charlie had no more than finished his warning when three or four of the orchestra members entered the auditorium with bundles of Cracker Jack boxes. Others laid out prizes along the front of the stage.

"Ten cents," they shouted. "For ten cents you get a prize in every box. Wholesome Cracker Jacks and a prize in every box!"

Charlie continued with his warnings. He explained that he had tried to stop the musicians, but that they outnumbered him. The best he could do was to warn the audience to be on their guard. "You're going to spend your money and be disappointed," he cautioned.

11

But even as he was speaking a man in the third row pulled a pair of women's underpants from his Cracker Jacks box, and everyone who saw it dissolved in convulsions of laughter. A woman in the back stood up and waved a piece of cardboard. "I won a set of dishes," she yelled and worked her way out of her row and down the aisle to the stage to claim her prize. She was followed a few minutes later by a young boy who came forward to claim his cuckoo clock.

Charlie continued with his warnings, but to no avail. He argued that there could not possibly be any more prizes of value left, but the words were not out of his mouth before someone pulled some ladies' lingerie from a box. By the end of the intermission Charlie had lost the battle. There was barely a seat in the house that did not hold someone munching on candied popcorn. The first ten minutes of the second act was marred a bit by kids testing out their newly won whistles and birdcalls.

By the end of the second act of the play, the appearance of additional conspirators had complicated the plot even more. The only thing the audience was certain of was that they were having a wonderful time laughing at the shenanigans of the performers and trying to guess who was the real thief.

The second intermission was a variation on the first.

When the final curtain closed everyone was satisfied. The likable young Jimmy Maloney proved to be a G-man in disguise. Reginald Wellington's manservant proved to be the elusive jewel thief Velvet Harry, whom Jimmy had been chasing for years. Only Margaret was upset when Jimmy proved that Reginald was in cahoots with Velvet Harry.

At the end of the play, Charlie stepped forward again and thanked everyone for coming and for their warm response to the actors.

"At ten o'clock," he announced, "the concert will start. It is the best concert we have ever carried," he assured his listeners. "You won't want to miss it. For those of you who don't have your tickets yet, the box office is open. For those of you who have tickets and don't want to go out into the rain to wait, the orchestra will entertain you while the ushers collect your tickets. To those of you who are not staying for the concert, we thank you for coming to the play and look forward to seeing you again this week." And again Charlie went quickly through the showboat's offerings for the rest of the week.

At ten o'clock the concert began. It was a typical vaudeville presentation of specialties and bits lasting about forty-five minutes.

The singers were good and the audience appreciated them. They especially liked Beulah and called her back for an encore. But the hit of the show was the blackface comic, little Eddie Paull.

As Eddie was finishing a comic xylophone solo, an actress planted in the audience called to Eddie, "These peanuts you-all sold me ain't no good. You got no pecans [pronounced pea-cans]?"

"No," Eddie answered, "but I'll get you a little cup."

That brought Charlie back on stage. "You can't say that, Eddie. That was a dumb thing to say."

"I was just trying to be helpful, Mr. Charlie."

"But you are always doing dumb things, Eddie."

"I ain't dumb, Mr. Charlie. She's dumb. I'se smart enough to take care of that 'fore I come to the theatre."

"I am going to show you how dumb you are, Eddie."

"Yes, sir, Mr. Charlie."

"If there are three rabbits sitting in a row and you shoot one of them, how many are left?"

"Dat's easy, Mr. Charlie. Dey is two left."

"Wrong! There is only one left."

"Dey's three rabbits, ain't der?"

"That's right."

"I shoots one of dem."

"You shoot one of them."

"I'se been to school, Mr. Charlie. I knows one from three leaves two."

"But I say there is only one rabbit left."

"I'se not dumb, Mr. Charlie. One from three leaves two. The teacher done rapped me on the knuckles until I got dat in my head. One from three leaves two."

"How many did you kill?"

"One."

"Then there's only one left. The others ran away. You think that over while we have a little more music."

"Hold a minute, Mr. Charlie."

"Yes, Eddie?"

"You say der's one dead rabbit?"

"Only one."

"De other two run away?"

"That's right."

"Den you's wrong and I'se right."

"How do you figure that, Eddie?"

"Dem rabbits dat run away, der was two of dem. That means der is two dat's left, see? Now you think dat over, Mr. Charlie, and you'll find you ain't as smart as you thought you was."

After the grand finale, Charlie came forward once more to say good night to the audience and to urge them to return for performances the rest of the week.

After the last cars had been pushed free of the mud, the last boats had putted off into the far reaches of the creek, and the performers had removed their makeup and changed their clothes, the showboat folks crowded into the still-hot galley for clam chowder. It was a tradition on the

Floating Theatre to have the third meal after the show. With the audiences gone, beer and wine bottles emerged from their hiding places—in 1926 Prohibition was still the law of the land—to help put the top on the evening.

Selb proposed a boat ride. "It's too damn hot to sleep," he declared.

Most agreed with him and piled aboard the towboat *Elk*. Captain Cannon had a late rendezvous scheduled with a young lady in Montross, so Selb captained the tug. Everyone took bottles with them, and cooled off in the light rain and flowing air.

Selb had no trouble following the dim shoreline out of the creek and into the Potomac River, but when he tried to find his way back into the creek, he wasn't certain of the narrow entrance over the bar at Icehouse Point. He elected to anchor for the rest of the night in Nomini Bay. No one complained. Some eventually found a nook or cranny in which to sleep. The rest partied all night. There would be time to sleep on the showboat after breakfast.

WEDNESDAY, AUGUST 18, 1926

The rain continued intermittently all week, but the houses continued to sell well.

Wednesday afternoon the clerk of Westmoreland County stopped by to write the license for the Floating Theatre—one dollar per performance, six dollars for the week.

"I missed your first two performances," he apologized to Selb. "But I'm coming tonight. I don't know if I ever told you," he continued, "but I saw George M. Cohan in that play you're doing tonight when I was visiting in New York back some twenty years ago. I hope you-all are as funny as he was."

FRIDAY, AUGUST 20, 1926

Friday afternoon a group of teenagers asked to see Charlie. They had a cherubic-looking black midget named Danny with them. They wanted Charlie to let the boy perform in the concert that night. He was a singing, dancing fool, they explained.

Charlie flipped his cigarette into the creek and invited them to come in. He told the midget to get on the stage and he sat down at the piano.

"What do you know?" he asked.

"I can dance to anything," Danny answered.

Charlie struck up an old Scott Joplin rag and then nearly fell off the piano bench laughing at the twirling antics of the dancer.

"You are some dancer," Charlie complimented him.

"Yes, sir, I am," Danny agreed.

14

"What can you sing?" Charlie asked.

"I know 'Shuffle Along.'"

"You start it and I'll pick you up," Charlie instructed.

Ten minutes later Charlie invited the little fellow to perform that night.

"Do I get paid?" Danny asked.

"No, you don't get paid," Charlie laughed. "I'll give you four passes for your folks for the concert."

SATURDAY, AUGUST 21, 1926

Saturday night the kids from Nomini came up with the money and the band was hired to play for the dance at Mt. Holly House after the showboat performance. They got twenty dollars for the night—and free booze out back during breaks—when the chaperons weren't looking.

SUNDAY, AUGUST 22, 1926

Early Sunday morning, with the *Elk* pulling and the *Trouper* gently nudging from behind to keep the big theatre in the channel, the showboat started out of Nomini Creek, heading for Leonardtown, Maryland, across the Potomac River. The skies were clearing. The fishermen promised that the day would be cool with a gentle breeze by noon. Most of the performers elected to stay on the boat to avoid the long, circuitous trip by car with its two-hour wait for the Potomac River ferry.

CHAPTER TWO

USS Playhouse

A LARGE THEATRE BOAT

*T*he local newspaper in Washington, North Carolina, reported on September 14, 1913, that some important things were happening at the W. M. Chauncey Marine Railway at the foot of Bonner Street. Bill Chauncey informed the *Daily News* that he had persuaded Johnny J. Jones, the carnival man, to winter both of his large shows in Washington, that he had a contract with Mr. R. S. Neal to build a seventy-foot barge, and that he had a contract with Johnny Jones's old carnival partner, James Adams, to build a "large theatre boat."[1]

Jim Adams, the man who gave Bill Chauncey the contract for the large theatre boat, first thought of building a showboat when his vaudeville company was touring West Virginia. He visited a river showboat and was impressed with the possibilities. "That looks like trouping as is trouping," he is reported to have said to his wife.[2]

As Adams continued to tour with his vaudeville show along the southeast coast, "he hung around the docks in his spare moments and talked with seamen and fishermen of the feasibility of a show boat in salt water."[3] He had advice pro and con, but in the end, as he always did, Jim Adams made up his own mind. One thing that impressed Jim about his new project was that he had no rivals. The river system of the Midwest was crowded with showboats, but his would be the first on the Atlantic Coast. One thing Jim hated about a good idea was the rivals it generated. One thing he liked about the Floating Theatre was the expense. It didn't cost much money to buy a tent and go touring by land, but not many could afford to build a floating theatre.

After Jim let his contract to Bill Chauncey, he went into the North Carolina[4] lumber camps to pick out his lumber. From the occupation of his youth, Jim knew wood. When he returned to Washington, he found the keel of his ship laid and the framing begun. Harry Van,[5] his right-hand man for many years, took Jim one evening to see the progress on the boat. "He saw the great bony skeleton of her looming up through the dusk and his heart

A view of the Floating Theatre sometime in its first four years, before the "pup" cabins were added on the roof. Photograph courtesy of Marguerite Young.

A September 1928 view of the Floating Theatre at Solomons, Maryland, after the "pup" cabins were added. Photograph courtesy of Jacques Kelly.

The first year Nina Howard owned the boat, she had it painted red and changed its name to the "Original Show Boat." Here, the theatre is shown in June 1933 with its new name and coat of red paint in the Redman and Vane Shipyard in Baltimore. Photograph courtesy of Jacques Kelly.

went into his boots. 'Good Lord,' Jim exclaimed, 'it will take all the lumber in the North Carolina woods to cover that!'"[6]

Chauncey did not use all the lumber in North Carolina, but he did build the boat solidly, with beams that ran the length of the boat without scarfs, "heavy thirty-two-foot planks across the bottom, a skin four inches thick, and drift bolted every two feet with twenty-seven-inch bolts."[7]

Jim himself drew up the plans for and oversaw the building of the theatre superstructure on the boat.[8]

Adams's theatre boat was launched on Tuesday afternoon, January 27, 1914. A crowd of curious townspeople gathered to watch. It was a large vessel, and the launching was an impressive sight. Adams named his theatre *Estelle.*[9]

That Friday there was an accident on the boat. Lynn "Jack" Johnson, a musician, electrical engineer,[10] and handyman who first joined Adams in 1909[11] when Adams was touring his vaudeville show, fell and gashed his head. The theatre was moored at Chauncey's Railway. Johnson was sleeping in one of the staterooms on the boat and got up at midnight, most likely to use the toilet. The toilet was located on the side of the stage. He was walking on the stage, the construction of which was not finished, when he slipped and fell into the "timber and rubbish" of the unfinished auditorium. The newspaper concluded that "he had a narrow escape from serious injury."[12]

On February 25, the *Daily News* ran a long article[13] on the impending opening of the Floating Theatre. Jim Adams was no longer calling his boat *Estelle.* It was now *Playhouse,* and by that name it was registered with the Coast Guard as a barge of 436 tons, 128.3 feet long, 34 feet wide, 4.5 feet from deck to keel, and having a crew of three.[14] Soon after the playhouse started on its tidewater treks, Jim was informed by the Coast Guard that a barge such as the *Playhouse* had to have identification painted on the sides of its superstructure. Jim painted: "James Adams Floating Theater,"[15] and that is what the theatre was called by its customers for the next eighteen years.

The *Daily News* first reported the cost of building the theatre as "at least $10,000."[16] Later, it reported the cost as $25,000.[17] In his first call in *Billboard* for players, Adams advertised that the theatre cost $40,000.[18] The most common sum reported by later writers was $8,941.42.[19] Jim may have exaggerated the costs of building the boat in the attempt to dissuade competitors from joining him.

Whatever the boat cost, the writer for the *Daily News* found it impressive:

> To the rear of the stage is situated eight comfortable and convenient living rooms for the performers; underneath the stage is

located a spacious and sunny dining room, also the cook room which is sanitary and airy. In this section of the boat is to be found the electric plant for the entire boat. Mr. Adams has on board his own water plant.

At the front end of the "Playhouse" is seen two offices, one being a ticket office and the other the private office of the owner. Between the two rooms is the main entrance to the theatre proper which is eight feet wide. Above the main entrance Mr. and Mrs. Adams have their living quarters, which are convenient and attractive, being Bungalow in style and finish. There are three large rooms, besides closets, bathroom, etc. These quarters are finished in Beaver board. The boat is provided with a telephone system running all over the boat.

The main attraction to the visitor, of course, is the main auditorium. This room is 30 by 80 feet, with a balcony running all the way around the room. The first floor is provided with steel folding self-righting opera chairs and has a seating capacity of 500 people. To the left and right of the stage is installed two boxes, having accommodations for five persons each. The . . . balcony is reserved for colored people exclusively and will seat 350 persons. Two boxes are also on this floor. The main auditorium is attractively finished with steel ceiling and the color scheme is surely one of good taste, being white, trimmed in blue and gold.

In the center of the auditorium has been placed an electric chandelier and also on the walls chandeliers of a similar design. When all these lights are turned on a person will be enabled to pick [up] a pin on the floor.

The stage has an opening of 19 feet and is equipped with scenery manufactured by John Herfurth & Co, of Cincinnati. An orchestra pit is located just in front of the stage. The "Playhouse" will carry a company of 25 people. The show will consist of first class vaudeville and drama. Mr. Adams has provided a ten-piece concert band and a six-piece orchestra . . .

All over the boat hot and cold water is provided, making the "Playhouse" not only the latest word in theatres but also in living quarters.[20]

The eight staterooms for the performers were located at the rear of the boat opening onto the back of the stage. They were arranged in two tiers of four rooms each. Each of the staterooms had a large screened window opening onto the rear deck of the theatre and an inside screened door for ventilation, and steam radiators for heating.[21] Each room had either a double bed that folded to make a couch for sitting or bunk beds, a sink with running water, a mirror, electric lights, and a small built-in table. The actors added curtains and other amenities.

Adams hired no unmarried women and allowed no small children to travel with the company. Married couples shared a room and bachelor men slept two to a room. Generally, the musicians slept in the upper rooms and the actors in the lower, so that the actors could use their rooms as dressing rooms for the plays.[22] The other members of the company, the deck-hands, ushers, and maintenance workers, slept where they were most comfortable on the boat—on the deck, on stage, in the auditorium aisles—depending on weather and insects.[23] The tug crews slept on the tugs.

The toilet was located on the side of the stage. The plumbing was typical of the times—a pull chain flush overboard into the river. The only bathroom, which contained the only bathtub on board,[24] was in Adams's apartment.

The actors kept their personal clothes in closets located outside the staterooms opening onto the back of the stage. The costumes for the plays were stored in closets behind the balcony. The actors' trunks were stored in the hold under the auditorium.[25] Stage furniture not in use was stored on the platform at the second level of the rooms, or it was flown on lines from the ceiling of the stage house in the area above the proscenium opening.[26] Other props were stored in "cubby-holes"[27] around the stage.

In the proscenium arch there appeared to be two doors, one on each side of the stage opening. The door on the audience's right was the door to backstage. The door on the left was a fake, put there only to balance the stage visually. There were ventilation openings above each of the doors. In the 1920s the openings were decorated with pictures of parrots. In the 1930s the openings were covered with fake organ pipes.

The door to the dining room and kitchen was through the orchestra pit. A grate in the stage floor helped with the ventilation of the dining room.[28] Electric fans were mounted on the walls of the auditorium and Jim had a large fan on a stand that he placed at the rear of the auditorium on hot nights. He advertised from the beginning that his theatre was cooled by electricity.[29]

Although the reporter for the Washington *Daily News* wrote of the dining room as being "spacious and sunny," not everyone agreed. The vertical clearance in the dining room was about five and a half feet. All the Adamses were short, and so had no problems, but taller people had to duck their heads when they walked to the dining table. In addition to the overhead grate in the stage floor, the area under the stage was ventilated by four portholes on each side of the boat and three in the stern.[30] The kitchen and the cook's quarters adjoined the dining room. Also under the stage was the ship's cellar, "containing the . . . steam heating plants, and a great thousand gallon boiler which supplies all but the drinking water, and a sort of junk and tool shop of things that may come in handy, including the commissary."[31]

New York *Morning Telegraph* reporter Maude McDougall, who visited the theatre in 1916, concluded that the dining room was "not the pleasantest place imaginable to eat . . . in."[32] On a rough passage with the ports closed, one may imagine not many people ate there.

From 1914 to as late as 1916,[33] the electric generators were under the stage near the steam heating plants. By 1920 they were located on the tugs, where they supplied the boat with twenty-four-hour electric lighting.[34] In the late 1930s, the generators were again located under the stage.

The drinking water for the boat was held in barrels in the galley that were filled by bucket at each port. Young boys vied for the privilege of carrying the water. They were rewarded with free tickets to the shows.[35]

Jim later changed the decor of the auditorium from the description in the *Daily News*. He trimmed it in silver and gold. The metal parts of the folding seats were painted silver.[36] As early as 1915, Jim advertised his theatre as the "house of silver and gold."[37]

In 1916, McDougall found that Jim had replaced the wooden seats[38] in the balcony with the same kind of folding opera seats he had on the orchestra level. She also found the orchestra boxes lit with red incandescent lights and the balcony boxes lit with green lights. She found the effect a bit bizarre.[39] By the 1930s, due to remodeling after several sinkings, the boxes had been removed.

The *Playhouse* had no propulsion of its own. It was towed from port to port by tugs. Most likely the first year Adams hired commercial tugs to tow the theatre. In October 1914, the Centreville, Maryland, *Record* reported that "A large tugboat from Baltimore arrived at Centreville Saturday night and towed the theatre to Queenstown Sunday morning."[40]

Wesley Stout reported that the shipping shortage of the First World War forced Jim to build his own tugs.[41] Adams's first towboat, the *Trouper,* was powered by a 30-horsepower gasoline engine. It is not clear when Adams secured the *Trouper*, because the boat was too small to require documentation. It is highly probable that Adams had secured it by 1915. In his 1915 journal, Leslie Waldorf lists "Captain" John A. Roberts as a member of the company. Jim certainly had the *Trouper* by 1916. In her article about the theatre that year, Maude McDougall refers to the "power boat that tows them."[42]

In 1918, Adams had a second tug, the *Elk,* built at the Johnson and Cockran Marine Railway[43] in Crittenden, Virginia. The *Elk* was larger than the *Trouper.* It was 20 gross tons, 47.8 feet long, 12 feet wide, had a draft of 5.2 feet, and was powered by a 70-horsepower gasoline engine.[44]

IN THE VAGABOND TRADITION

On Monday, March 2, 1914, Jim moved his Floating Theatre from Chauncey's Marine Railway to Fowle's dock for the opening performance of his new venture. He was almost late for his appointment with history. Despite the fact that his boat was designed with a shallow draft—empty of audience it drew only fourteen inches—the water was too low to move the boat to the wharf. The tide rose enough for Jim to get the boat moored just in time for the performance to start. A crowd of people was waiting for the boat, clamoring for tickets.[45]

When Jim Adams opened the doors to his Floating Theatre, he was following in a long tradition of traveling theatres in America. One historian characterized the early acting companies in America as "literally a band of strollers."[46] Even with the development of American cities, most actors still had to travel to make a living.

The nineteenth century saw the growth of theatre stock companies. Initially the companies roamed without pattern seeking their audiences. But by the end of the nineteenth century two forms of traveling stock companies had become dominant. The circle stock company performed one play each week, playing in a different town each night. They went back to the same towns each week. The repertoire stock company carried six or more plays in its repertory and played for a week in the same town, a different play each night. At the end of the week they moved to a new town, and usually played in each town only once a year.

By the beginning of the twentieth century producers saw the potential of making money by exploiting the popularity of individual actors and actresses. A group of business men formed the theatre Syndicate, and strove to control both the talent and the theatres in which they performed. The name actors either signed with the Syndicate or lost all earning power. Theatre owners across the nation, too, either signed with the Syndicate or lost the popular shows for their theatres.

Two developments in the early part of the twentieth century led to the decline of theatre outside of New York: One, the smaller markets couldn't support the flood of high-cost traveling theatres the Syndicate and its rivals were sending out from New York; and two, films became increasingly popular and were much less expensive for theatre managers to present than live theatre. Gradually the theatres in the small towns were converted to cinemas, and the New York–based "road"companies played only in a few theatres in the large cities.

A group of performers emerged to fill the gap. They found eager audiences in small towns and rural areas for live theatre, areas which the New York–dominated theatre had found unprofitable. By the 1910s these performers identified themselves as the "Repertoire"movement, and the Repertoire page of *Billboard* magazine became their communications center.

Because the threatre print media were centered in New York, the small theatre companies of the Repertoire movement labored in theatrical obscurity. They played in the ubiquitous small-town opera houses, in city halls, on showboats, and in tents. But the small, for the most part nonunion, traveling Repertoire companies were the main sources of theatrical entertainment for the small towns of America in the first four decades of the twentieth century.

During its heyday, the Repertoire movement was a not-insignificant part of the American entertainment world. *Billboard* estimated that in 1926 there were 400 tent companies, touring 16,000 communities, playing to 78 million customers, and providing employment to 8,000 performers. *Variety* (the voice of the New York theatre) was more modest in its estimates, putting the figures at less than half those of *Billboard*. But even *Variety*'s more modest estimate suggests that, financially, the "rep" movement was more than holding its own in competition with the New York–based theatre industry. [47]

The performers with the repertoire companies came from many backgrounds. For some it was their first break in acting, and they went on to more notable careers in New York or Hollywood—Clark Gable and Milburn Stone got their starts with tent companies.[48] Many of the players came to the reps from small-time vaudeville or burlesque. A few had careers playing in the secondary theatres in New York or on the road. For example, Walter Sanford, who was with James Adams in 1915 and 1917, had a long and successful career first touring as an actor throughout the United States, Australia, and South Africa, and later managing secondary theatres in New York.[49] But most of the performers worked their entire careers in the opera houses, tents, and showboats of rural America.

The James Adams Floating Theatre followed in the tradition of the repertoire theatres. In the organization of its company, in its choice of audiences, in its choice of plays, and in the other elements of its operations, the James Adams was a repertoire stock company touring by water.

SHOWBOATS

The James Adams also followed in another American tradition, that of the showboat.

Primarily because of the popularity of Edna Ferber's novel, *Show Boat*, and the movies and musical based on it, showboating raises a strong feeling of romantic nostalgia in people today. Before Ferber, the showboat was just another way for the struggling itinerant actor to try to make a living.

In the nineteenth century, the river systems of the Midwest and South provided a major mode of transportation. The early itinerant actors traveled the rivers from town to town. They soon discovered that they could use the boats they travelled on as their stages.

Showboating was primarily a phenomenon of the Midwestern rivers. Philip Graham lists fifty-three major showboats that were built in the United States between the years 1831 and 1939.[50] Fifty of them were on the

Mississippi and its tributaries, one was on the Erie Canal, one was on the Hudson River, and one—the James Adams—was on the tidewater of North Carolina and the Chesapeake Bay.

THE PLAY'S THE THING

The opening bill on The James Adams on March 2, 1914, was *Under Western Skies*, a comedy-drama in four acts—with specialties. Admission prices that night were ten cents for general admission, fifteen cents additional to sit in one of the two hundred "reserved" seats and twenty-five cents additional to sit in one of the hundred "choice reserved" seats.[51]

In offering specialties with his plays, Jim was following the practice of most repertoire theatres of the time. Touring actors—troupers—were expected to be skilled at more than just acting. They had to have specialties. The term is from vaudeville. A vaudeville performance was made up of "bits and specialties," played alternately. "Bits" were the jokes and comic routines. "Specialties" were the skilled presentations: singing, dancing, juggling, magic, tumbling, etc. The specialties in a repertoire performance were presented between the acts while the scenery was being changed and the candy and drinks were being sold.

The plays for the rest of the opening week were: Tuesday, *The Girl Ranchman*; Wednesday, *Sunset Trail*; Thursday, *The Boy Detective*; Friday, *Tempest and Sunshine*—all presented with specialties between the acts. For the Saturday matinee the theatre offered vaudeville, and, on Saturday night, *The Devil's Partner*, followed by vaudeville.[52]

The plays Adams presented in 1914 were typical of the offerings of the repertoire theatres of the period. By modern taste we would describe them as melodramas. In the strictest definition, however, they were not all melodramas. There were some of those, some comedies, and an occasional farce, but most were comedy-dramas. During the 1920s and '30s, repertoire comedy-dramas developed as a special form of theatre. In the mid-1910s, however, the form was still closely related to the melodrama of the nineteenth century.

There are many views of melodrama, but Clayton Hamilton writing in *The Bookman* in 1911 provided a good working definition for our purposes: "a serious play in which the incidents determine and control the characters."[53] He went on to explain that "in melodrama the heroine and hero are not clearly characterized; they are represented not as particular people, but merely as *anybody* involved in the situation of the moment."[54] Hamilton believed that melodrama had special appeal to ordinary people.

> The devotees of cheap melodrama are workaday people to whom, in the orderly procession of the days, nothing noteworthy ever hap-

pens; and in the theatre they demand the sort of play in which surprising and startling adventures will happen not only to the
people on the stage but to themselves . . . [They] love to lose themselves in an irresponsible train of circumstances which conceivably
might happen to themselves . . . This point—perhaps the most
important that we have to consider—is that the abiding mood of
melodrama is an absolute and dauntless optimism. The world of
melodrama is a just and lucky world where all things fall out fitly.[55]

Hamilton was an admirer of melodrama. He believed it answered one
of the "most profound of human needs: it ministers to the motive which phi-
losophers term the will to believe."[56] He was concerned because melodrama
(in 1911) appeared to be a dying form. It was being replaced by the new psy-
chology based drama of writers like Henrik Ibsen. He used *Hedda Gabler* to
make his point. "Hedda Gabler interests us merely as a specimen; and what
happens to her does not in any real sense happen to us. The fact of what she is
convinces us that she must ultimately kill herself; but if we were flung into the
same position, we should crawl out by some easier way."[57]

Hamilton also noted, as most students of the form have noted, that
"because it casts its emphasis on action, rather than on character," melodrama called for "an exhibition of the uttermost mechanical equipment of
the stage."[58] This uttermost use of mechanical equipment is most often described by scholars as "the sensation scene." The sensation scene usually
came at the climax of the play. Some famous sensation scenes included these:
two small orphans drifting on the ice of a half-frozen river; the hero bound to
the railroad tracks with the train seen rapidly approaching; the heroine caught
in a building engulfed in flames; and the heroine lost in the woods in a blind-
ing snowstorm. The producers of melodrama prided themselves on the realism of their sensation scenes and the audiences thrilled to the effects.

The melodrama contained no "message" beyond the truism that good
triumphed and evil was punished. Good and evil were presented in forms that
were acceptable to the audience and that often appealed to the audience's
deepest convictions and prejudices. For example, in a melodrama presented in
England, a figure of malevolence might be an Irishman. In the same play in
America the man might be an Indian. The actions of the plays involved stigmas, some of which could be overcome and others of which could not,
based on the mores of the audience. In this way, a man of the upper classes
might be able to defy convention and marry a woman of the lower classes,
but only if it were clear that her family was "of good stock." He could never
marry her if her father were a criminal, unless, of course, it were shown in
the last act that he had been falsely convicted.

The rewards won by the virtuous in melodramas were almost always in the form of material wealth—an inheritance, property, or a gift. An

important aspect of American mores in the nineteenth century was the triumph of materialism. Herbert Ross Brown explained it this way: "At a time
when things were in the saddle, and America was in the midst of a boastful
materialism, the sentimentalists felt a need of enveloping the new indus-
trial order in an aura of approval. Accepting without critical scrutiny the
sanctions of the philosophy of acquisition, they dangled the tempting bait
of material prosperity before the eyes of every reader."[59]

Two plays produced in 1914 by the Floating Theatre serve to illus-
trate the evolution of melodrama. The first, *Mabel Heath*, presented at the
end of the season in Elkton, Maryland, is an example of the nineteenth-century melodrama. The second, *Sunset Trail*, presented on Wednesday in the
first week of the season, is an example of a transitional play, similar in some
ways to the melodrama, but showing many of the characteristics of the later
repertoire plays of the 1920s and '30s.[60]

Mabel Heath is in four acts, has a sensation scene, has just six characters, who are presented only as types, and makes no social or psychological
statement.

The play is set in the countryside outside of London, but Adams
might well have set it outside of Philadelphia or Baltimore. The play takes
place in rooms in two different farmhouses, and by a church in a snowstorm. The characters are so narrow of type and undefined that the play
could be set anywhere there are farmhouses and a church in a climate
where it is cold enough to snow.

The story has some subplots involving comic characters, but the
main story concerns Mabel's problems with her father and her husband
Frank. Frank has sworn Mabel to secrecy about their marriage because he
has told her his father will disinherit him if he discovers that Frank has
married the daughter of his father's sworn enemy. Mabel wants to tell her
father so that she and Frank can live honestly. Frank writes a letter to
Mabel's father telling him that Mabel thinks she is married to him (Frank),
but that in fact she is not because he faked the marriage. Mabel's father is
blind and cannot read the letter. Mabel reads it to him because she is honest
and will not lie. The father drives his daughter from his house because he
believes she is living in sin.

The rest of the play is built upon similar twists of plot as Frank
seeks to get Mabel's father's property and the comic characters try to help
Mabel and her father to reconcile. In the third scene of the third act (the
sensation scene), Mabel leads her blind and homeless father through a
snowstorm. He does not know his benefactor is his daughter. Frank appears and attacks Mabel and tells her father who she is. Her old, blind
father defends her physically against Frank, but when she is safe, he again
rejects her and the complications continue. In the end, Mabel and her father are reconciled and recover their property from a thwarted Frank, the

light-comedy couple agree to marry, and the broad-comic servant is rein-
stated by Mabel. All ends happily.

Mabel Heath clearly is a melodrama. Most theatre audiences today
would also consider *Sunset Trail* a melodrama, but it has elements that are
more modern.

Sunset Trail concerns two young women living in the West. Their
uncle, an Army officer, has been murdered. One of the sisters (the female
lead) is being courted by a soldier and by an Indian. The soldier killed the
sisters' uncle and the Indian knows it. The Indian is silent about the murder
because his sister has had a child by the soldier and wants to marry the
soldier. The Indian will be silent if the soldier agrees to marry the Indian's
sister. If the soldier will not marry her, the Indian threatens to kill the soldier. The soldier attempts to frame his buddy, an Irishman, for the murder.

The Indian foils the soldier's plot to frame the Irishman. The soldier
tries to kill the Indian. The female lead arrives in the nick of time and attempts to save the Indian, but is thwarted by the soldier. At the last moment
the Irishman arrives and saves both the female lead and the Indian. For
some reason—most likely to ensure that there will be a last act—nothing is
done about the soldier's attempts to murder the female lead and the Indian.
In the last act, the Indian reveals that his sister and her child have died and
he is ready, rather than to kill the soldier, to testify against him in court. The
Irishman arrests the soldier. The characters work through some heavy
social stigmas, and everyone, we assume, lives happily ever after.

The sequence of coincidences, unmotivated entrances, and unrealis-
tic time gaps would make the play unacceptable to modern audiences. The
play has many melodramatic elements but is not, by definition, a melodrama.

In form, *Sunset Trail* is in three acts. A melodrama is usually in four
or five acts. *Sunset Trail* has no sensation scene.

In content, *Sunset Trail* challenges stigmas and does not reward the
"winners" monetarily. The Indian, John Swiftwind, is presented human-
istically and sympathetically. Although the script is not sociologically or
anthropologically accurate in its depiction of an Indian, it is sensitive to
Indian customs and mores. The romance between John and the female lead,
Naoma St. Clair, explores the cultural differences between the two. In the
end, the two work through their differences and agree to marry, knowing
full well that their marriage will meet with disapproval from both cultures.
The other two sympathetic characters in the play also agree at the end to
marry. They are the light-comic characters, Naoma's sister, Eleanor St. Clair
(who disapproves of Naoma and John's marriage), and the Irishman, Jerry
O'Donnell. The fact that Jerry is Irish is a stigma to Eleanor. But Eleanor
reveals in the last act that she has a seven-year-old child by a previous marriage, which, to Jerry, is a stigma. In the end, romance triumphs, but the two

couples have only their love as rewards. In the traditional melodrama they would have inherited an estate from the women's murdered uncle, but in *Sunset Trail* he was only a poor Army officer with no money.

While *Sunset Trail* is typical of plays produced by the repertoire theatres after 1910, it is more socially conscious than most. The tradition of Indians as characters in plays goes back at least to Edwin Forrest's production of *Metamora, the Last of the Wampanoags* in the 1830s.[61] The Indian was usually portrayed either as a noble or a vicious savage. In *Sunset Trail* John Swiftwind is neither. He is a man of a different heritage who is confused, angry, hurting, and in love. He is reasonable and intelligent, but capable of both honest and dishonest responses. The one stereotypical trait the playwright gives him is his inability to control his reactions when he is under the influence of alcohol.

The marriage between John and Naoma is not presented as an unnatural act that is bound to offend God and produce that creature of almost universal loathing in nineteenth-century American drama, the half-breed. Instead it is presented as a social concern of about the same seriousness as Naoma's sister's marriage to an Irishman.

THE PERFORMERS

It is unfortunate, but we do not have a complete list of the performers on the Floating Theatre in 1914. The reviews in the *Daily News* listed three who performed in the specialties, the Martyne Sisters and Mr. Calvin Clark.[62] A later article identifies one of the Martyne Sisters as Dottie Martine of Kansas City.[63] The orchestra was most likely under the direction of Harry Masten from Thurmont, Maryland. Harry played the violin and baritone horn. His wife, Della, was the cornet soloist and played the piano.[64] We can assume, because of their previous service with Adams, two others were with the theatre that year: Jack Johnson, clarinet player; and Harry Van, drummer and advance man.

As the opening night audience crossed the gangplank and crowded aboard the *Playhouse*, they were greeted by Captain Jim. Standing nearby was his wife Gertie. Both were small of stature but handsome in appearance. Gertie's blue eyes shone with good humor in a round face framed with short, wavy brown hair. Her body had begun to pick up weight, but still showed the grace of a former athlete.

Jim was a man to match the romance of his new vessel. As a reporter described him two years later:

> He is a good-looking little chap, is Jim—blue eyes, wavy dark hair, just touched with gray, neat clean cut features, neat clean cut figure, built to scale and in first rate condition. So far as looks go Jim

would make a popular leading juvenile, perhaps even a matinee idol. But he lacks the instincts for that. He says he can't act—not a little bit . . .

He has always been a showman—and he looks the part—clothes rather conservatively "sporty" and a diamond on his little finger that makes you blink. It must be nearly half an inch across, that diamond. Oh, yes, it's real enough—a bit yellow, perhaps, and not very deep. But even so it's rather dazzling.[65]

For twelve years, Jim had been a showman. Before he built his showboat, he had tried his luck with circuses, carnivals, and vaudeville.

CHAPTER THREE

Circus, Carnival, and Vaudeville

THE ADAMS FAMILY

*J*ames Even Adams was the fourth of eight children born to Demos and Rosedell Westbrook Adams. Jim was born in Ohio, though his family moved when he was eighteen to Saginaw, Michigan, in 1891.[1] From all accounts the family was extroverted and their gatherings were times of fun and good feelings.[2] Contemporary accounts indicate that the Adamses enjoyed being with people and were pleasant to be with.[3] It would seem appropriate that at least five of the eight siblings found their way into show business.

The oldest of the children was Hattie Mae, born in 1867.[4] Although her career in the theatre was probably not extensive, she did at one point advertise herself as part of the vaudeville acting team of Beard and Adams.[5] Jim Beard was the second of her three husbands and he appears in the advertisement as a blackface comic, she as an ingenue.

After Hattie, Harry Joel was born in 1869. He died in 1909 at the age of 40 leaving no evidence of a show business career.

Selba was born in 1871. For sixteen years Selb was the business manager for his brother Jim's showboat.

The fourth Adams child, James, born in 1873, was the first of the family to enter the entertainment world and he provided the center for those who followed him.

Mary Eva, born in 1878, apparently resisted the call of the stage. She died in 1900 at the age of 22.

Susie, born in 1887, formed an act with her niece Rose, Hattie's daughter. They billed themselves as the Adams Sisters and played both the circus as a revolving ladder act[6] and vaudeville as a song and dance act.[7]

The youngest of Demos and Rosedell's sons, Claude, born in 1888, lived only a month.

The youngest of their daughters, Beulah, born in 1892, went on to the longest career in the family as a performer. She began in her brother James's vaudeville show when she was a young girl and continued uninterrupted until she retired in 1940 at the age of forty-eight. Her most glorious years were those she spent as the star of Jim's showboat.

As young men, Selba and Jim worked in Shepherd, a small town close to Saginaw where their family lived. Shepherd, Michigan, at the time, had much of the feeling of the frontier, just a few decades removed from the Indians. It was surrounded by forests and its main industry was lumbering. In 1887, though only six blocks square, it supported a clothespin factory, a stave mill, a heading mill, and a planing mill, in addition to such non-lumbering enterprises as a cider mill, coal kilns, a canning factory, and two cheese factories.[8]

Jim apparently found working in the sawmills not to his liking. He moved to Bay County, Michigan, where in 1895 he married Gertrude Powlson of Mayville, Michigan. On their marriage license, Jim listed his occupation as farmer, and Gertie listed hers as seamstress.[9]

THE JAMES ADAMS NEW CENTURY SHOW

About the time of their marriage or shortly after, Jim and Gertie trained as aerialists. Although Jim had fled the routine of the sawmills, he was drawn to another routine fathered by a by-product of the mills: saw-dust. The Saginaw area produced a number of acrobats and aerialists be-cause of the lumbering industry[10]—performers who could not afford a net trained over the sawdust piles that lined the Saginaw River. Around the turn of the century, Jim and Gertie joined the Wixam Brothers Circus, a small Michigan-based troupe.[11] But Jim's entrepreneurial self was no more satisfied with being a performer for a paycheck than he had been as a mill hand. In Bay City, sometime in the spring of 1902, Jim bought ten horses being retired from a streetcar company.[12] He added a few wagons and started a tour of central Michigan with his little circus, which he named the James Adams New Century Show. They played one-day stands in small towns. The week of May 26, for example, they played, Monday through Saturday, in Henderson, Elsie, Bannister, Eureka, Maple Rapids, and Hubbardston.[13]

The troupe's problems were not limited to the rigors of constant travel in rickety wagons. Their audiences were not especially receptive:

> It was heartrending business at first. Their modest wagon train
> brought yells of derision wherever they went. Street crowds
> shouted 'gypsies' at them, and matters reached the point where,
> when the outfit neared a town in which a show was to be given,
> the troupe climbed down from the wagons and took a roundabout
> way to the spot where the tent was to be pitched.[14]

James E. Adams, circa 1914, when he opened his Floating Theatre. Photograph courtesy of Marguerite Young.

Gertrude Powlson Adams as a young woman. Photograph courtesy of Marguerite Young.

The Adams family, at about the time Jim built the Floating Theatre. Left to right, back row: Jim Adams, Jim's niece Rose (Hattie's daughter), Jim Beard (Hattie's second husband), Jim's sister Susie, and Jim's brother Selba. Front row: Jim's sister Hattie, Jim's great-niece Dorothy (Rose's daughter), Jim's mother Rosedell with Jim's great-niece Beulah (Rose's other daughter) on her lap, Selba's son Delmar, and Selba's wife Clara. Missing from the picture are Jim's sister Beulah and her husband Charlie Hunter. Photograph courtesy of Marguerite Young.

The "Adams Sisters." Susie is on the left, Rose on the right. Photograph courtesy of Marguerite Young.

Jim and Gertie were performing as trapeze acrobats when this picture was taken circa 1902. Photograph courtesy of Carlista Golden.

James Adams's first Vaudeville Show, circa 1910, in Charlotte, North Carolina. Jim is seated in the middle of the picture, behind the other men. Photograph courtesy of Marguerite Young.

THE HATCH-ADAMS MIGHTY MIDWAY AND CARNIVAL CO.

The last reference in the *Billboard* Routes section to Adams New Century Show was August 16, 1902, although Jim may have continued his season longer without sending his routes to *Billboard*. The next mention of Jim in *Billboard* is January 3, 1903: "Hatch and (Frank) Adams opened their own company on December 27 to tour Florida. They now have four shows and a Ferris wheel."[15]

It was Jim's first foray into the big time, and the paper got his name wrong. Frank Adams was an established circus manager in the Southeast, and the mistake is understandable. But the Adams in Hatch-Adams was Jim and the Hatch was J. Frank Hatch.

The news item was listed in *Billboard* under "Street Fair Notes." Although the nature of the institution has changed over the past ninety years, today we would recognize a "street fair" as a carnival.

In 1903, carnivals were a growing phenomenon. While giving a nod to the early pagan sources of the carnival, the later Christian festivals that tried to reform the beast, and its various manifestations in Europe and early America, Joe McKennon traces the beginnings of American carnivals as we would recognize them today to 1893:

> A History of the American Collective Amusement Industry, commonly and fondly called The Carnival. First conceived in 1893 at the back of Buffalo Bill's Wild West Show on the dirty streets of Chicago, the sturdy gem of the American Carnival survived a couple of still births, several miscarriages and an abortion or two. Finally, in 1899, fathered by a complete outsider, a town mark, she was born full-blooded and ready for action. Action that was destined to thrill and shock and change the amusement pattern of all North America as her midways were set up on the streets, the fair grounds and the cow pastures of the continent.[16]

The 1893 event to which McKennon refers was at the site of the World's Columbian Exposition in Chicago. The story of the carnival, however, was not on the exposition grounds, but outside it.[17]

It was the practice of performers and operators of concessions, games of chance, sideshows, and like enterprises to work independently. Each would contract with county fairs and circuses for employment. At the Chicago Exposition, a number of these independent showmen, who had failed or had not tried to win a contract with the promoters of the event, set up shop outside the gates of the midway. They did quite well economically even when the exposition, with higher overhead costs, was struggling. Otto Schmidt, a German painter employed as a scenic artist by a Chicago theatre, got the idea of organizing the independent showmen. He found financial backing for his idea and took The Chicago Midway Plaisance Amusement Company, composed of many of the independent attractions from the unofficial exposition midway, out on the road. He met with more failure than success, but the seed was planted.[18]

In the years that followed, others attempted to organize the showmen, but the first to succeed was a hotel keeper, Frank W. Gaskill. In the summer of 1898, the Elks clubs of Akron, Zanesville, and Canton, Ohio, were planning street fairs and Gaskill was the chairman of the committee to book attractions.[19] The events were so successful that Gaskill and the Exalted Ruler of the Elks, George Chartier, decided to organize and book the talent for street carnivals elsewhere. They planned to start in 1899, but Gaskill went out on his own in the fall of 1898. The next year they each organized a carnival. Gaskill's Canton Carnival Company opened in Chillicothe, Ohio, on May 30, 1899. Two weeks later, Chartier's Exposition Circuit Company was on the road.[20] Thus was launched the street fair carnival as an organized industry.

The concept of the street fair carnival was simple: An entrepreneur contracted for a variety of attractions. These might include daredevil acts, such as the slide-for-life and the leap-the-gap; traditional skill acts, such as aerialists, jugglers, and magicians; vaudeville performers; animal acts; minstrel shows; concessions, including food and souvenirs; games of chance; at least one band; amusement rides, such as the carousel and the Ferris wheel; and sideshow performers, including "freaks" of various natures, figures of curiosity, such as the tattooed lady or the lone survivor of an earthquake, and performers with arcane skills, such as eating fire or swallowing snakes. The street fair always featured at least one "free act." It was usually a daredevil act that required a lot of space and complicated paraphernalia, like the slide-for-life (the performer slid down a long wire from a height, usually through fire); leap-the-gap (the performer rode a bicycle down a long ramp, through a loop, and jumped a gap at the end of the ride); or a high dive (the performer dove into a shallow pool from a great height, often into water covered with flames). The free act could be seen by anyone without buying a ticket, and served as a come-on for the other attractions. The free act performer received a cut of the other admissions.

The manager of the carnival sometimes owned one or more of the acts, but typically he contracted with independent showmen for his attractions. After he had his attractions signed—and sometimes before—the manager booked sites for the carnival to play by contracting with civic groups in the towns to sponsor the fairs. The civic groups got a cut of the gate and in turn advertised the event and made the local arrangements (land, license, and electricity). Ideally, the carnival played in a town for a week, Monday through Saturday, and moved a reasonably short distance on Sunday to a new town to open again on Monday. Ideally, also, the weather cooperated, the townspeople were friendly, and the railroads ran on time.

Conditions, however, were seldom ideal. Managers stole dates from each other. The attractions jumped to other carnivals that promised more work or higher percentages, or, worse, performers decided that managing a carnival looked easy and started their own in competition, jumping ahead to steal dates the former manager had already contracted. The games of chance were often dishonest gambling devices ("grift") used to "bilk the marks." The dancers in the sideshows made extra money from the men of the town. The sponsoring civic groups failed to provide the services promised. Or, most common of all, the manager was unable to book consecutive weeks and everyone lost money from being idle.

There were so many dishonest men in the carnival business and dishonest practices in the games of chance and sideshows, that eventually the Elks, who had been foremost in starting the carnivals, announced that their clubs would no longer sponsor street fairs.[21]

But there were plenty of marks eager to be bilked and swains eager to learn love's lessons from exotic women, and there were also honest men who ran honest shows, and so the carnival as a form of entertainment survived and flourishes in various forms today.

In 1903, the season Hatch and Adams opened their carnival—only four years after Gaskill first played Chillicothe—McKennon reports that there were twenty-two organized carnivals in the United States, every one of them traveling by railroad.[22]

James Adams was twenty-nine when he joined with Frank Hatch; Frank could not have been any older. In 1900, Frank had an office in Cleveland and booked his own acts for county and street fairs.[23]

In late December 1902 and January 1903, Hatch and Adams toured Florida, Georgia, and South Carolina.[24] By the end of January they were in winter quarters in Spartanburg, South Carolina,[25] preparing for their first full season. In an expensive display ad in *Billboard* on March 21, Hatch and Adams announced the grand opening of their carnival at Tarboro, North Carolina, for the week of April 14.

The Hatch-Adams carnival played a full season in 1903, starting in North Carolina, touching one week in Petersburg, Virginia, then into Pennsylvania, Ohio, and New York, closing in Cortland September 26. Although shows reporting to *Billboard* often exaggerated their success, by all appearances Frank and Jim made money. They started the season in ten railroad cars,[26] and by the end of the season they had purchased more.[27] Throughout the season they advertised for new attractions. On June 13 they reported to *Billboard* that they had not had a losing stand all season.[28]

Despite the carnival's success, on September 26, Hatch and Adams announced that the following year, instead of running a carnival, they planned to put out an eight-car circus.[29] From later developments in Jim's career, one can surmise that the reason for the announced switch from carnival to circus was that Jim was not entirely comfortable managing a carnival. But two months later Hatch and Adams made an investment that kept them in the carnival business. It was either too good a deal to resist, or Frank overcame Jim's resistance. On November 17, they bought the bankrupt Wright's Carnival to add to their own so they could "enter the Carnival Season of 1904 as one of the largest and best equipped Carnival Companies on the road."[30]

When the 1903 season closed in October, Jim went to San Francisco, most likely to visit with Gertie's family, and Frank went to Chicago for the winter.[31] The carnival was sent first to winter in Lansing, Michigan,[32] and then, in January 1904, to Washington, Indiana, site of the Wright Carnival. There the two units were consolidated for the new season.[33]

It was there that the Hatch-Adams Carnival Company opened the season on May 2, 1904. When the carnival completed its week and went on its way, it left behind contented customers.

> Viewed as a whole the carnival was a success. In every feature for the city of Washington it was a success, even financially, as the carnival managers and their people during the last several months have left several thousand more dollars in the city than they took away.
>
> From the standpoint of an attraction the exhibition was all that could be desired. New, clean and interesting shows generally attracted large crowds. The managers of the outfit, Hatch-Adams, were both clever, affable men and in all deals were honest and business-like. The performers and others with the company were also a nice lot of people and while in Washington made many friends. Several families with the company expect to make this their future home and when the company goes into winter quarters, which will be in the south next year, very likely, will return to Washington.
>
> The company left yesterday on the B. & O. S. W. with their fourteen cars for Columbus, Ind.[34]

The number of acts Hatch-Adams offered in 1904 was twice what they had offered in 1903. Two of the acts were of special interest to James. The first was his wife, Gertrude, who performed on the trapeze, most likely in the "Roman Coliseum Circus," with a man named Ansel.[35] Unfortunately, in July, in Pennsylvania, Gertie was injured in a fall.[36] There is a strong possibility that she did not perform again after her fall.

The other act was the "Adams Sisters,"[37] Jim's sister Susie and his niece Rose Leach (Hattie's daughter), performing either their revolving ladder act in the "Roman Coliseum Circus" or their song and dance act in the "Vaudeville Show." Susie later married Frank Hatch and there is a good chance that Jim objected. She was only seventeen. Later Jim prevented his sister Beulah from marrying Charlie Hunter until she turned eighteen. When Hatch married Susie in December 1905,[38] he and Jim were no longer partners.

In 1904, the Hatch-Adams Carnival Company probably was financially successful. One indicator of the success of an entertainment company of the period was its consistency in reporting its dates to *Billboard*. Successful companies liked the publicity, while unsuccessful companies kept their itineraries secret to avoid competition. Throughout 1904 Hatch and Adams reported their routes regularly.

But not everything was going well. They had a number of important defections, among them the advance man who left to front another company.[39] As a result, Hatch had to go out on the road.[40] One of their big free attractions, the Two Hewitts, a balancing act, defected to the Big Open Air Circus.[41] And in October they had to close the season three weeks early when they were quarantined in Tarboro, North Carolina, because of outbreaks of diphtheria in Wilson, Goldsboro, and Kingston, North Carolina, where the carnival had previously played.[42]

In September, the company advertised for performers for a minstrel show it planned to open November 1. Hatch and Adams may have planned to run the minstrel show during the winter when the carnival was closed, or as a part of the carnival. But for reasons discussed below, the new venture never materialized.

There is one curious note to the season. In June, in Steubenville, Ohio, Jim and Frank were riding the Ferris wheel together. Jim fell out. "But luckily he controlled himself and his feet struck the ground first," *Billboard* reported. Jim, of course, was a trapeze performer and no doubt his athletic ability served him well in the incident. But most curious is *Billboard*'s final note to the event. "The affair was a result of an attempt on Mr. Hatch's part to have some fun with Mr. Adams."[43]

Whatever the reasons—Jim's discomfort with carnivals, his concern for Susie, his differences with Frank, or the difficulties of the season—on October 1, Hatch advertised that all the property of the Hatch-Adams Carnival Company was for sale.[44] Two months later the notice followed in *Billboard* that Hatch and Adams had dissolved their partnership.[45]

In 1905, and for many years afterward, Frank continued alone with his carnival, The Great J. Frank Hatch Shows. Jim went on to a new partnership. The same issue of *Billboard* that announced the end of Hatch-Adams contained a note that the Jones-Adams Exposition Shows had played to good business the week of November 14, 1904, in Georgetown, South Carolina.[46]

THE JONES-ADAMS CONGRESS OF NOVELTIES

Johnny Jenkins Jones was a wiry Welshman from Pennsylvania, smaller in stature than Jim Adams and a year younger. Johnny sported a large flowing mustache. He dressed well, always wore a hat, smoked a cigar, and was fond of alcohol until he "got religion" and gave up drinking in his later years.[47]

Jones started working in a coal mine when he was ten, but he soon quit the mines to sell newspapers. Then he moved up to sell his papers as a "news butcher" on passenger trains. He did well enough on the trains that by the time he was twenty-one he owned and operated a cane-rack concession stand at fairs. Four years later he bought a miniature railroad amusement ride and built himself a Ferris wheel. His big break came in 1903 when he went into partnership in the Columbus Carnival Company with a man named Bert Hoss.[48]

In August 1903, *Billboard* noted that Jones had purchased Bert Hoss's interest in the Columbus Carnival Company and would change the name to the Jones Carnival Company.[49] Fifteen months later Johnny went into partnership with Jim Adams.

In January and February 1905, the Jones-Adams carnival sported a rather cumbersome name, reported both as "The Jones-Adams Congress of Novelties, Pure Food Show and Theatrical Exposition Co.,"[50] and "The Jones-Adams Congress of Novelties and Merchants Pure Food and Advertising Show."[51] The show played only in Florida and operated under "one top."[52] Most likely Jones and Adams, in the effort to accrue capital for the 1905 summer carnival season, were running what is commonly known as a medicine show.[53] Medicine shows took many forms, but primarily they combined carnival or vaudeville type entertainment with a pitch to sell one or more products, usually "patent" medicines. A good orator could take in more money selling a crowd a product to heal their physical and emotional woes than the show could take in from admissions.

On February 16, in Gainesville, Florida, the company gave Jim a surprise party for his thirty-second birthday. Jim reported the party to *Billboard*.

> Mr. Johnny Jones, my esteemed partner, and Mr. James Howard, manager of Fairyland Theatre, called at my office tent, requesting me to come to Fairyland Theatre and see a new film tried. On entering I saw the entire company, and the band struck up "Dixie." The surprise was complete. Immediately following, Mr. Tom Moss made a short and eloquent address on behalf of the company and presented me with a precious souvenir, in the way of a handsome solid gold watch with chain and diamond locket, and friendly greetings, and wished me many more happy and successful years.

The surprise was so complete I hardly knew what to say. However, I responded with a few words of thanks, which but feebly expressed my appreciation. I shall always remember this occasion as one of the happiest moments of my life, and preserve their gift as a priceless pearl, that which money can not buy.[54]

In March, the carnival went into winter quarters in Dillon, South Carolina, preparing for the new season. It advertised for attractions for the opening in Dillon on April 3.[55]

In 1905 the Jones-Adams carnival played every week of the season, traveling through South Carolina, North Carolina, Virginia, Maryland, Pennsylvania, and West Virginia, ending in December in Georgetown, South Carolina. Despite the usual defections, the company grew in size during the season. In August Jones and Adams reported that they had had only one losing stand, and that was in Baltimore, where they played three weeks. They also reported that there had been only two accidents: "One was in Alexandria, Va., where one of our lady trainers was bitten by a bear, and the other was at Benwood, W. Va., where two riders missed the landing of the gap on account of a bad board."[56] In September they bought more wild animals and Jim, drawing no doubt on his experiences in the sawmills of Shepherd, personally supervised the construction of the cages.[57]

THE JONES AND ADAMS NEW CENTURY RAILROAD SHOW

Despite their apparent success with the carnival in 1905, in 1906 Jones and Adams changed their format to that of the circus. In February *Billboard* reported they were in the North buying animals, new cars, tents, and an electric light plant for their new operation.[58] In May they advertised for acts and musicians.[59] Gertie was apparently no longer performing, because in July they advertised for an aerial act, "man and wife preferred."[60]

The circus opened in Greenville, South Carolina, in May. It was not a good year. Following the common practice of struggling shows, the partners stopped listing their routes with *Billboard*, and in July they ran the following notice in Billy Boy's routes department: "Jones & Adams New Century: Publication of Route prohibited. Any mail addressed in care of The *Billboard* will be forwarded promptly."[61] Part of their problem may have been market saturation. McKennon reports that there were twice as many shows out in 1906 as there had been three years earlier.[62]

In September, Jones severed his connection with the organization.[63]

He went back to carnivals, and opened the Johnny J. Jones Big Trained Wild Animal Exhibition[64] (most likely operating with the cages Jim Adams had built). Jones went on to become one of the greatest names in popular entertainment. He died in 1930,[65] but his son continued his work, and the name "Johnny J. Jones" marked major carnivals in the United States for more than fifty years.

After Jones left, Jim revived the name of his first circus, the James Adams New Century Show.[66]

Although Jim had twice found financial success running carnivals, at the end of each carnival year he had shown the desire to replace the carnival with a circus. Because his two ex-partners continued for years with carnivals, I have to conclude that the pressure to change came from Jim. I can only guess at the reasons. The enterprises about which Jim later expressed his greatest pride were his vaudeville shows and his Floating Theatre. They were small, self-contained units, fully controlled by the manager. They appeared to have had a family atmosphere. It seemed that to Jim the simple amenities of life, such as hunting and entertaining friends, were of prime importance. He appeared to like things human-sized, and the carnivals may have been too hectic and unwieldy for him.

Carnivals are big, sprawling operations, filling blocks of city streets with many fronts and individually managed tents. The carnival manager cannot possibly keep a rein on all activities. Unscrupulous operators can introduce prostitution and crooked gambling; the performers in the tents—sold by suggestive ballyhoo out front—can deliver inside what is advertised outside without the approval or knowledge of the manager. Even though Jim and his partners had run clean operations (their shows probably fell into the category which the carnies label a "Sunday School Show"[67]) there were enough rough edges to have made Jim uncomfortable. Certainly later with his Floating Theatre he prided himself on providing shows to which a gentleman could, without embarrassment, bring his wife and children.

The circus was more to Jim's liking. There the manager hired and fired the performers, and the emphasis was on skill and entertainment and not chance and suggestion. Although the circus carried sideshows and concessions, they were limited and more regulated. The audience came and went in an orderly fashion and sat on bleachers. A customer might visit the sideshows, but he came primarily to see the animals, the clowns, and the aerialists, and to listen to the band.

Jim did not do well financially with his circus. Although he announced in October that he was doing a good business in South Carolina, had bought a new tent, and planned to play all winter,[68] the circus played mostly one-night stands. It was tough going, but on July 5, 1907, Jim reported one happy occurrence to *Billboard:*

Members of the James Adams Show enjoyed one of those festal occasions, which serve to dispel the tedium with the show that never closes. Commemorative of the twelfth anniversary of Mr. and Mrs. Adams and Mrs. Adams' birthday, after the performance, large tables were erected in the "big top," and with magic-like rapidity the caterers spread a bounteous repast of good things to eat and drink. Mr. and Mrs. Adams were the recipients of several handsome and valuable presents from members of the company, and Mrs. Adams received from her husband a beautiful two-karat diamond ring.[69]

At the end of 1907, Jim went broke and closed his show. He had to sell his house to pay his debts and to raise enough money to start again.[70]

THE JAMES ADAMS VAUDEVILLE SHOWS

In the spring of 1908, Jim launched his vaudeville shows, two separate companies playing in tents in small towns, a week at each stand. The first listing for the companies in the Routes section of *Billboard* was for the week of March 9, 1908. Company Number 1, James Adams, manager, played at Wadesboro, North Carolina. Company Number 2, C. F. Haraden, manager, played at Edgefield, South Carolina.[71] For the next four years the two units crisscrossed the Southeast, from Florida to Maryland, and as far west as Tennessee, Kentucky, and Alabama.

Admission was ten cents. Overhead was small; there were only about twenty-five people in the company, including the band and the canvas men.[72] They traveled in two railroad cars, the people in one, the gear in the other.[73]

Judging from reviews in local newspapers, the company offered more than traditional vaudeville fare. In 1910 in Gastonia, North Carolina, Adams assured his audiences that the trapeze artist, Mr. Rizard, who had been injured at Gastonia the year before, was entirely recovered and prepared to perform again. The company band entertained in the town square at noon and 7:00 P.M. all week.[74] Later that year in Washington, North Carolina, the *Daily News* reported that on Friday night Adams presented the play *Ten Nights in a Bar Room,* and performed it exceedingly well. "This bill has been presented in this city several times by different companies, but last night far exceeded them all."[75]

Although Jim was no longer performing on the trapeze, he was still performing.

A new sensational feature of the show is Mr. Adams' wonderful and astonishing "electrical act." Mr. Adams has a current of electricity, 150,000 volts strong, passed through his body, and paper and any other combustible coming in contact with his body immediately catches fire and burns.[76]

Later Jim claimed that he pioneered the ten-cent traveling vaudeville tent show in the Southeast. His biggest problem was that the idea was too good. According to Wesley Stout, "His success was so spectacular, in fact, that each year the bulk of his company left him and started rival ten-cent shows until the golden goose was cooked."[77]

Jim was successful enough that by the end of 1911 he had made his fortune and decided to retire. According to Maude McDougall, Jim and Gertie returned to Michigan, bought property near Detroit where in 1916 they still claimed their residence, and went to California to visit Gertie's folks.[78] Their whereabouts for the next few years are not clear. For the years 1912 to 1915 Jim and Gertie were listed in the Charlotte, North Carolina, *City Directory* as living at 219 Elizabeth Avenue in that city. The Adamses invested extensively in property in Charlotte. In a record of sale in September 1916,[79] they were still listed as Charlotte residents. By 1920, they were listed as living in Philadelphia.[80]

But wherever he was living in the summer of 1913, Jim got bored and decided to start building his Floating Theatre.[81]

CHAPTER FOUR

The First Ten Years: Places and Events

A GOOD START

*F*or most of its history, the James Adams Floating Theatre played in small towns and its performances were not reviewed in newspapers. Its initial performances in Washington, North Carolina, in 1914 were among the exceptions. After opening night, the reviewer for the *Daily News* reported that "high praise is being heard not only for the uniqueness and well appointed Floating Theatre but the performance presented."[1] Singled out for special notice were the Martyne sisters and Calvin Clark: "They were artists in their line and did much towards the conspicuous success of the performance."[2]

After the second night's performance, the *Daily News* reported:

"The Girl Ranchman" was presented to a packed house on the "Playhouse" last night and all present seemed to be well pleased with the performance. The entire company was again at their best and did the stunt with the skill of veterans. The audience enjoyed every moment of the production which was conspicuous for thrilling climaxes, witty sayings and scenic effects. The specialties were again pleasing, receiving hearty applause.[3]

The reviews for the remaining performances were equally approving. After the Friday night performance of *Tempest and Sunshine,* the feature play of the week, the *Daily News* reported that "People had to be turned away from the doors as they could not be provided with seats."[4]

THE ITINERARY

The theatre's itinerary for 1914 is difficult to trace. Adams listed his route in *Billboard* for only four weeks that year. There are very few surviving local papers, and Jim advertised in very few of those.

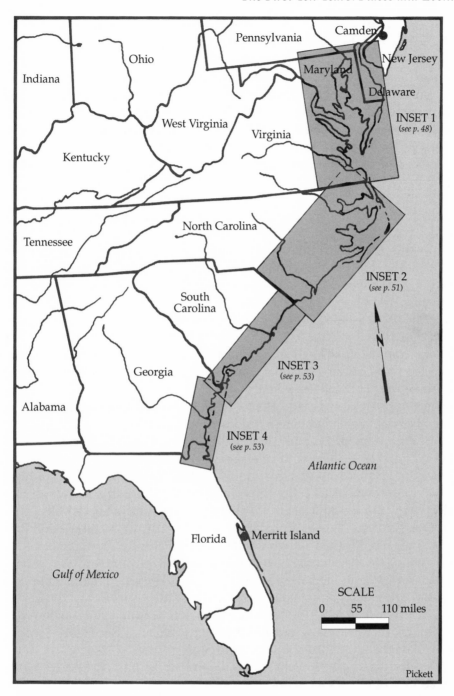

The Floating Theatre played at one time or another in at least 142 locations in eight states, traveling as far north as Camden, New Jersey, and as far south as Merritt Island, Florida. For most of its history, however, the theatre played primarily to towns on the Chesapeake Bay and in the Albemarle region of North Carolina.

45

From 1915 to 1937, the theatre's itinerary is well documented. For three years, 1915 to 1917, a musician on the boat, L. D. Waldorf, kept in his journal a complete list of the ports of call. From 1918 to 1937 the management regularly listed its routes in *Billboard*. There are some conflicts of evidence and omissions, but most of these can be resolved by local newspaper articles and advertisements. The itinerary from 1938 to 1941 is, like that of 1914, more difficult to establish. The theatre published no itinerary in *Billboard*, so most of the ports I have identified for the later years I found through local papers.

In 1914, after completing its opening week in Washington, the Floating Theatre went up the Pamlico River to Greenville, North Carolina, for a week. It returned to Washington for a single performance on Monday, March 16, and then went downriver for two days each at Bath and Aurora and a week at Belhaven.[5]

After the theatre's last performance in Belhaven March 28, the next performance documented in a newspaper story is in Irvington, Virginia, on May 18, seven weeks later. It is, however, possible to project the theatre's route from March to May.

In 1914 the section of the Intracoastal Waterway running from Albemarle Sound to the Pamlico River by way of the Alligator and Pungo rivers was not completed.[6] The Floating Theatre had to go north through the less protected Pamlico and Roanoke sounds. The major steamboat wharves on that route were at Belhaven, where the boat called the week of March 23, Middletown in Hyde County, and Sky Cove on Roanoke Island.[7] Mildred Gibbs[8] remembers the theatre playing at Middletown and P. D. Midgett[9] remembers it stopping at Roanoke Island before 1920. It did not return to Roanoke Island until 1921 and to the Middletown area (Engelhard) until 1935.

The next steamboat wharf north of Roanoke Island was in Elizabeth City. If the showboat took the same route in 1914 that it is known to have followed in 1915 from Elizabeth City—half a week each in South Mills, North Carolina, and Deep Creek, Virginia; and a week each at Hampton, Smithfield, and Crittenden, Virginia—it would have arrived at the Rappahannock River in the middle of May. It may have called in Mathews County in 1914, because a woman writing in the Baltimore *Sun*[10] in 1939 remembered it playing there in 1914, but I found no mention in 1914 in the Mathews *Journal*.

The week of May 18, the Floating Theatre was in Irvington; the week of May 25, in Urbanna;[11] and the week of June 1, in Reedville.[12] It most likely played also at Tappahannock and Sharps.[13]

After Reedville, it went across the Bay to the Eastern Shore where it played in Virginia at Onancock.[14]

Sometime in June or July the theatre played at Tangier Island, Virginia, for the first and only time. It most likely played there the week of June 8, on the way from Reedville to Onancock, and McDougall described the visit:

Ever been to Tangier Island? It is a friendly little place . . . [but] it is rather a problem to get up to it. They came as near as they could with their own power boat towing them. Then they got a whole fleet of little oyster and fishing boats, built for those particular waters, and hitched onto them and said, "now, all together pull!" "It was a mosquito fleet for fair," according to the authority . . . quoted. "I reckon those boats carried about half-a-horse-power engines. But they got us there—at flood tide. And when the tide went out—well, we were very much there!"[15]

Billboard reported the showboat at Saxis, Virginia[16] (for the first and only time), and at Snow Hill and Pokomoke City, Maryland.[17] But the Crisfield *Times*[18] reported it at Crisfield from July 6 to 11, the week *Billboard* had the theatre in Saxis. The *Times* reported that the theatre played at Deal Island the week after Crisfield.[19] The Wicomico *News* had the theatre in Salisbury, Maryland, on July 20, the week following Crisfield.[20]

After Salisbury there is no documentation for the theatre's itinerary until September 7, when it was in Annapolis. In the intervening six weeks it probably played the ports on the Nanticoke River: Vienna and Sharptown, Maryland, and Seaford and Laurel, Delaware. I think it then went to Honga and Solomons, Maryland.

After Annapolis it played at Port Deposit[21] and Elkton.[22] In October, after it left Elkton, it visited the Chester River, where it played at Chestertown,[23] Centreville,[24] Queenstown,[25] and Rock Hall.[26] It may also have played at Georgetown on the Sassafras.

On November 2 the theatre opened a week's run at St. Michaels, Maryland,[27] the only town the theatre visited every one of its twenty-seven full seasons.

The next week, November 9 to 14, the theatre was at Denton, Maryland, on the Choptank River.[28] My guess is that Adams finished out his season on the Choptank, stopping possibly at one or more of the following: Hillsboro, Greensboro, Secretary, Cambridge.

At the end of the 1914 season, the theatre was towed to Elizabeth City, where Jim Adams produced a special winter season opening January 18, 1915, and closing February 13. The season featured seven plays: *His Daughter's Honor*,[29] *Tempest and Sunshine*,[30] *Her Shadowed Past*,[31] *The Moonshiners*,[32] *A Woman's Warning*,[33] *Why Girls Leave Home*,[34] and *Wedded and Parted*.[35] Each play was presented for three consecutive nights. The plays featured the showboat's new star, Kathleen Wanda, supported by her own company. One of the plays, *A Woman's Warning*, was written especially for Miss Wanda by her director, costar, and husband, Walter Sanford.[36]

Adams began his 1915 regular season in Elizabeth City February 27. He did not begin it without some embarrassment. His advertisement in the

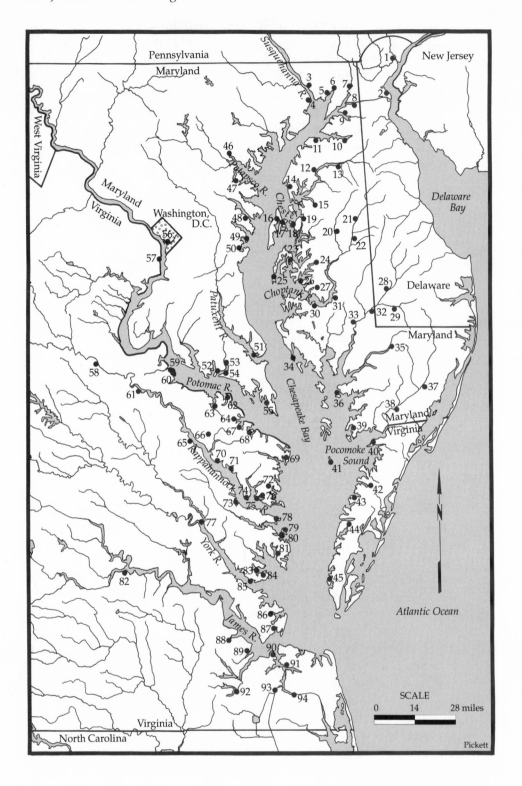

Pennsylvania
Maryland

Susquehanna R.

New Jersey

1

3

6 7
5 8
4 9

West Virginia

46

Patapsco R.

11 10

12

47

13

Maryland

Virginia

Washington, D.C.

48

14

Chester R.

15

16
17 18 19
20
21
22

Delaware Bay

49
50

56

23

57

24

28

Delaware

25 26 27

Choptank R.

Patuxent R.

30 31

33

32 29

Maryland

35

51

58

59

52 53
54

34

Potomac R.

60

61

55

36

37

63
62
64
67

38

Maryland
Virginia

65 66

70

68

39

69

Rappahannock R.

71

Pocomoke Sound

40

41

72

42

74
73 75

76

43

77

78
79
80

44

York R.

81

82

83 84

45

85

Atlantic Ocean

86
87

James R.

88
89

90

91

92 93
94

SCALE

0   14   28 miles

N

Pickett

Virginia
North Carolina

KEY

1. Wilmington	25. Tilghman	49. Mayo	73. Urbanna
2. Delaware City	26. Oxford	50. Galesville	74. Bertrand
3. Port Deposit	27. Trappe	51. Solomons	75. Weems
4. Havre de Grace	28. Seaford	52. Compton	76. Irvington
5. Charlestown	29. Laurel	53. Leonardtown	77. West Point
6. North East	30. Cambridge	54. Britton	78. Deltaville
7. Elkton	31. Secretary	55. Wynne	79. Gwynns Island
8. Chesapeake City	32. Sharptown	56. Washington, D. C.	80. Cricket Hill
9. Benton Manor	33. Vienna	57. Alexandria	81. Williams Wharf
10. Georgetown	34. Honga	58. Fredericksburg	82. Hopewell
11. Betterton	35. Salisbury	59. Potomac Beach	83. Glass
12. Chestertown	36. Deal	60. Colonial Beach	84. Lady
13. Crumpton	37. Snow Hill	61. Port Royal	85. Gloucester Point
14. Rock Hall	38. Pocomoke City	62. Alliton's Wharf	86. Langley Army
15. Centreville	39. Crisfield	63. Mt. Holly	Air Force Base
16. Stevensville	40. Saxis	64. Kinsale	87. Hampton
17. Chester	41. Tangier Island	65. Tappahannock	88. Smithfield
18. Grasonville	42. Onancock	66. Warsaw	89. Crittenden
19. Queenstown	43. Harborton	67. Lodge	90. Portsmouth
20. Hillsboro	44. Wardtown	68. Bundick	91. Norfolk
21. Greensboro	45. Cape Charles	69. Reedville	92. Suffolk
22. Denton	46. Baltimore	70. Sharps	93. Deep Creek
23. St. Michaels	47. Green Haven	71. Morattico	94. Great Bridge
24. Easton	48. Annapolis	72. Kilmarnock	

The Floating Theatre tied up at McGuire's Wharf, Nomini Creek, Virginia, in September 1922.
Trouper *is moored at the theatre's stern. Photograph courtesy of the Mariners Museum,*
Newport News, Virginia.

Advance announced that the theatre would open on the nonexistent date of "Feb. 30th."[37] He corrected it in the next edition of the paper.[38]

In 1915 Adams began to explore the ports of the Albemarle and for the next six years—through 1921—the Floating Theatre played only in the Albemarle Sound area of North Carolina and in the Chesapeake Bay. In the Chesapeake it played mostly on the western shore of Virginia, the lower Potomac River, and the upper Eastern Shore of Maryland, and less regularly on the Eastern Shore of Virginia. On the western shore of Maryland it played no farther north than Solomons; the exception was an occasional visit to Havre de Grace.

Adams sometimes dropped a town and replaced it with another. He told an interviewer that he dropped a town if he experienced two losing nights there in one week.[39]

The major stops in those years were, on Maryland's Eastern Shore: North East, Elkton, Chesapeake City, Georgetown, Chestertown, Crumpton, Centreville, Queenstown, Stevensville, Oxford, and St. Michaels. On the western shore the chief ports of call were Port Deposit, Solomons, and Leonardtown.

In Virginia, the major stops for the theatre were, on the western shore: Reedville, either Irvington or Kilmarnock, Urbanna, and Tappahannock. Further south, the boat stopped in Mathews County, usually at Williams Wharf, and at Smithfield, Crittenden, and Deep Creek. On the Eastern Shore of Virginia, the major stop was at Onancock.

In North Carolina, the major ports for the showboat were Elizabeth City, Hertford, Edenton, and Columbia.

For the first four years, the Floating Theatre wintered in Elizabeth City at the end of the season, although it offered no winter entertainment after the first winter. At the end of the 1918 season, the boat stayed north for the winter. It closed the season at St. Michaels on October 26, and then went to Baltimore for repairs. Adams took his showboat to the Redman and Vane Shipyard,[40] an unusual establishment. According to Robert Burgess, "One would not expect to find a shipyard that could be described as quaint and serene. Yet there was such a yard in the middle of all the waterfront activity at the port of Baltimore." Redman and Vane were "specialists in repairing wooden ships."[41] The Floating Theatre, after springing a leak in Leonardtown from a grounding at low tide,[42] had first visited Redman and Vane the year before, at the end of August 1917,[43] the year the shipyard opened.[44]

When the Floating Theater left Baltimore in 1918, it went to Elkton for the rest of the winter.[45]

The showboat wintered in the north two more times before 1925. At the end of the 1920 season, it wintered in Oxford,[46] and at the end of the 1922 season, it wintered again in Elkton.[47] The end of the other seasons— 1919, 1921, 1923, and 1924—it wintered in Elizabeth City. In October 1923, the Elizabeth City *Independent* announced, "The Adams crowd are going to winter

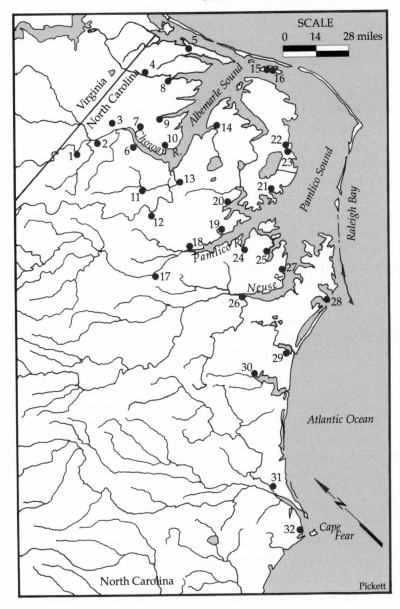

KEY

KEY

1. Murfreesboro	9. Hertford	17. Greenville	25. Vandemere
2. Winton	10. Edenton	18. Washington	26. New Bern
3. Gatesville	11. Windsor	19. Bath	27. Oriental
4. South Mills	12. Williamston	20. Belhaven	28. Beaufort
5. Coinjock	13. Plymouth	21. Swan Quarter	29. Swansboro
6. Colerain	14. Columbia	22. Engelhard	30. Jacksonville
7. Tyner	15. Manteo	23. Middletown	31. Wilmington
8. Elizabeth City	16. Sky Cove	24. Aurora	32. Southport

it in Elizabeth City because this is the cheapest place they have found to tie up. They claim they can get more work done for the money at the local shipyards than in the cities further north of us. That is why the ark will be repaired here."[48] Two years later, however, Adams temporarily abandoned Elizabeth City and wintered his theatre in Crittenden, Virginia, at the end of the 1925 season, and again at the end of the 1926 season.

In 1922 the nation experienced an economic recession. *Billboard* reported that it was "one of the leanest of theatrical years" for the rep shows.[49] Adams made major changes in his itinerary. In North Carolina he began to explore the upper rivers of the Albemarle, playing at Colerain, Murfreesboro, Winton, Windsor, Plymouth, and Williamston. In the early 1920s Adams also added several Chesapeake Bay towns to his list of regular stops, including Rock Hall and Chestertown in Kent County, Maryland; Mt. Holly and Bundick on the Northern Neck; and Glass in Gloucester County, Virginia. He also dropped some of his regular stops in Maryland. The last year he called at Port Deposit was 1925; he played at Queenstown irregularly after 1921, at Stevensville only once after 1923, and at Georgetown only twice after 1922.

The ten years between 1914 and 1924 were successful for Adams and his showboat. He solidified his audiences and made money. The years, however, were not without incidents.

HAPPENINGS AND ADVENTURES

There is a note in the Kent *Shoreman* that illustrates what the Adamses must have experienced at many of the ports when the Floating Theatre visited for the first time. The author of the note is mistaken in his dating of the incident, but he places the event in Fredericktown, Maryland, which Adams listed in his route as Georgetown.

> A friend told me this tale: "After the boat was tied to the wharf
> Mr. and Mrs. Adams looked the small town over. Mrs. Adams sat
> down and cried. She was sure the coming week would be a total
> loss. Much to their surprise they played to a full house every night
> for the next six nights."[50]

Belinda Selby of Aurora remembers that in 1914 the Floating Theatre had a bear aboard.[51] There is no mention of the bear in the Washington, North Carolina, *Daily News,* and Mrs. Mason Lumpkin of Irvington, Virginia, who attended a performance on the boat in 1914, does not remember the bear.[52] But Miriam Haynie in her history of Reedville, Virginia, quotes a resident of that town, Carrol K. Vanlandingham: "When the floating theatre tied up they used to have a big black bear they would put on the wharf—chained to his cage. He would drink Coca-Colas as fast as you gave them to

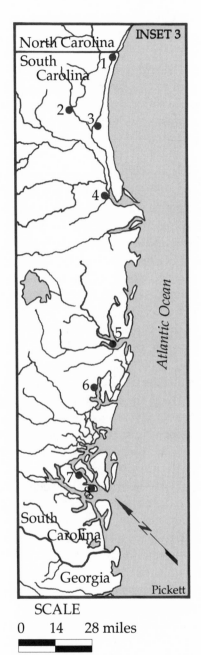

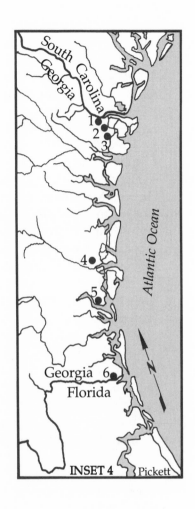

KEY FOR INSET 3

1. Little River
2. Conway
3. Socastee
4. Georgetown
5. Charleston
6. Yonges Island
7. Beaufort
8. Parris Island
   Marine Base

KEY FOR INSET 4

1. Savannah
2. Thunderbolt
3. Isle of Hope
4. Darien
5. Brunswick
6. St. Marys

SCALE

0   14   28 miles

him. He was in a wrestling act in the show."[53] Vanlandingham does not give the year that he saw the bear, but many of his memories are from 1914.

In August 1915 in Chesapeake City, the boat was almost sunk by a flooded bridge. Maude McDougall described the incident:

> Mr. Adams was awakened one morning by shouts from shore and getting into a bathrobe went out to discover what was up and found that his good ship was—way up and straining madly at her leash—or rather hawser. The gangplank was standing on end, and a native was drawling excitedly that they'd better get out or the bridge would fall on them.
>
> They had tied up just a little below a bridge, and a glance at that showed Mr. Adams that the native had reason on his side. The stone foundations were rocking and the water was apparently about to lift the body of the bridge from its moorings. They got out in a hurry—and not much else—and were taken care of in the village while they waited to see if the bridge was due to collapse or not. It didn't. After a while it settled down again as the river fell. They lost a couple of anchors, however, and the "great big hitching post was pulled out by its roots, and some winches and things went overboard." That description is not technical, but it certainly describes. It is the way the soubrette put it, and she was there.[54]

In 1916, on its second visit to Fredericksburg, Virginia, the theatre company suffered a casualty. The current in the Rappahannock River at Fredericksburg can be quite swift, especially after a heavy rain. The boat carried four dogs aboard: a toy poodle belonging to the cook and three little blue Beltons, two bitches and a male, which Mr. Adams planned "to shoot over in the fall." Unfortunately, the male puppy was washed overboard.[55]

There was a fire on board the theatre in Smithfield. Segar Dashiell in her book, *Smithfield, A Pictorial History*, described the incident:

> [The showboat was] a fine old fire-trap, if there ever was one. And it actually did catch fire on one occasion and gave the town quite a scare. It was during a Saturday matinee, when in the middle of "St. Elmo" flames burst out from under the stage and everybody made a break for the single exit at the other end of the auditorium. Mercifully, there was a very small audience, most of them school children, and everybody scuttled to safety without mishap—except a tall girl who leaped from the balcony and broke a couple of ribs. The fire did practically no damage, but had it occurred at a night performance with a full house the result could have been appalling.[56]

Dashiell, who as a young girl was in the theatre at the time of the fire, remembers that a black girl fell from the balcony. She also remembers trying to open a window and discovering that the windows in the auditorium didn't open. She noticed that as a boy ran through the stage to escape he was handed a horn by a musician and asked to save it.[57]

Ann Wilmer quotes Adelaide Gee, another observer of the fire: "As the play was in progress, flames suddenly leaped through the stage flooring. Everyone screamed and in fear started for the entrance and the gangplank. The aisles were just crowded—children pushing children . . . We made it safely to the outside and needless to say, I never went on that boat again."[58]

The descriptions suggest that it was a grease fire in the cookstove, located directly under the stage. There was an open ventilation grate in the floor of the stage. The cook was probably preparing dinner which the cast and crew ate at 4 P.M. It is a safe bet that dinner was burned that evening.

I cannot date the fire. The theatre produced *St. Elmo* in 1915 and 1924, but may have revived it as a matinee offering any year. Dashiell places the fire closer to 1915 than 1924.

In the early years Adams briefly found himself competing with two rivals. The first was in 1915 at Leonardtown, Maryland, where Adams played for the first time on June 28.[59] A little more than a month later, the July 31 St. Mary's County *Enterprise* reported: "Leonardtown is to have a novelty of its own, in the shape of a floating moving picture show, if the plans of Mr. R. E. Van Pelt materialize. Mr. Van Pelt has purchased and now has at Leonardtown wharf a large barge about 75x25 feet, upon which he will at once erect a commodious and model show house."[60] Two weeks later the *Enterprise* reported:

> Robert Emmett's new novelty floating theatre, vaudeville and picture show boat will be completed, it is expected, about August 30th, and will open in Leonardtown.
>
> The show will be under the personal management of Mr. Parker Donegan, the well known black-faced comedian, whose performances proved a source of amusement to many people during the recent series of entertainments here on the James Adams' Floating Theatre. Mr. R. E. Van Pelt will be assistant manager, while Captain Anthony Van Pelt will have charge of the nautical end of the business.[61]

Al Gough, Jr., who has researched the history of the Floating Theatre in Leonardtown, wrote that Anthony Van Pelt moved to Leonardtown from Charles County "around the year 1913." He bought "an acre and a half of land across from Leonardtown Wharf known as part of Buzzards point."[62] Gough doesn't identify what relation R. E. (Robert Emmett)[63] Van Pelt was to Anthony or who the original Robert Emmett was for whom the boat was named.

The bow of the theatre in August 1917 while it was in dry dock at the Redman and Vane Shipyard, Baltimore. On the first level, **left to right**, are an entrance to the balcony, a screened window, the door to an office, the theatre entrance, another office door and a screened window, and a second entrance to the balcony. On the upper level are the living quarters, from 1914 to 1916, for James and Gertrude Adams, and, from 1917 to 1932, for Selba and Clara Adams. The "pup" cabins had not yet been built on the roof. Photograph courtesy of Jacques Kelly.

The Floating Theatre in Baltimore, December 1939, where it played the longest stand in its history. Photograph by A. Aubrey Bodine, courtesy of the Mariners Museum, Newport News, Virginia.

The September 11 *Enterprise* printed a progress report on the *Robert Emmett:*

> Although handicapped by many unsurmountable difficulties in the way of lack of advertisement, weather conditions, counter attractions, etc., the Robert Emmett Floating Theatre began its career at Leonardtown wharf on Saturday night last and, true to previous announcements by the management, the performance was clean, moral and up-to-date. A concert on Sunday night was followed by a variety and vaudeville show on Monday.
>
> Wednesday, the theatre left for Rock Point, River Springs and Colton's and after giving performances at these places will return to this city, where a series of entertainments will be given during Court week.[64]

Parker "Jake" Donegan, the comedian, character actor, and tuba player,[65] who was to direct the entertainment for the Van Pelts, apparently did not make the switch. He was still with Adams at the end of the 1915 season.[66] (He did not, however, work for Adams in 1916,[67] or apparently ever again.)

The *Robert Emmett* returned to Leonardtown, as announced. The company performed on Monday, Tuesday, and Wednesday evenings, September 20 to 22.[68]

Adams, who hated competition, was aware of his rival on the Potomac. The ads for the James Adams Floating Theatre in the Leonardtown papers in 1916 included a statement that he used nowhere else in his advertisements that year, or any other year: "The Only Floating Theatre That Counts!"[69]

But Jim did not need to worry. The *Robert Emmett Floating Theatre* was in business for less than two weeks. The *Enterprise* marked the theatre's death knell. According to the newspaper, the performances were "first-class in every particular" and, unfortunately, "worthy of better patronage than they received."[70]

Compared to the three-state sweep of Adams's first season, Van Pelt's entry into the repertoire movement was modest in territory. Colton Point was at the entrance to the next river north of Leonardtown, and River Springs was a few miles north of Colton Point. Rock Point, Van Pelt's most distant port, was barely in the next county, a few miles north of River Springs. The pattern suggests that Van Pelt may have been trying to establish a circle stock on water. Most likely, however, he didn't understand show business well enough, and he apparently accrued more debts with his enterprise than profits. In September he sold his house and lot on Wharf Hill for two hundred dollars, "subject to the existing liens."[71] Within three years he had sold his last holdings in St. Mary's and had left the county.[72]

The Robert Emmett Floating Theatre wasn't Jim's only rival in the early years. Wesley Stout wrote of a secondhand clothing dealer in Elizabeth City, who,

> seeing Adams' harvest in the drama, built a boat in 1917 to play vaudeville and pictures over the same territory. The newcomer was neither a seaman nor showman. A devout churchman, he would not move on Sundays, therefore losing most of his Monday-night performances. The ten-horse-power motorboat he used for towing was inadequate. On the first voyage he set out for Roanoke Island, a forty-mile stretch, much of it open water. The towline caught in the launch's propeller and put it out of business early, and a westerly gale coming up, the show boat let go its anchor. The old wire cable snapped and the theatre went lurching drunkenly off before the wind.
>
> "I reckon you were sort of scared?" the mate of a lumbering schooner asked the secondhand clothing man later.
>
> "Scared, nothing!" he retorted. "The wind was driving me just the way I wanted to go."
>
> Sure enough, he had, by the grace of Neptune, waltzed right up to the desired landing on the old Sir Walter Raleigh homestead.[73]

This second rival lasted longer than the first. According to Stout, "The boat survived three seasons, then was sold to a logging company, which junked the superstructure and converted the hull into a barge."[74] Entries in *Merchant Vessels of the United States* suggest that the secondhand clothing merchant's venture into show business lasted longer than that. *Merchant Vessels* identifies a barge of 454 tons named *Floating Movies*, which was built in 1915 in Elizabeth City and was abandoned in 1924.

At the end of April and the beginning of June 1918, Adams played a week at Langley Army Air Force Base in Earnest, Virginia. The United States had been at war for just over a year, and no doubt Adams visited the newly organized air base as a patriotic gesture. In a note to *Billboard* he claimed, nonetheless, to have done "excellent business." They also had fun. "The entire company was entertained by the officials as well as by many of the aviators during the engagement."[75] Adams may have overstated his financial success at the base, or he may have encountered security restrictions, but for whatever reasons, it was the only visit the Floating Theatre made to a military installation during the First World War.

In 1919 the boat sailed south from Elkton, Maryland, where it had spent the winter. During the week of July 4 at Solomons, Maryland, among the audience attending the theatre were Mrs. Alfred Gwynne Vanderbilt and Secretary of the Navy Josephus Daniels and his wife, from Washington, D.C.[76]

There were, however, disappointments in the 1919 season. Twice the theatre cancelled engagements, first in September on the Rappahannock River, and again in October in the Dismal Swamp Canal. It was because of the interrupted 1919 season that Elizabeth City, North Carolina, and Tappahannock, Virginia, cannot be counted with St. Michaels, Maryland, as towns the theatre played every season.

Adams's troubles that year began on the Rappahannock. He announced that the theatre would play for the first time near Warsaw, Virginia. Warsaw, at the center of the Northern Neck, is the Richmond County seat. For the first five years, the only stop the theatre made in Richmond County was at Sharps. The stop apparently was not profitable for Adams because after 1918 he stopped playing there. In 1919 he planned to play Richmond County at Totuskey Bridge, where the road from Warsaw to Lancaster County crossed Totuskey Creek approximately three miles from Warsaw. Adams advertised that his band would give a free open-air concert at Warsaw at 2:30 on the afternoon the theatre was to open.[77]

The boat never arrived. The following Friday, the Northern Neck *News* announced that the "Adams Floating Theatre had to go on the dry dock at Norfolk for repairs and could not come to Totusky Bridge this week and will not be able to come before next summer." In fact, the boat did not attempt to play again at Warsaw until the 1921 season, when it played at Totusky Bridge for the first and only time.

Before its scheduled visit to Warsaw in 1919, the boat played at Kilmarnock, August 25 to 30,[78] and for the first and only time at Morattico, September 1 to 6. At the end of what the Rappahannock *Record* reporter, at least, considered a successful week, Adams announced that the boat needed repairs and was being taken to Norfolk.[79]

Although there is no clear record, there is the possibility that the showboat may have been in an accident. A Michigan newspaper in 1937 gave a description of a 1919 mishap, based on an interview with Selba Adams after he left the Floating Theatre. The reporter confused several events and described them as if they were one. Amid the confusion, he included this description of the 1919 mishap, which I was unable to confirm with any other source: "Two tugs were towing the theatre with a Y-shaped tow line when one of the hawsers broke. This swerved the boat into the bank where a hidden log tore a hole in the bottom. The show boat settled in about four feet of water, enough to spoil the decorations and seats and spoil the prospects of continuing the show that year."[80] The description is similar to the sinking of the boat in the Dismal Swamp Canal in 1929 that took place after the season had closed, while the theatre was being towed by only one tug. It is possible, although I have no corroborating evidence, that on the way from Kilmarnock to Morattico, the theatre swerved into the bank of the Rappahannock and sank. It is difficult to believe that if the theatre had suf-

fered extensive damage, however, that the management could have continued playing for another week.

Whatever happened to the boat in 1919, it was significantly refurbished
after it was towed to Norfolk. In 1920 Adams advertised that he was "Coming
this Season with Enlarged Stage, New and Better Scenery, New Unexcelled
Lighting System, New Opera Chairs, New Private Boxes."[81] The changes in
the boat suggest that decorations and seats had been spoiled. Also, it was in
1920 that Adams moved his generators from under the stage to the tugs.

According to *Billboard,* the theatre resumed its tour four weeks after
Morattico in 1919, playing the week of September 29 at Crittenden[82] and the
next at Deep Creek.[83] From Deep Creek, the boat returned to Crittenden
where the season was abandoned. Late in November the boat was towed to
Elizabeth City for the winter.[84]

The reason for the final interruption of the 1919 season is clear.
Rosedell Adams, mother of Jim, Selba, and Beulah, died on October 17, and
the family gathered in Saginaw for the funeral. Rose had been ill for two
weeks,[85] and there must have been some prescience of her pending death,
because Adams closed in Deep Creek on the eleventh and moved the short
distance back to Crittenden rather than forward the only slightly longer
distance to Elizabeth City. Despite the interruptions to his season, Jim reported to *Billboard* that 1919 was "one of the most profitable and pleasant"
in the boat's history.[86]

The next year, on July 4,[87] the boat and crew suffered a harrowing
experience in a terrible storm on the Chesapeake.

When the boat was crossing to Reedville from Onancock on the Eastern
Shore of Virginia[88] it was struck by a severe storm near Tangier Island, one of
the widest areas of the Bay. The tow rope parted.[89] The crew on the Floating
Theatre threw "fourteen hundred pounds of anchor"[90] overboard but the anchors, reporter Rose Marvin wrote, "failed to hold and the cruising coliseum
was swept across the bay before a howling wind."[91]

Wesley Stout described the way the boat "strained at its anchors for fourteen hours, . . . waves breaking over the roof of the theatre."[92] Marvin reported
one of the theatre's tugs "developed engine trouble and not being able to
steer it became a menace to the other. The serviceable tug finally was cut
loose from the disabled one and with Mr. [Selba] Adams on board drew up
alongside the show boat. Mr. Adams made a wild leap from the tug and
sprawled on the deck of the playhouse striking his head on the boards. The blow
dazed him, but he was kept from sliding back in the bay by a workman."[93]

Marvin further described the disaster: "During the transfer of Mr.
Adams from the tug to the show boat the larger craft, in one of its lunges,
had punched a hole through the side of the tug above its water line. It then
became necessary for the injured tug to make a run across the bay for repairs. So the show boat was left to weather the storm alone."[94]

"A fisherman crept out of the lee of the island to the rescue, but lost its wheel and had to run for it . . . ,"[95] according to Stout. "It . . . was . . . towed back to port by a sister fishing smack,"[96] in Marvin's account.

"Distress signals were hoisted" on the Floating Theatre, "and at dawn two fishing boats towed them into port. Once safe in Reedville harbor," asserts the 1926 Minneapolis newspaper story, "half the theatre's company and help, including the cook, packed up and departed for parts unknown."[97]

Near the end of the season in 1921, when the theatre was playing Elizabeth City, Adams went into temporary partnership with an airplane company.

For six days from Wednesday, November 16, until Monday, November 21, Aeromarine Airways, Inc., had one of their flying boats at Elizabeth City, carrying passengers aloft to view the city—at five dollars per passenger for a six-minute flight.[98] The passengers for the seaplane boarded from the Floating Theatre. "We sat in the cockpit and watched them take parties out in the hydroplane from the floating theatre," wrote Adele Hersey, who observed the proceedings from the yawl *Cachalot* anchored in the harbor.[99]

The seaplane and the showboat were the source of some humor, as well. In "Girl Falls Overboard Much Comedy Results," the *Daily Advance* reported:

> An accident, a rescue and feats like one sees in comic strips in the movies were pulled off here Friday afternoon . . . A party of young folks . . . went out in a motor boat to view the landing of the hydroplane . . . When well out in the . . . harbor, one of the girls, climbing about the rail of the small craft, lost her balance and fell overboard. The young man, . . . leaving his engine running, dashed to the deck and dived over after her. In a moment he recognized that the girl was one of the best swimmers, masculine and feminine, in the city, and they turned about to swim toward Adams Floating Theatre . . .
>
> Meanwhile, the accident, witnessed from the shore, had created a commotion there. One man with a skiff, in his excitement put one foot on the edge of his boat and the other on the dock . . . The skiff inevitably moved off shore, and the man fell overboard. Watching this further excitement, another man on the floating theatre leaned over too far, and fell into the water, wildly pulling three others with him.
>
> The crowd aboard the boat whence the first fall overboard had occurred meanwhile were having troubles of their own. In an effort to turn their gas boat around, they had broken their steering gear, and were drifting helplessly about. And all the while the girl who first fell in, and the swimmer who went in after her, were pad-

dling their way calmly and leisurely toward the shore, and watching the comedy in progress on all sides.[100]

On Monday, November 21, the hydroplane flew south, and the Floating Theatre followed, and so did the Herseys, who sailed south of Manteo to Wanchese, on Roanoke Island. According to *Billboard*, Adams finished out his season with a week each in Hertford, Edenton, and Columbia.[101] But if Mrs. Hersey is correct, Adams altered his schedule and went instead to Manteo to stay with the seaplane. "We sighted an areoplane, it flew down & landed at Wanchese Wharf," she wrote. "The Floating Theatre is at Manteo. They went out with parties 5 times."[102]

CHAPTER FIVE

The First Ten Years: Performers

THE COMPANY

*A*ctors for stock companies were hired by type. Many of the plays written for the early stock companies identified the characters, not by physical or social description, but by actor type. The types were identified in pairs, male and female. For serious parts there were male and female leads, male and female characters, male and female juveniles (the females were often called ingenues or soubrettes), and the male and female heavies. The words hero and villain were not used. The invitation to "cheer the hero and hiss the villain" was issued later by satirists of the old plays. The stock companies presented their plays with sincerity and their audiences received them seriously.

The comic characters were even more specialized. In general, comic characters were defined as light comic or broad comic. There could be light or broad comic characters of either sex or of any age, but comic actors usually specialized in one particular type. There were three primary comic characters in the repertoire theatre: the G-string, the blackface, and the Toby. There was a female equivalent to the Toby, Sis Hopkins, but no female comic types emerged with the specific identity of the G-string or blackface, although there were, of course, comic roles that called for elderly or blackface women. Often, however, the female comic blackface roles were played by men. The soubrette or the character comic woman was usually described simply as light or broad (or low).

The G-string character was an old man. He evolved from the nineteenth-century comic Yankee character, sometimes with a dose of the frontiersman character thrown in. He was characterized by a squeaky male voice (from which, theatre troupers have argued, the name G-string came), and a goateelike beard.[1] The cartoon Uncle Sam is a G-string character. The G-string did not have a specific personality. He could be cantankerous or pleasant, wise or gullible, according to the bent of the actor; but like almost all of the repertoire comic characters, he was commonsense smart.

The blackface character was built on stereotypes the white theatre establishment identified as being "typical" of black people. The stereotypes were built on such characteristics as slowness, laziness, dishonesty, and sometimes good humor and loyalty, especially to white employers. In the title of his history of blacks in American films, Donald Bogle summarizes the stereotypes: *Toms, Coons, Mulattoes, Mammies & Bucks.* Amos and Andy were blackface comics.

Black actors, such as Stepin Fetchit, Rochester, Bojangles, and Butterfly McQueen, who were able to break into films in the industry's early years did so only by presenting blackface stereotypes. In tribute to their talents, the black performers had to be exceptionally talented to be able to struggle through the barriers of bigotry they faced. Bogle argues that they "elevated *kitsch* or trash and brought to it arty qualities if not pure art itself."[2]

The Adams company featured a blackface comedian, often in the plays, and always in the concerts.

Both the G-string and the blackface were developments from the nineteenth century, but the Toby was a development of the twentieth century. He was based on the smart country rube, which in precedent went back to Roman comedy, and had appeared frequently in nineteenth-century American drama as a silly or mischievous kid. But in the early twentieth century a series of actors gave special identity to Toby,[3] creating a character recognizable to rural audiences. Toby was a dumb hayseed, usually with red hair and freckles, who was commonsense smart. In the end, no one got the better of him. Red Skelton's Clem Kadiddlehopper is a Toby. Some of the playwrights producing works for the repertoire companies created plays especially for actors who specialized in playing Toby.[4] The Toby became so famous in the twentieth century that many writers have referred to repertoire plays and companies as Toby plays and Toby companies.

Repertoire companies adapted plays to suit the specialties of their stars. For example, there is a play, *Mister Jim Baily,* written in 1910 by Charles F. Harrison, a man who deliberately avoided writing Toby characters into his plays. In fact, if he knew a company had introduced a Toby into one of his plays he would recall the play.[5] In this play, Jim Baily is married to a woman he loves but whose mother has made her discontented with him because he is a simple farmer from Oklahoma and doesn't fit into the society his mother-in-law wants for her daughter. Jim's father, who is more country than Jim, visits, and his visit upsets both women. In the original version, Jim's father is a G-string character. I have seen a script[6] in which the father has been rewritten—despite the playwright's admonition—as Jim's brother, so that the part could be played by a Toby.

In 1915, James Adams's sister Beulah and her husband Charles Hunter joined the showboat cast. They did not immediately become the stars of the show, and, in fact, they even left the boat for a period. But by the mid-1920s, they were the mainstays of the show and remained as such until the end of the 1936 season. Beulah was an ingenue and Charlie was (primarily, but not exclusively) a G-string, and that determined the basic nature of the plays the showboat presented. The company hired blackface comics, leads, heavies, characters, and even sometimes Tobys. But the plays were chosen or adapted to feature the ingenue, the G-string, and the blackface.

Following are descriptions of the companies of the Adams Floating Theatre in 1915, 1916, and 1917. The information is quoted from the journals of L. D. Waldorf.[7] Preceding the descriptions are these brief definitions of words and abbreviations used by Waldorf:

Advance: Advance man, went before boat, posted notices, etc.
Alto.: Played the alto saxophone.
B. &. O.: Played in both the band and the orchestra.
B. Drum: Played the bass drum.
Baritone: Played the baritone horn.
Bass: Played the string bass.
Bits: Performed bits in the the comic sections of the vaudeville.
Capt.: Captain of the towboat.
Char's.: Performed character roles, e.g., older people.
Cor.: Played the cornet.
Elec. Eng.: The electrical engineer, who operated the electrical generator.
Gen. Bus.: General business, played parts in plays not assigned to main actors.
Heav. or Heavies: Played malevolent characters, villains.
L. Com.: Played low or broad comic characters.
Mail: Collected and distributed mail at each stop. Also, sent news and routes to *Billboard*.
Mgrs.: Managers of the theatre.
Pea. But.: (I have no idea. Maybe he liked peanut butter.)
S. Drum: Played the snare drum.
Soubr.: Soubrette, played young girl roles.
Spec.: Performed specialties in vaudeville performances.
Traps: Played traps, e.g., snare drum with cymbals, etc., attached.
Trom.: Played the trombone.

Company—1915 Season

Mr. & Mrs. James Adams—*Owners*
Mr. & Mrs. Walter Sanford—*Leads*
Mr. & Mrs. Charles Hunter—*L. Com., Cor., Spec.*
Mr. & Mrs. James Shadrick—*Heavies, Char's.*

Mr. & Mrs. Ed Bellows—*Heavies, Char's.*
Master Albert Bellows—*Spec.*
Capt. John A. Roberts—*Capt.*
Mr. Harry Van—*Advance, B. Drum*
Mr. L. D. Johnson—*Clarinet, B. & O.*
Mr. W. H. Arledge—*Trom., Pea. But.*
Mr. Parker Donegan—*Blackface, Tuba*
Mr. E. E. Markham—*Cornet, B. & O.*
Mr. R. E. King—*Drums, B. & O.*
Mr. Wm. H. Theis—*Violin, Baritone*
Mr. L. D. Waldorf—*Piano, Trombone*
Mr. & Mrs. Ed Miller—*Cooks*

(*Notes:* Mrs. Walter Sanford was Kathleen Wanda. Mrs. Charles Hunter was Beulah Adams. Mrs. James Shadrick was Julia Talbot. Mrs. Ed Bellows was Dolly Temple. Albert was their son. He had a unicycle act. He went to school in Elizabeth City for several winters and "caused quite a stir on the streets as he rode his unicycle back and forth to school."[8])

Company—1916 Season

Mr. & Mrs. James Adams—*Owners*
Mr. & Mrs. A. E. Bellows—*Heavy, Leads*
Mr. & Mrs. Charles Hunter—*Lead, Gen. Bus., Cor.*
Mr. & Mrs. Frank Roberts—*Lead, Gen. Bus., Tuba*
Master Albert Bellows—*Bits, Spec.*
Mr. Rube Freeman—*Blackface, Char., Gen. Bus.*
Capt. W. E. Freeman—*Capt.*
Mr. Harry Van—*Advance, B. Drum*
Mr. L. D. Johnson—*Clarinet, B. & O.*
Mr. W. H. Arledge—*Trom., Pea. But.*
Mr. Carl E. Neel—*Cornet, B. & O., Mail*
Mr. William H. Theis—*Violin, Baritone*
Mr. L. D. Waldorf—*Piano, Trombone*
Mr. & Mrs. Carl Clover—*Leads, Chars., Cor.*
Mr. M. D. Jacobs—*Blackface, Gen. Bus.*
Mr. Chas. Raymand—*Blackface, Gen. Bus.*
Mr. Harry Herring—*Drums, B. & O.*
Mr. George Wazo—*Magic, Janitor*
Mrs. George Wazo—*Cook*

(*Notes:* Mrs. Carl Clover was Crystal Clover. The Clovers apparently replaced the Roberts later in the season. There were three blackface comics

The band of the Floating Theatre brought their instruments to Betterton, Maryland, in 1917, although the boat didn't stop there that year. Left to right, back row: *L. D. Johnson, Charles Hunter, Pop Neel, possibly William Stohlmann, and George LaVale.* Front row: *Harry Van, L. D. Waldorf, W. H. Arledge. Photograph courtesy of Maisie Comardo.*

A view of the stern of the boat, showing the double tier of staterooms, each of which has one window. The picture was taken at Solomons, Maryland, by Bob Hoskins, circa 1929. Photograph courtesy of Al Gough, Jr.

Selba Adams, Jim's older brother, managed the Floating Theatre after Jim "retired" in 1917. Photograph courtesy of Robert Struble.

Clara Struble Adams, Selba's wife, served as housekeeper for the Floating Theatre from 1917 to 1932. Photograph courtesy of Robert Struble.

Delmar Adams, Selba and Clara's only child, was seventeen when his father became manager of the showboat. Delmar spent summers on the boat and winters in school. Photograph courtesy of Robert Struble.

Charles M. Hunter was director and character actor on the James Adams Floating Theatre. Charlie's wife Beulah was Jim Adams's sister. Photograph courtesy of Marguerite Young.

L. D. Waldorf, a musician with the Floating Theatre 1915–17, kept a journal listing the company, itinerary, and repertoire of the theatre for each of those years. Photograph courtesy of Maisie Comardo.

Beulah Adams, Jim's sister and star of the James Adams Floating Theatre, was known as "the Mary Pickford of the Chesapeake Bay." Photograph courtesy of the Mariners Museum, Newport News, Virginia.

in 1916, each succeeding the one listed previously. George Wazo did magic acts before the play and in the concerts.)

Company—1917 Season

Mr. & Mrs. Selba Adams—*Mgrs.*
Delmar Adams—*(Job unknown)*
Mr. & Mrs. Walter Sanford—*Leads*
Mr. & Mrs. Harry Schuman—*Char's., Heav.*
Mr. & Mrs. Charles Hunter—*Char., Cornet, Heavy, Soubr.*
Capt. & Mrs. William Allen—*Capt. and Cook*
Mr. William (Billy) Stohlmann—*Alto., Comedy*
Mr. Harry Van—*Advance, B. Drum*
Mr. James Bratton—*Blackface, S. Drum*
Mr. George La Vale—*Traps, Baritone*
Mr. Louis (Musical) Webster—*Violin, Bass, Spec.*
Mr. L. D. Johnson—*Elec. Eng., Clarinet, B. & O.*
Mr. W. H. Arledge—*Trombone, Pea. But.*
Mr. Carl Neel—*Cornet, Bandmaster, B. & O.*
Mr. L. D. Waldorf—*Trombone, Piano*
Mr. and Mrs. John L. Mets (*Violin, Piano*) left at Deep Creek, Va. Apr. 7.
L. D. Waldorf joined at South Mills Apr. 4 and Musical Webster at Smithfield Apr. 9
Roland Ward (*Waiter, Janitor*) left at Urbanna, Va. May 12.
Mr. and Mrs. Harry Schumann left at Onancock, Va. June 20 and Mr. and Mrs. James Bratton joined there the same date.
Mr. and Mrs. Walter Sanford left at Rock Hall, Md. Sept. 15 and Mr. and Mrs. Phil Maher joined there the same date.
Delmar Adams left Oct. 11 at Queenstown, Md. for Shepherd, Mich., to attend school.

(*Notes:* This was the first year Beulah Adams was listed as the soubrette. Mrs. Selba Adams was Clara. Delmar was Clara and Selba's son. In 1917 he was 17 years old. The Sanfords were back from the 1915 season. It is reported that Roland Ward was asked to leave the boat at Urbanna because he had expressed an "unnatural" fondness for some of the men in the orchestra.[9])

Two aspects of a repertoire company are illustrated by the information in Waldorf's journals. The first is that the performers had to be versatile because they were expected to do more than one job. On the Floating Theatre the performers had responsibilities Waldorf didn't list. Many of the orchestra members sold candy and other refreshments for the commission they got from the sales. They also performed as "general business" if the management chose to present a play with a cast larger than the usual four men and three women. For example, in 1932 in Norfolk, in a production of W. C. Herman's *Where the River Shannon Flows*, Harry Van appeared in a few brief bits as an Italian laborer who constituted "a one-man gang." [10]

Management had other ways of solving the problem of a large cast. One was to double cast, that is to have one actor play more than one role. Another was to combine or eliminate characters, often with interesting results. A trouper with a circle stock company tells of touring one year with a reduced cast. One of the local boys they hired to help unpack the truck and set up the scenery was disappointed with the small number of actors the troupe carried. "Is the villain going to be on the telephone again?" he asked. [11]

The second aspect of trouping illustrated by Waldorf's list is the changeableness of the company. Troupers were independent people. They had to be because there was no security in their work. If they liked their working conditions, including roles, food, housing, pay, management, and colleagues, they would stay. If not, they moved on.

The turnover rate on the Floating Theatre was no better or worse than the average touring company. In years of national prosperity, the turnover rate was higher than in years of recession or depression, because in good years the performers had more employment choices. Most performers stayed with Adams for a season. Some stayed for many years, some stayed for a few weeks or months only, some came and went and came back years later for another season.

Many male troupers belonged to the Elks. Wherever they toured they could always find a welcome at the local Elks club. Many Floating Theatre actors and musicians were affiliated with the Elks club in Elizabeth City, North Carolina.

After the turn of the century, the marketplace for troupers was *Billboard* magazine in Cincinnati. *Billboard* began publication in the middle 1890s as a trade paper for bill posters, that is, for the men who went before the circuses and other traveling companies and "posted the bills," or pasted up the posters. At the turn of the century, *Billboard* was sold and the new management campaigned to make it the voice of professional entertainers. The paper's initial target was the circus. It wanted to surpass the *Clipper* as the voice of all tent show workers. By the time Adams built his Floating Theatre, *Billboard* was the newspaper for troupers. It carried news from New York and other entertainment centers. It carried news of every segment of the entertainment business, including the film industry, vaudeville, and the music industry. In these areas *Billboard* had significant rivals, including *Variety*, but after 1910, it was the only voice for the repertoire actor. When a repertoire or circle stock company wanted performers, it advertised in *Billboard*. When a repertoire performer was at liberty, he or she advertised in *Billboard*. Following is a typical ad for the Floating Theatre:

JAMES ADAMS FLOATING THEATRE WANTS

Team for General Business, some Characters, must do Specialties; Blackface Man to do Parts, to put on Nigger Acts. This is not a Musical Comedy, but a Dramatic show, with a Concert. Offer a long season, sure money and good accommodations, In return you must be able to troop.
Harry Fuller, wire.
Week of May 9th, Chestertown, Md.; 16th, Crumpton, Md.[12]

Troupers prided themselves that they were professional entertainers. They made their living under the worst of conditions. They were underpaid, often cheated of wages by unscrupulous managers, unemployed as often as employed. But despite all, they paid their bills, put their kids through college, and saved for their retirement. Troupers had no use for amateurs, for people who performed for self-expression, or for kids who learned to act in college. A trouper wasn't foremost an "artiste," he was a professional, who knew how to leave his audience wanting more.

The artistic conditions under which the troupers labored would appall even the most hardened dinner theatre actor today. Typically the actors rehearsed one week preparing six plays. On Monday morning they rehearsed play number one, on Monday afternoon, play number two. Tuesday they rehearsed plays three and four, Wednesday plays five and six. Thursday through Saturday was a repeat of Monday through Wednesday. On Sunday, when there was no rehearsal, they memorized any lines for the plays they did not already know. On the following Monday, they rehearsed play number one during the day and performed it that night. They did the same with each of the other plays during the rest of the week. After that there were no more rehearsals unless the management replaced a play or decided to carry more than six.

Even adding an extra play was sometimes done without additional rehearsals. In his autobiography, rep actor Neil Schaffner told the story of the rep company manager, Doc Rucker, who claimed that his company could perform any play requested by the audience.

> There's an old story, not hard to believe, about one such request for *Trilby*. Doc is supposed to have called the company together and asked, "Any you birds ever played *Trilby*?" None of them had.
> "Nevertheless," Doc said, "tomorrow night we play *Trilby* and the first sonofabitch that calls her Kathleen is fired."

He was referring, of course, to *Kathleen Mavourneen,* a grand old repertoire bill that every rep actor and most audiences knew.[13]

During the same week they rehearsed the plays, the company also prepared the specialties to be performed between the acts or during the concerts that followed the plays. These performances had to be different every night because they would be playing all six nights to essentially the same audience. A performer's specialty might be singing, so she would sing different songs every night. The experienced trouper's rehearsals were simply a matter of making sure the orchestra knew her key and tempos, didn't play too loud, and knew when to apply any special effects. Any amateur who had talked his way into the company[14] and had faked his way through the plays was in big trouble when he found himself expected to know (without rehearsal) how to set up the comic for the "barbershop" routine or the "whisky gag"—something every trouper had seen a thousand times and knew by heart.

Part of the trouper's disdain for the amateur was because the amateur had not paid his dues. Being an actor, especially a touring actor, carried no respect outside the profession. The apocryphal story of the sign on the boardinghouse that read, "No Dogs or Actors Allowed," was not far from the truth. Everyone knew that actors were Gypsies at heart and if given a chance would steal, rape, and pillage, and otherwise cheat storekeepers and landladies, and corrupt unsuspecting daughters and wives.

The following appeared in *Billboard* in 1910:

> Little Virginia Hassell, aged 4½ years, has been turned out of Miss Woodward's fashionable private school in Boston. She was not bad, but her father was an actor.
>
> Mrs. George Hassell, the mother, took the little girl to school two days. When she came on Friday she was summoned into Miss Woodward's office and told that Virginia could not continue going to school there.
>
> "We cannot have children here unless they are from old and well known families," said Miss Woodward.
>
> Mrs. Hassell was amazed.
>
> "I came from an old Kentucky family," she said with spirit. "I was a Murray of Louisville. Mr. Hassell's father is a colonel in the British Army. Do you mean to eject Virginia because her father is an actor?"
>
> "Well," admitted Miss Woodward, "that has something to do with it."[15]

Maisie Comardo remembers that as a child she was shunned by some of her schoolmates because she was known to associate with the actors from the Floating Theatre.[16]

Despite the hardships of being an actor, life on the Floating Theatre offered many amenities for anyone who knew his job. After the shows were mounted, except for performances, the performers' time was their own. In 1920, an actor promised to write to *Billboard* in June about life on the tidewater, but he didn't send his article to "Billy Boy" until November. "Possibly a lapse of four months," he wrote, "might not be construed as an 'early date,' but for those who enjoy bathing, boating, fishing, oyster roasts, and fish frys on moonlit beaches after the show, time is an obsolete article. Months merge into weeks and weeks into days with a rapidity that is startling to say the least."[17] If the author had been on the theatre in its earliest days, he might have mentioned baseball as one of the amenities. For the first few years Jim, who loved baseball and played well, fielded a troupe team and challenged local teams. His wife made him quit when he was badly spiked by a player from a local college. The college team was losing.[18]

The members of the company engaged in the usual leisure-time activities, such as reading, letter writing, sewing, and cleaning, and, of course, playing games. Two popular games were horseshoes and pinochle. Waldorf wrote:

> Jim Adams would very often, right after dinner, come out of his room and send out a challenge.
>
> "I am the best pinochle player on this boat." Somebody backstage would call him a liar and then have to prove it. L. D. "Jack" Johnson, Harry Van, and I would call his bluff and the whole afternoon would be spent in Jim's room playing pinochle.
>
> The year 1916 we had four more pinochle players among the company and that year there were some really hot games.[19]

And, of course, a big activity was eating. The cooks prepared a big breakfast at ten every morning and a dinner at four in the afternoon. The food was rich, plentiful, fresh, and fattening. Around midnight, after the performance, there was always more to eat, especially rich soups and chowders.

One dissenting voice regarding the relaxed comradeship of the performers on the Adams Floating Theatre is Philip Graham's. He wrote:

> Some of those employed thought they did not enjoy the same privileges as others more favored by the management. A caste system prevailed over much of the boat's territory, and something that closely resembled it appeared on board. Those who had been with the Adams for many years were accustomed to the meticulous following of even trivial conventions and could understand and even sympathize with what appeared to newcomers as social affectation. It seems that the management had the habit of taking along

on holiday excursions only the chosen few, and also of admitting only this same select group to the social functions on board.[20]

Graham continued to describe the low wages Adams paid, and then quoted a letter of an actor on the boat advising a friend not to take a job there because of the low pay: "Remember, twenty is the limit and no banners or candy to help."

Despite Graham's assertions, he documents nothing, and the letter he quotes, also without documentation, does not address Graham's contention that the boat had a caste system. I have found nothing in my research to support such a contention.

As to the complaint of the letter writer, it is true Adams paid low wages. The average salary in the early days was perhaps ten dollars a week. He offered ambience and pleasant living, not high wages, and he never went union.

Two important people who traveled with the Floating Theatre were the scene painters, Jim Wilson and his son Hal. For many years Wilson also ran the concessions on the boat. They followed the showboat in Jim Wilson's cabin cruiser *Nandi.* Jim Wilson's wife, daughter, and grandchild traveled with them.[21] Maisie Comardo remembers Hal as a good-looking guy who had many of the girls in Elizabeth City pining for him.[22]

SELBA, CLARA, BEULAH, AND CHARLIE

Jim Adams built the Floating Theatre, but after three years of managing it, he was ready to retire again. Tradition has it that one of the major influences pushing him to retire was Gertie. She had had her fill of trouping in the earlier years, and living on a boat was no more attractive to her than living on a train.

Jim turned over the active management of the theatre to his older brother Selba at the beginning of the 1917 season,[23] after which Jim spent his time managing his extensive real estate investments in West Philadelphia,[24] including the management of the Rivoli movie theatre;[25] entertaining friends;[26] hunting, especially at the hunting lodge on Kent Island, Maryland, he shared with friends;[27] and following the Floating Theatre around the Chesapeake Bay in his private yacht.[28]

Jim owned at least two motor yachts, one after the other. The first was the *Marion,* which he owned as early as 1922,[29] and then came the *Sispud II,* which he owned in 1926[30] and for many years after he sold the Floating Theatre.

Although Selba and his wife Clara lived in the apartment on the Floating Theatre and between them handled the day-to-day business operations of the theatre, Jim was still calling the shots. His picture was on the heralds, where he was identified as "owner and manager." As late as 1920 the notices the theatre put in *Billboard* for performers were signed "James Adams." Between 1921 and 1926 they were not signed, but Jim's Philadelphia address was often given. Only after 1926 were the notices signed by Charles Hunter. All local newspaper notices were signed "James Adams." For example, in July 1928, when the theatre was playing at Fredericksburg, Virginia, the mother of Estelle Pellette, one of the actresses, became seriously ill and the actress left the theatre for several days to be with her in Detroit.[31] The theatre's announcement in the paper that performances would be cancelled was signed "James Adams, Mgr."[32] Whether Jim issued the notice or Selba issued it in Jim's name, it is clear that the theatre was still Jim's.

Selba, or "Selb," as he was called by his family and friends, was less than eighteen months older than Jim. As teenagers they had worked together in the sawmills in Shepherd. In 1899, Selba married Clara Struble,[33] the daughter of the Shepherd postmaster, John Bartley Struble.[34] Both before and after his marriage, Selba lived with the Strubles[35] and continued to work in the stave mill in Shepherd until Jim called him East to manage the Floating Theatre.

Selba, like Jim, was short, but he was heavier. He resembled Jim in facial appearance, but "was more rugged looking, not as handsome."[36] Like Jim, he was athletic and he loved to play baseball. Selba smoked cigars and had a habit of hitching his pants up with his elbows.[37] He also was good-natured. As one actor put it, "The manager is a regular human being."[38] According to Maisie Comardo, "He was friendly and outgoing and very good at small talk. He would stand in the lobby before curtain time, informally dressed in a white shirt, coatless, greeting patrons and old friends."[39]

Selba's sense of fun was much more extroverted than Jim's. An article in the Shepherd, Michigan, newspaper in 1933 described one of his practical jokes.

Selb and his son Delmar rigged a microphone to a radio, and then hid in another room and "broadcast" false news reports to unsuspecting neighbors gathered to listen to the radio. Among the news items Selb and Delmar issued were that Uncle Sam was discontinuing rural mail service to save money; a young woman in the town who had borrowed a friend's car was wanted by the police for car theft; and the sugar factory in a nearby town had been blown up. The news of the sugar factory explosion had local people driving eleven miles to see the ruins.

The pranksters got into the national news as well. They announced that a well-known Detroit churchman noted for his political talks on radio had been shot, and that President Roosevelt had been hit in the head with a billiard ball. They also blew up the Capitol Building in Washington.

Their best fun came at the expense of the local constable when their radio news flashes sent him on a chase after supposed bank robbers.

A writer describing Selb's exploits predicted that, although Selb's shenanigans had been exposed this time, everyone expected him to invent new mischief in the near future. "Having spent many months of each year in an atmosphere of make-believe as manager of a theatrical showboat," the writer concluded, "his training and a bubbling sense of humor fit him for his waggish role as nature adapts a duck to water."[40]

A humanizing story about Selba was told by his great nephew as follows: "After he retired from the theatre, Selba bought an expensive deer rifle. When the season opened, he went out with friends to hunt. He had no trouble locating a deer, but when he raised the rifle to his shoulder and aimed at the animal, he was struck by a severe case of buck fever. He couldn't bring himself to shoot. Despite the ragging by his friends and relatives, Selba came home empty-handed and put his new toy up for sale."[41]

Sometime during his sixteen years on the Floating Theatre, Selba lost his left thumb. On "formal" occasions he wore a tin prosthesis, which his grandson thought looked worse than no thumb.[42] When anyone asked him about his thumb, his usual answer was, "It got run over by a showboat."[43]

Selba's wife Clara was small and somewhat plain. She wore glasses and appears to have been friendly and motherly, but a quiet person; quiet, perhaps, in contrast to Selba. She fit into life on the boat and like Selba got along well with everyone. She always went to her apartment after the plays started because she did not enjoy watching them more than once. She kept a sewing machine in the apartment with which she kept the costumes in repair.[44] She was listed as the housekeeper for the theatre in Waldorf's journal.

Clara was not without a sense of humor. (She probably needed one to live with Selba.) Sometime after 1943 Beulah wrote a letter to a friend in Elizabeth City in which she described Clara's attempt to keep from becoming seasick when the boat was caught in a storm.

> She was advised to place a newspaper over her chest, which she did, but to no avail, for she had a spell of seasickness. After it was over they asked if she had put the newspaper over her chest. She said she did as she was told, but it didn't do any good. She said it *must* have been an *old paper*.[45]

By the 1920s,[46] the artistic management of the Floating Theatre was clearly in the hands of Charles Hunter, Jim and Selba's brother-in-law. Charlie's earlier relationship to the enterprise is a little confusing.

Stout, writing in the *Saturday Evening Post* in 1925, records that Hunter had been with the showboat from the first,[47] and many later historians of the showboat have quoted Stout. L. D. Waldorf, who was with the theatre from 1915 to 1917, corrected that impression in an article in 1954. He remembered that Beulah and Charlie first joined the cast for the second season, in 1915.[48]

Most historians of the James Adams Floating Theatre have recorded that in 1917, when Jim turned over the business management of the theatre to his brother Selba, he also turned over the artistic management to his brother-in-law Charlie. That is not accurate. The director of the plays for most of the 1917 season was Walter Sanford.[49] The director in 1920 was Hal Stack.[50] I found no identification of the director in 1918 or 1919, but I do not think it was Charlie. Charlie and Beulah were not on the boat for the first half of the 1920 season, and they may not have been on board for part or all of the 1919 season. They rejoined the theatre in Leonardtown in July 1920.[51] There is some evidence to suggest that Charlie's directing the plays was a condition of his return to the showboat in 1920.[52]

Charles M. Hunter was born June 3, 1885,[53] in or near Huntington, West Virginia. He followed his older brother, Sam, a musician and comedian, into show business.[54] Charlie's father, Peter Hunter, served in the army of the North during the Civil War. Peter Hunter's brother fought for the South.[55] After the war Peter worked on the rivers as a pilot and tug captain. By the early 1900s he had come ashore at Ironton, Ohio, where he worked as a carpenter and building contractor.[56] Peter died in 1939 at the age of 90, one of the last of the Civil War veterans in the area.[57]

Charles M. Hunter was a tall, thin man, bent in posture, a chain-smoker with terrible eyesight. He often took off his glasses to look younger. When he acted without his glasses, he first had to memorize the scenery. When he went onstage to speak before the play and between the acts he held onto the curtain to make sure he found his way back.[58] It was his poor eyesight that kept him out of the army in the First World War. Charlie was a friendly person, but not as gregarious as the Adamses.

There is some controversy about Charlie's drinking habits. Almost everyone I spoke to who knew Charlie in the 1930s mentioned his steady drinking. An actress onboard the Floating Theatre then remembers, "He always had a bottle of whiskey in his room, but he didn't show the effects of drinking."[59] He was not an offensive drunk, although a man in Tappahannock, Virginia, remembers, on more than one occasion, seeing Charlie in the morning vomiting from the deck of the theatre.[60]

Maisie Comardo, who knew Charlie in the 1920s, disputes the description of Charlie as a sot. She thinks it may have been true in the later years of the showboat when things were not going well for him, but in the glory years he drank very little, if at all. She remembers Charlie as a complex and sensitive person who, in the 1920s when he had the responsibility for the boat's success on his shoulders, had difficulty sleeping and often wrote and worked in the early hours of the morning. She thinks that in the later years he may have drunk to try to sleep.[61]

Before Charlie became an actor he earned his living as a musician. Waldorf described Charlie's playing:

> Charlie Hunter played trumpet in the band but once in a while when Charlie would get worried, or have something preying on his mind, the rest of the company would enjoy a real treat. Charlie would get his flute and walk back and forth across the stage playing the most beautiful music you ever heard. Most of it was improvised to suit Charlie's mood, and everything was still and quiet—listening.[62]

Charlie was also well-read for a self-educated musician and actor. His correspondence with Edna Ferber revealed a man of broad, if not deep, literary interests.

Charlie had a strong imagination and a talent for storytelling. "He was a storehouse of anecdotes, jokes, and yarns about life in the entertainment business."[63] He adapted many of the plays the showboat presented. But his imagination, as delightful as it must have been, presents difficulties for the historian. When Charlie latched onto a good tale that had potential for publicity, he worked it to make it better. All of his autobiographical stories have germs of facts buried in them; the problem for the scholar is to separate the facts from the imagination.

In an interview in 1936 Charlie claimed that his father "was a captain of showboats on the Ohio and Mississippi in the old days, and the first theatrical performance [he] ever saw was aboard one of his [father's] ships."[64] Although this is possible, since Peter Hunter was a pilot and captain on the rivers, I think the claim is probably not true. Philip Graham, in his history of showboats, does not mention Peter Hunter. I found no mention of him in my research on showboats. It is more probable that Peter Hunter worked on a towboat than that he managed a theatre. Most probably, at the time of the interview, Charlie was lost in the nostalgia of what should have been.

Charlie also claimed that he started his show business career on a showboat. "[The arrival of the showboat] was indeed a colorful picture—one which made such an impression on me as a lad, that when the time came for me to spread my wings and earn my own living, I joined a showboat. And I have been a showboater ever since."[65]

Charlie grew up on the Ohio River where Ohio, Kentucky, and West Virginia meet. The area was a hotbed of showboating. It is highly probable that he started his career on a showboat, and he may have been a showboater in spirit ever after, but not always in deed. During his early career Charlie worked the tents as well.

Charlie claimed that he took Jim Adams to see his first showboat and persuaded Jim to build one. Charlie most certainly knew Jim Adams before

1913, and very well may have introduced him to showboats when the vaudeville company was in West Virginia. I rather imagine, however, that no one persuaded Jim where to invest his money.

The first mention I found of Charlie as a performer is in 1906, right after Jim Adams and Johnny Jones ended their partnership. Jim announced that he was taking his circus south for the winter. Sam Hunter was with the show and "Charles M. Hunter had charge of the band."[66] Charlie was 21 at the time.

How long Charlie stayed with Adams after 1906 is not clear. I have a strong feeling he was with Adams's vaudeville show in 1911. On April 11 of that year, Charlie married Beulah Adams in Goldsboro, North Carolina.[67] Tradition in the Adams family holds that Beulah performed as a young girl with her brother's vaudeville company. There is a picture of her at about age sixteen playing in a tent with a man made up as a black woman[68] and Goldsboro was one of the cities Adams played with his vaudeville show. Unfortunately, the Goldsboro newspapers from 1911 were lost in a fire in the newspaper office, so I cannot verify that the show was there in April. However, the man who secured the license for Charlie and Beulah was Harry Van, and there is every reason to think Van was with Jim's vaudeville show.

Adams family legend holds that Charlie wanted to marry Beulah even earlier than 1911, but that Jim prevented the marriage until she was eighteen.

Why Charlie and Beulah were not with Adams in 1914, the first year of the showboat, and where they were, I cannot discover. Waldorf lists them with the cast in 1915, 1916, and 1917, and I assume they were on the boat in 1918.

In July of 1920 Charlie and Beulah visited the editorial offices of *Billboard* in Cincinnati. They had just closed with the Milt Tolbert Number 2 tent show at Lawrenceburg, Tennessee, and were on their way to join the Adams Floating Theatre in Leonardtown. "Mr. [Hunter], who has been playing leads and directing with Miss Adams, will act in the same capacity [on the showboat]."[69]

When and why Charlie and Beulah left the showboat may never be answered. In the interview in *Billboard*, Charlie expressed his regrets at leaving the Tolbert show. "It was the first break in the company in eighteen months . . . and we were sorry to leave."[70]

If the Hunters had been with the tent show for eighteen months, then they were not on the showboat at all in 1919. If so, they may have left the Floating Theatre because Jim would not let Charlie direct and Milt Tolbert offered him a job directing Tolbert's second show.

Another possible explanation is that when the showboat had repair problems in the fall of 1919 that curtailed the season, the Hunters had to look for other work so they joined the Tolbert show. This theory is bolstered by a want ad Tolbert ran in *Billboard* on October 18, 1919,[71] the week the Floating Theatre ended its season in Crittenden. The ad offered a perfect situation for Beulah and Charlie. Tolbert sought an ingenue and a piano player for his Number 2 show, starting November 3.

The Hunters were not with the Floating Theatre for the first half of the 1920 season. They may have stayed with Tolbert because of their contract, but it is difficult to believe that they would have stayed with the tent show if they had really wanted to be on the showboat.

The timing of the Hunters' return in 1920 is interesting. From the notices in *Billboard*, Jim appeared to have had trouble that year holding onto a cast. On February 7, he ran his usual beginning-of-season notice.[72] On February 28, he ran another notice, calling for performers in all lines "because of disappointment."[73] He advertised again on April 17,[74] May 8,[75] and July 3.[76] On July 5, he limped into Reedville and lost many of his cast because of the stormy crossing from Onancock.[77] If there had been a disagreement between Jim and Charlie, it was clear that Jim now needed Charlie and was willing to meet his price. On the other hand, it could simply have been a serendipitous event: Charlie and Beulah were available, and Jim needed a cast. In either case, Charlie and Beulah were back to stay for sixteen years.

If Charlie was something of an enigma, Beulah was not. Many considered her prettier than her photographs. She was, in the early years, tiny, though in her later years she picked up weight, probably from eating the many late-night suppers on the showboat. She was also fond of beer.[78]

As a young friend and admirer described her: "Her hair was dark and abundant, her eyes blue and brilliantly expressive, her nose a bit sharp. Her greatest asset as an actress was her voice, . . . melodious and yet a bit brassy. She could sound like Judy Garland doing Dorothy, with a sob and a cry, or she could ring out like Ethel Merman."[79] An actress who played with her in the later years describes Beulah's voice as "shrill."[80]

Offstage, Maisie Comardo remembers Beulah as "a warm, outgoing, happy lady with a zest for life."[81] She appeared to make friends everywhere the theatre played, and she appeared to have problems only with people who didn't know how to relax and have a good time.[82]

CHAPTER SIX

The First Ten Years: Performances

THE PLAYS

When Charlie took over as director, he brought with him a definite conviction about what kind of plays the theatre should produce. A writer who interviewed him in 1925 wrote:

> The plays used by the Floating Theatre Company are usually adapted by Mr. Hunter.
>
> "We tried giving royalty plays from Broadway," he explained, "but [the audience] didn't care about them. I don't believe we would get half a house the first night if we were to put on 'What Price Glory,' for instance. After the first evening we would play to empty seats.
>
> "And the play with the tear is sure to be popular. They say people like to laugh, but the sort of drama that holds its popularity is the one that ends happily of course, but allows the people to leave the theatre, smiling through a mist, furtively wiping their eyes, and declaring they 'never enjoyed anything as much in their lives.'
>
> "We tried all sorts of things, musical shows, comedies, vaudeville. And we've found that the drama with the tear is the one that makes the real hit."[1]

Charlie, as usual, overstated the case when he insisted that the showboat management had tried many different forms of theatre before they discovered the play "with the tear." From its first year the Floating Theatre played the comedy-dramas from the repertoire movement. The showboat was never a vaudeville or musical comedy theatre, as Charlie's comments might suggest. They presented vaudeville either between the acts or after the plays, and sometimes as a Saturday matinee, but the vaudeville was always subordinate to the plays. However, Charlie may have been referring to Jim Adams's experience with his vaudeville shows between 1908 and 1911. Jim appeared to have experimented with different entertainment formats then and may have discovered that the rep plays were his best-sellers.

As to "royalty" plays, the Floating Theatre presented them occasionally, but not often. They were too expensive. The reason Hunter chose the plays he did was every bit as dependent upon his budget as upon his audience's taste.

The rep managers' goal was that the plays they presented each season worked as a pattern. They wanted a mix of styles, types, and subjects designed in such a way as to draw the customers back every night of the week. One manager suggested the following formula:

> *Monday* (opening): A play with heart interest, a strong vein of comedy and "dress"—at least one act in which the entire company could appear in its finest attire. Most important, a play with "after draft"—an indefinable quality that made them say to one another, "Gee, that was good!" but not so much that customers would get their fill and not want to come back.
>
> *Tuesday:* A family comedy, to appeal especially to the women because it is the women who pull the men back the second time.
>
> *Wednesday:* A hillbilly or mountain play—a change of pace, enjoyable but not too substantial.
>
> *Thursday* (feature night): A play with a strong, dramatic story line and settings to permit a more elaborate production than others in the rep; a play to be talked up from opening night.
>
> *Friday:* A light comedy or warm-hearted story like *Jack O' Diamonds.*
>
> *Saturday:* A farce, to leave them laughing.[2]

The offerings of the James Adams Theatre did not follow that pattern. Throughout the history of the Floating Theatre its feature night was Friday, not Thursday. Also, the James Adams presented a western and a mystery most seasons. But Charlie, like all rep managers, was always concerned that his season be balanced. To do that, he needed a supply of scripts from which to draw.

In the first two decades of the twentieth century, when the tent reps were relatively new, finding affordable scripts was something of a problem. All the managers had the same needs: a small-cast play with simple scenery that would play well to rural and small-town audiences. The rep managers usually adapted nineteenth-century melodramas or wrote disguised or updated versions. The managers leased the "new" plays to each other, and they also stole them from each other. The less scrupulous managers played the same plays every year under new titles. Even the most responsible managers occasionally changed the titles of plays to make them appear new.

Adams's bill in 1916, as described by Maud McDougall, was typical of the offerings of the period. "Not a thing is repeated from last year except *East Lynn,* and that by request. Not a thing they will have to pay royalties on; for even *East Lynne* is a version no other manager would recognize, let alone claim."[3]

East Lynne was based on the 1861 novel by the English writer Mrs. Henry Wood, and was a mainstay of theatre during the last half of the nineteenth century and the beginning of the twentieth. Even theatre audiences today may recognize the title. The story chronicles the adventures of an orphan, Lady Isabel Vane, who is brought back as a bride to her family estate, East Lynne, by Archibald Carlyle, the estate's new owner. Unscrupulous friends cause Isabel to doubt Archibald's love, and she runs away with another man. Too late she learns the truth. At the end, she returns to East Lynne, broken in health and disguised as an old governess, to nurse her ailing child.

Another mainstay of the early repertoire theatre was *Lena Rivers,* a play based on the 1856 novel by the American writer Mary J. Holmes. Like *East Lynne, Lena* is a twist on the Cinderella story. Lena and her granny are forced to seek refuge with a relative. They fall under the machinations of the man's wife, who cares only for her daughter's social aspirations and treats Lena as a servant. Durward Bellmont, who comes to court the daughter, sees Lena's worth, and courts and marries Lena instead of the daughter.

As with other "classics" it presented, the Floating Theatre had its own version of *Lena Rivers.* When the Montross, Virginia, Community Theatre put on a production of *Lena Rivers,* the director and adapter of the play publicized his adaptation as "authentic" and "entirely unlike the Floating Theatre play of the same name."[4]

Charlie, with his usual sense of fun, explained to one curious young man who asked where the plays came from that he had several writers on contract. One was in New Orleans. When the playwright wanted to write a new play, he checked into a hospital and took dope, under medical supervision, for his inspiration.[5]

Fortunately, Charlie did not have to resort to such convoluted means to procure plays. After the First World War a new breed of writers emerged to supply the needs of the repertoire theatre. Some were company managers, some were actors, and some were just writers.

One of the most prolific of the new writers, and a favorite of the Adams Floating Theatre, was Robert J. Sherman. In the profession, Sherman was known as "Young Bob" because there was a theatre manager/playwright named Robert L. Sherman, who, as one might guess, was called "Old Bob."

Young Bob joined the Repertoire movement as an actor around 1911.[6] By 1915 he was writing plays and trying to distribute them to rep companies.[7] His career as a writer began to flourish after his discharge from the Army in 1919.

In 1923, *Billboard* chronicled Sherman's early success:

... After his discharge from the army, his list contained but seven plays. These were accepted readily by most of the recognized tent repertoire companies, and all are said to have proved successful. In 1920 six more bills were added to the list and his business increased accordingly. An addition of seven plays were made last season, and this spring Sherman comes forth with fourteen new ones. The Mae Edwards Players topped all business in St. Johns, Canada, with the *Bronze Goddess,* which Sherman is offering this season as a feature bill. It is said by some that a complete repertoire of one man's plays is not a good thing as they are all written in the same vein. This is said to be one of the notable features of Sherman's plays, that they all differ in plot and style of construction. The second most pleasing feature to managers being that he writes nearly all plays to be told in one setting, cutting down the expense for the show instead of seeing how much he can elaborate on scenery ...

Anything worth doing is worth doing well, and Sherman has dropped all other lines of work and maintains an office in Chicago, devoting all his entire time to writing new plays.[8]

One of Young Bob's early plays was *The Scarlet Nemesis.* He released it in the fall of 1920, and Adams leased it for the following season. It well may have been the first of Sherman's plays the showboat produced. (They may have done one in 1919; I did not find their repertoire from that season.)

From his office in Chicago, Sherman represented other playwrights as well, including some who previously had been represented by the big name among play publishers, Samuel French.[9] In 1923, Sherman teamed up with a tent show manager, Karl Simpson, who was ready to retire from trouping, and opened a second office in Kansas City.[10] Sherman and Simpson expanded into representing talent[11] as well as scripts. In 1927 Sherman turned the Kansas City office over to Simpson and moved his Chicago office to his hometown, Susquehanna, Pennsylvania.[12]

Sherman found success quickly in his new profession, but he was not a pioneer in developing the form of the new rep plays. The rep manager-writers had developed that before Sherman came on the scene. One of the most "modern" of the early writers was Charles F. Harrison, who as early as 1906 was writing and producing his own plays in Texas and the Southwest. Before Sherman's success, Harrison did not attempt to distribute his plays widely to other managers, but in 1924 he teamed with his business manager from the tent, J. D. Colgrove, and opened a play bureau in Colorado Springs.[13]

Charlie Hunter made up as a G-string and an unidentified actress. Photograph courtesy of Marguerite Young.

Beulah Adams and an unidentified man in blackface, circa 1910. The background suggests that they were performing in a tent show, possibly Jim's Vaudeville Show. The man bears a resemblance to Jim Beard, who also appeared in the show. Photograph courtesy of Marguerite Young.

In the mid 1920s, other bureaus, most smaller than Sherman's and Harrison's, some older, and many newer, provided plays and talent for the rep companies. There were many plays for managers like Charlie Hunter to choose from.

There were several things all repertoire plays shared in common.

The royalties were low, much lower than for "royalty" plays from New York. A rep company performed a play once a week for at least thirty-five weeks. A royalty play could cost a company hundreds of dollars for the season. Schaffner recalls that in 1932, in the depth of the Depression when prices were generally low, he leased two royalty plays, *The Family Upstairs* and *Some Baby*, for $150 each for the season.[14] The plays from the repertoire play bureaus were much cheaper. In 1924, during the most popular period of the Repertoire movement, Sherman offered his stable of plays for $30 apiece for the season, six plays for $150.[15] Adams took advantage of the offer. That season he trouped with three plays from the Sherman bureau.

The plays written for the traveling repertoire company typically required four men, three women, and one set. There were plays written especially for Tobys and G-strings. There were plays of different styles, including mysteries, farces, and modern melodramas. But most were comedy-dramas. The comedy-drama had at its core a serious event, but the play also featured comic characters, and always had a happy ending.

The playwrights were sensitive to the mores of the rural audiences. They knew how to titillate without shocking the country folks. The "bark" of the title was infinitely worse than the "bite" of the play. Some of the intriguing titles included: *Don't Lie to Your Wife*, *Why Girls Walk Home*, *Cheating Woman*, *Modern Wives and Absent Husbands*, *Nice Girls Don't*, *The Love Racket*, and *Why Wives Worry*. The content of the plays was only vaguely relevant to the promise of the title. Boob Brasfield, who produced *Why Girls Walk Home* on the Floating Theatre in 1937, wrote the following to *Billboard*: "The *News Leader* reporter . . . brought up a point that is always embarrassing. 'Why did the girl walk home?' As usual, I referred her to Neil Schaffner. He wrote it. We only follow his script. It's a good title anyway."[16]

A good example of a comedy-drama written for the repertoire theatre in the 1920s is *The Balloon Girl*,[17] by Robert J. Sherman. Sherman released the play in 1922 and the James Adams Floating Theatre first produced it in 1925. *The Balloon Girl* was a natural choice for the Floating Theatre, a company that featured an ingenue. Sylvia, the balloon girl, and her twin sister Mazie, were carnival performers and, although one was honest and the other was a thief, they were both, under the surface, good at heart. But most important of all, *The Balloon Girl* was written for one actress to play both sisters. What ingenue could resist that delight?

The story of *The Balloon Girl* is centered on three plot developments. In the first, Sylvia, as a free act for the carnival in town, parachutes from a balloon and lands on the roof of the parsonage. The parson is delighted to discover her there and helps her down, but he is embarrassed that she is dressed in tights. (The playwright warns the producer that for audiences in smaller towns she should be dressed in a ballet effect, which was the choice made on the Floating Theatre.[18]) The parson asks Sylvia to hide in another room when some of his parishioners come visiting. She agrees, but she is annoyed because she does not think her costume is indecent; she doesn't find the human form indecent. Despite their differences of opinion and the many misunderstandings, Sylvia and the parson fall in love.

The second plot complication involves the parson's younger brother Phillip, who agrees to give a con man from the carnival the combination to the safe at the bank where Phillip works. Phillip chooses to help the con man in order to get money to cover funds he has embezzled from the bank. The con man's accomplice in the robbery is Sylvia's twin sister, Mazie.

The third complication involves a rich and proper parishioner, Mrs. Chapman, who is trying to convince the parson to marry her attractive young daughter Patience.

The three plots interweave with delightful, though predictable, developments, aided by two comic characters, a bragging but not incompetent G-string constable, and a young Toby, whom the author indicates can be cut without damage to the story.

There are plenty of complications. Mrs. Chapman used to be married to the con man, who, unknown to Patience, is Patience's father. Phillip embezzled the money to spend it on Patience, who is a nice young lady but enjoys her fun—in another town. The burglary goes awry and the parson tries to save his brother even if it means the parson must sacrifice his career. Phillip is ready to put the blame on anyone he can, including Sylvia and Patience. The con man and Mazie confess their part in the crime to save Sylvia from prison and force Phillip to do the same. Sylvia and the parson agree to marry.

There are melodramatic elements to *The Balloon Girl*. The play is plot centered, rather than character or issue centered, and the plot is filled with coincidences and unmotivated character changes. But in tone the play is far from *Mable Heath* or even *Sunset Trail*. There are no villains, just misguided or weak people. Although superficially done, the play addresses moral issues. And the play exists in a definable world, that of the Midwestern small town. The setting is not arbitrary. The ethical issues explored in the play grow out of the social world of its setting. The play is closer to *Hedda Gabler* than to *Mable Heath* in structure and style. The differences are that Sherman did not have Ibsen's talent and insight, and each wrote from different motivations. Sherman wrote to entertain small-town and rural audiences in the United States in the 1920s; Ibsen wrote to create new forms of theatre through which he could explore the character of his country and times.

Despite Sherman's inadequacies as a writer, the issues he explored were important and timely to his audiences.

In 1887 the Methodist church established a ban on all entertainment: "The *Discipline* stated that a member could be reproved or even expelled from membership for patronizing certain amusements, including the theatre."[19] In 1889, the Baptist Association adopted a resolution "requiring church members to abstain from attending theatres."[20] The Methodist and Baptist churches, of course, were the churches of the repertoire theatre's audiences.

The bans were more ignored than obeyed. If they hadn't been, there would have been no Repertoire movement. But the issue was there, and many good and intelligent citizens were troubled by the theatre. As a consequence, the repertoire theatres presented many "preacher plays." *The Balloon Girl* is one. An earlier preacher play was Charles F. Harrison's *Saintly Hypocrites and Honest Sinners* (presented by the Floating Theatre in 1934). The chief theme of the preacher plays was hypocrisy. Sometimes the preacher was a hypocrite; sometimes he confronted the hypocrites. The basic point was that what some called sin was only different values, and it was better to be an "honest sinner" than a hypocrite who held strict standards for others while concealing his own indiscretions. Usually at the center of the preacher play was a concern for some aspect of the entertainment industry to which the hypocrites were giving a hard time.

THE CONCERTS

Just as the plays offered by the repertoire companies in the early years were based on the melodramas of the nineteenth century, so, too, the practice of including musical presentations with the plays grew out of the melodramas. By definition the Victorian melodrama included music, not only between the acts, but also as a part of the play. When the rep theatres changed their fare from melodramas to comedy-dramas, they continued to include music as a part of their performances. Because many of the performers were skilled vaudevillians, the musical presentations resembled vaudeville shows more than Victorian melodramas.

Adams, who came to rep theatre after managing vaudeville companies for four years, in 1914 offered vaudeville type entertainment between the acts. On Saturday of the first week he offered a variation: vaudeville alone for the matinee and a vaudeville performance after the play at night. Jim called the postplay performance a "concert."

I do not know how often Jim presented the concert during the first season. He may have played it only on Saturday nights; he may have played it less or more often. Thanks to a second version of the diary Waldorf kept in 1915,[21] we do know how often Jim offered the concert the second year.

Initially he was inconsistent. In Hertford, North Carolina, the week of March 1, he presented the concert on Tuesday, Thursday, and Saturday nights. Four weeks later in Elizabeth City, he offered no concerts. A week later during a split week in South Mills, North Carolina, and Deep Creek, Virginia, he presented the concert every night. As the season went on, Adams presented the concert more frequently. By the end of the 1915 season, he presented it almost every night.

The next year, 1916, McDougall wrote as if the concert were a regular feature. She made no mention of specialties between the acts.[22] It is most probable that, by the third year, specialties were a thing of the past and the concert was an established regular feature.

THE AUDIENCES

The Repertoire theatre movement, of which the James Adams Floating Theatre was a part, began at the end of the nineteenth century and ended at the beginning of the Second World War. There were companies that preceded the 1890s and companies that survived into the 1950s and '60s and even longer. But essentially the movement had a life span of forty years. Those four decades were fertile with change, change driven primarily by technological developments, including the automobile, the airplane, the telephone, the motion picture, the radio, and the television.

By the end of the First World War, the United States had become a "filiarchy." The word is Gilman Ostrander's. He defined it as rule by the young:

> In a continually developing technological environment, a society which relies on the young to acquire the new skills necessary to maintain and further re-create the environment; a society, furthermore, where social values are in continual process of reinterpretation in relation to the changing environment, and where the young, as social products of the new environment are superior to their elders in adaptability to the environment and in their understanding of it, and on that basis are qualified to act as authoritative exemplars of social change.[23]

Ostrander describes the 1920s:

> Filiarchy visibly became the new order in American society following World War I, and it was this new filiarchal order that gave the 1920s its distinctive character . . .
>   The flapper was the authentic personification of the twenties: a happily motherless child, smoking, boozing, petting, necking, joyriding,

doing the Charleston and Black Bottom; living for the moment; trying out every new thing and discarding every old thing. Against this fast-stepping flapper, the moral forces of the day—sobersided Progressives and concerned parents, as well as fundamentalists and prohibitionists—strove fruitlessly to save old values . . .[24]

The traveling rep theatres were not the only purveyors of entertainment to rural America. There were, of course, the circuses and carnivals. Like the theatres, they were challengers to the old values. There were two institutions that reinforced the established values: the Chautauqua and the camp meeting.

A local reporter at Reedville, Virginia, reported in 1916: "Reedville is resting today after three weeks of unusual activity and rush. The Chautauqua, protracted service at Bethany and Floating Theatre, each followed closely the other, have departed, all expecting to come again."[25]

The Chautauqua movement was established commercially in 1912, an outgrowth of the much older summer program at Chautauqua, New York. Chautauqua was organized in circuits throughout rural America, and provided various forms of uplifting entertainment, including concerts and lectures. Many of the best-known figures of the time—artists, authors, musicians, politicians, actors, and religious leaders—performed at some time on a Chautauqua circuit.

Chautauqua was a big family time. In many locations the Chautauqua committee maintained an elaborate campground where families could rent cabins or tents, or pitch their own tents, for the week of Chautauqua. There were events for the entire family throughout the day, including games and entertainments for children, special lectures for teenagers, and the featured events for adults. In the evenings there were always major lectures or performances, often featuring famous singers from the world's opera houses.

In 1922, a longtime observer of the Chautauqua wrote, "If ever you wonder what counterweight America has to the growing volume of radicalism, think of the Chautauqua. In its chairs and on its platform prevails not only the most conservative but the most conventionally moral influence of our national life. More than once I have smiled in thinking that it is something beyond all this, that it is the most monotonously moral agent I have ever observed among men."[26]

During the second week at Reedville, the 1916 newspaper reporter wrote, there was "protracted service at Bethany," or, in simpler terms, a camp meeting or religious revival at a local "camp." I cannot write personally of the Chautauqua because it ended as a movement in 1925, before I was born. But as a child I was taken to many camp meetings. The revival movement was established to bring the Christian community back to the fundamentals of faith. The days at camp were heavy with classes and sermons. As a small child I failed to grasp the higher moral purposes of the event and found the experiences anything but monotonous. There was constant activity. In the morning there were other children to play with and a marvelous woods and stream nearby to explore. Meals were eaten in a large open tent, and I thought that was how the Indians must have lived. There were lessons in the afternoon of which I can now recall nothing, and gospel music in the evening, which, fifty-five years later, still rings in my ears. My uncle played clarinet in the band, and I used to go with him to listen to the musicians rehearse. I cannot hear gospel music today without remembering a time when I thought the world was simple and families were happy and all was right with the world, but I don't think that was exactly the lesson the teachers tried to teach us in the afternoon sessions.

Following revival week at Reedville in 1916 there was Floating Theatre week. The lessons of Chautauqua and camp meeting were not the lessons of the Floating Theatre. Although the "entertainment" was imported from outside, the Chautauqua and the camp meeting were run by local people. The showboat was an intruder, an interloper. So the challenge Adams faced was to make his theatre an accepted part of the communities in which he played.

There were three parts to Adams's problem: Two of them were people's perceptions that the theatre as an institution was sinful and that actors as people were sinful. The third was that both the theatre and the people in it were strangers.

By the standards of much of the audience, theatre as an institution was sinful. It was sinful to blaspheme, to swear, to smoke, to drink, to lie, to cheat, to lust, to steal, and to kill; and the theatre showed people doing all those things.

One can argue that representing sins on the stage is not the same as being a sinner. An actor can play a drunkard without being one in life. Much of Adams's audience, however, had difficulty accepting the aesthetic distance which is an essential part of viewing modern theatre. A story Charlie Hunter reported many times, changing the locale of the incident to suit his listeners, bears repeating here:

> Our audiences are enthusiastic. They lose themselves in the plays just as if they are witnessing a real scene. One night we were up on the Perquimans River, playing a Hertford audience. The play was "The Little Lost Sister." The heroine had been lured from her home to a gay cabaret in the city. The villain tried to make her take a drink into which he had dropped a powder. As the girl was slowly raising the glass to her lips, a farmer's wife arose suddenly in her seat, as if she had been playing in the act, and waving her arms commandingly shouted in a loud voice:

"Don't you drink that stuff, little girl."

The company got nervous, some thinking that the interruption might break up the play. But it didn't. Beulah caught the situation, and as if it had been a part of the play, she threw the glass to the floor, and cried:

"You're right; I won't drink that stuff."[27]

People who saw the world in such concrete images made good religious fundamentalists, but suspicious theatregoers.

Adams argued, as did most of the rep theatre managers, that the performances on his stage were moral and clean, that the actors did and said nothing offending, and that the plays presented moral stories. For the first four years he printed the words "high class, moral, clean, and refined" in most of his newspaper advertisements. And he exercised censorship to make certain the performances stayed that way. A former resident of Urbanna, Virginia, remembers, "My father [a minister] was given special passes, good for every one of the six performances. Dad was always informed by [the] dapper advance man of the high moral tone of each play . . ."[28]

In 1924 the theatre must have employed a comedian who didn't understand Jim's priorities, because in March 1925 he advertised for a comedian "who can get laughs without profanity."[29] It was always a judgment call, both in the plays and in the concerts, as to what would or would not offend the audience.

It was also true, by the standards of the communities the Floating Theatre played, that actors were sinful. Most actors were decent, moral people, but as a group they were "modern" in their outlook. They smoked, drank, and cursed freely. They partied all night and slept late in the morning. Alcoholism was common among them, as was syphilis.[30]

To counteract the general reputation of actors, Adams insisted upon a strict code of behavior on the Floating Theatre, and his efforts brought quick results. After the theatre's second visit to Elkton, Maryland, a writer for the Cecil County *News* praised the demeanor of the company. "It is a pleasure to speak a good word for the members of the company, who not only gave good performances, but who were in every respect so obliging, courteous and refined. Seldom do strangers make such a good impression in a community."[31]

Philip Graham quotes from a letter an actor on the Floating Theatre wrote to a friend complaining about the restrictive moral atmosphere on the boat. "You don't dare chase any [girls]," he warned his friend, "as [the Adamses] are very particular about that." Graham concludes that the "members of the company were as meticulous in their private lives as in their characters and lines."[32] Jim was most concerned about the public image of his company, but Graham was apparently unaware of the social life that the players shared with established friends in the towns the boat visited. Jim's code of behavior was not designed to stop the actors from enjoying themselves when they were with their own or with people from the community who shared their sense of fun. Dorothy Barlow's journal of her visit to the showboat in 1926 records a constant parade of parties, including the observation that at Solomons, Maryland, she attended a dance every night. Also, in the midst of Prohibition, she had no trouble getting a glass of wine whenever she wanted one.

Jim also sought the approval of his audiences by committing his theatre and troupe to community and patriotic causes. He was a major supporter of the July 4th celebration in 1916 in Reedville. As a local reporter noted, "The managers of the affair are especially indebted to Mr. James Adams, owner of the Adams Floating Theatre, for excellent band music furnished for the occasion, as well as for the financial aid at night."[33] In 1917 he aided the Red Cross drive in Leonardtown. "A percentage of receipts . . . will be donated to the local Red Cross societies. Don't miss the opportunity to enjoy a few hours of rare entertainment and at the same time help a worthy cause."[34] In 1918, as part of his contributions to the war effort, Adams gave a benefit performance for the Red Cross in every port the theatre visited."[35] In Mathews Courthouse that year, his band was one of the main attractions at a patriotic meeting. Part of the poster advertising the event read as shown, *opposite*.[36]

The list of community efforts supported by Adams—by participation of the theatre's talent, by direct financial contributions, and by benefit performances—is great in length. It simply was a matter of policy for the theatre to support the communities in which it played.

One might suppose that all traveling theatres made similar contributions. Many did, but many did not. *Billboard* was the recipient of periodic complaints from rep theatre managers about the shabby practices of some of their colleagues on the road. In 1927 Harley Sadler, a tent manager in Texas, complained to "Billy Boy" most vehemently about the problems caused by "Mr. Wiseacre," his pseudonym for the troublemakers in the business.

Sadler described how Mr. Wiseacre made fun of the "hicks," refused to make civic contributions to the towns, and employed underhanded tricks to "bilk the marks" of everything he could get.

Sadler summarized Mr. Wiseacre's philosophy: "Be hard-boiled with the public. Insist on your company doing the same. Take no interest in civic affairs. Insult the intelligence of all with whom you come in contact. Give as little as possible in all directions. Get the money today; to hell with the future."[37]

Adams was no Mr. Wiseacre. He made friends of his audiences. As the years went by, the regular members of the company built special and long-lasting relationships with people in the communities. A major portion

GRAND PATRIOTIC MEETING

Mathews Courthouse, Va.
Saturday, May 11th, 1918
Beginning at Two O'clock in the Afternoon

★ ★ ★ ★ ★

To Celebrate The Unfurling Of
OUR HONOR FLAG

★ ★ ★ ★ ★

Every Patriotic Citizen in Mathews County
is Urged to be Present that Day

★ ★ ★ ★ ★

Through courtesy of Manager Adams,
the Fine Concert Band from

JAMES ADAMS' FLOATING THEATRE

Will be Present to accompany a Chorus of 2,000
Voices in Singing Patriotic Songs

★ ★ ★ ★ ★

Through the courtesy of the same management
Miss Della Masten,
America's Leading Female Cornet Soloist,
will also be Present to Render a Number of Selections

of Dorothy Barlow's journal is the record of friends she made while visiting the showboat.

Despite Jim's good efforts, the showboat and its actors did not escape all moral criticism. There were those who took the church ban on entertainment seriously. Miriam Haynie, Reedville historian, wrote of how, in the early days of the Floating Theatre before Adams won over many of the morally cautious, the superintendent of the Sunday school called the boat "the hell-hole of iniquity."[38] Another churchman declared that "since the devil can't get to us by land, he is coming by sea." Norris Parks, a former resident of the Northern Neck, is convinced that the boat stopped coming to Kinsale, Virginia, because of the prejudice toward it there. He remembered that his parents disapproved of the boat and that his grandmother wouldn't go aboard even to look at the theatre, let alone to attend a performance. On the boat's last visit to Kinsale, however, Parks's parents weakened. His sister wanted a pony, but she agreed to forget about the pony in exchange for being allowed to see the plays each night.[39]

An identifiable critic of the showboat was John Beale of Hague, Virginia. Beale wrote the Westmoreland County news column in the 1920s for the Northern Neck *News.* Beale signed his columns "Seldom." According to Beale's nephew, Beale considered himself a devout churchman. He wrote his column as a way of compensating for his lack of financial success as a farmer.[40]

Beale was not vicious in his criticism of the Floating Theatre. He professed not to understand the popularity of the boat.

> Adams Floating Theater is heading this way and I want our church members to read what a writer in the Virginia *Citizen* [a paper in Kilmarnock, Virginia] has to say: "We agree with the Fleets Bay correspondent in regard to the Floating Theatre. A few from this section, but very few attended, and from the songs we hear them singing and from the vulgar jokes they say they heard we think they would have been much better to have remained at home. If any church member was better off by the things they saw and heard we would like to hear from them."[41]

After the boat arrived in the county, Beale wrote, "Adams Floating Theatre is attracting an unusual crowd each night to McGuires Wharf, but I have not seen the first man or woman who was much pleased."[42] A few years later, Beale was more ironic in his comment. "Large crowds are rushing each night to Adams Floating Theatre at Nomini. Those who go seem to think they get their money's worth."[43] The following year Beale put his concerns in juxtaposition: "Large and responsive crowds flock every night to Adams Floating Theatre. Very few from here have attended Kirkland Camp this year. Rev. Mr. Lumpkin, of Reedville, is with Rev. T. W. Ogden in a revival this week at Carmel and they are hoping for a good meeting."[44]

From Beale's position, the forces of righteousness appeared to be losing out to the secular attractions of Beulah Adams and company. It was, perhaps, just a sign of the times.

Ironically, the change in the times that brought the Floating Theatre increasing acceptance and popularity during the 1920s helped lead to its decline in the 1930s.

BLACK PEOPLE

There is nothing in Jim Adams's history to suggest that he was a bigot. Maisie Comardo claimed that Jim "loved black people."[45] He employed a plantation show in his carnival, and the first year he operated the Floating Theatre he advertised that the balcony was "reserved for colored people exclusively."[46] Seating black and white people together in the same theatre, even separated by levels, was not common practice in the smaller towns of the South in 1914, and Jim's gesture met with criticism from conservatives.

The second year Jim dropped the announcement from his advertising, but not because of criticism. In 1925 Adams explained to Wesley Stout that he had been disappointed by the response of black people to his theatre. "The negroes viewed the Adams with a hostile and a suspicious eye on its early appearances," Stout wrote. "Whether maliciously or as a joke, a rumor was set going that the floating theatre was a diabolical invention to lure the black population aboard, lock them in and transport them back to Africa. The alarm was passed along the coast by shanty wireless and dogged the boat at every landing for a season." Stout added, "The 20-35-50 cent scale is a bit beyond the range of the bulk of the negro population. Most of them loiter on the wharf, listen to the music inside, and wait for the fifteen-cent concert after-show."[47]

Although Adams opened the balcony to white customers in 1915, as long as he owned the vessel, blacks were welcome in the audience. They sat in the back of the balcony, and possibly in the back of the auditorium.[48]

Maisie Comardo remembers that in the late 1920s and early 1930s, more blacks attended the plays than the concerts. Her feeling was that either they could not afford to pay the extra for the concert, or they did not want to linger in the white part of town as late as the concert ended.[49]

Judging from part of a letter that Charlie Hunter wrote to Edna Ferber in 1925, he shared the basic racist perceptions of his time, but, like most show business people, showed no animosity to blacks.

> The town of "white negroes" is Winton, N. C. [which the Floating Theatre played each year between 1922 and 1930], and believe me they are white, so white in fact that we didn't attempt to separate them from the whites but would let them make their own separation which they always did. It was funny our first time there. When we got in on Sunday the boat was crowded with sight-seers, and I was politely answering all questions, assisting them up and down stairs, with much hat tipping and bowing and 80 per cent of the time I had a negro, which was cause for much merriment among them, but I didn't know then what the "giggles" were about. As one man remarked to me when I mentioned the fact of so many "white negroes": "There is many a father sitting downstairs among the whites with a daughter in the gallery among the colored." But it would be as much as my life is worth to make that remark where any one there could hear it.[50]

After Adams sold the boat in 1933, there were fewer blacks in the audience. Rachel Seymoure, who was with the theatre from 1933 to its end, remembers no blacks on board.[51] Some who attended the performances on the boat in the 1930s remember some blacks in the audience. At least once in 1940, late in the career of the Floating Theatre, when the Adamses and the Hunters were no longer associated with it, the management advertised that the Floating Theatre "Caters to White People Only."[52]

At no time in the history of the Floating Theatre were blacks employed as part of the regular cast or orchestra. They were employed only as menials. In the early seasons there were no blacks at all. The first cooks, Mr. and Mrs. Miller in 1915, Mr. and Mrs. George Wazo in 1916, and Mrs. William Allen in 1917, were all white. The first documented reference to black cooks appeared in 1925, when Aggie Scott and Joe Gunn, possible models for Edna Ferber's Queenie and Jo in her novel, *Show Boat,* were aboard. In the 1930s there was a black cook, Rose Teel, and her black assistant, Roscoe James.

Even though blacks were never regular members of the cast or orchestra, there was at least one black person who one season performed specialties in the concert.

In 1926, when the showboat was playing at Mt. Holly, Virginia, on Nomini Creek, a group of teenaged boys in the neighborhood persuaded Charlie Hunter to allow a black midget to perform in the concert. The midget was Daniel Webster Montague of Hague, Virginia, at the time a teenager. Montague often entertained the kids in the area with his singing and dancing.[53] Charlie Hunter apparently liked Danny's performance, because the following week when the show boat was in Leonardtown, Maryland, Danny shipped on board.[54] At the end of the 1926 season Dorothy Barlow listed the names of all the performers on the boat, and Danny's was not among them. He was, however, still on the boat when the season closed because he rode to Michigan with Dorothy and her family.[55] Most likely Danny earned his passage in 1926 by working in the kitchen. Performing specialties in the concert was something Hunter allowed him to do, not something he paid him to do.

Ed Newton, one of the boys who persuaded Hunter to see Danny, remembers that several years later Montague returned to visit in Hague. A big Hudson sedan drove up to Newton's farmhouse. It was driven by a white chauffeur, but Newton couldn't see who was in the back. The door opened and Montague stepped out. He carried a cane and sported a diamond stickpin. After they greeted one another, Montague informed Newton that he was now performing with Billy Rose's midgets in New York City.[56]

Danny sang and danced. Joe Gunn played the harmonica. And there was a rumor of a black man on the Floating Theater at one time who played the piano. Such musicians might on occasion have the opportunity to perform before the show or in a special slot in the concert, as long as the audience understood that the black performers were talented menials and not a part of the company. Such were the prejudices of the time.

Daniel Webster Montague, right, with an unidentified little girl. The picture was taken when Danny was visiting the Adamses in Michigan, most likely in the late 1920s. Photograph courtesy of Robert Struble.

Two cooks in the galley of the Floating Theatre. Photograph courtesy of the Mariners Museum, Newport News, Virginia.

In the heyday of the Floating Theatre, blacks did not appear on the same stage as whites. McArthur points out that before 1920 "no black actor achieved prominence on a Broadway stage," and that "mixed companies were rare."[57] They were more rare in the provincial South than in New York. The only "acceptable" employment for black performers before the 1920s was in black minstrel shows, or plantation shows as they were often called. McArthur records that the overwhelming majority of the 1,490 blacks listed as performers in the 1890 census were working in all-black minstrel shows.[58]

Although the Floating Theatre employed no black performers, it employed the blackface comic as its chief humorous figure. Not all rep theatres of the period used blackface comics. For example, the Schaffner Players, a Toby company, never in its history used a blackface in its plays or concerts.[59] For some understanding of the nature of the performances on the Floating Theatre one needs a sense of the origin, development, and use of blackface humor.

It is difficult today for most audiences to view without embarrassment early films in which white actors in blackface or black actors portrayed stereotypical Negro comic figures. It is difficult for many to understand the appeal of such humor to an earlier audience.

Rourke reported that from the earliest days of the nation, Americans were fascinated by the humor and musical skills of blacks.

> A western poet declared that "among the earliest original versus of the West were sundry African melodies celebrating the coon hunt and the vicissitudes of river navigation." The Negro was to be seen everywhere in the South and in the new Southwest, on small farms and great plantations, on roads and levees. He was often an all but equal member of many a pioneering expedition. He became, in short, a dominant figure in spite of his condition, and commanded a definite portraiture.[60]

That portrait, however, was not created by black performers. It was created by whites who added the "coon" to the "Yankee" and the "frontiersman" in the pantheon of native American humorous types. Some of the early actors, such as Edwin Forrest and Thomas D. Rice, worked for realism in their portrayals of blacks,[61] but audiences wanted the plantation stereotypes. For example, in 1822, in New York City, the actor playing Hamlet in the all-black African Theatre Company was interrupted by the audience in the middle of a soliloquy. The audience demanded that he sing "Possum up a Gum Tree."[62]

Ironically, a character which over a hundred years later became a bitter symbol of segregation was developed in the late 1820s by actor Thomas D. Rice from his observations of the dancing of a crippled old black man who ended his impromptu performance with the line, "Every time I wheel about, I jump Jim Crow."[63] Rice's portrait of the man, by all reports, was honest and compassionate, but through such performances the stereotypical patterns of black characters developed into what became the minstrel show.

The only significant reprieve blacks were given onstage from stereotypical comic portrayals was with the dramatization of *Uncle Tom's Cabin* in the 1850s. When after the Civil War segregation became more pronounced than before the war, the only theatre companies in which white and black actors were mixed with some regularity were the ubiquitous "Uncle Tom" touring companies.[64]

In the latter half of the nineteenth century the minstrel black became the black of the theatre, and the only means of entry for black performers into the theatre was to continue the minstrel stereotype. In so doing the black performers reinforced the black caricatures in the minds of whites.[65] The state of affairs reached the point where, in 1886, the editor of *The Theatre* responded to an inquiry regarding the lack of successful black actors with the following:

> There is not, nor is there likely to be . . . The negro is naturally disqualified as an actor of the better order of character, and even in his native antics—the songs and dances peculiar to plantation life— he finds a superior on the stage in the imitation darkey of the white man. He is entirely unfitted to represent the finer thoughts, sentiments and emotions.[66]

The best blackface comics, in the tradition of jesters throughout history, used their material to comment on the state of society. The foolish "darky" was allowed observations and sentiments which, if they were expressed by the actor sans blackface, would have aroused the wrath of portions of his audience. It is doubtful, however, that the blackface comics employed by the Floating Theatre had the insights of a Will Rogers or a Lenny Bruce, or even of a Freeman Gosden or a Charles Correll ("Amos and Andy"). Every contemporary commentary on the performances on the showboat suggests that the comics were content to mine the clichés of the times. It is not that the comics were vicious or mean in their portrayals of blacks. They were insensitive, and contributed through humor to the continuing suppression of the aspirations of black people by showing them as servile, stupid, lazy, and dishonest but often lovable children.

It is ironic that the first production in New York of the musical *Show Boat*, despite the innately racist elements in the story, helped create opportunities for blacks to portray themselves in forms other than the accepted minstrel clichés. Predictably, however, the part of the tragic mulatto Julie was played by a white actress in each of the three films made of *Show Boat,* despite the fact that for the 1951 revival Lena Horne pleaded with MGM to allow her to play the role.[67]

It is especially ironic, as the play has been repeatedly revived on stage and in films, that while producers have worked to reduce the story's racism of language, they have succeeded primarily in suppressing the legitimate racial issues the story raises. On one hand, for example, in the lyrics of "Old Man River," blacks were originally identified as "niggers," and later as "darkies"; later still, the racial references were removed altogether. On the other hand, the portrayals of blacks in the 1936 and 1951 films are products of two entirely different social worlds. In the 1936 film, blacks are very much in evidence and Hattie McDaniel as Queenie is pushed around by no one, black or white. In the 1951 version, the blacks primarily stand about docilely in the background singing beautifully on cue.

CHAPTER SEVEN

Edna Ferber

OCTOBER 1924

O n September 24, 1924, Edna Ferber and George S. Kaufman's dramatization of her short story Minick opened in the Booth Theatre in New York. The show was received with ambivalence by both audience and critics. The play's reception earlier during its tryout in New London, Connecticut, was even more disheartening: The audience, which filled only half the house on opening night, was subjected to the aerial antics of bats that inhabited the upper reaches of the auditorium.[1]

Later that night, during the postmortem in his hotel room, the producer, Winthrop Ames, suggested that for the next play they wouldn't bother with tryouts. They would just charter a showboat and perform on it.[2]

That was Ferber's introduction to showboats. The idea that plays were being performed on the rivers fascinated her and, after her play opened in New York, she threw herself into researching showboats.[3]

Ferber apparently made inquiries of several showboats in hopes of visiting one. Captain Bill Menke, of the showboat *Goldenrod,* claimed to have received such an inquiry from her. In 1927 he had a telegram posted in the ticket office of his boat. It read:

Captain Bill Menke
Show-Boat Golden Rod
At River Landing

GIVE ME YOUR ROUTE
VERY ANXIOUS TO VISIT YOUR THEATRE

Edna Ferber

"I never heard of her so I never sent her no answer," was Captain Bill's explanation as to why Ferber did not use his boat for her research.[4]

Captain Bill may not have heard of her, but Edna Ferber was not an unknown author when she sent that telegram. She was a prolific short story writer and novelist from the Midwest who had begun her career as a newspaperwoman, but found her life's work in writing fiction. She published her first short story, "The Homely Heroine," in 1910 in *Everybody's* magazine,[5] and was soon experiencing early renown with her short stories about Emma McChesney, a traveling saleswoman. By 1924 she had moved to New York and had written approximately seventy-five short stories, most of them published first in major magazines, and then in collected volumes. *Minick* was her second play, and by 1924 she had also published three novels, the third of which, *So Big*, would win the Pulitzer Prize the following year. Ferber was to write her most famous novels after 1924—including *Show Boat, Giant, Cimarron,* and *Saratoga Trunk*—but the woman who walked onto the deck of the James Adams Floating Theatre in the fall of 1924 and introduced herself to Charlie Hunter was far from unknown.

According to Ferber, she found the boat in a little village in North Carolina. When she arrived at the boat and introduced herself, Charlie immediately recognized her as the author of the Emma McChesney stories and called for Beulah to join them. The showboat people warmly welcomed her, but, according to Ferber, because the season was ending and the boat was leaving in half an hour, there was no time for a visit.[6]

Ferber described a charming first encounter between herself and the Hunters which later events suggest was accurate. However, other aspects of her story are not accurate. I can only assume that she confused the details of her second visit to the Floating Theatre, in April 1925, with her visit in the fall of 1924. In 1925 she met the boat in Bath, North Carolina, but in the fall of 1924 she could not have met the boat in North Carolina because the Floating Theatre was then touring the towns of the upper Eastern Shore of Maryland.

In 1951, in an interview for the Richmond *Times-Dispatch*, William Cannon, who from 1925 to 1941 was the captain of the *Elk*, recalled that, the year before he joined the crew of the showboat, he ushered Ferber aboard the Floating Theatre at Crumpton, Maryland. "I'd happened to be visiting on [the showboat] at Crumpton, Md., when Edna Ferber first came aboard her before she went to work on her novel, and I happened to be the one that showed her aboard."[7] Cannon's memory is corroborated by a newspaper clipping from 1930. "The show boat will leave Centreville Landing early next Sunday morning for Crumpton, in the upper part of the county, which is said to be the first place Miss Ferber paid a visit to the Adams when looking for a setting for her story."[8]

There are several pieces of evidence that suggest that Miss Ferber's stay in Crumpton may have been longer than the few minutes she described.

Following an interview in 1937 with Selba Adams, a reporter in Michigan wrote, "Three years before Miss Ferber's famous novel appeared,

Miss Ferber appeared on the boat while it was fulfilling an engagement at a Maryland town. She seemed greatly pleased with the entertainment and show boat life and told Mr. [Selba] Adams she would like to spend more time on his boat collecting material and atmosphere for a story. [Selba] assured her that she would be a welcome guest—to drop in at any time and stay as long as she liked. There matters dropped."[9]

Selba's sense of the visit having lasted for more than a few moments gives support to the oft-told story of Edna Ferber beginning to light a cigarette in a lunchroom on the Eastern Shore, and stopping when she saw the shocked expressions on the faces of her showboat hosts.[10]

APRIL 1925

In *A Peculiar Treasure*, Ferber recalls that at the end of her 1924 visit to the Floating Theatre she made plans to visit it again in 1925 at the theatre's first stop in Bath, North Carolina.[11] Selba recalled the circumstances a little differently. "Two years later at Bath, N. C., [I] received a telegram asking if it would be all right for her to come right away. An affirmative reply produced her the following day."[12]

Which account is accurate is difficult to determine. Selba is undoubtedly wrong in recalling that there were two years between the visits. But I doubt that Selba or Charlie, in October 1924, could have precisely foretold their itinerary for April 1925. Because of the unpredictabilities of weather and casting, the boat was not consistent in its starting time each spring. (The theatre had not played on the Pamlico River in eleven years, since its first season in 1914. The boat's appearance at Bath in 1925, therefore, was also not a routine event that Charlie could have anticipated with great accuracy.)

There is also a conflict concerning the telegram. Selba claimed that he had received a telegram from Ferber when the boat was at Bath. She wrote that she arrived in Bath two days before the theatre did.[13]

The evidence regarding the differences in the two accounts is a little confusing. During the week of April 13, the week Ferber was with the Floating Theatre in Bath, she and members of the cast and crew signed their names to the guest book of the St. Thomas Episcopal Church in Bath. Ferber dated her signature April 18 (Saturday), but some members of the cast and crew dated their signatures April 13 (Monday), five days before Ferber's signature. Since the theatre was scheduled to begin its performances in Bath on Monday, the evidence superficially suggests that Selba was right and Ferber wrong, but Ferber's description of her wait for the boat to arrive suggests most strongly that it was not there at the beginning of the week.

My guess is that the Floating Theatre, which two weeks earlier had opened the season in Elizabeth City, North Carolina, had run into difficulties making the long trip down through Pamlico Sound. (The Intracoastal Waterway canal between the Alligator and Pungo rivers was not yet open.[14]) The cast usually drove their cars from port to port, and probably had arrived ahead of the boat and were waiting for it, as was Ferber.

Ferber wrote that while she was waiting for the showboat she stayed at the only boardinghouse in the town.[15] According to North Carolina historian Michelle Francis, the building Ferber indicated is on Water Street and was known as Ormond's boardinghouse.[16] It is now known as the Palmer-Marsh House and is an "historic site under the administration of the North Carolina Division of Archives and History."[17]

After learning that the Floating Theatre was delayed by one or two days, Ferber wrote that she spent two uncomfortable days waiting.[18]

According to Michelle Francis:

H. N. Roper, Bath's postmaster, gave Edna a tour of the town. At Ormond's boardinghouse he cleared a path through the underbrush so she could view the old Palmer-Marsh family graveyard. He also took her to visit St. Thomas Episcopal Church, where she signed the church register. Built in 1734, St. Thomas is the oldest church in North Carolina and once contained the state's first public library . . .

The next day Roper's son took the author across Back Creek to Plum Point, once the home of Edward Teach, the notorious Blackbeard the Pirate. Ferber paid the young Roper 50 cents for his time and trouble.

Edna also talked to some of the town's residents. One elderly man in particular eagerly shared his knowledge of Bath's history. At the end of a long conversation Ferber, wanting to pay him for his time and information, allegedly thrust into the bewildered gentleman's hand a $100 bill.

Mrs. Nancy Roper, a lifetime resident of Bath, was asked in June of 1979 what she knew of the $100-bill incident. She related that soon after the showboat left Bath in 1925, a man came into the post office to see her husband, H. N. Roper. The man wanted to know how Roper felt about the $100 bill Edna gave him. Roper replied that he had not seen any $100 bill and that Edna Ferber had not even made a donation to the church! According to Mrs. Roper, the money was given to the showboat's manager, Charles Hunter, not to her husband. Ferber's stay in Bath was brief but not soon forgotten by some of the town's citizens.[19]

Ferber described the boat's arrival in *A Peculiar Treasure*.[20] It is a charming description of the boat and its crew at work. There are, however, some curiosities in Ferber's account. She refers to the boat as "The James Adams Floating Palace Theatre." There is no historical basis for the use of the word

"Palace" in relation to the James Adams. There were several showboats on the Mississippi system that employed the name: Spaulding and Rogers' Floating Circus Palace, Robinson's Floating Palace, Lightner's Floating Palace, and the New Grand Floating Palace.[21] The showboat in Ferber's novel, however, is named "Capt. Andy Hawks Cotton Blossom Floating Palace Theatre."

It is possible that when Ferber wrote her autobiography, her memory of her experience on the James Adams may have been influenced by the memory of what she wrote in *Show Boat*. Such a possibility seems reasonable. She wrote *A Peculiar Treasure* thirteen years after her visit, and in the intervening years the novel *Show Boat*, the musical based on it, and the two films based on the musical had filled the minds and imaginations of much of the American public. On the other hand, it may be evidence of Ferber's influence that writers since have referred to the James Adams as the Floating Palace Theatre. Even in *Showboat Centennials*,[22] a national newsletter on the history of showboats, the James Adams has been called the James Adams Floating Palace Theatre.

Another example of fiction possibly informing history is that Ferber quoted Hunter as saying the James Adams sometimes played a new town each night. Hunter may have been telling her stories about the Mississippi boats, because the James Adams rarely played one-night stands. The only incidents I have documented were those when the theatre played or planned to play a town more than once in a season. The *Cotton Blossom*, on the other hand, did play one-night stands.

There is also a question as to how much Ferber travelled with the showboat. The theatre opened the season in Elizabeth City on April 4.[23] The boat was due in Bath on April 13.[24] According to Ferber, it arrived two days late. That would have put Ferber on board April 15. If she stayed for four days, as she indicated she did, she would have left Saturday, April 18. The boat would have been in Bath all four days. Late Saturday night, or more likely Sunday morning, it left Bath for Belhaven where it spent the next week.[25]

There is evidence supporting the fact that Ferber travelled to Belhaven on the boat. In 1974, a Washington, North Carolina, writer quoted a woman who had visited the theatre when it arrived in Washington after its week in Belhaven. The woman was hopeful of meeting Edna Ferber, whom she had heard was on board. Charlie informed her that Ferber had left the boat in Belhaven.[26] Also, in an account Ferber gave the *Woman's Home Companion* in 1926 acknowledging her indebtedness to Charlie, Ferber stated that she talked with him in Belhaven.[27]

The boat, then, may have been two days late for its engagement with Ferber, but it must have been three or four days late for its scheduled appearance at Bath, if Ferber spent only four days on the boat and was onboard when the Floating Theatre moved to Belhaven.

But the central story of Ferber's visit to the Floating Theatre was a conversation she had with Charlie Hunter. She had difficulty getting Charlie to slow down enough to talk with her, but when he finally did, she wrote that she filled sheets of paper with notes of his tales and descriptions of life on showboats, notes that she later drew upon in writing her novel.[28]

THE NOVEL

Ferber's novel, *Show Boat,* was first published as a serial in the *Woman's Home Companion*, April through September 1926. In August of that year it was published in book form by Doubleday.

Briefly, the story chronicles three generations of the Hawks family, headed by Captain Andy and his wife Parthy. The Hawkses become the owners and managers of the showboat *Cotton Blossom*. The story centers on the love of the Hawkses' daughter, Magnolia, for a handsome gambler, Gaylord Ravenal. The novel tells of their marriage and the birth of their daughter Kim. It describes the Ravenals' move from the showboat to Chicago, the problems in their marriage because of Gaylord's gambling, and Magnolia's return to the showboat. An important subplot in the novel is the difficulties that two performers on the boat, Julie and Steve, have with the law because they are married: he is white and she is a mulatto passing as white.

Harriet F. Pilpel, trustee of Edna Ferber's literary trust and knowledgeable admirer of Ferber's writing, finds that one of the many strengths of Ferber as an author was her ability to incorporate in original and imaginative ways the feelings of the locales she researched in preparation for writing. Pilpel suggests that Ferber's stories are charged with the atmosphere of the original settings, but that she did not slavishly reproduce them. Ferber used her research to enrich, but not to limit, the development of her fiction.[29]

It is my opinion that Ferber's novel *Show Boat* reflects the atmosphere of the James Adams Floating Theatre. In the discussion that follows, I will suggest some possible connecting links between the novel and the historic James Adams. I do not mean to infer that Ferber literally reproduced in her novel any of the sources cited. Her use of the material was adapted through the richness of her imagination to meet the unique needs of her story.

One critic wrote of *Show Boat*: "Perhaps the best chapters are Five and Six, which contain almost no action at all, but rather a deeply loving sketch of life aboard the *Cotton Blossom*."[30] Most of the details in chapters 5 and 6 appear to be culled from life on the James Adams.

In *A Peculiar Treasure*, Ferber described the bedroom in which she slept on the Floating Theatre.[31] Francis suggested that Ferber's description of the Hawkses' bedroom in Show Boat "is reminiscent of Charles and Beulah Hunter's room on the *James Adams*. The Hawkses sleep in two large square

Jim Adams's first yacht, **Marion.** *Photograph courtesy of Marguerite Young.*

Beulah Adams, left, and Edna Ferber. Date and location are unknown. Photograph courtesy of Marguerite Young.

Charlie Hunter working on a script in his stateroom, probably several years after Ferber visited the boat. Photograph courtesy of the Mariners Museum, Newport News, Virginia.

rooms located over the forward section of the showboat. Each room holds a bed, dresser, rocker, and stove; dimity curtains hang at the windows."[32]

One of the interesting things about Ferber's account in *A Peculiar Treasure* of her sojourn on the Floating Theatre was her omission of any mention of Selba and Clara Adams. By all accounts, the apartment behind the balcony, originally built for Jim and Gertie, was occupied by Selba and Clara from 1917 through 1932. Maisie Comardo remembered that Charlie and Beulah had one of the center rooms on the first floor behind the stage. The room Ferber remembered, with four windows, was most certainly in the apartment. It may have been that Selba and Clara shared the apartment with Charlie and Beulah, but it was a room in the Adamses' apartment in which Ferber slept. Ferber wrote in *A Peculiar Treasure* that an iron wood stove and a washbowl and pitcher were in the room. But the James Adams was heated by steam and had piped hot and cold water for washing in the rooms. Ferber does not mention the radiator in the room nor the sink with running water. The chances are her description in 1939 of the room she slept in in 1924 on the Floating Theatre was another example of her memory of the *Cotton Blossom* in her novel influencing what she remembered of the James Adams.

Ferber's description in *A Peculiar Treasure*[33] of the dining room on the James Adams, with its entrance through the orchestra pit, is accurate. It is interesting that her description of the dining room on the *Cotton Blossom* in *Show Boat* is very similar. Her description of the arrangement of the bedrooms behind the stage on the *Cotton Blossom* also brings similarities to mind of those on the James Adams.[34]

In *A Peculiar Treasure* Ferber wrote of her visit to the churchyard in Bath.[35] Francis described how Ferber may have used the churchyard in her novel.

> In one scene from the book Gaylord Ravenal, claiming descent from the Tennessee aristocracy, shows Andy Hawks and Magnolia the churchyard and tombstone where one of his ancestors, Suzanne Ravenal, is buried. The tombstone inscription is a verbatim transcript of the 1765 epitaph of Mrs. Margaret Palmer, wife of Robert Palmer. Mrs. Palmer was interred to the right of the altar in St. Thomas Episcopal Church. The epitaph was copied during Ferber's 1925 visit to Bath.[36]

Francis pointed out, also, that there is one direct reference to Bath in *Show Boat*. "In a letter to her daughter, Parthenia Hawks says, 'We're playing the town of Bath, on the Pamlico River.' Ferber does not explain to her readers," Francis continued, "that the Pamlico is in North Carolina, states removed from the *Cotton Blossom*'s Mississippi River."[37]

In the novel, after Andy Hawks died, Parthy was left alone to run the showboat. Most of the performers and crew rebelled and refused to work for a woman. But she took over the business with a vengeance and made a success of the enterprise. She later moved the boat for a time to the East Coast. She wrote to Magnolia about the new towns the boat visited, including Bath on the Pamlico and Queenstown on the Sassafras.[38]

While recognizing that Ferber was writing a novel, and could create any geography she wanted for her fictional world, it is interesting to compare what she wrote with the mundane world. "Queenstown on the Sassafras" is a delightful phrase, rich in consonance. The reference, however, suggests Queenstown, Maryland, which, although close to the Sassafras, is actually on the Chester River.

It is also interesting to project, in the mundane world, Parthy's feat of transporting the *Cotton Blossom* from the rivers of the Midwest to the East Coast and back again, for in the novel she returned to the Mississippi River system after her sojourn in North Carolina and Maryland.[39] It is, of course, unnecessary in a work of fiction for an author to conform to historical reality. The delight of fiction is that it transcends the workaday world through flights of imagination. But if Parthy, in the real world, had moved the *Cotton Blossom* from the Mississippi to the Pamlico, it would have been a magnificent accomplishment: an awkward, flat-bottomed barge with a high superstructure, ornate trimmings, and large windows, pushed by a small river steamboat navigating hundreds of miles of open water, through the Gulf of Mexico, around Florida, and up the Atlantic Coast. Such a trip conjures up images of great adventure, images worthy of another novel by someone with Edna Ferber's imagination.

Francis[40] also found a similarity between Ferber's description in *A Peculiar Treasure* of her ride from Washington to Bath in a Ford[41] and Ferber's description of Kim and her husband driving to the *Cotton Blossom* near the end of the novel.[42]

Francis addressed another incident in the novel, one regarding the marriage of Julie and Steve, but the story is better explored through another source.

In the novel, Steve Baker, a tall, handsome, but untalented actor, was married to Julie Dozier, a dark-haired mulatto beauty who was passing for white. They were the character team on the showboat. Steve was jealous of other men's attentions to Julie. Pete, the engineer of the towboat *Mollie Able*, was stuck on Julie, sent her presents, and courted her attention. Steve confronted Pete and in a fight threw him into the river. Pete discovered that Julie was part black and was passing as white and gave the information to the local sheriff. The sheriff came to the boat to arrest Steve and Julie for the crime of miscegenation—cohabitation of a man and woman of different races. But when the sheriff started pounding on the door for admission, Steve realized what was happening, drew a knife, made a cut on Julie's finger, and sucked the blood from the wound into his mouth. When the sheriff entered,

Steve thwarted him by declaring that he had black blood in him. The others, who had witnessed Steve's actions, swore that he spoke the truth. The sheriff was persuaded that the marriage was between persons of the same race and let the couple go free. But Julie's secret was out; she and Steve could no longer stay with the showboat.[43]

Ferber may have based the story on an incident suggested by Charlie Hunter. Following is a letter Charlie wrote to Ferber from St. Michaels, Maryland, October 20, 1925 (five months after Ferber's visit to the boat).

> Glad to hear from you even if it was a "request number"... I enjoy talking to you much more than writing, in other words we like Miss Edna Ferber "human" and not the name on the back of the book, oh shucks, I'm all tangled up like a cat in a ball of yarn.
>
> Now wait until I get that letter of yours and try to get them in rotation.
>
> Now we'll take the "miscegenation" case.
>
> All Southern states have a miscegenation law, but very few Northern states—I know my home town in Ohio there are quite a few cases of white women married to Negro men, but I don't know a case of the condition being reversed. In the South it would be a pretty hard thing to find a case of a white woman and a Negro man, in fact I never heard of such a case. But I can't say as much for the Southern men. Between me and you there is plenty of mixed blood in the South and it isn't all confined to the lower classes by any means. Thomas Dixon in his Sins of the Fathers didn't exaggerate but drew a very mild picture of what all Southerners know exists, but ignore.
>
> The "drinking blood incident" (doesn't that sound "piratey") actually happened and I knew all the parties concerned. It happened about 20 years ago and it was in Charlotte, N. C.
>
> At the time I was a musician in the band with what was called a "rag front" carnival. You see some of the carnivals at that time had elaborately carved wooded fronts to their shows, but the smaller outfits simply had painted banners pulled up on poles in front of their attractions, hence the name of "rag fronts."
>
> One of the attractions was "The Old Plantation," or "The South Before the War." All carnivals had one of these attractions in the old days, and still have. The show was an all Negro one and consisted of songs and dances, something like a colored minstrel, but they all ended the same, that is with "Uncle Eph's Return." Uncle Eph would be the best dancer in the troupe, and he would supposed to come back from up North after a long absence, and to lead up to one sure-fire laugh, the old "mammy" would introduce

each of them as one of Uncle Elph's children grown-up, but there would always be one small "pickaninny" hiding behind mammy's skirts and Uncle Elph would discover it last and when he would begin to question mammy about this one she would give him this answer.

Eph: "Mammy, who is dat button headed youngster hidin' behind you all?"

Mammy: "Why Eph! Dats dat postal card you sent me."

Well, "our man" had one of these "Plantation Shows." His last name was Henry; I never heard his first name. He was a quite gentlemanly sort of fellow, a big man with sandy hair. He knew that it was general knowledge on the show that he was associating with this "yellow girl" so he never thrust himself on anybody.

This girl, Bessie, was a good looking "high yaller," and the thing that I remember most about her was when the season was getting along in cold weather I would see her out on the "ballyhoo" (now do I have to explain "ballyhoo"?). Well, this was a platform in front of the show where all the performers would come out and give the crowd a sample of what was to be seen inside. She would be on the "Bally" in an evening dress, low neck and short sleeves, and, of course, powdered until she was almost white, but wearing a short pair of "red woolen mittens." I can see those mittens yet waving in the air, and hear her singing "Can't You See My Heart Beats All For You."

Henry would be on the "ticket box" watching her every move as he was violently jealous of the "bass drummer."

We had never known of him actually living with this woman until Charlotte, N. C. where he discharged one of his employes. It seems that he was living out in the Negro quarter with her, and this man reported to the authorities. Henry was tipped off by one of his men that they were going to arrest him, and he knew what the penalty was in the South, and the colored boy who done the tipping is the one that told us that he saw him take a needle and prick her thumb and suck the blood. For in the South, one drop of Negro blood makes you a Negro.

Henry went to the stand and swore that he had Negro blood in him. I didn't hear the case but they tell me that the Judge scorned him unmercifully, and told him that if he had sworn to a lie to evade the law he had worse than Negro blood in him.

Of course that settled his connection with the carnival, but we learned later that he continued to live with her as man and wife although they were not married, until she deserted him for a big black Negro who worked for him called "Capudine Bill" from the fact that Bill would take a 25 cent bottle of Capudine headache medicine and drink it straight down to get a kick out of it.

And that's that. I can't squeeze another thing in it to save me.[44]

In *A Peculiar Treasure*[45] Ferber gave credit to one of the character actresses on the James Adams for the story of the "snuffing" of Magnolia when she gave birth to Kim. When Magnolia was having trouble with the birth, the midwife, much to the confusion of the young doctor in attendance, put snuff in Magnolia's nose, and in the resulting sneeze, Kim was delivered.[46]

Michelle Francis explored Edna Ferber's experience with Bath, North Carolina. Another writer, Al Gough, Jr., developed some interesting stories about the connection between Leonardtown, Maryland, and Ferber's novel. Ferber never visited Leonardtown, but the two black cooks on the Floating Theatre in 1925, Aggie Scott and Joe Gunn, were from Leonardtown. The cooks in Ferber's novel, Queenie and Jo, may have been suggested by Aggie and Joe.

Many older residents of Leonardtown still remember Joe Gunn with great fondness. Virgil Swales, who remembered "Uncle Joe" from his youth, recalled that he was "the singin'est, dancin'est, cookin'est man I ever knew."[47]

Joe was born in 1871 to former slaves. He had no formal education and listed his profession at various times as "oyster tonger, driver for St. Mary's Hotel, and cook." In 1925, when Ferber came aboard at Bath, Joe and Aggie were working for the first year on the Floating Theatre.[48]

One of Gough's most delightful stories is about a recipe that was native to Leonardtown.

There was one other dish that Joe and Aggie served and Edna Ferber described it in her novel. It was Easter time—Easter fell on April 12 that year—and Aggie and Joe prepared a special treat. It is the description of this treat that helps tie in the real Joe Gunn of the Adams Floating Theatre with the fictional Jo of the *Cotton Blossom*.[49]

The recipe was for stuffed ham, a very special stuffed ham in which many spices and greens are pushed into the ham with a sharp knife. The ham is stuffed with this mixture until it is doubled in size. When the ham is cooked and sliced, the spices and greens form a mosaic pattern in the slice. Gough describes the dish as a favorite in St. Mary's County in Southern Maryland.[50]

In the novel, Magnolia learns the recipe from Queenie. Later, when Magnolia's daughter Kim is an actress in New York, she has her cook prepare the dish for her famous theatre friends.[51]

Jo and Queenie are not the only characters Ferber may have developed from people on the James Adams. Selba and Clara Adams are possible models for Andy and Parthy, although the part of Andy that appeared on stage to make the announcements before the plays could haven been taken from Hunter. Selba was full of fun and Clara was motherly and business-like, although she wasn't overweight as Parthy was.

Ferber most likely based some of the actors on the *Cotton Blossom* on the actors she met on the James Adams. However, our knowledge of the James Adams acting company in April 1925 is limited primarily to what Ferber wrote about them in *A Peculiar Treasure* and to the signatures in the guest book of St. Thomas Episcopal Church in Bath, North Carolina. Those who signed, in addition to Ferber, were:

> *Charles Hunter*
> *Beulah Adams*
> *Frank L. Root and wife*
> *J. B. Stevens*
> *Ralph Hayes*
> *Frank Kramer*
> *Connie Lehr-Fuller Kramer*
> *Clara and Selba Adams*
> *Marguerite Wooley*
> *Oscar Wooley*
> *Mrs. H. W. Riedel*
> *Lucille Hooker*
> *Harold Marshall*
> *W. S. Cannon*

Billboard indicated in March that, because of the number of rep companies touring that year, there was a shortage of actors.[52] Charlie apparently was not satisfied with the hand he drew at the beginning of the season, for in the same letter in which he elaborated on the miscegenation case, he wrote Ferber, "We have replaced four people since you were here and we have a much better show, at any rate the box office says so and that is the thermometer of approval."[53]

An actress from the Floating Theatre who retired to raise a family in Reedville, Virginia, lived with the rumors, according to her daughter, that she had been the model for Julie.[54] The rumors were false. That actress, Jackie Mayo, was not on the Floating Theatre in 1925. Her first year on the boat was 1927. But Jackie had dark hair and was petite. Also, she was an actress who had been divorced. That was enough to make anyone a subject for gossip in a small town in the early 1930s.

Finally, there are Beulah and Charlie. After the novel was published, Charlie claimed that he and Beulah were Ferber's Gaylord and Magnolia. There are two levels to Charlie's claim.

The first is simply that he and Beulah were the models for the characters. "Edna Ferber spent several weeks on board when writing her famous 'Showboat' and the characters of 'Ravenal' and 'Magnolia' are still with the show in the persons of Charles Hunter and Miss Beulah Adams, the leading man and lady."[55]

There is reasonable argument for projecting Beulah into Magnolia. They were both ingenues. They both were attractive without being raving beauties. They both had good singing voices. They both had a combination of sweetness and grit. It is difficult, however, to see the handsome, charming, irresponsible rascal Ravenal in Charlie, who was tall, thin, bent at the shoulders, nearsighted, friendly, and hardworking.

The second level of Charlie's claim is the more interesting one:

If you have read the story of Miss Ferber's Show Boat, or have seen the motion picture—or the Ziegfeld musical show of that title you remember the characters of Magnolia and Ravenal. I think I may say with truth and modesty that these characters portray the courtship of myself and my wife. If you remember, their trysting place was the "water barrel" on the upper deck of the show boat. This water barrel played quite an important part in our lives—as I will explain . . .

At the time I was courting my wife my standing with her parents who owned the show boat, was not what you would call very high, so our meetings had to be arranged secretly. One of our regular meeting places was at the water barrel. Every night she would make it a point to come to the barrel to get a pitcher of water to take to her parent's room. My room was close to the water barrel. When I would hear the lid to the barrel click I would step out hoping it would be my sweetheart. As a rule it would be someone else—So I would have to take a drink of water to make everything look all right. I think the company was aware of this little plan of ours for sometimes I would be forced to drink a gallon of water before I succeeded in kissing my sweetheart good night. But perseverance will have its reward. I won the little girl and still have her. And tho we are perfectly happy, I have been bitterly opposed to "water as a beverage" ever since.[56]

Charlie's story is a charmer and it had a strong impact on the theatre's audiences. Even today, one of the first things people who remember the boat want to talk about is Charlie's courtship of Beulah at the water barrel. Unfortunately, one of the occupational hazards of writing history is skepticism.

Some facts: Beulah's parents did not own a showboat. They lived in Saginaw, Michigan, far from the Mississippi River, and Beulah's father died in 1909, two years before she married Charlie.[57]

Some people, clinging to the myth, suggest that it was on Jim's showboat that Charlie courted Beulah. That perception of the myth and the nineteen years' difference in their ages have persuaded some people that Jim was Beulah's father. Facts: The James Adams was the only showboat Jim owned and it was built almost three years after Beulah and Charlie were married.

The next claim is that it was Charlie's father Peter who owned the showboat on the Mississippi. Fact: By 1903, when Beulah was only ten years old, Peter Hunter was ashore in Ironton.

Perhaps we can throw the parental element out and put Charlie and Beulah on a showboat on the Mississippi with a captain who was determined to protect the chastity of his young ingenue. However, it is highly unlikely that Beulah's mother or older brothers would have allowed her to go off into show business by herself as a young girl. She was only eighteen when she married Charlie.[58]

With what are we left?

Beulah was most likely performing with Jim's vaudeville show. Charlie was probably playing in the orchestra or doing some acting. Jim didn't want Beulah to marry until she was eighteen and told Charlie so. The rest—the marvelous details of the water barrel on the showboat—is Charlie's invention. He may have given the story to Ferber, or he may have taken the story from Ferber and made it his own.

One statement in Charlie's story that, by all accounts, has the ring of truth is ". . . I have been bitterly opposed to 'water as a beverage' ever since."

Initially, I think, Charlie concocted the story of his courtship for publicity purposes. Ferber had done her research on his boat, but, despite the fact that the novel was filled with the essence of the James Adams Floating Theatre, the showboats reaping the largest rewards from Ferber's book's popularity were those on the Mississippi. Hunter needed something that would focus the public's attention on the James Adams. The courtship story touched people's hearts. Charlie and Beulah repeated the story so many times over the years that I think they came to believe it themselves. In an interview in Michigan in 1948, eleven years after they left the Floating Theatre, Charlie and Beulah were still telling the story.[59]

Ferber wrote nothing about the courtship story in her novel having been Charlie's, but she did confirm using another of his stories. In a letter, she wrote that the description in her novel of Magnolia and Ravenal's wedding was based on the stories she had heard of Beulah and Charlie's wedding.[60]

Because I have taken away one of the myths of the Floating Theatre—Charlie courting Beulah at the water barrel—I hope readers will take the time to look up Ferber's description of Magnolia's wedding.[61] It is a less dramatic story than the courting, but we have Ferber's word that it is one of the authentic links between her novel and the James Adams Floating Theatre.

CHAPTER EIGHT

More on Show Boat

SHOW BOAT, THE MOVIE

Charlie Hunter's involvement with *Show Boat* did not stop with Ferber's novel. It continued into the first filming of the story.

Screen rights to Ferber's novel were purchased by Universal Pictures on October 26, 1926, only two months after the book's publication. Ferber sold the rights for $65,000,[1] a tidy sum for the period. It is important to note, however, that the films of *Show Boat* were based more on the musical than on the novel itself.

Many people today think that the movie released in 1936 with Irene Dunne, Allan Jones, Charles Winninger, Paul Robeson, Helen Morgan, and Helen Westly was the first film version of *Show Boat*. It was not. The first version was released in March 1929. Both versions were made by Universal under the supervision of Carl Laemmle. Laemmle produced the first film. His son, Carl Laemmle, Jr., produced the second.

Laemmle, a major pioneer in the film industry, created Universal Pictures. "Uncle Carl" was a man of energy and vision. He bought the rights to *Show Boat* with the determination to make it into a major motion picture, a "jewel," in the parlance of Universal Pictures.[2]

Laemmle's ambitions were, for a time, thwarted. He succeeded in 1936, but his dreams for the 1929 production faded under an avalanche of miscalculations and frustrations.

The cast of the first film included Otis Harlan as Captain Andy; Laura La Plante as Magnolia; Joseph Schildkraut as Ravenal; Stepin Fetchit as Jo; Gertrude Howard as Queenie; and Jane La Verne as Magnolia as a child and Kim. But the screenwriters tried to cover too much of the sweeping story and the director, Harry Pollard, was unprepared to handle the plot's complications.[3]

The film was initially shot as a silent picture. In 1909 Laemmle had tried to introduce to the industry a synchronized talking picture system from Germany. The attempt failed,[4] and he lost faith in talking pictures. So Universal Pictures wasn't prepared for the "talkies" revolution that came in

October 1927 with the release of Warner Brothers' *The Jazz Singer.* Laemmle also was unprepared for the success of Ziegfeld's musical version of *Show Boat* that opened onstage in New York in December 1927. Before Uncle Carl could get his film finished, the public wanted only a talking, singing version of the story.

Universal did not have the recording devices in its studios to compete with Warner Brothers, and scrambled to improve them. Laemmle held up the release of *Show Boat* until he could film it again with sound. Kreuger, who has chronicled the history of *Show Boat,* concludes, "The activities at Universal in preparing an early sound picture were performed in utter chaos and confusion."[5]

In the end, Laemmle produced three versions of the film: a silent version, a part-silent/part-talkie version, and a talkie version with music from the Ziegfeld production performed as a prologue and injected in various spots in the story. The film finally premiered in March 1929 in Florida, and in April in New York.[6] For all the confusion of its conception and birth, the film played surprisingly well. After the triumph of the 1936 version, however, the 1929 version drifted into obscurity. Many people today think of the later version as the "first" *Show Boat* movie.

In January 1927, three months after Ferber sold the movie rights to her book, Charlie Hunter went to Hollywood to serve as an adviser on the film.[7]

I have not been able to put together the full story of Charlie's involvement. Universal Pictures sold its interests in *Show Boat* to MGM, and later Turner Entertainment bought out MGM. All the companies involved have cooperated with me in my efforts to find documentation of Charlie's involvement, but what records might have shown his contractual arrangements with Laemmle have faded into obscurity with the film itself.

Charlie and Beulah were in Hollywood in the winter of 1927. On their way back East, the Hunters and Jim and Gertie Adams stopped at Robert J. Sherman's offices in Chicago where Charlie leased three of Sherman's plays for the 1927 season. *Billboard,* which reported the Hunters' visit to the Windy City, also reported his contribution to the film: "During his stay in Hollywood, Hunter acted as technical director for the picture *Show Boat,* being made from Edna Ferber's novel of the same name."[8]

What kind of involvement Charlie had with the film in January 1927 is difficult to surmise. The best guess is that he was advising the writers. According to Kreuger, the first writer assigned to the project, Charles Kenyon, finished his first "treatment" of the story on January 13, 1927. Kenyon didn't begin continuity scripts until March.[9] There certainly was no filming taking place in January.

In a story in the Elizabeth City *Independent* in April 1928, a year after the Hunters returned from Hollywood, Charlie gave an interview to the daughter of the newspaper's publisher. She wrote:

Universal pictures sought Mr. Hunter himself and offered him the leading role in the Screen production; it was his big chance to get into the Movies and get away from a little floating theatre that played the small towns on the inland waters of North Carolina, Virginia and Maryland.

Charles Hunter might have signed up with the Movie folk and quit the floating theatre forever. This was in January 1927. But by chance he picked up a copy of The American Magazine and read one of the most dramatic appreciations of small town life written in recent years: "In The Valley of the Shadow I Found the Golden Key," by W. O. Saunders. But let Mr. Hunter tell the rest of it.

Said Mr. Hunter: "I read that article telling about how much friends meant to Mr. Saunders, and it gave me food for thought. That night I told Beulah, my wife, that friends did mean more to a person than anything in life. And I said, my place is with the show boat, we are going back to North Carolina where we have friends.

"Everything in Hollywood seems artificial; people coming and going all the time, and no one is genuine. One sees so many strange faces. I like to be where I know people and where people know me."

And so Charles Hunter and his wife did not stay in Hollywood; they returned to the show boat, and they are happy. This is where their hearts are and where they have friends.[10]

As is the case in most of Charlie's stories, there is in the above, I think, some truth and some hyperbole.

Facts: Charlie was in Hollywood in January 1927. W. O. Saunders's article in *The American Magazine* was published in January 1927.

Assumption: That Charlie read Saunders's article when he was in Hollywood and found himself in agreement with the values of small town living that Saunders espoused. Charlie expressed his opinions to Beulah and they both agreed that the Hollywood life was not for them.

Hyperbole: That Charlie was supposedly offered a contract to "star" in the movie, or even to have a role in it. What role would he have played? Captain Andy or Ravenal? He wasn't the acting type for either. (It also doesn't appear that Laemmle was casting as early as January. Kreuger indicates that the first casting notices from Universal were announced eighteen months later, in June of 1928.[11])

My guess is that when he was interviewed by Elizabeth Saunders, Charlie wanted to say something nice about her father, W. O. Saunders, the publisher of the Elizabeth City *Independent* and writer of the magazine article. Charlie had every reason to do so. Saunders and his newspaper were good friends of the Floating Theatre. Charlie had read Saunders's article in *The American* and was moved by its sentiments. The business of Universal offering him a role in the movie was Charlie's natural way of enriching a tale. The reporter, of course, focused on it because it was the juicy part of the story. If the reporter were to have interviewed Charlie three years later, she would have discovered that the story had grown with time. By 1931, Charlie had "assisted in the direction of the 'Show Boat' scenes."[12]

Several months after Charlie's visit to Hollywood, Bill Menke reported to *Billboard* that his showboat *Goldenrod* was being used for the filming of *Show Boat.*

PADUCAH, Ky., March 5.—The Showboat Goldenrod, which has been tied up in the "Dick's Nest" on the Tennessee River here, with her sister boat, French's New Sensation, since last November, will leave here shortly with a company of motion picture people aboard under the direction of Lynn F. Reynolds, director of the Universal Pictures Corporation, for the filming of Edna Ferber's well-known novel, *Showboat.*

T. E. Dean, assistant producing director of Universal, arrived here recently with his wife, to make final arrangements for the filming of the picture. The other motion picture people, who are at present in Canada, filming *Back to God's Country,* are scheduled to arrive here within a few days. Dean stated that during the filming of the scenes of *Showboat,* which are laid on the Ohio and Mississippi rivers, the entire company will remain aboard the Goldenrod.[13]

Nothing in the *Billboard* article corresponds to the research on the making of the film reported by Kreuger. It is ironic to think that, after Bill Menke rejected Ferber's visit because he didn't know who she was, the film of her novel would be shot on his showboat. What, if any, filming was done that spring, I do not know. The unit may have been doing background shots. Kreuger reports that the final version of the film was, in typical Hollywood manner, shot on a showboat built by Universal for the movie and launched on the Sacramento River at Knights Landing, California.[14]

SHOW BOAT, THE MUSICAL

According to a biographer of Oscar Hammerstein II, Kern and Hammerstein, as part of their preparation for writing the musical of *Show Boat,* visited the James Adams Floating Theatre in the fall of 1926. The biographer, Hugh Fordin, wrote that the men went to Baltimore and then took a train to where the boat was moored in Maryland. When the vistors arrived they found that the men were on shore shooting, but the women greeted them graciously and invited them to dinner. The visitors were pleased with

A 1914 view of the auditorium of the Floating Theatre, before Adams remodeled the balcony. Photograph courtesy of Vivian O'Leary.

The stage of the Floating Theatre in the early 1920s. Photograph courtesy of Vivian O'Leary.

A view of the auditorium after the balcony had been remodeled, most likely after the Floating Theatre sank in 1927. Photograph courtesy of Marguerite Young.

The auditorium in December 1939, after the balcony had been remodeled again, probably after the Floating Theatre sank in 1938. Photograph courtesy of Jacques Kelly.

their visit until they witnessed the play that night. They found that the players were not "bad actors but they didn't care. They ran through their lines mechanically and had no feeling for the theatre at all." According to Fordin, Kern and Hammerstein "sneaked away" before the performance was over without saying good-by to their hosts.[15]

If Kern and Hammerstein went to Baltimore from New York to get to Chesapeake City, as Fordin suggested, they had a very poor travel agent. Most likely they got off the train at Elkton, the same place they got on the train the next day. And if they walked out of the performance, they hung around that night and the next morning, had lunch with their hosts, and were driven to the train after lunch by the business manager of the theatre.

I am in no position to dispute Fordin's interpretation of Kern and Hammerstein's aesthetic judgments, but Dorothy Barlow was an eyewitness to their visit and reports the facts a little differently.

Chesapeake City, Maryland
Wednesday, November 10, 1926

The boys went rabbit hunting . . .
Mr. Jerome Kern, the song writer, and Mr. Oscar Hammerstein, the musical comedy producer [sic] came. Had dinner and stayed for the show. Had lunch and Uncle Selba took them to Elkton to catch the train . . .
Had rabbit and partridges for lunch.[16]

Interestingly, the New Yorkers did not get to see a typical showboat performance. The play they witnessed on Wednesday night was *George Washington, Jr.*, written by their Broadway colleague and rival, George M. Cohan.

Hunter did not have the involvement in the musical that he had in Ferber's novel or even in the first film. His only participation in the stage production was as a member of the audience.

Ziegfeld's production of *Show Boat* opened on December 27, 1927, almost a year later than he had originally planned. It was an instant success, meeting with unqualified praise from both critics and audiences. Brook Atkinson, the drama critic for the *New York Times*, wrote, "This superlative praise of 'Show Boat' does not seem excessive."[17]

When the musical opened in New York, Hunter had other matters on his mind. About a month before, on Thanksgiving Day, the James Adams Floating Theatre had sunk in the Chesapeake Bay.

On January 3, Hunter wrote to Ferber congratulating her on the success of the play and apologizing for not having been able to see a performance.[18] In the letter, Hunter described for Ferber the disaster that had befallen the boat, but more importantly he asked permission from her to cash the check she had sent to him with an autographed copy of her *So Big* after her visit to the Floating Theatre two and a half years earlier. Hunter, according to Ferber, pasted the check in the book and wrote if he ever needed to cash it he would ask her permission.[19]

In early January 1928, Hunter asked permission to cash the check:

> I think I am going to destroy whatever good opinion you had of me, that is if in your different sphere you bothered to have any opinion at all.
>
> When you very generously gave me a check that I have treasured very highly you made the remark that you hoped that some day I would be so "broke that I would have to cash it" which as I know was just an idle remark, but, may I ask your permission now to cash it?
>
> After my "grand gesture" I do feel rather caddish in suggesting such a thing and if I receive no reply to this letter I think it will get just what it deserves.[20]

Ferber's response to Hunter, unfortunately, has not been preserved. But from his letter to her dated January 17 we learn that she gave him permission to cash the check.

> Your wonderful letter received, and it was just like your own impulsive self speaking. I have done as you said. I have cashed the check, that is, I put it in for collection. It may be too old and I don't care if it is. And now that that disagreeable topic (to me at least) is over with we will continue.[21]

Hunter went on to praise Ferber's talent, especially for what she had done to bring showboats to public awareness. "They have only been in existence about sixty years in this country, and they were discovered by Edna Ferber. Your name should rank along with Amundsen, Byrd, and Peary."[22]

Ferber in her letter had invited Hunter and his family to come to New York as her guests to see the Broadway show. Hunter replied:

> How I would love to see 'Show Boat' and how proud I would be to sit in a box with you, but I believe it will come true. In spite of all the hard knocks I have had, and all the illusions, 'My dear Public' has taught me to believe in human nature.[23]

I do not know when the Floating Theatre people went to New York, but Ferber's biographer wrote that they did go, as Ferber's guests, and attended a party where they met Ferber's important friends in the theatre world.[24]

There is one more incident in which Laemmle's efforts to finish his first filming of *Show Boat* touched Charlie.

At the end of November and the beginning of December 1928, the James Adams finished its season on the lower Eastern Shore of the Chesapeake. On November 22, the newspaper in Onancock, Virginia, reported the following:

> The James Adams Floating Theatre is in Crisfield this week. Manager Mercedise of the Broadway Theater, New York, was down on Tuesday to sign a contract with the entire company for a ten weeks' engagement on Broadway which begins following their appearance in Onancock and Harborton. This contract, it is believed, is the result of the popularity of Edna Ferber's novel and great play which has had such a long run in New York.[25]

In 1928 and '29, while Laemmle was waiting to get his first *Show Boat* picture patched up, he tried to keep interest in it alive by producing a performance by a showboat company in New York. The result was eight performances in the Belmont Theatre between January 21 and January 29, 1929, of *The Parson's Bride*, the play described in Ferber's story. The company was Norman Thom's from the Ohio River showboat, *Princess*. *The Parson's Bride* ran for that week and was followed the second week by Thom's production of *Shadow of the Rockies*.[26]

There is no record of the Adams company playing in New York. It is also not clear whether or not the offer made to Hunter to bring his company to New York was made by Laemmle's people or by a rival who wanted to upstage him. Nor have I been able to document a reason for Mercedise's contract not having been honored, but I suspect it was because the James Adams was not an Actors Equity company, and by 1928 Equity had New York solidly unionized.[27] Whatever the reason, New York audiences, in their first exposure to a showboat company, saw Norman Thom, "the John Drew of the Rivers,"[28] rather than Beulah Adams, "the Mary Pickford of the Chesapeake."

ON THE MISSISSIPPI

Despite the fact that Edna Ferber sailed her *Cotton Blossom* on the Mississippi, the essence of the James Adams shines through not only in the novel, but in the original production of the musical and in the first two movies (1929 and 1936). However, the James Adams fades away in the third (1951) movie, the version most available today.

One of the elements that separates most people's perception of Ferber's *Cotton Blossom* from the historical James Adams Theatre is the nature of the boat itself.

Ferber preserved the original in her novel. When she described the *Cotton Blossom*, she described the James Adams, a flat-bottomed barge that looked like a house sitting on the river.[29]

Ferber's *Cotton Blossom* was, like the James Adams, without its own power. It was pushed by the paddle wheel–driven steamboat, the *Mollie Able*.[30]

The 1929 movie preserved much of the James Adams. The *Cotton Blossom* Universal built was a barge, more ornate than the James Adams, but still a barge of similar proportions that needed to be pushed from port to port. Universal's first *Cotton Blossom* had three full decks, the topmost one open. The railings and pillars supporting the balcony that surrounded the second deck were more ornate than anything on the James Adams, but nothing like what the later movies presented.

There was one incongruent element in the *Cotton Blossom* of the 1929 movie, based most likely on a misinterpretation of the "pup" or "pop" cabin Jim built in 1918 on top of the barge for Pop Neel, who lived aboard year-round. On the top deck near the bow of the *Cotton Blossom* there was a pilot-house in which was a large steering wheel. Although this *Cotton Blossom*, like the James Adams, was a barge with no means of propulsion, incongruously it had a rudder and could be steered.[31] The pilothouse and steering wheel were also incorporated into the sets for the 1927 musical.[32]

By 1929, the pilothouse was projected as part of the James Adams. A North Carolina writer, describing Ferber's experiences on the James Adams, mistakenly reported that the floating theatre had been destroyed by fire. (And in the program of the New York musical in 1928 there was printed a notice that the showboat had burned.[33]) The writer curiously concluded, "The main part not burned was the pilot house, in which the mahogany pilot wheel, five feet in diameter, was undamaged."[34]

For the 1936 movie, *Cotton Blossom* became a spacious triple-decker with enough space in the galley to hold a dance and enough room in the staterooms to entertain friends. The showboat was still a barge pushed by the *Mollie Able*, but the only views of the boats moving on the river are confusing and it may appear to some viewers that the *Cotton Blossom* is a self-propelled stern-wheeler.

In the 1951 film there is no vestige left of the James Adams. The *Cotton Blossom* is what one can only assume is one of the largest and most ornate, twin-stacked, steam-propelled stern-wheelers ever to navigate the inland rivers.

The producers of the *Show Boat* films had no responsibility to portray the historical James Adams Floating Theatre. But the fact that they did not was a source of pain to Charlie Hunter. He tried for years to persuade people that the James Adams was the original showboat, but images of a Mississippi riverboat created by the novel, the musical, and to a greater extent by the popular 1936 and 1951 films, made the task monumentally difficult.

A writer in Elizabeth City described the problem in 1930:

> Because Miss Ferber's famous novel had its setting on a Missis-sippi River showboat, it has been said repeatedly that Miss Ferber got the background for it on a Mississippi showboat. And some have gone so far as to say that the showboat on which Miss Ferber got the background for her novel was named the "Cotton Queen," or some such fanciful appellation.[35]

Ferber corroborated the fact that she drew her information on show-boats from her visit to the James Adams. In a correction of a UPI story in 1962 identifying the *Goldenrod* as the source of her information, Ferber stated without equivocation that she was on the James Adams, and that she never visited or saw any other showboat.[36]

Ferber, however, most likely would not have been disturbed to hear that people believed her *Cotton Blossom* navigated the Mississippi and not the Pamlico. If Bill Menke's story is true, she may have used the James Adams because she was unable, because of schedule or opportunity, to visit a showboat on the Mississippi. In her writer's mind, she saw her showboat on the rolling Mississippi, not on a lazy tidewater creek in North Carolina. She wrote in *A Peculiar Treasure*, describing the genesis of her project, that it was not only the theatre that fascinated her, but the glamour of life on the Mississippi. In contemplating her fascination with rivers, she conjectured that in a previous life she may have been a Jewish slave girl on the Nile.[37]

There were influences in her present incarnation, as well, that drew Ferber to the rivers of the Midwest. For one thing, more than a third of the novel was set, not on the river at all, but in Chicago. That was a city Ferber knew well and had used as the location for many of her stories before 1925. It was not a difficult trip physically or emotionally from the Mississippi to Chicago, certainly not as difficult as from the Pamlico to Chicago.

In an article in *Liberty* written before she published *Show Boat*, Ferber explained that her writer's soul drew its material from the middle class, from the Midwest, and mostly from Chicago.[38]

Ferber's soul put the showboat on the Mississippi, and her heart put the guts of the story in Chicago. But she was not unmindful of her debt to Charlie. In 1926, the year after her visit with Charlie and thirteen years be-fore she wrote her autobiography, she wrote a piece for the *Woman's Home Companion* generously giving Charlie his due.

All sorts of people and things would be found strewing the path that trails back to the starting point of *Show Boat*. Certainly Winthrop Ames, who first told me about show boats, would figure largely there. So would that delightful person, Charles Hunter, juvenile lead of the James Adams Floating Theatre. When I'm ninety and toothless I'll remember still an April afternoon spent with him two years ago down in Belhaven, North Carolina. I had gone there especially to see a show boat and get the proper setting for the book. For three days (spent on the show boat as a guest of the company) I tried to pin Charles Hunter down to a long talk. He knew show boats from stem to stern, from pilot-house to cook's galley; he knew the river from Minnesota to the Gulf. But he was busy, what with the rehearsing, acting, directing, for he was not only the juvenile lead on this boat but also director and frequently author. His wife is Beulah Adams, ingenue lead on the Adams boat. There probably isn't a more fascinating talker in the world than this same Charles Hunter. A fascinating person altogether, for that matter, whether he is playing the piano (something of his own composition perhaps) at midnight after the show, when the company, relaxed, is gathering sociably on the stage in that hour of ease that precedes bedtime, or playing the dashing young hero to his wife's ingenue lead.

Finally one afternoon, just as I had despaired of cornering him for any length of time, he slumped his lean length into a rocker up in the bright cheerful bedroom off the balcony, lighted the preliminary cigarette in a great procession to follow and began to talk. He talked for hours. He talked until evening came on and the hour for the night's performance approached. And as he talked I repeated a silent prayer, "Oh, Lord, don't let him stop talking!" Tales of river. Stories of show boat life. Characterizations. Romance. Adventure. River history. Stage superstition. I had a chunk of yellow copy paper in my hand. On this I scribbled without looking down, afraid to glance away for fear of breaking the spell.

From those readers who do not like the novel "Show Boat" as it now stands, I crave the boon of another chance. For it seems to me there is a fair-sized volume that could be made up entirely of rich bits told me by Charles Hunter that April afternoon, and that, somehow, never got into the book at all.[39]

As long as Charlie was on the Floating Theatre, a copy of the article was printed in the the the theatre's programs.

130

CHAPTER NINE

Trials and Tribulations

LICENSE FEES

*B*efore 1920, the Repertoire theatre movement was growing. In the early 1920s, it was temporarily slowed by a national recession. In the mid-1920s, it was in stride again, but by the last half of the decade it ran into obstacles.

Many of the causes of the decline of repertoire have been chronicled: the development of new forms of mass entertainment including films, radio, and eventually television; the improvement of transportation including increased ownership of automobiles and the construction of roads and bridges; and finally, the coming of the Great Depression followed by the Second World War.

All of these conditions had their impact on the Floating Theatre. In addition, the James Adams contended with the decline in steamboat traffic and the accompanying decay of wharves the theatre needed for mooring.

Another issue in the 1920s was the institution of punitive taxation against the traveling theatres. The local, county, and state governments instituted the taxes, but the enemy identified by the rep managers was the movie industry. One manager argued:

> The individual owner and operator of the local movie theatre is not responsible. He is only part of the chain. Indeed, many movie owners have found it necessary to combine against the system of which they are a part, for the protection of their own interests. When the movie was in its infancy the local picture showman was content to compete with the traveling attractions and collect his nickels, dimes and quarters, and be satisfied with fair rivalry, but when Wall Street was convinced that the movies were worth considering from the viewpoint of backing them with real money, they, at the same time determined to brook no opposition.[1]

The rep managers observed that the new syndicates, the film companies, were squeezing out live entertainment. For example, Billy Boy, in a call for the rep managers to organize, reported:

> Several weeks ago the operators of a chain of theatres in a section of the country where repertoire shows are very popular, but are being shut out of more towns each year, took over the road-show house in town and closed it.
>
> They signed a 10-year lease on the playhouse at $500 a month.
>
> Even the poorest business man knows that no firm is going to pay out $500 a month unless it expects to get just as much or more in return.
>
> In other words, the theatregoers in this town must pay in the extra $500 monthly at the movies—*without getting anything for it.*
>
> With the closing of the theatre in question the repertoire company which had been booked to play there . . . found itself without a house in that town.[2]

The movie moguls shut out the New York and circle stock touring companies by leasing the available theatres, but the tent theatres needed only a vacant lot. Bernheim described the response of film interests to the tents.

> They are exerting their utmost influence to have laws and ordinances passed prohibiting the appearance of tent shows within town and city limits. Failing this they seek the establishment of license fees so high as to tax the tent shows out of existence. In some instances they have been known to lease all available lots for tent locations.[3]

In 1927, Robert J. Sherman released for production a play entitled *Tildy Ann*.[4] The play is a typical repertoire comedy-drama with a Cinderella theme, but it also is a propaganda piece presenting the rep managers' position in the conflict with the movie chains.

The orphaned Tildy Ann is being raised by her uncle and aunt. Her uncle, John Brewer, owns and manages a theatre, but his business is failing because of the competitive practices of the other theatre in town, part of a large chain. Brewer has used some of the trust fund, left by her mother for Tildy Ann, to support his business. He has no way of paying the money back, and he feels the guilt of his actions. Tildy Ann's aunt treats her like a servant and does everything she can to further the social ambitions of her own daughter, Annabelle, who has her sights set for the most eligible, rich young bachelor in town. Mrs. Brewer has no qualms about using more of Tildy Ann's trust fund to assist Annabelle.

Brewer brings a major motion picture star to town to judge a local beauty contest at his theatre. The conclusion of the story is that the movie star falls in love with Tildy Ann; she goes to Hollywood for a screen test; she forgives her uncle's embezzlement of her funds because his heart is honest; and Annabelle and her mother are miserable.

Early in the play Brewer and young Hamilton, the object of Annabelle's affections, have a discussion about theatres. Hamilton's father is Brewer's competition.

Young Hamilton brags about the efficiency of the "consolidation" in eliminating competition. Brewer, who tries to bring live entertainment to the town, admits that they are beating him. Hamilton explains how the consolidation is forcing live theatre out of business by such means as punitive taxation. Brewer can't believe that the movie people can succeed with such a plan.

> Hamilton: "Can't we? Do you know that right now, even in the smallest towns—that is, most of them—the tent shows pay ten, twenty, thirty, and fifty dollars a day to operate?"

> Brewer: "That isn't just—isn't even lawful."

> Hamilton: "What do we care as long as we can make them do it?"

> Brewer: "But the general public in these towns wants this class of show."

> Hamilton: "The general public in a small town has no more to say about what they will have or will not have than the people of a large city. The town council is supreme, and in most cases by working through the right channels we can handle them."

> Brewer: "If the people of the town put it to a vote, they would vote twenty to one for the traveling show."

> Hamilton: "That's where we have the people licked to death. They don't get to vote on it. The town council says high license, and high license it is. The people can like it or lump it."

What possible arguments would persuade town councils to pass blatantly discriminatory laws against one form of entertainment in favor of another? The answer, which had plagued traveling entertainers from the very beginning, was exacerbated by the increasingly difficult economic times of the late 1920s. The answer was expressed with eloquent simplicity by the

133

Maine farmer in 1819 after he shot Hachiliah Bailey's show elephant Old Bet: "She was taking too much money out of town."[5]

The argument was simple and persuasive. When itinerant entertainers came into town, the townspeople gave good money to them. When the entertainers left, they took the money with them. The answer was as simple as the problem: Buy local. Support your local movie house rather than give your money to strangers who care nothing about your town.

The rep managers argued that such a theory was false. J. Frank Marlow presented his position in *Billboard:*

> The movie theatre equipment is purchased outside of the village, and practically all that is used in the movie theatre goes to help enrich the manufacturer in some distant city. The moving picture man spends practically no more in the small town where he is located than the amount necessary for living expenses for himself and his family, and in some cases these theatres are operated in chains with headquarters in some city, and managed by men locally who are no more than office boys. Employment given by the moving picture houses is notoriously limited. Contrivances have actually been invented to operate even the curtain from the box office or the picture booth, requiring no one behind the stage.
>
> In addition to license fees, lot rent, light bills and numerous incidentals, the average tent show with a personnel of 20 or 25 leaves an average of $500 in hard cash in every town visited, besides a modicum of pleasure.[6]

It is not coincidental that Sherman's *Tildy Ann* was a part of the James Adams repertory in 1927. The Floating Theatre encountered incidents of discriminatory licensing in each of the three states in which it had played most of its career.

The earliest account I have found is in Leonardtown, Maryland. Al Gough described the event:

> On July 14, 1922 a special meeting was held by the commissioners of Leonardtown, with the full board present. At the meeting Article 26 of the Town ordinance was amended and a motion was made and seconded to "fix the tax on the Adams Floating Theatre for playing at the town wharf at fifteen dollars for each evening performance and ten dollars for each matinee or afternoon performance."[7]

This was in addition to the county tax of two dollars a performance. Adams's answer was to play outside the town, at Foxwell's Point, for two years. Gough concluded that "by 1924 they must have worked things out,

134

for the St. Mary's *Beacon* reported in August of that year that the Floating Theatre had played to capacity audiences at Leonardtown wharf."[8]

They would have had to have worked things out before Adams would have returned to the town wharf. Leonardtown was always one of the most profitable stops for the theatre, but Jim and Selba would not have tolerated paying a tax of fifteen dollars a performance. The theatre could not have survived such a tax, let alone prospered under it.

Adams had no tax problems with the small towns of Virginia. The state license was one dollar per performance, payable to the counties. The one time he ventured into the big city, however, he was stung. In 1932 he played four successful weeks in Norfolk, but the Floating Theatre never returned there. Under pressure from the movie interests, the daily city license was "hiked to $100 a day."[9]

North Carolina had the most complicated license structure of the three states. It was a formula based on state, county, and local taxing rights. Over the years the formula changed, but always in the direction of more punitive taxes. For example, in 1913, a company playing one-night stands was taxed $5 by the state. If the company played a week and charged no more than ten cents a ticket, it was taxed $5 the first day, and $1 each additional day. However, the towns and counties could also charge as much as, but no more than, the state.

In 1923, companies in licensed halls were charged less than those playing in tents (and showboats). Those in tents were taxed $10 the first day and $2 each additional day by the state. The towns and counties could charge the same.

By 1929, the state tax was $300 a year, or $25 the first day and $25 for the rest of the week. The towns could tax up to $20 a day, but, fortunately for the troupers, the counties could no longer levy license taxes.[10]

By 1936, license taxes in North Carolina had gotten so high that the Floating Theatre skipped the state entirely in the fall[11] and tried its luck in South Carolina, Georgia, and Florida.

The Adams Floating Theatre, like the tent shows, was not immune to the pressure of the movie chains and the charge that it took money out of town. In the theatre's heralds for 1930 and 1931, Adams printed his side of the issues:

> The idea that the FLOATING THEATRE "takes all the money out of towns" is absurd. We expect to make legitimate profit for the operation of our business the same as a dealer who sells you an automobile, a pair of shoes, or a pound of coffee. The major portion of your purchase goes out of town, and the manufacturer probably doesn't even know your town exists.
>
> Our business is to manufacture entertainment and amusement. We bring our factory and our workers with us. While in your town

everything they need for their comfort is purchased from you. Food as well as little luxuries, gas and service for their cars and small purchases that can not be enumerated means money spent in your community. We pay taxes in the way of town, county and state license and dock rent.

The FLOATING THEATRE has a drawing radius of from forty to sixty miles. This brings hundreds of people to your town which is bound to be of some benefit to your merchants as well as advertising for your community.

At the present time the entire amusement industry is dominated by the "talking picture." The public has no choice, the chain controlled theatres give them what they want them to have, and force the public to accept it by denying them any other form of entertainment.

If the time comes that our judgement tells us that our public prefers "mechanical entertainment" we will bring it to you. But until that time comes, we shall continue to bring you our company of thirty people. Flesh and blood actors and musicians, which we believe is of more benefit to your community than **"five thousand feet of celluloid and a phonograph."**

JAMES ADAMS

T. R. M. P. A.

Early in 1926, a group of repertoire theatre managers met in Chicago and organized the Tent and Repertoire Managers' Protective Association, the TRMPA[12] Its purposes were to collectively fight the enemies of the rep companies, to clean up the operations of the rep companies, and to improve working conditions for both management and performers.

The TRMPA had a short and stormy history. Rep theatre managers were, on the whole, independent men and women. They did not have a strong herd instinct. They had made it alone in a difficult field and they didn't trust giving authority to an organization.

In its brief existence the TRMPA worked closely with Actors Equity to unionize the tents,[13] it arranged for the major play-licensing companies in New York to give discounts in royalties to organization members,[14] and it worked to secure group fire and theft insurance for performers.[15]

But the major activity of the organization was fighting licensing abuses.

In 1927 Alabama passed a state law that raised taxes on tent shows from \$35 to \$300 a week.[16] The TRMPA mobilized its forces to defeat the law. It organized a boycott of Alabama cotton (tents used a lot of cotton),[17] collected money for a war chest, and sent tent companies to the state to

Some members of the cast, orchestra, and crew of the James Adams Floating Theatre, circa 1927. Left to right, back row: *possibly Captain Cannon (Elk), Captain Crocket (Trouper), Eddie Paull, Tim Lester, Jim Adams.* Middle row: *Charlie Hunter, Pop Neel, four unidentified men.* Front row: *Delmar Adams, Selba Adams, Clara Adams, Gertie Adams, Hazel Paull, Beulah Adams Hunter, Jackie Mayo Lester. Photograph courtesy of Florence Mayo Haynie.*

Members of the company in 1932. Left to right: *Jack Pfeiffer, an unidentified actor and actress, Beulah Adams Hunter, Gladys Pennington Pfeiffer, Marion Hayworth, an unidentified actress, and Seabee Hayworth. The two on the far right are newlyweds Dick Mason and Pearl Austin Mason. Photograph courtesy of the Mariners Museum, Newport News, Virginia.*

challenge the law. The law was repealed.[18] The problem was that non-organization tent managers—who didn't hire Equity actors, who had no interest in using "royalty" plays at any cost, and who didn't care if their actors had fire and theft insurance—benefited by the organization's efforts as much as the members did.

By 1929 the TRMPA was dead. Each rep company stood alone to face the forces of change and economic depression. Sadly, Paul English, the man who served longest as its president, and who for many years owned and operated one of the biggest and strongest tent companies in the Deep South, was out of the repertoire business by the early thirties.[19]

Jim and Selba Adams and Charles Hunter, like the overwhelming majority of the four hundred or so[20] rep managers in the country, chose not to join the TRMPA.

THANKSGIVING, 1927

Adams's chief problem in 1927 came not at the hands of conspirators or impoverished audiences, but from the caprice of nature.

The year was a normal season, until the end. The theatre opened in Elizabeth City in April, played the towns of the Albemarle as far upriver as Murfreesboro and Winton, returned to Elizabeth City for a week's stand, and then went into the Chesapeake through the Dismal Swamp Canal, playing at Deep Creek. In July and August it played the western shore of Virginia and north to Leonardtown and Solomons, Maryland. From Solomons it crossed the Bay to Oxford and St. Michaels and then played the towns of the Chester River, ending its season on November 5, at Queenstown.

It was a successful season. On Monday nights they offered Robert J. Sherman's new comedy, *The Come Back;* on Tuesday nights, Hunter's satire of the movie *It,* featuring Beulah as Clara Bow. On Wednesday nights it was a mystery, Sherman's *The Crimson Nemesis* billed as *Mickey.* On Thursdays it was a revival of the 1914 hillbilly comedy-drama *Kentucky Sue* by the veteran rep writer W. C. Herman. On Fridays the featured play was Sherman's propaganda piece *Tildy Ann.* They closed the week on Saturdays with Sherman's Western comedy-romance *The Rose of Mexico.*

Business was good and the theatre had its share of praise from the local newspapers. The Centreville, Maryland, *Observer* remarked, "The annual visit of the showboat is . . . like the return of an old friend and neighbor."[21]

When the season ended, the performers scattered. Two musicians, Harry Masten—who had been on the Floating Theatre for the 1914 and 1918 seasons—and the young drummer, Jimmie McCallum, went to Norfolk to find work. Harry's cornet-playing wife, Della Mae Masten—who was about to become his ex-wife—and the current leader of the Adams's orchestra, Van Browne, joined the Clint and Bessie Robbins Company in South Dakota. The little comic, Eddie Paull, and his comedienne wife, Hazel Arnold, went home to Boston. Actor Herman Mohlenkamp went home to Toledo. The magician, Heverly the Great, went to Philadelphia. Selba and Clara went home to Shepherd. Charlie and Beulah left to visit family in Ironton and Saginaw. Musicians Pop Neel and Jack Johnson stayed onboard to see the vessel into its winter quarters in Elizabeth City.[22]

Jim hired a commercial towing company to pull his theatre back to North Carolina. The theatre was picked up by Captain Miller of the steam tug *W. H. Hoodless*[23] and added to the two barges he had already under tow.[24]

In the lower Chesapeake Bay, on Thanksgiving evening, November 24, the Floating Theatre struck a "submerged object with sufficient force to stove in a hole in her bottom of about 20 square feet."[25]

The first Jack knew of the accident was when water soaked his bed-clothes. Without waiting to pull on his trousers, he hurried to the roof. There he found Pop.[26] They hurried to the stern, "grabbed a tow rope, pulled a small skiff alongside, and piled into it without ceremony." The next morning they were rescued from the frail craft, heavy seas, and cold winds by the crew of the tug.[27] When the survivors got ashore at Norfolk, they wired their friends in Elizabeth City: "Ark sank five miles above here. Nothing saved except Pop and Jack."[28]

Captain Miller strove to get the boat to shallow water, but was hampered in his efforts by the other two barges he had in tow. He radioed for assistance from the Coast Guard, which sent the cutter *Carrabasset* and two patrol boats to the sinking theatre's assistance, but to no avail.[29] The vessel sank on Friday in sixteen feet of water four miles southeast of Thimble Shoals Light, outside the entrance to Norfolk harbor.[30]

The boat sank in a heavily trafficked area and had to be salvaged at once or risk being destroyed by the Coast Guard.[31] For the next two days high winds and heavy seas delayed salvage and ripped apart the superstructure.[32] Finally, on Sunday, salvagers raised the hull,[33] and the *W. H. Hoodless* towed it to the Norfolk Shipyard.[34]

The hull of the James Adams was still under water as it was towed, and it dragged along the bottom of the harbor, cutting two gas lines running between Norfolk and Berkley, its neighbor across the Elizabeth River. It also cut the Western Union telegraph cable "carrying wires to the entire South and part of the North."[35]

One person who was not distressed by the sinking of the boat was John Beale of Westmoreland. Beale, as columnist "Seldom," had opposed the Floating Theatre playing on the Northern Neck of Virginia. He wrote to the editor of the Northern Neck *News* expressing the hope that the Floating Theatre would stay sunk.[36]

The secretary of the Elizabeth City Chamber of Commerce, Dick Job, rushed to Norfolk to try to be of assistance to Adams and to persuade him to tow the boat to the North Carolina port to be rebuilt.[37] Adams agreed, and after it was raised on pontoons by the Norfolk Shipbuilding and Dry Dock Company and the hole in its bottom repaired, the theatre continued its journey to Elizabeth City to be rebuilt in time to start the 1928 season.

Jim Adams was always close about money, but a reporter in February estimated that the rebuilding of the boat cost Jim $30,000.[38] Three years later the Mathews, Virginia, *Journal* reported the cost as $22,000.[39] Both figures suggest that it cost Jim more to repair the boat than it had to build it in 1914.

The next two seasons Jim advertised on his heralds, "Every piece of scenery, mechanical device, and electric equipment is entirely new this year and no expense has been spared to make the James Adams Floating Theatre the finest show boat in America." He also made it clear that none of the loss he suffered in the sinking was covered by insurance.

Jim's financial loss was substantial, but so was that of the actors who had planned to return the next season. The contents of their trunks stored in the hull, and their clothes in their rooms, were destroyed. The worse loss was the trunks. Rep actors were expected to provide their own costumes and often advertised for work with references to the costumes they could provide. Often actors and actresses became known in the profession as much for their wardrobes as for their skill. In his autobiography, Neil Schaffner wrote upon first becoming a professional rep actor, "At the last minute I acquired the most important of all my equipment: a flat-top Taylor trunk." Schaffner also listed the bare essentials an actor needed to put into that trunk:

> Broad-brimmed hat
> English walking suit with a round-cut coat reaching to the knees
> Prince Albert coat with satin lapels
> Windsor tie
> Formal dress outfit
> Western outfit, complete with chaps, spurs and leather wristlets
> Satin square cut, with lace foils in the sleeves and a lace collar, knee
>   britches and white hose for French costume drama
> Oil cloth boot tops, worn over regular shoes to look like miners' boots[40]

In his January 3 letter to Edna Ferber requesting permission to cash her check, Charlie Hunter wrote about the loss of his and Beulah's trunks.

> All my personal belongings were lost, as well as Beulah's. I did
> find two of her trunks but everything in them, of course, was

ruined. In opening one trunk that I hadn't been in in years, I opened a little package done up in silk and tied with ribbon, and there was something that I hadn't seen in sixteen years. Our marriage certificate from the little church in Goldsboro, N. C.

I was all alone (Beulah is with her people in Saginaw Mich). I chopped those trunks open with an axe as I had no keys, and as I lifted the soggy water soaked articles out it seemed like death. Yet I found things that re-kindled our romance. A little pair of diamond earrings about the size of the head of a pin that I had given her years ago that she was tremendously proud of at the time, poetic outbursts that I had written to her which I really didn't blush to read again, things that she had treasured that I had forgotten all about.

So, in spite of the financial loss, I really found something that I had lost and didn't know it, if you get what I mean.[41]

There have been guesses as to the value of the check Ferber wrote for Hunter. Francis suggested it might have been for $100,[42] Wilmer that it might have been $1,000.[43] Whatever the amount, probably none of it went to the repair of the theatre itself. Jim was affluent enough to handle that. Charlie no doubt used Ferber's check to refurbish Beulah's and his wardrobes.

Another loss from the sinking of the theatre surfaced in an advertisement Charlie ran in *Billboard* the following March:

PLAYS WANTED

★ ★ ★ ★ ★

All my files and correspondence were lost with the sinking of the James Adams Floating Theatre. Would be pleased to receive lists and plays from authors and bookers, particularly Harrison and Colegrove and Century. CHAS M HUNTER, care of Adams Floating Theatre, Elizabeth City, N. C.[44]

In October 1928, almost a year after the James Adams sank, the program for the stage musical *Show Boat* reported the loss of the boat. The Ziegfeld description of the event, although allegedly based on Charlie Hunter's letters to Ferber, was curiously distorted, as can be seen in the program notes below.

The account is most likely the invention of a press agent, but it was the source of continuing rumors. In my research, I encountered many accounts of the burning of the Floating Theatre (while it was still active) and the close escape of its cast. No one was ever quite sure where it happened, but many testified to the fact.

THE ORIGINAL OF "SHOW BOAT" HAS PASSED ON
WATERS CLOSE OVER THE RIVER CRAFT
WHICH GAVE EDNA FERBER
MATERIAL FOR HER MASTERPIECE.

Down at the bottom of the muddy Pamlico river in North Carolina rests what was once the pride and joy of the Mississippi River hamlets—the hull of the James Adams Floating Theatre, queen of "showboats" and progenitor of the musical success at the Ziegfeld Theatre.

It passed into oblivion recently while it was being towed upstream to another "stand." Fire caught in the hold and the little band of players seized their belongings and made way to shore in rowboats. The crew did their best, but the fire was too much for them, and the troupe of roving Thespians stood on the banks and watched what was once their home and their playhouse blaze and then sink beneath the waters.

It was an event of such seeming insignificance that no mention of the tragedy was seen in the metropolitan press, and it was not until Edna Ferber, author of "Show Boat," received a letter from Charles Hunter, owner, manager, and leading man of the organization, that she knew the James Adams Floating Theatre was no more.[45]

DISMAL SWAMP CANAL, 1929

The 1928 season passed without major traumas. One minor problem was the illness of actress Estelle Pellette's mother. Estelle went to Detroit to be with her, and Jim cancelled performances for two nights while she was gone. Her mother recovered.[46]

Another problem was Pop Neel's teeth. He had them pulled and he discovered that he could not play his cornet with false teeth. Selba sent to Norfolk for a bass fiddle and in short order Pop was back in the pit but at a different stand.[47]

The publicity theme of the year was Charlie's decision to reject Hollywood and stay with the Floating Theatre. The story appeared in various forms in the local newspapers.

One feature of the season was the return of Jolly Bert Stevens, "a peppy little fellow with an uncontrollable laugh." Eddie Paull worked that season as advance man.[48]

The next year, 1929, was exceptionally successful financially. Hunter presented a royalty play, *Smilin' Through*, as his Friday feature, and it proved to be one of the most popular plays in the Floating Theatre's history. They presented it three seasons—1929, 1934, and 1938—always to great audience approval.[49]

Stern view of the "sunken" Floating Theatre in the Dismal Swamp Canal, November 1929. Photograph courtesy of the Mariners Museum, Newport News, Virginia.

The front of the auditorium, the stage, and the two tiers of stateroom doors (usually unable to be seen) photographed while the partially submerged Floating Theatre was at a thirty-degree list after it sank in the Dismal Swamp Canal, November 1929. Note the furniture floating in the water. Photograph courtesy of the Mariners Museum, Newport News, Virginia.

Smilin' Through is a dual love story covering fifty years. It begins with a prologue in which the ghosts of the dead mothers of the two lovers hope their children will be able to overcome the prejudice keeping them apart. In the first act, an old man, John Carteret, is bitterly opposed to his niece marrying the son of an old enemy. The second act is fifty years earlier. It is John's wedding day, but the father of the young man John's niece wants to marry fifty years later is insanely jealous and, in an attempt to shoot John, accidentally kills the woman they both love. The third act is in the present again. The young man returns wounded from the First World War, and claims he doesn't love the young girl anymore to spare her being burdened with his physical injuries. John brings them together, however, when the spirit of his dead fiancée imbues him with the ability to forgive the crime done to him and to her. John dies, peacefully, as he falls to sleep over a game of dominoes. His dead fiancée greets him. "Is this what they call dying?" he asks. "Yes, isn't it glorious?" she answers. "They'd go smilin' through the years," she explains, if people "knew what they'd find at the end of the road."

The play is cleverly constructed so as to motivate romantic music being played throughout much of it. Chief among the tunes is the song "Smilin' Through."

> There's a little green gate
> At whose trellis I wait
> While two eyes so true
> Come smilin' through.
> I'll be there
> Waiting
> Just at the end of the road.

Beulah played the dual roles of the two young women, Kathleen Dungannon and Moonyean Clare, roles created for the New York audiences in 1920 by the beautiful Jane Cowl, who was coauthor of the play.[50]

Maisie Comardo saw the production as a young girl. She cried so hard during the show that she told Beulah afterwards—in all seriousness—the play should have been called "Cryin' Through." Beulah loved the idea. From then on that was how the cast referred to it.

Pop Neel, mixing his metaphors, remarked that after the show, "There wasn't a dry seat in the house."[51]

The joy of the season, however, was diminished when the Floating Theatre sank again. The Elizabeth City *Daily Advance* reported the accident on November 16:

The James Adams Floating Theatre met with disaster in the Dismal Swamp Canal Saturday morning and now rests at the bottom about a half mile below the South Mills locks with its hull impaled upon a submerged stump.

The floating theatre passed through the locks on the night before and had started on the last lap of the journey to Elizabeth City for its regular winter lay up in tow of its consort, the tug Elk, when at about 7 o'clock its port bow ran high on a snag, which under the great weight gradually crushed the bottom. Navigation through the canal will be suspended until the show boat is floated.

As it now lies it has a list of about 35 to 40 degrees to starboard at the bow, which still rests upon the stump, with a flatter angle at the stern, giving the whole structure a twist which has caused the roofing to buckle over the entire length. The water on the low side reaches almost to the balcony deck and the interior is flooded, unsecured furniture and odds and ends of timber floating in the auditorium . . .[52]

At the time of the accident, Pop Neel and K. C. Terry were aboard the theatre, Captain Britt Richardson was on the *Elk*, Jack Johnson was on the *Trouper*, and a "negro cook"[53]—probably Joe Gunn—was on one of the tugs. The tug *Sparrow* followed the James Adams through the locks, but because of the accident had to leave its tow in the canal and turn back.[54] A boat came out from Elizabeth City to pick up the men on the Floating Theatre, but Pop Neel was insistent on remaining with the sunken craft. The boat also took off the personal baggage, most of which this time had been stored well above the waterline.[55]

A week later the *Daily Advance* reported the successful salvage of the theatre.

Mud stained and twisted from its six days' repose on the bottom of the Dismal Swamp Canal but structurally sound the James Adams Floating Theatre arrived at the yards of the Elizabeth City Iron Works & Supply Company at 7 o'clock last night [Thursday, November 21] in tow of the [pump boat] Picket and Elk.

In response to the well planned operations of the salvage crew of the local iron works under the direction of Brad Sanders, difficulties in the way of raising the unwieldy hulk of the show boat from the bed of the narrow channel in which it was wedged, which to many appeared well nigh unsurmountable and caused many predictions of failure, faded away, and the James Adams was floated, disengaged from the stump which had stabbed through its hull, and was under tow a full day ahead of the earliest estimate for the completion of the work.

Two days of hard work beneath the cold water of the canal in diver's dress by Grover Hill of the local shipyard was the necessary preliminary to the beginning of operations which freed the hull of water. Groping beneath the black juniper water Hill located and sealed 17 openings in the show boat below the water line, working in the dark by sense of feeling. Within the hull a watertight bulkhead was built around the jagged hole made by the stump.

All was made tight by Wednesday night and at 9 o'clock Thursday morning the pumps of the Pickett and Cutter were started and were soon discharging 2,100 gallons of water a minute over the side. An hour of suspense followed while the workers watched anxiously to see if the comparatively light upper structure of the show boat which was below the surface would hold under the pressure of the water without.

Soon the show boat stirred and then gradually rose as its buoyancy increased and at last a shout from the spectators greeted the deck as it broke water. By 12 o'clock the hull had been drained of water. Some of the vertical planking at the bow which was still hung on the stump was sawed away, the show boat was hauled clear by a windlass and its journey to Elizabeth City begun.

The tow down the river was made at a slow rate of speed without mishap although the show boat in its warped condition was unwieldy and trouble was narrowly averted in negotiating the narrow draw of the Norfolk Southern bridge. A pump was kept going to clear out water which still seeped in through cracks where the planking had been sprung and men stood by all night.

The show boat was hauled out on the marine railway this morning and it is expected that it will settle down on the blocks and eliminate the twist in the hull by its own weight, after which it will be caulked, braced and structural repairs made.

Considerable damage has been done inside by the water, the wood veneer seats and backs of the auditorium chairs being damaged beyond repair, and all material below the balcony level water soaked.

"Pop" Neel, veteran trouper who has spent 60 of his 71 years in show business and has made his home on the James Adams for the past 11 years, set foot ashore last night for the first time in nearly two weeks. "Pop" stuck by the ship during its stay on the canal bottom and refused to take a pessimistic view of the future even when the situation seemed most discouraging. Last season had been the best in the show boat's history and Pop expects to see many more.[56]

The Mathews *Journal* reported Jim Adams's financial loss from the sinking as $12,000. W. O. Saunders's paper, the Elizabeth City *Independent,* reported that Jim had considered suing the government, which had recently taken over the management of the canal, for damages. But Jim must have realized he didn't have a case. The canal was not officially open for traffic. Boat owners were allowed to use it at their own risk.

For the second time in three years the boat was seriously damaged. The greatest frustration was that the new auditorium seats and other capital improvements made in the spring of 1928 had to be replaced anew. But Jim rebuilt the "ark" again, and by the middle of March the troupers were rehearsing for their opening in Elizabeth City on March 29.[57]

MORE LOSSES

In 1930 the theatre presented plays by three veteran repertoire theatre writers: *Gossip* and *S'manthy* by Robert J. Sherman, *Mr. Jim Bailey* by Charles F. Harrison, and *The Girl Who Ran Away* by Eli Whitney Collins. But, following the pattern of the highly successful 1929 season, Charlie chose for the Friday feature a royalty play, *Peg O' My Heart*. Beulah played the role of Peg, the Irish lass whose common sense and strong will put some spirit in her stiff-lipped, rich, English relatives. The role was made famous in 1912 by Laurette Taylor.[58]

Peg O' My Heart does not appear to have had the drawing power that *Smilin' Through* did. It was, perhaps, too subtle for Adams's audiences. The theatre never presented it again after 1930.

One sign of a declining box office is that Hunter tinkered with his route. Early in the season he played at Manteo on the outer banks of North Carolina. The Elizabeth City *Independent* reported it was the first time the theatre had played at Manteo. There is a strong probability it was the third, the first in 1914 when the theatre played at Sky Cove, and the second in 1921 when it followed the airplane to Roanoke Island.

In 1929 Hunter expanded his ports on the western shore of Maryland, playing at Galesville on the West River. In 1930 he played at Annapolis for the first time since 1914. He also played at Cambridge on the Eastern Shore in 1929 and 1930.

In Fredericksburg, Virginia, on Saturday, July 12, 1930, citizens of the city presented members of the company and staff with a large birthday cake surmounted by 17 candles, one to indicate each annual visit. Inscribed on the cake was the significant phrase, "Many happy returns."[59] The citizens who presented the cake were either most generous, poor in arithmetic, or desirous of persuading the theatre company to come to Fredericksburg more regularly, because in seventeen seasons the James Adams had played there only eight times.

When the theatre visited Centreville, Maryland, it moored sometimes at the estate of John J. Raskob, chairman of the Democratic National

Committee. During the 1930 visit, Raskob brought with him as his guest to the theatre a friend from New York, Al Smith, the Democratic presidential nominee two years earlier.[60]

Charlie had planned to close the season on November 15 at Cambridge, Maryland.[61] But he announced to a reporter for the Cecil *Democrat* that the boat would leave soon for Washington, D. C., for the winter. In Washington it would give performances under the sponsorship of the Kallipolis Grotto, a Masonic affiliation.[62] For opening night Jim expected a "number of distinguished guests, and among them . . . Edna Ferber, author of Show Boat."[63]

At the time of the announcement, Charlie and Beulah were having Sunday dinner with Jim and Gertie in the Adamses' house in Chesapeake City, where Jim and Gertie had lived for the past two years.[64] (The Floating Theatre at the time was en route between Chestertown and St. Michaels, Maryland.)

The boat arrived at the Seventh Street wharf in Washington sometime on Friday, November 20. Selba and Charlie planned to open in the nation's capital the following Monday, but Deputy Fire Marshal Charles G. Achstetter and the harbor police had other ideas. The James Adams was denied "a license for public performance because of the arrangement of exits and other structural qualities" which did not "comply with the District's fire code."[65]

Selba and Charlie moved the boat across the Potomac to the Cameron Street wharf in Alexandria. In order not to arouse fears in potential audiences that the Floating Theatre was a fire hazard, they advertised that the boat was moved "because of easier wharf facilities."[66] According to Milford Seymoure, future owner of the boat, who was not aboard at the time, they had to refund $1,200 of advance sales.[67]

Because of the move, the theatre did not open on Monday, as planned. They opened a day later, on Tuesday, November 24. There is no record that Edna Ferber was present for the opening.

To capitalize on the pre-opening publicity in the District, Adams provided free bus service from the United Bus Terminal in Washington to the theatre in Alexandria. Buses left at 7:00, 7:30, and 8:00 each night.[68] The performances started at 8:30. To accommodate the late opening, Adams dispensed with the concert after the performance and went back to the earlier practice of specialties between the acts.[69]

This was the Floating Theatre's first venture into a large city. It was their first winter season since 1915. And it was their first attempt at running as a stock company, playing each play for a week. All of these changes suggest that financially the theatre was not doing well.

Charlie had planned to keep the theatre running all winter,[70] but by Christmas, despite enthusiastic reviews in the Washington press, it was closed.[71] They rehearsed the new season in Alexandria in April,[72] but they did not play there, nor did they ever return to the upper Potomac. The new enterprises were apparently not promising enough.

As omens of troubles to come, perhaps, there were two accidents that winter. In December, Raymond Cooke, an actor visiting from the Eddinger-Cooke Stock Company of Trenton, New Jersey, "sustained an ugly scalp wound when, while running up the gangplank, his head struck a low arch, caused by the extremely low level of the boat in the water. He was removed to the Alexandria Hospital, where several stitches were required to close the gash."[73] In April, Beulah was unable to appear with the company for some weeks because she had broken her leg in an accident during the winter while she was visiting her niece Rose in Saginaw.[74] When she was finally able to limp through a small role, Charlie explained to the audiences in his precurtain speech that because of her broken leg he had written in a small part for her "rather than shoot her."[75]

In 1931, Hunter presented no royalty plays. It might have been because of the poor showing of *Peg O' My Heart,* or it might have been to save money. He presented mostly old and tried rep plays, including Freda Slemens's 1907 potboiler, *The Sweetest Girl in Dixie.* The only new script was Robert J. Sherman's *Chickens Preferred.*

The 1931 route was unique in the boat's history. It opened the season in Leonardtown on April 27, played the lower Potomac River, and then went north via Solomons, Galesville, and Annapolis. It played at North East, and then dropped south to play the ports of the Chester River. It next played at St. Michaels, and then crossed the Bay again to play the only time in its history at Mayo on the South River (presuming it did not play there in 1914). The boat then returned for second visits to two of its most dependable stops, Solomons and Leonardtown; played Kinsale on the Potomac for the first time since 1914; and then worked its way south via its usual stops on the western shore of Virginia. This was a theatre again in search of an audience.

The Northern Neck *News* enthusiastically welcomed the theatre's return to Kinsale,[76] but a week later the best it could report was, "Despite the depression a fair-sized crowd greeted the Adams Floating Theatre at its first performance here Monday night."[77] Audiences were no larger farther south. The Mathews *Journal* reported, "The crowds, which early in the week were small, have increased each night."[78] In addition to the financial problems of the times, the weather was abominable. The area suffered through the hottest July in thirty years.[79]

But none of the problems could have prepared the company for the events of September 28, when there occurred the worst personal tragedy in the theatre's history.

Lynn D. "Jack" Johnson was born in Wisconsin in 1869. He moved to Clear Lake, Iowa, in 1892. In 1908, at the age of thirty-nine, he joined the

Gollmar Brothers Circus as a musician. In 1909 he joined the Adams Vaude-ville Company, and he had been with Jim ever since.[80] In 1914 he was the man who fell from the unfinished stage of the boat when it was under con-struction. He had many jobs with the Floating Theatre. He sometimes lived all year on it with Pop Neel, and he was with the theatre when it sank in 1927 and 1929. One of his responsibilities was to maintain the electrical generators.

On Monday, September 28, while the Floating Theatre was moored at Urbanna, Virginia, Jack was working on a generator on one of the tugs.

> [He was] in cramped quarters when his clothing was set ablaze, it is thought, by sparks which ignited gasoline. It was with almost superhuman effort that he crawled from the corner below decks where he was working with his clothing on fire from neck to knees and plunged overboard.[81]

Jack was sixty-two years old.

On advice of the attending doctor, Selba moved Jack on the *Elk* seventy-five miles to the Marine Hospital in Norfolk.[82] He lived for twelve days in the hospital and died on October 12.[83] His sister, Mrs. Edith Wood, came East from Iowa to accompany the body home to Ocheyedan for burial.

The Floating Theatre continued its season. No doubt mindful of the problems the boat had had the last time it was in the Dismal Swamp Canal, Adams returned to North Carolina by way of the Elizabeth River, where he played at Coinjock and then went on to Manteo.

Leaving Manteo, the boat was hit by a strong northerly wind that blew the showboat out of the channel, and it could not be maneuvered back in by the tugs. For two days it sat, anchored two miles out in the sound.[84] The season had been too much for Selba. His patience was at an end. He "decided to get into Elizabeth City and tie up for the winter as soon as possible."[85]

It was a disheartened company of troupers who celebrated the end of the season when, after the last performance, the band, without Jack John-son, played the traditional "Auld Lang Syne." Charlie Hunter took the mo-ment to relate to a reporter from the *Independent* the list of friends the Floating Theatre had lost in recent years.[86]

The first to die had been George LaVale, a musician who played the traps and the baritone horn on the James Adams for five years, and who had joined the company in 1917. He was found dead in his room on Christ-mas night, 1922. He had been in poor health for eighteen months, but was feeling fairly well at the close of the 1922 season and had gone to Rutland, Vermont, for the winter.[87]

Charlie's brother Sam, who had been a comedian with Adams in the circus and vaudeville days, was the second. Sam died in Ironton in 1923 after an extended stay in a sanitarium suffering from paralysis[88] brought on by syphilis.[89] Sam was forty.

The third was Frank Root, an actor who was with the theatre when Ferber visited it in 1925. Root died in January 1926 in the Grand View Sanitarium in Oil City, Pennsylvania. He had been ill for three years. Root was forty.[90]

The fourth to die was Linden Heverly. Heverly the Great was a magician and character actor who had a long career in vaudeville and repertoire. He was with Adams in 1927 and 1928. After he left Adams he went with Norman Thom on the *Princess* and appeared with the company on Broadway in *The Parson's Bride*.[91] Ironically, Heverly died less than a week after the play closed. He was 40 years old.[92]

The fifth, Frank Kramer, died only a month before Jack Johnson. He had been with the theatre when Ferber visited, but at the time of his death he was preparing to produce a burlesque show at the Casino in Philadelphia. Kramer died at Margate City Beach, New Jersey. He was thirty-seven.[93]

1932

Charlie and Beulah returned to Elizabeth City in 1932 earlier than was their wont. They had been in the habit of vacationing in Florida, but Charlie found conditions there depressing. "Florida is a playground," he explained, "and folks just naturally haven't any money to play on now. Consequently, Florida is on its back. Two big night clubs in Miami began the season with New Year's Dances and not one couple showed up at either place. All the clubs and hotels are broke."[94]

It was a tough year in which to plan a showboat season, but Charlie had two new strategies in mind. He would extend his itinerary beyond the little towns dependent on agriculture and the water for their economies. He would seek out manufacturing areas where he hoped there would be more money. It was his plan to take advantage of the recent improvements in the Chesapeake and Delaware Canal, which was now wide enough for a boat the size of the Floating Theatre, and test the cities of Delaware Bay, such as Philadelphia, Camden, and Trenton.[95]

Charlie's second strategy was to update the concert. He had several ideas in mind,[96] but his final choice was to turn the concert into a tab show. There were many forms of the tab show, but the most common was a short musical review, based on a story, and including a chorus line. The tab show was a big change from the vaudeville format of bits and specialties, but it was more modern and might draw audiences in the new areas Charlie planned to play.

The innovation was handled with care. Since Charlie still carried no unmarried women on board, the chorus line was small—three or four women—and they were modestly dressed in character costumes. They showed a little leg, but no tights or short shorts. Charlie did not want to scandalize his old customers in the effort to win new ones. The first director of the new musical review was Leonard "Seabee" Hayworth. Seabee was a blackface and Toby comedian, who, when he wasn't working with the Floating Theatre or another rep show, toured his own tab show, the *Pepper Box Review,* through North Carolina and points south.[97] Seabee replaced Eddie Paull in 1931 as the number two man aboard, and like Eddie, he came complete with a comedienne wife, Marion Andrews.[98]

In February, Charlie announced that the theatre would open later than usual in 1932 because of the "uncertain conditions in the field of entertainment."[99]

The James Adams opened in Elizabeth City on May 12, and played there for three nights. Skipping the Albemarle completely, it moved up the Dismal Swamp Canal and played for three nights in South Mills and three nights in Deep Creek. Then, for the first time in its history, it stopped at Norfolk.

On May 19, Ziegfeld opened a revival of *Show Boat* in the Casino Theatre in New York. The new production, with most of the original cast (the notable exception was that Paul Robeson replaced Jules Bledsoe as Jo), opened to great fanfare.[100] Adams tried to take advantage of the publicity for the Norfolk appearance, and the rest of the season, by changing the name on his theatre to the "James Adams Show Boat."[101]

Charlie apparently hoped to play for three weeks in Norfolk: he scheduled each of his plays for a three-day run. But the stay was more profitable than he had expected, and the boat stayed four weeks, reviving two old standbys to fill the extra week: the comedy-drama, *Carry Me Back to Old Virginny,* and the melodrama, *Was She to Blame?*

The showboat's stay in Norfolk was sponsored by the Quota Club of Norfolk as a benefit for the Norfolk Museum of Arts and Sciences.[102] Charlie was able to get the Norfolk papers to carry only one ad for the theatre because of opposition from the movie houses,[103] but through the influence of the women of the Quota Club the Floating Theatre received excellent coverage in the feature columns of the *Ledger Dispatch,* which carried an article almost every day.

Because of the Depression and the shortage of work for musicians and entertainers, the showboat carried one of the best companies in its history in 1932. A veteran rep company couple who joined that year, Jack Pfeiffer and Gladys Pennington, stayed on with the boat for the next four years and became close friends with Charlie and Beulah. Another couple, talented dancers as well as actors, were Dick S. Mason, Jr., whose father managed his own tent company for years, and Pearl Austin. Dick, Jr., and Pearl had been married for only a few months before they joined the company, and considered the showboat tour their honeymoon. During the season, Pearl became pregnant.

Charlie took further advantage of the public's revived interest in *Show Boat* while in Norfolk and arranged for the theatre's orchestra to broadcast each day on a local radio station.[104]

After Norfolk, the showboat went to Suffolk for the first time for a week's engagement. After Suffolk it played its usual stops on the western shores of Virginia and Maryland, as far north as Galesville. One observer remembered a robbery and shooting at Galesville, most likely in 1932. A man held up the ticket office, but when the thief tried to flee, the ticket agent pulled a gun and shot the thief dead. No doubt the pickings were too thin in 1932 for the management to have much tolerance for sharing its income with a thief. The same observer remembered the Floating Theatre crushing a smaller boat when the larger boat was blown against the little one at the dock.[105]

After Galesville, the theatre crossed the Bay to St. Michaels, then north to North East and Chesapeake City, skipping all the usual stops on the Eastern Shore. The Sunday it arrived in Chesapeake City, now Jim's hometown, the showboat orchestra gave a concert onboard for the benefit of the Parish House fund of the Church of the Good Shepherd.[106] The following Sunday, before the boat entered the Chesapeake and Delaware Canal, "Captain" Jim and Gertie entertained the entire company

> at their beautiful home 'Linger Longer'. . . Bridge, pinochle and rummy were in full swing, with a waffle luncheon one of the later highlights. "Seebee" Hayworth and "Cowboy" Gwynne [trumpet player] won the waffle-eating contest, with Dick Mason running 'em a close second.[107]

The first stop in the Delaware was Delaware City at the east end of the canal. Then the boat went to Camden, New Jersey, but not without incident. While pulling into Cooper Creek, it "jammed into the middle of the Pennsylvania railroad draw bridge, due to the low tide. The jam-up tied up five crack passenger trains for more than an hour." Charlie wasn't averse to the publicity the accident generated. He rigged up a public address system for the orchestra to entertain the curious people the newspaper stories brought to the riverfront.[108]

Selba and Charlie's problems, however, were nothing compared to those of a rival showboat owner in the area.

In the mid-1920s, A. A. Leyare operated a "store boat" on the Chesapeake Bay. In an interview in 1926 he claimed to tour his store from Bristol, Pennsylvania, to Beaufort, North Carolina.[109] Troupers from the James Adams visited the store boat in Chestertown in October 1926.[110] That same year, Leyare bought an old navy wooden-hulled steam freighter, the *Mahanna*, with the intention of turning it into the "largest showboat afloat."[111] The *Mahanna* was 286 feet long, 45 feet wide, and originally had a draft of 23 feet 6 inches.[112] The steam engine and other machinery had been removed from the ship, which must have reduced the draft considerably for Leyare to think he could tour a boat that size to the small towns on the Chesapeake Bay. Leyare moored the *Mahanna*, renamed the *Million Dollar Joy Boat*, in Baltimore at the foot of Andre Street and began refitting, a task he never completed.

It was Leyare's plan to build a restaurant, a carnival midway with a Ferris wheel and caterpillar ride, a wax museum, and a 1,500-seat auditorium and stage in the ship, and tour his showboat from Pennsylvania to North Carolina.[113] He tried to finance the conversion of his *Joy Boat* by selling shares,[114] but by January 1929 he had made little progress with his project. The boat was still at the foot of Andre Street in Baltimore with a few new portholes cut into her sides and a few stairs built inside. In the spring of 1929, Leyare was planning to move his *Joy Boat* across the Patapsco River to Brooklyn, Maryland.[115]

A year later, in May 1930, Leyare moved his still-incomplete showboat across the Chesapeake Bay to Georgetown, Maryland, where he announced he would operate it as a dance hall with a restaurant and floor show.[116] One resident of Georgetown remembered that the boat was docked at the town for several years, but that it could hardly be described as a Million Dollar Joy Boat. It was, in the observer's words, a wreck. It was open amidships and astern, and poorly maintained. When it was open for business, which was not on a regular basis, it drew a "rough, beer drinking crowd." When it left Georgetown, it was towed out by a tug.[117]

Leyare announced in May 1932 that he was taking his ship through the Chesapeake and Delaware Canal to play in New Jersey waters.[118] It was a choice he may have made because Adams had the Chesapeake sewed up, and the Delaware looked like virgin territory. He probably did not know Adams was headed in the same direction that year.

Adams's plans, however, were, in the end, of no concern to Leyare. When Charlie and Selba and company got to New Jersey, Leyare was already in dire straits. He reached New Jersey by midsummer, and in the effort to raise money to complete the conversion of his craft, took people aboard for sight-seeing.[119] In October, when he was anchored in the river off Burlington, he was instructed by the mayor to purchase a license. Leyare couldn't afford the license, and was fined $10 and costs. When he couldn't pay the fine, he was jailed, but was released when he promised to remove his boat from the Burlington area. When he tried to move it, he ran it aground.[120] The James Adams had left New Jersey and was in Wilmington, Delaware, before the *Million Dollar Joy Boat* was afloat again.

Charlie had hoped to run in stock through much of the winter in Camden,[121] but business did not hold. When Selba was approached by a group of women from the Board of Managers of the St. Michaels Home for Babies in Wilmington to come to their city to play benefits for the hospital, he readily accepted their offer.[122] After three weeks in Camden, the showboat moved across Delaware Bay to Wilmington and on Monday, October 24,[123] opened a four-week run.

The ambience of the performances in Wilmington was the headiest in the theatre's history. There were two society columns in the Delmarva *Sunday Star*. One was for the ragtag run of society folks. The other, "The Society Hour Glass," by Ann Shipley, chronicled the activities of the duPonts, the Carpenters, and such sundry. The folks who sponsored the showboat were of such sundry. Ann Shipley even recorded the names of people who bought tickets for the performances.[124] The society editor for the Wilmington *Morning News* did the same.[125] As part of the fun, a group of local aviators put on a display of stunt flying over the city as publicity for the showboat. The planes took off from duPont Field. Among the pilots were Felix duPont, Jr., Mrs. Felix duPont, Jr., Lammot duPont, and Berlin duPont.[126] During the last week of the showboat's stay in the city, Ann Shipley recorded that "Mrs. Pierre S. duPont, who was in New York early last week, has returned to 'Longwood.' Mrs. duPont arranged for the entertainment of the Show Boat company last Wednesday afternoon when a delightful organ program was given."[127]

It was not all duPonts and organ recitals, however. Some of the bad luck of the past five years followed the theatre. On the Friday before the last week, "a fierce gale . . . inundated the wharf where the boat was docked and threatened to swamp the vessel . . . Nine members of the troupe were carried to safety by firemen. They spent the rest of the night at the firehouse."[128]

The boat survived the storm with no major damage, and on November 20 was towed back to Chesapeake City for the winter.

Jim claimed that 1932 had been an extremely good year financially for the showboat.[129] But the patterns of the year suggest the opposite.

That winter, Jim put his Floating Theatre up for sale.

CHAPTER TEN

Under New Management

1933

The Easton, Maryland, *Star-Democrat*,[1] the Cecil *Democrat* of Elkton, Maryland,[2] and *Billboard*[3] recorded the sale of the James Adams Show Boat. All the stories were dated either May 19 or 20, 1933.

The new owner was Nina B. Howard of St. Michaels, Maryland. She bought the boat for her adopted son, Milford Seymoure, also of St. Michaels, to manage.[4] The Elizabeth City *Independent* reported that Mrs. Howard

> used to travel thru the inland waterways in a small yacht and had frequent contacts with James Adams' Floating Theatre while so doing. One season she followed the show boat from place to place simply because she enjoyed the company of those aboard it. She became fond of the floating theatre, and expressed a desire to purchase it, but the owner would not consider an offer. Finally she got the opportunity to purchase the show boat and she did.[5]

Howard's yacht, in which she followed the showboat, was the forty-three-foot *Jennie M. II*. After she bought the theatre, she sold the yacht to Louis Bennett, Jr., of Severna Park, Maryland.[6]

Seymoure later reported that Adams wanted $40,000[7] for the boat, but the price was reduced in negotiations. Seymoure also later claimed that the showboat and tugs represented an outlay of $90,000.[8]

In 1936, three years after Howard bought the boat, Louis Azrael, columnist for the Baltimore *News Post*, wrote an article about the new owners. They were as adept as Charlie Hunter at embellishing tales, and their story sounds somewhat like a play from the theatre's repertoire.

This is Azrael's story of the "showboat mother."

> The "Original Floating Theatre" probably wouldn't be floating now if it weren't for a tall, vigorous, dignified lady named Mrs.

Nina Howard with one of her dogs. Photograph courtesy of the Mariners Museum, Newport News, Virginia.

Milford Seymoure. Photograph courtesy of Jacques Kelly.

Rachel Seymoure with magician/musician Bob Fisher. Photograph courtesy of the Chesapeake Bay Maritime Museum, St. Michaels, Maryland.

157

In 1932, the last year he owned the boat, Adams renamed it the James Adams Show Boat. Here it is moored at Chesapeake City, Maryland, near the end of the season. Photograph courtesy of Jacques Kelly.

Adams's two tugs, Elk *on the left and* Trouper *on the right, towing the theatre in Pamlico Sound, North Carolina. The 1936 picture was taken by Robert Blakely, a musician with the company. Photograph courtesy of the Mariners Museum, Newport News, Virginia.*

158

Nina Howard. Or, to be more accurate, it probably wouldn't be floating if it weren't for a ragged little boy who came to Mrs. Howard in her hour of grief and threw his arms around her. But let's start at the beginning—

Nina von Bach was the daughter of a German army captain and she married a wealthy New Yorker who was killed a few years later in an auto accident.

Some time after, while traveling restlessly about, the young widow came to St. Michaels, Md., and met Capt. Charles Howard, an official of a Baltimore financial house. Soon they were married. They bought a beautiful estate near St. Michaels. They were very happy.

It was during this time that Captain Howard gave a petty job to a ragged fourteen year old Milford Seymoure, whose parents had gone away, leaving him in the questionable care of old impoverished grandparents. The Howards took a fancy to Milford, but he went off without even telling them about his plans, and they thought no more about it.

For a year and a half Captain and Mrs. Howard were happy. Then he died of cancer. Rich in money, rich in grief, Mrs. Howard was alone.

The next day the ragged boy came back.

"I just had to tell you how sorry I am about Captain Howard," he cried. "Is there any way I can help you; anything I can do?"

And Milford Seymoure, after that, ran errands for Mrs. Howard; worked around the place; drove her around. She educated the boy. He traveled on her yacht. He grew up as her son.

Five years ago it was time for Milford to get into a career. She wanted him to go into business. He loved the water. And just at this time Capt. Jim Adams was about to give up the showboat that he had operated for eighteen years. It was an ideal solution—business on the water. So Mrs. Howard bought it for Milford Seymoure to manage.

Now, five years later, Milford is the manager and the former Rachel Fairbanks, whom he married three years ago, handles the box office. But Mrs. Howard has expanded her proxy motherhood; it now includes not only the boy but everyone on the boat.

She doesn't have to work; she could sit at her home overlooking the Miles river and live an enviable life. But next Saturday, when the showboat starts its five or six month trip through the South, Mrs. Howard will be at every town. She doesn't travel on the boat. She drives from town to town each week. Partially because she has to take care of some business affairs. Primarily, though, its because she doesn't like to take her three dogs on the boat. One dog is seventeen years old; the two others are ten, and, next to Milford and the boat, few things are dearer to her. So, many a midnight, when Saturday's show is over, Mrs. Howard and a few others in the group who go by auto start out through the night to a town farther down the river.

When the boat is in harbor, Mrs. Howard lives on it, in a comfortable room arranged for her.

Little children know her at the sleepy towns and come to greet her. Often she lets them in to the show. Like a mother, she watches over the performers, supervising diets, hearing their troubles, helping, counseling.

And every Monday, often in the dawn hours, she stands on the dock of a river town, waiting to see the big white boat approach; waiting to greet the young man she learned to love when he was a ragged boy; the troupers who help him; the business into which she has put her heart.

"Sometimes," she told me, "I get awfully, awfully tired, but that passes."

There's no room for weariness in a mind that is filled with interest; in a heart that is filled with love.[9]

Here are a few facts to augment Azrael's romance: Milford Seymoure was born Milford Seymour in or near St. Michaels, Maryland. He added the "e" to his name later because he wished to distance himself from his Maryland relatives. His parents divorced when he was small. His father stayed in St. Michaels, and his mother moved to Baltimore. Seymoure was raised by his grandparents, who took good care of him. His grandmother would have been distraught to have heard him described as "ragged." Milford quit school to go to sea with Captain Terrance Burroughs of St. Michaels, who worked for the Grace Line and was responsible for a number of young boys getting started in commercial shipping.[10]

Nina's second husband, Charles Howard, was a police captain. He died before Nina bought the estate on Long Haul Creek. When Howard fell ill, Milford was home, having quit the Grace Line, and looking for work. Howard hired him as a chauffeur. After Howard died, Milford continued to work for Nina. Although she treated him as if he were her son, she never legally adopted him.[11]

Azrael's mention of Howard's dogs raises an interesting point. Although there were never small children on the boat, there seem to have always been dogs. I mentioned Jim Adams's dogs in chapter 4. Selba and Clara, when they managed the theatre, had two small dogs named Sodom and Gomorrah. Maisie Comardo thinks they were named in reaction to the Floating Theatre being dubbed, by at least one religious person, the "Hell-Hole of Iniquity."[12] Two of Howard's dogs, cocker spaniels named Ruby and Jenny, died when the boat was in the South one year. Howard had coffins built for them and brought their bodies back to St. Michaels to be buried.[13]

When Milford Seymoure took over the management of the Floating Theatre, he had no background in show business. He was, however, because of his experiences with the Grace Line, skilled on the water. It was his passion for the water that motivated his foster mother to buy for him first the *Jennie M. II* and then the James Adams.[14]

When she started the 1933 season, Howard changed the name of the theatre to the Original Show Boat. Rachel Seymoure remembers that Adams had wanted a royalty for the use of his name on the theatre, and that Mrs. Howard would not pay it.[15] Howard also had the boat painted with "a rakish coat of vermillion."[16]

When Jim put the theatre up for sale, most of the performers looked for work elsewhere for the next season. Some, however, stuck with the showboat, most notably Charlie and Beulah. Charlie continued as manager.[17] Because neither Howard nor Seymoure had any show business experience, it was to their advantage to keep him. The Floating Theatre was Charlie's life, and he had nowhere else to go. Beulah continued as the boat's star. Pop Neel,[18] Jack Pfeiffer, and Gladys Pennington also stayed with the theatre.[19] The comedian and director of the concert that year was Pat Gallagher.[20] With him was his actress wife, Mickey. Also joining the company in 1933 was Rudolph Paul, a handsome leading man with a beautiful singing voice.[21]

When she bought the boat, Howard announced that she expected to open the season in June in Chesapeake City,[22] but she instead took the boat to the Redman and Vane Shipyard in Baltimore for repairs.[23] It was there, most likely, that the boat was painted red and the new name painted on the sides. The Original Show Boat officially started the season in Galesville, Maryland, on June 12.[24]

Before the boat went to Baltimore, however, the company gave a private performance. On Wednesday, May 24, the New Century Club of Wilmington, Delaware, held a bridge luncheon at Benton Manor, the estate of R. R. M. "Bob" Carpenter on the Bohemia River[25] and the evening entertainment was provided by the showboat. After the show, one of the guests came backstage and met the actors, who immediately recognized Libby Holman even though she did not identify herself.[26]

Libby Holman was an actress and torch singer who rose to prominence in her profession in the late 1920s. She was perhaps best known for introducing the song "Body and Soul" in *Three's a Crowd* in 1930. Late in 1931 she married Zachary Smith Reynolds of the Reynolds Tobacco family. In July 1932 Reynolds was found dead, shot in the head. Libby and a servant, Albert Walker, were accused of murdering him. The trial dragged out through the summer and fall of 1932, when the Reynolds family had the charges dropped. Libby fled to Delaware to hide from the publicity. In January of 1933, she gave birth to Reynolds's son; in April she was hospitalized. When she visited the Floating Theatre in May, no doubt she was in great need of anonymity.

The plays the Floating Theatre presented in 1933 were as follows: On Monday, W. C. Herman's 1921 comedy-drama, *When Dreams Come True;* Tuesday, a royalty play, Kaufman and Connelly's 1923 comedy, *Merton of the Movies;* Wednesday, W. C. Herman's *The Shoplifters;* and Thursday, J. C. Angell's 1909 Western, *The Serpent and the Dove.* The Friday feature was Mabel Keightly's 1914 romantic comedy-drama, *The Broken Butterfly.* The Saturday closer was a melodrama, *The Parson's Bride,* the play featured in Ferber's novel.

After Galesville, the theatre crossed the Bay to play in the new owners' hometown, St. Michaels, then crossed the Bay again to play the old standbys, Solomons and Leonardtown, followed by the usual stops on the western shore of Virginia. By the time it got to Mathews County, the management was advertising the boat as the Original Floating Theatre, instead of the Original Show Boat. The name on the side of the boat, however, was not changed until the 1934 season, most likely during spring haul-out.

In Mathews County the boat called at Cricket Hill off Milford Haven instead of its usual stop at Williams Wharf on the East River. Three months after buying their new enterprise, the owners of the Floating Theatre got a strong taste of the vicissitudes of operating a seagoing showboat. On Tuesday night, August 22, while the theatre was moored at Cricket Hill, a hurricane swept across tidewater Virginia. The headlines on the lead story in the Mathews *Journal* give a picture of the disaster.

COUNTY SWEPT BY DESTRUCTIVE NORTHEAST STORM

Northeast Gale and Tidal Wave Leave
Wide Area In State of Devastation

Horses, Hogs, Cows, Sheep and Thousands of Chickens Drowned.
Smoke-houses, Barns, and Corn-Cribs Swept Away. Meat and Provisions Destroyed. Fishermen and Farmers Facing Serious Situation.

Growing Crops Ruined—Homes Flooded.

Hundreds of Acres That Never Before Tasted Salt Water, Submerged Beneath High Seas Whipped by Terrific Hurricane. Furniture Washed Away. Homes Left Plastered in Mud

And Sand. Wrecked Boats, Pound Stakes and Other Wreckage Piled Up In Fields Everywhere. New Point, Sandbank,
Bayside and Cricket Hill Wharves Wrecked. Heavy Damage
at Mobjack, Williams Wharf, and Diggs Wharf. Stores at
Court House Flooded. Gloucester Point and Yorktown De-
molished. Ferry Landing Wrecked. Hampton Roads Cities,
Beaches, Peninsula and Northern Neck Counties Hard Hit.[27]

The full fury of the storm hit after the close of the show that night.
Seven years later, a Baltimore writer reported Seymoure's version of the
events:

There was an inch or so of water over the beach and the men in the
audience had to carry the women to the waiting automobiles.
Next morning the automobiles belonging to the boat which were
parked on shore were covered with water; the engines wouldn't
start; the cruiser and small tug had broken away from their moor-
ings and the players watched helplessly as they floated off. The
showboat tugged and pounded at the dock, pulling it to pieces,
and the captain decided they must get loose and anchor out or be
pounded to bits. With the water churning in great waves around
them, Mr. Seymoure jumped overboard and fought his way to the
dock, to turn the boat with a hawser so she could pull out and anchor. That was a little too much real drama to please the cast,
especially the landlubbers from inland.[28]

Rachel Seymoure remembered that the *Trouper* was blown out of the
creek, and then, when the wind veered, it was blown back in.[29]

The theatre was scheduled to play next at Gloucester Point, but it
was delayed a week to allow for repairs both to the theatre and to the wharf
at Gloucester Point.[30]

John Wilson suggests that the hurricane of 1933 reduced even further an already limited steamboat service in Virginia by destroying many
wharves.[31] The Floating Theatre was dependent upon the steamboat
wharves, and their destruction was one more frustration the management
faced. An immediate effect was felt the next year at Tappahannock, a town
the theatre visited every year but 1919. The steamboat wharf was unusable,
and the theatre had to moor at the Hoskins Creek bridge, south of town.[32]

At the beginning of the 1932 tour, Hunter had expressed interest in
playing at Richmond, Virginia.[33] The theatre had a following from Richmond who usually drove to Tappahannock to see the plays.[34] Then he abandoned the idea, most likely because of the unexpected length of the
theatre's run that year in Norfolk. But since the theatre couldn't return to

Norfolk in 1933 because of punitive license fees, Hunter chose to play as close to Richmond as he could. On September 18, the theatre opened a two-week stand at Hopewell. The boat also returned to Smithfield after a six-year absence, and played at Portsmouth for the first and only time.

The theatre returned to North Carolina via Coinjock and the Elizabeth River. In the Albemarle area it played at Elizabeth City, Manteo, Plymouth, Columbia, and at Williamston for the first time in ten years. The *Independent* anticipated that the theatre would return to winter in Elizabeth City, but, because the Alligator River canal had been widened the year before,[35] it kept going south, to the Pamlico, where it played at Belhaven and Bath.

After the Pamlico, the boat continued south, exploring new territory. It made stops at New Bern, Beaufort, Swansboro, and Wilmington, North Carolina. It played a week each at the first three ports, and five weeks at Wilmington, under the patronage of the American Legion.[36] Hunter apparently planned to play only three weeks at Wilmington, because he ran each play for three nights. For the last two weeks he revived some old favorites, *The Girl Who Ran Away*,[37] *The Sweetest Girl in Dixie*,[38] *The Country Boy*,[39] and *Where the River Shannon Flows*.[40]

The Floating Theatre presented ten plays in the 1933 season, and not one of them was a new script. Among the many problems rep theatres faced in the early 1930s was the scarcity of new plays. The established writers were fading away. Virginia Maxwell died in 1927,[41] Charles F. Harrison in 1928.[42] Hunter's favorite playwright, Robert J. Sherman, lived until 1939, but by 1933 he was more occupied with managing a restaurant in Susquehanna, Pennsylvania, than he was in writing plays.[43] There were people still writing for the rep players, but not in Charlie's style. Most notable of the new writers was Neil Schaffner, but Schaffner was a Toby and wrote Toby plays. While Charlie was director, the Floating Theatre presented few plays that starred a Toby.

1934

In February and March the Floating Theatre was refurbished in a shipyard in Wilmington, North Carolina. Hunter had the ceiling of the auditorium rebuilt to improve the acoustics.[44] He also had the boat painted again—its customary white with green trim.

The theatre opened on April 2 in Wilmington, still under the auspices of the American Legion, and played for three weeks. The company was basically the same as in 1933, but the 1934 season included three royalty plays. The newest, written in 1926, was the Friday feature, *The Rosary*, a domestic drama by Edward E. Rose. On Wednesday nights, the theatre presented a revival of its earlier success, *Smilin' Through*. On Thursdays they presented Bayard Veiller's 1912 melodrama, *Within the Law*. On Mondays they did Charles F. Harrison's 1915 preacher play, *Saintly Hypocrites and Honest Sinners*, on Tuesday and Saturday the comedies *Tamed and How* and *The Go Getter*.

Throughout the season, *Smilin' Through* was as popular as it had been in 1929.

After Wilmington, the theatre moved north rapidly. In North Carolina, it played only in Beaufort, Belhaven, Manteo, and Elizabeth City. The boat rushed through North Carolina because of the license fees. Hunter explained to a reporter from the *Independent*:

> The state imposes a tax of $75 per day upon amusements of this nature. Then the County comes along and imposes a tax. The City, anxious to get its finger in the pie, adds its tax making the total tax burden almost unbearable. Forced to pay taxes to the extent of $1,000 a week, more or less, exclusive of sales tax, the Show Boat simply cannot make any money in North Carolina without capacity houses every night, and such things do not happen in these times.[45]

The Floating Theatre was still charging the admission prices it had charged in 1914: reserved seats for 40 cents; 15 cents extra for the concert.[46] Hunter occasionally tried to get more money where he felt the traffic would bear it. For example, in Alexandria, Virginia, in December 1930, he advertised "Reduction in prices, 50¢, 75¢ and $1.00."[47] In the midst of the Depression, though, there were not many places where he could "reduce" his tickets to $1.00.

From Elizabeth City the Floating Theatre went directly to Smithfield, followed by two weeks in Hopewell, a week at Gloucester Point, and then over to the Eastern Shore of Virginia for the first time in six years. It played at Onancock, and then went up the Pocomoke River to Pocomoke City for the first time in nineteen years. It then went up the Nanticoke River to Laurel, Delaware. Unless it had played there in 1914, it was the theatre's first visit.

From Laurel, the theatre crossed the Chesapeake Bay again to the Northern Neck of Virginia where it played the major stops, and on up the western shore to Galesville, Maryland. From there it went to the head of the Bay to Chesapeake City, where Charlie and Beulah had a chance to visit again with Jim and Gertie.[48]

From Chesapeake City, the boat went south to the Chester River, then to St. Michaels, and then farther south on the Eastern Shore to the Choptank River, where it played at Denton and Secretary for the first time since 1921. It then went north again to Easton, where it had not played in five years, and then south to Salisbury on the Wicomico River, where it arrived a day late because of high winds.[49] It was the first time the theatre had played at Salisbury since 1914. From Salisbury it went to Cape Charles, for the first time, unless it played there in 1914. From Cape Charles, the theatre was towed back north to St. Michaels where it was moored for the winter in Long Haul Creek in front of Mrs. Howard's house. Today the estate is the location of the Miles River Yacht Club.[50]

The Floating Theatre was searching for audiences. It opened new territories, tried to revive unprofitable markets that it had abandoned years before, and clung to the few towns in which it could still draw large crowds. It was driven out of one-third of its itinerary by taxes. Jim Adams had known well in 1932 that the heyday of the showboat was over. Only Mrs. Howard's money allowed it to keep operating.

1935

In April 1935, Mrs. Howard sent the boat to Redman and Vane in Baltimore for the spring haul-out. While it was on the slips, Hunter gave a reporter from the Baltimore *Sun* a tour of the theatre. Hunter used the interview to set the theme for the year's publicity: Edna Ferber and nostalgia for the great days of showboating on the Mississippi, of which he claimed to have been an integral part.[51]

There were changes in the company and the orchestra, but the Hunters, the Pfeiffers, the Gallaghers, and Rudolph Paul were still aboard. The season was heavy in plays by Charles F. Harrison: *I Want the Moon, Mr. Jim Baily, The Only Road,* and *Why Wives Worry.* They also presented Eli Whitney Collins's *Lure of the City,* and a new comedy-drama by Michael Dickerson, *The Man from Texas.*

The itinerary for 1935 was similar to that of 1934, in reverse. The theatre opened the season in the southern end of the Chesapeake Bay, in Onancock and Cape Charles, which it played for the second and last time. It then crossed to Smithfield, played Gloucester Point, and then played the major stops along the western shore. It played at Fredericksburg, Virginia, for the first time in five years. (Apparently the "birthday" cake the city gave the boat in 1930 had not been an effective lure.)

Rachel Seymoure remembered the heat in Fredericksburg. The company hosed off at the icehouse to keep cool. She also remembered the beauty at night when the moon shone through the three arches of the bridge there.

In one of the visits to the town in the midthirties, Pat Gallagher had a terrifying experience. He was fishing off the stern of the theatre while one of the theatre's tugs was revving its engine. The water flowing from the prop flushed a dead body out from under the stern of the theatre. Pat screamed. The body was that of a black deckhand who several days before had fallen from a large ship in port and drowned. The swollen body was hauled onto the deck of the theatre by the authorities.[52]

After Fredericksburg, the theatre continued its route up the western shore to Galesville. It then went north across the bay to Chesapeake City, and then south to Crumpton, St. Michaels, Denton, and Secretary, then north to Easton, and south to the Choptank again, where it played Cambridge for the first time in five years.

From Cambridge the boat went to North Carolina, passing through the Elizabeth River and playing Coinjock and Manteo. In the Albemarle area, it played at Elizabeth City, Plymouth, and Columbia. It also played at Colerain, for the first time in six years.

Despite the taxes, the theatre continued south through North Carolina, to Belhaven, Washington, Engelhard (its only time), and Swansboro. In Swansboro there was as much drama among the cast as there was on the stage: a love triangle, jealousy, and an attempted suicide.

Jack Pfeiffer had come to believe that his wife, Gladys Pennington, had fallen for the handsome leading man with the beautiful singing voice, Rudolph Paul. Gladys was beautiful. Rudolph was handsome and a flirt.[53] Jack was a character actor and a heavy with a dark and rugged face appropriate for his chosen profession. Jack became intensely jealous, probably not without reason, an actress on the boat at the time suggested. Jack attempted suicide by drinking a bottle of iodine. An ambulance was called and he was rushed to the hospital. His stomach was pumped, and he was back on the boat the next day. Fortunately, the night he was in the hospital he did not have a large role in the scheduled play.[54]

All three of the performers saw the season through, but Rudolph Paul did not come back the following year.[55]

The boat was due into Wilmington December 29, but was delayed by the weather. It opened on New Year's Eve, played for two weeks, and ended the season.

1936

There were many changes in the cast of the showboat in 1936. The Hunters were still there, and the Pfeiffers, but the Gallaghers were gone. Pat was replaced as director of the concerts by Marshall Walker.

Marshall Walker was a big name in tab shows. For many years he had toured his own company, the Whiz-Bang Review, on the Gus Sun Vaudeville Circuit.[56] Early in his career, Bob Hope toured with Walker.[57]

Walker wrote his own material[58] and the Whiz-Bang Review, with its more suggestive humor and emphasis on the chorus line, was a large step toward more modern entertainment for the Floating Theatre. Later developments suggest that Walker was hired by Seymoure, and not Charlie.

Also with the company in 1936 was Beulah's "niece," Beulah Adams Barlow Pendell Dutcher.[59] Little Beulah, as she was called, was the daughter of Beulah's niece, Rose, who was the daughter of Beulah's oldest sister, Hattie. Rose had teamed with Beulah's sister Susie in vaudeville as the Adams Sisters. Little Beulah as a teenager had visited the showboat often but, unlike her older sister Dorothy, she did not keep a diary. Maisie Comardo remembers a party on the boat around 1930, when Little Beulah, after dancing all night, threw herself in a chair and exclaimed, "Flaming youth has done gone out!" In 1936 Little Beulah was married to a trumpet player in the Floating Theatre orchestra, Lloyd "Dutch" Dutcher.

Hunter chose an unusually light season in 1936, including two Charles F. Harrison comedy-dramas, *Man's Will and Woman's Way*, the Friday feature, and *Shooting Gold*, the Saturday closer. Monday's offering was a fairly recent royalty comedy, *The Big Shot*, by John McGowan. Tuesday's was a royalty farce, *Breakfast for One*. Wednesday Charlie presented the rep show standard, *Tempest and Sunshine*, which the Floating Theater was producing for the fourth time. *Tempest and Sunshine* chronicled the romantic adventures of two daughters, one sweet and kind, the other hot-tempered and jealous. The play also featured two blackface comic characters which no doubt fit into Charlie's emphasis on a season of comedy. The Thursday offering was *Frisco Jenny*, the play some rep troupers associate with Mae West.

The 1936 season began much as the 1935 one did. The boat moved quickly through North Carolina with Hunter complaining about taxes.[60] He stopped long enough in Elizabeth City to give a talk on Edna Ferber and *Show Boat* at the Carolina movie theatre where the just-released 1936 version of the film was playing.[61]

Walker wrote to Billy Boy in May about the skipper of the *Elk:*

> Captain W. S. Cannon is a grand fellow. We call him Wonder Bar Cap, as he can find more sand bars in Chesapeake Bay than anybody in the world. His chief ambition is to land us high and dry in the middle of nowhere on some dark night and wait for the tide to get us afloat again.[62]

Walker passed judgment on Cannon by hearsay, because when he wrote the note, the Floating Theatre had not yet reached the Chesapeake Bay.

After leaving North Carolina, the theatre spent five months on the Chesapeake. It went up the western shore of Virginia and Maryland to Galesville. At the end of August, it was again in the Redman and Vane Shipyard in Baltimore.

One of the promotional themes of the season was the false promise of air conditioning.

Chugging down the Southern Potomac after a week at Colonial Beach, Capt. Charlie Hunter, pilot for 23 years of one of the few remaining floating theatres, wiped his brow and made one of the big decisions of his life.

"The time has come," he said, "to put in air-conditioning."

Carl (Pop) Neel, the show boat's 76-year-old pit musician, stopped polishing his bass fiddle.

"What," he asked, "is that?"

"Air-conditioning," explained Capt. Charlie, "is something that cools the temper of the hottest crowd, makes 'em enjoy themselves and causes 'em to come back."

Pop shook his head.

"That's a definition of *East Lynne*," he said.[63]

Needless to say, Charlie never installed air-conditioning on the boat.

When it left Baltimore, the Floating Theatre played for the first time in the Patapsco River area, in Green Haven on Stony Creek. It then went north across the Bay to Chesapeake City and started down the Eastern Shore. The first week in November it was at Onancock.

From Onancock it headed toward the Deep South for the first time. It passed through North Carolina, stopping only to pick up a hitchhiker at Masonboro Sound, near Wilmington: a Norwegian who was traveling in a twenty-two-foot sailboat with his dog. He left the theatre at Little River, South Carolina, where the showboat opened its southern tour.[64] In South Carolina the theatre played also at Conway, Georgetown, Yonges Island, and Beaufort—all, of course, new territory. At Beaufort it played for the marines at Parris Island.[65] At the end of the year it was in Savannah, Georgia. The Floating Theatre opened the new year at the Isle of Hope resort in Georgia. It then went deep into Florida and played a week at the new resort at Merritt Island.

The boat didn't stay long in Florida. Walker reported to Billy Boy that they "encountered three showboats between Jacksonville and [Merritt Island]. There are reported to be several others between Cocoa and Miami."[66]

Coming north again it played at St. Mary's, Georgia, where "Wonder Bar Cap" ran the boat onto a sandbar.[67] Then it played at Brunswick, Georgia, and closed the season at Darien, Georgia.

Somewhere between Savannah and Darien, Charlie and Beulah quit the Floating Theatre.[68]

For twenty-one years, with only one break from 1919 to 1920, Charlie and Beulah had made the Floating Theatre their career and their home for most of every year. Even after Jim sold the boat, they stayed on. But at the end of the 1936 season they quit.

I have found no published explanations for their actions, but there is both testimonial and circumstantial evidence to explain what happened.[69]

Charlie and Marshall Walker had strong differences about the nature of the entertainment the Floating Theatre should present. The argument focused on the concerts, and people on the boat took sides in the conflict. Both Charlie and Walker were established and experienced showmen, but Walker had much more national prominence. Charlie was known along the route of the Floating Theatre, but that route was changing and in the new itinerary Charlie was unknown. Walker's name wasn't a household word, but it was more widely recognized than Charlie's. Also, if the Floating Theatre had followed strictly along the lines Charlie wanted, it surely would have gone broke. Marshall offered new possibilities of success with his more up-to-date musical reviews.

A year later, in September 1937, Louis Azrael of the Baltimore *News Post*, gave an insight into the nature of the conflict. He wrote about the plays the theatre was presenting, and then observed:

> The audience waited outside until the 'concert' which was merely something about a ranch boss who falls in love with the ranch owner's daughter and won her from a mean Mexican rival. It was tempered with skits by dancing girls and all that modern stuff. The audience applauded and hissed and laughed. That's what they seem to want, say the Show Boat folk, and it must be presented no matter how it hurts the players' artistic consciences.[70]

When Charlie and Beulah left, Jack Pfeiffer and Gladys Pennington went with them.

CHAPTER ELEVEN

The Last Hurrah

1937

The 1936 season ended in Darien, Georgia,[1] on February 3, 1937. Neither of the two adversaries, Charlie Hunter and Marshall Walker, returned to the Floating Theatre for the 1937 season.

The boat arrived in Elizabeth City at 6:00 on Friday evening, February 19. The only people onboard were Pop Neel and the Howard family: Nina Howard; Milford Seymoure; Milford's wife, Rachel Seymoure; and Mrs. Howard's sister, Mrs. Charles Merritt.[2]

Pop Neel announced in April that the showboat company, which had been kept "practically intact," was barnstorming through Georgia before coming to Elizabeth City.[3] But the 1937 company that arrived for rehearsal, with the exception of Pop Neel, was a total change from the 1936 company.

One question for which I have no answer is exactly when the Hunters left the Floating Theatre. If the company that appeared for the 1937 season was the company to which Neel referred, and it had finished out the 1936 season on the Floating Theatre, then Charlie and Beulah left the company before the end of the season. Neel supports that argument with the report that the Hunters left shortly after Christmas and that Charlie was managing a tent show "of the Redpath Lyceum chain."[4]

If the company that appeared in Elizabeth City was new, and had never been on the boat before, then the Hunters probably quit after the boat's appearance in Darien. Marshall Walker was on the theatre in Darien,[5] and he was not with the new company. In lieu of confirming evidence, I am of the opinion that the Hunters stayed on until Darien. Seymoure's new company was a package deal, and *Billboard* reported (*see below*) that in the spring of 1937 they were appearing for the first time on the Floating Theatre.

According to *Bill Bruno's Bulletin*, a Kansas City–based rep company newsletter, in the chorus were Peggy Miller, Opal Lyle, Dillie [Dawn Fangio] Angelo, Rachel Seymoure, Connie Matthews, and June Martin. The

---

BRASFIELD SHOW TAKES TO WATER

Company moves intact from Rome, Ga., onto Original Floating Theatre.

Boob Brasefield's Comedians have just concluded a two-year engagement in Rome [Georgia] for the Lam Amusement Company and the company is moving intact to the Original Floating Theatre for the summer . . .

With the exception of Wayne and Bessie Bartlett and Gus Schulze, the cast will remain intact for the showboat engagement. Several new faces and a line of six girls will be added, and the orchestra will be augmented to nine pieces.

Present roster includes Boob Brasfield, Thayer Roberts, Pup Shannon, Angelo Fangio, Chester Hughes, Vern Spofford, Leslie Lyle, Neva Brasefield, Dot Dumas, Dillie Dawn, Bonnie Brasfield, Peggy Miller, Connie Matthews, Opal Lyle and Maxine Darie. Pup Shannon's Swingcopators will furnish the music.

Concert features will include Fangio and Dawn, dancers; Miller and Matthews, sister team, and Thayer Roberts, dancer.

Opening bill will be Why Girls Walk Home, by Neil Schaffner.[6]

---

orchestra consisted of Chet Hughes, Vern Spofford, Leslie Lyle, Angelo Fangio, Johnnie Rupee, Pop Neel, and Pup Shannon, director.[7]

Seymoure's hiring of Boob Brasfield and company marked a major change in the style of the showboat. The Floating Theatre's presentations were still of the same format as they had been under Charlie. Format differences among rep companies were few. Some offered a variety show of some sort after the play, as did the Floating Theatre. Others offered their variety between acts to allow more time to sell drinks, candy, ice cream, and such, which in the 1930s had become as important a source of revenue as the admissions.[8]

With Boob's coming, however, there were important changes in other aspects of the theatre. It was the first year that the showboat employed an Actors Equity company. The concerts emphasized the chorus line even more so than under Walker. The herald for 1937 pictured the "Stream-lined Stylettes," a chorus line of ten women, eight of them in short skirts. Beside the picture were the words, "Girls, Girls, Girls—Sing, Swing, Sing." Newspaper ads in the new markets, the larger cities—but not in the old, smaller towns—referred to "A Bevy of Beautiful Girls."[9] With the new emphasis, the theatre, for the first time, hired unmarried women.

With the additional performers the boat carried, the concert, although more risqué, was of high quality. (Fangio and Dawn had performed at the Century of Progress Dallas Exposition.) A feature of the Wednesday concerts was Thayer Roberts's Dance of the Golden Siamese Gods, in which he dressed in a loincloth, lei, ornate headdress, and large hoop earrings, his body painted gold.[10] On Fridays he performed the Dance of Death.

Because red-faced, freckled Boob was a Toby, he put several Toby shows in the repertoire, although he complained about it to *Billboard*.

> Show opened here [Elizabeth City] to a half house Monday, but business had a decided increase as the week progressed. These toby shows are a disgrace, but we are figuring on using at least one on the week; don't know which one. None of the cast has ever worked in a toby bill, as all are Guild actors.

Boob continued his letter with the kind of news a comic would typically write.

> Toby Shannon started out playing tennis and broke his racket, then played golf until he lost his ball, and finally went back to his original pastime of catching catfish from his stateroom window.
>
> There were two mishaps Tuesday when the second dinner bell rang. Dot Dumas got tangled in Pop Neel's fiddle, broke the G-string and skinned her ankle. Chet Hughes forgot to duck and suffered a bruised skull. [He was probably bald-headed.]
>
> Harry Dicker, retired showman, who helped to build this boat 24 years ago, was a visitor. He tells good stories about its past history. He and Pop Neel are like two kids out of school. They even wrestled on the top deck yesterday.
>
> Everybody is having a good time: rehearsals are over and shows going smoothly. There is plenty of fish and beer. Where is the grouch that does not like show business?[11]

Boob is not well known today, but in his time he had a large following, particularly in the Southeast. His brother, Rod Brasfield, was better known. For many years Rod was the comic who played Uncle Cyp on the Grand Ole Opry radio shows from Nashville. Boob occasionally was a guest on the show.[12]

Boob began his career in 1913 working in several different wagon shows, went into vaudeville in 1915, and a few years later was working on Broadway as an assistant stage manager. In the 1920s he played in both legitimate and touring repertoire shows, and in vaudeville and burlesque.[13]

Others in the company were not as well known. Dot Dumas was a much-traveled leading lady, married to the orchestra leader, Pup Shannon. She was known to have advertised for work, "available with or without

Left to right, *Ellen Douglas, Thayer Roberts in makeup, and Rachel Seymoure. They are on* Trouper, *tied up next to the Floating Theatre. Photograph courtesy of Jacques Kelly.*

Actress Opal Lee Lyle, one of the "Stream-lined Stylettes," lounging in her state-room. Photograph by A. Aubrey Bodine, courtesy of the Mariners Museum, New-port News, Virginia.

Peggy Lennox posting a rehearsal notice. Photograph by A. Aubrey Bodine, courtesy of the Mariners Museum, Newport News, Virginia.

Pup."[14] Thayer Roberts was a young actor-dancer who started in vaudeville when he was five, and had worked with several major dance companies. He had done legitimate drama with the Jitney players at Vassar.[15] Neva, an acrobatic dancer, was Boob's wife and Bonnie was his daughter, married to a musician in the showboat orchestra, Vern Spofford. Peggy Miller was a tall, leggy, dark-haired singer-dancer who reminded one actress onboard of Ann Miller. Peggy displayed pictures in the lobby of herself dancing with Ann Miller.[16]

I am familiar with only two of the six plays the theatre offered in 1937: *Lena Rivers* and *Why Girls Walk Home,* a Toby play by Neil Schaffner.

Tobias Tolliver is "a freckle-faced hog buyer" on his way to Chicago. He stops at the Golden Pheasant Inn for gas and a meal. He gets mixed up with bootleggers and helps solve things in the end with the help of (1) a minister who is trying to stop the bootleggers who use his shell-shocked brother to embarrass him before a newspaper reporter, and (2) a society matron who, in fact, is a federal agent in disguise.

By a delightful coincidence, the script of the play I read was the one Boob used on the Floating Theatre.[17] The roles were cast as follows: Boob as Tobias; Thayer Roberts in the dual roles of the minister and his brother; Dot Dumas as Sara Ford, the love interest (for the minister); Pup Shannon as the bootlegger's not-too-smart son; and Neva Brasfield as the bootlegger, who, for the production, was changed to a woman and named Jesse instead of Beef.

The other four plays are unfamiliar to me. The Saturday closer was *Toby Goes to Town,* and the other three, *Johnnie's in Town, Sin Takes a Holiday,* and *The Rent's Due,* probably had Toby lurking around somewhere. The Friday feature, *Lena Rivers,* hopefully escaped from Toby's clutches.

In another of Boob's reports to Billy Boy, he wrote:

New pulp factories in this section have improved business considerably. We are enjoying the best fishing in years.

. . . Pup Shannon's Swingcopators play a dance each week.

Had a swell time at the Herring Catcher's Ball in Colerain. Chet Hughes has his schonozzle buried in a lot of concert music but found time to catch real fish in Plymouth. [Hughes was probably a clarinet player.] The game warden of Bertie County paid the boys a visit.

. . . Toby Roberts, Toby Shannon and Toby Angelo went swimming Sunday. Peggy Miller and Fred Radcliffe were married Sunday. Connie Matthews and Johnnie Rupee are that way about each other, too. Capt. Seymoure is worrying about how to fix the staterooms.[18]

The reporter for the local paper in Windsor, which the showboat visited for the first time, reported Peggy and Fred's marriage with more feeling:

> Windsor's balmy May climate, plus the calm beauty of the Cashie [River], combined to work their spell on the romantic-minded troupers of the cast of the Show Boat, playing here all week.
>
> In the small hours of Sunday morning—at 2:00 a. m. it was— Register of Deeds L. S. Mizelle was awakened by the couple who were bent on marriage there and then. And so, the two—Fred Allen Radcliffe of St. Michaels, Maryland, and Miss Norma Ardella Cox, of Salina, Kansas, were tied in matrimony in the stillness of the early morning, before dawn, and their honeymoon is on board the floating theatre, amid the scenery and paraphernalia and foot lights and melodrama—soon to float away to entertain the natives of other towns having waterways and docks to tie up to.[19]

It would appear that Norma Cox's admiration for Ann Miller went further than just pictures. She borrowed her last name as well.

While the showboat was getting itself sorted out for the season, Hunter was already in performance. Pop Neel said that Charlie was working for the Redpath Lyceum, but I have found no other evidence supporting the claim. He may have been in the winter, but by the end of March[20] he was touring his own show, the Show Boat Players. The company featured Charlie, Beulah, Jack Pfeiffer, and Gladys Pennington from the Floating Theatre.

For the first few months of the season the Show Boat Players performed in school auditoriums.[21] As did the Floating Theatre, they featured a Toby. In their heralds for the first part of the season they printed a picture of Bob Demorest, Jr., identified only as "Toby."[22] The herald advertised three plays, *Charlie McCarthy's Big Broadcast, Rebecca of Sunnybrook Farm,* and *The Sweetest Girl in Dixie.* None of these is a Toby play, but any play could be adapted as such. The chances are, however, that Toby was featured in the concert.

Toby may have been a gimmick to attract schoolchildren to the plays. When they played in school auditoriums Hunter and Pfeiffer distributed "Teachers' Courtesy Tickets" to the teachers in the schools. The tickets instructed the teachers to urge the students: "Let us try to have this room represented one hundred percent—bring your admission to me if you like and I will take care of it for you, and our room can go in together. Don't forget now." Hunter and Pfeiffer assured the teachers that the plays "are not only entertaining but educational as well."[23]

On May 13, while Boob and company were still in the Albemarle area of North Carolina, the Smithfield, Virginia, *Times* reported that:

A performance on the Floating Theater in the middle or late 1930s, after Adams had sold the boat. Note the fake organ pipes over the air ducts on each side of the stage. Photograph courtesy of the Chesapeake Bay Maritime Museum, St. Michaels, Maryland.

Beulah Adams Hunter (seated) with the 1936 chorus line. Left to right: *Beulah Adams Dutcher, Esprit Lowery, Gladys Pennington Pfeiffer, Beulah Walker, and Martha Kaye. Photograph courtesy of Marguerite Young.*

Charlie Hunter's and Jack Pfeiffer's Show Boat Players Under Canvas will open on the Thomas Lot at Smithfield Monday, May 24th, according to present plans.

The company plans to present shows of the type that have been given for many years on The Original Floating Theatre, later known as "The Show Boat."

. . . The company has been in Smithfield for several weeks, painting scenery, equipment, building chairs and rehearsing in preparation of the grand opening.

A brand new tent 50X100 feet seating 700 people is coming from Winston-Salem, N. C. Lumber, hardware, and trucks have been purchased locally.

The Company will play week stands in the section where they are known.[24]

The company opened, as scheduled, on May 24. The Smithfield *Times* reported that "the opening play, *The Girl in the Taxi*, seemed to meet with the approval of the audience by their constant applause."[25] Segar Dashiell was in the audience that night, and she remembered the event differently. She thought the cast probably had not taken enough time to rehearse the play. "The performance was terrible. The audience laughed. Finally Beulah and Charlie joined in the laughter because they realized how bad the show was."[26]

Rachel Seymoure thinks that the financing for Charlie and Jack's tent had to have come from Jim Adams, because Charlie was poor at handling money and never saved anything. Jack Pfeiffer may have put up half the capital, but Charlie's half probably was a loan from Jim.

The only play the Show Boat Players retained from their school auditorium tour was *Rebecca of Sunnybrook Farm*. The other plays they presented in tents were *The Country Boy, Brother against Brother, Ten Nights in a Bar Room*, and *Arizona*. Charlie had produced all the plays previously on the Floating Theatre except possibly *Ten Nights in a Bar Room*. It was a conservative season, and stood in strong contrast to the repertory the Floating Theatre offered. The concerts most certainly reflected the same contrasts.

When the Show Boat Players left Smithfield, they continued up the western shore of Virginia to Leonardtown, Maryland.

The Floating Theatre reached Smithfield almost a month after the Show Boat Players. Charlie not only was ahead of Seymoure in schedule, he probably wasn't playing fair. Seymoure found the need to send letters to the papers in the areas where Charlie was touring:

There is a rumor going around that the Floating Theatre will not return in your vicinity this year, and I do not understand how this rumor got around.

We are bringing to our public this year, an entirely new cast and orchestra, and shall be around the usual time of year.

There will be, more than likely, a tent show out, under the name of Original Show Boat Players, and we wish to state that we in no way are connected with this organization.

Capt. Milford Seymoure[27]

As the Floating Theatre made its way into Virginia, Boob appeared less concerned about things than Seymoure. Boob reported that in Hopewell the Richmond *News Leader* "ran a half-page story with a flock of pictures of the boat. Dot Dumas and the Showboat Streamline Stylettes taking a sun bath on top deck was a real drawing card. Even the photographers came back to see the show."[28]

Boob also bragged a bit to Billy Boy about his value to the Floating Theatre. "If you want a tonic for your show go to Alabama and Georgia and get a cornfed boy that knows the answers."[29]

In June the showboat expanded its cast. "Red and Marie Corley joined this week, adding one more sax and clarinet and one more streamlined stylette to our musical review."[30]

Despite Boob's jolly mood, when the Floating Theatre arrived in Chesapeake Bay country, where the Show Boat Players were trouping just a few weeks ahead, Seymoure felt the competition. The newspaper advertisements for 1937 reveal the rivalry. Although neither mentions the other theatre in its ads, the size of the ads tells the story. Both managers took out eighth-page and occasionally quarter-page ads in each county's papers. The Floating Theatre in previous years sometimes bought a two-column ad, but nothing like those in 1937. Clearly benefiting from the rivalry were the newspaper publishers.

Seymoure ran into a setback at Urbanna. The city had raised its license fee. In order to play in Middlesex County, Seymoure took his boat to Deltaville, for the first and last time.[31]

In a letter she wrote from Reedville to her brother, Rachel Seymoure reported that business was good. They had a sellout every night but Tuesday. She also reported that Boob's father had suffered a stroke and Boob had had to leave the company temporarily. They wired for Pat Gallagher, who had been on the boat from 1933 to 1936 but had since retired to run Pat's Showboat Grill in Easton, Maryland.[32] Pat came "right away," Rachel reported. "He's going over good. He always was a favorite down this way."[33] Pat had hoped to launch his own tent show that year to play the Chesapeake Bay,[34] but settled for a short stay on the Floating Theatre instead.

Charlie, running up the western shore ahead of Seymoure, may have played dirty in Leonardtown, one of the most consistently profitable stops for the showboat. Maisie Comardo, however, thinks that it was more likely that Jack was the instigator, not Charlie.[35]

The Sunday before the Floating Theatre had opened in Leonardtown in 1936—the year Marshall Walker directed the concerts, concerts Charlie disliked, but which were tame compared to those Boob was producing in 1937—Father Joseph Sheridan Knight, the pastor of the St. Aloysius Catholic Church in Leonardtown, preached a sermon in which he referred to the "women in spangled tights" on the showboat, and urged his parishioners to boycott the Floating Theatre.[36]

Father Knight got tougher in 1937. On Wednesday, July 7, the week before Charlie was scheduled to bring his tent show to Leonardtown, the commissioners of Leonardtown reacted to a letter from Father Knight. Al Gough quoted their response:

> Reading letter from Rev. J. S. Knight, S. J. protesting against the Commissioners of L'town issuing a license to the floating theatre because of the immoral type of show the theatre shows known as their concert. The Commissioners were heartily in accord with Father Knight's views and the clerk was instructed to write to Father Knight to this effect and that they are going to the limit of their authority to see that any and all performances shown shall not reflect upon the morals of the public.[37]

Father Knight was not opposed to theatre. In fact, he had established a theatre program for the youth of his parish, and had directed them in plays and minstrel shows.[38] There is no record of his opposing the showboat before Walker took over the concerts. He simply didn't like women in spangled tights. Neither did Charlie, which made Father Knight and Charlie natural allies.

At the time the commissioners were meeting, the showboat was six weeks away from Leonardtown. Charlie and Jack's company was across the river in Colonial Beach.

The following week, July 12, Charlie moved his show into Leonardtown with no difficulties. In the minutes of the same meeting of the commissioners in which they responded to Father Knight:

> The clerk was further instructed to get in touch with Mr. Hunter of the "Show Boat Players" tent show, and have him confer with the president of the board before any license shall be issued for show as advertised for the week commencing July 12th; the conference being solely for proving and guaranteeing a moral type of performance. Thru any failure of this guarantee, the license, if issued, shall be rescinded.[39]

180

There was not much chance that Charlie wouldn't agree to the commissioners' conditions. And I can't think that the commissioners thought there was much risk. Charlie's Floating Theatre had brought "moral" performances to Leonardtown for twenty-two years. Seymoure's was the one peddling the "immoral" stuff.

I can't prove that Charlie had a hand in getting Seymoure banned from Leonardtown, but circumstantial evidence is strong. There was the motivation: Charlie had opposed the changes in the concerts so strongly he left his beloved showboat because of them. There was opportunity: Charlie, most likely, was aware the year before of Father Knight's feelings. And there was the magnificent coincidence of timing: Father Knight and the commissioners had had a year to act against the showboat, but they waited until Charlie was off the boat and on his way into town with a "moral" alternative. Charlie often worked as advance man for his company, even when he was on the Floating Theatre, and he may well have been in Leonardtown when Father Knight wrote his letter and when the commissioners read it.

Banning the Floating Theatre from Leonardtown may have shaken up the elements a bit, because on Tuesday night "one of the worst electrical storms in the memory of the oldest inhabitant"[40] hit the area. Charlie had to cancel his performance. Gough wrote:

> Eddy Stokel, who was in the tent at the time, recounts that when the lightning struck the electrical transformer located a short distance from the tent the patrons sitting on the back row of the bleachers were knocked from their seats. Eddy was one of them and his friend Tommy Shadrick was knocked unconscious.[41]

When the Floating Theatre arrived at Leonardtown in the middle of August, Seymoure found his way barred. He moved on to Solomons, and advertised in the Leonardtown papers that the theatre was providing a free ferry across the Patuxent, "Leaving Millstone Daily at 7:30 P. M., and Returning at 11 P. M."[42] The ferrying, no doubt, was done on the *Elk* and the *Trouper*.

After Leonardtown, the Show Boat Players continued up the western shore, then across the Bay, no doubt on the Annapolis-Matapeake ferry, to the Chester River towns. They went north to Chesapeake City, then south again to Chestertown and Easton.

Pat Gallagher, who helped out the Floating Theater in Reedville, visited the Show Boat Players in Chestertown with his wife Mickey. They came to see their daughter, Lana Lois Gallagher, who was a performer with Charlie and Jack's company. Also visiting the show at the time were Jim and Gertie Adams, who had bought a "living trailer," and intended to follow the tent show for awhile.[43]

Two weeks after their engagement in Easton, the Players were in Elizabeth City, North Carolina.

The Floating Theatre continued the season without any more recorded grief. It toured up the western shore to Green Haven, then went to the head of the Bay, where it played at Havre de Grace for the first time in seventeen years. It went down the Eastern Shore as far as Cambridge. Before the season ended, Pup Shannon and Dot Dumas left the boat. Red Corley[44] was promoted to orchestra director, and Bonnie Brasfield Spofford took over Dot's roles.[45] At the end of the season the theatre returned to St. Michaels to winter again in Long Haul Creek.[46]

Seymoure did not get over being banned from Leonardtown. Two years later he complained about it to Eugene Warner, a reporter for the Washington, D. C., *Times-Herald*. "Listen, we show all up and down the Atlantic Coast, from Florida to New Jersey, but that darned little town of Leonardtown wouldn't let us in! And me a taxpayer in Maryland! Can't even run a business in my own State!"[47]

Seymoure was bitter about the Hunters leaving him, too. "They walked out on us and went with a tent show . . . After we gave 'em their start."[48]

1938

Boob did not return in 1938. He went back to trouping in Alabama and Georgia.[49] Although Boob and Neva did not return, some of the cast from 1937 stayed on, including Thayer Roberts, who was promoted to director of the plays.

One of the problems in reporting the history of the last few years of the showboat is in evaluating statements made about the boat by Nina Howard and Milford Seymoure. For example, in the spring of 1938, in an interview for a Baltimore newspaper, Howard reported that Thayer had directed the plays in 1937. In the same article she claimed that she bought the boat in 1930, that Red and Marie Corley had been on the boat for five years, and that Edna Ferber did her research for her novel when the Floating Theatre was in Florida.[50]

In 1938 the showboat advertised "Thayer Roberts and his Players Right from Broadway."[51] Most likely Thayer continued the practice started by Boob of hiring Equity actors. Charlie, when he had directed the plays, favored scripts by contemporary repertoire writers featuring ingenue roles. Boob had favored Toby plays. Thayer brought a legitimate theatre bias. Half of the plays presented by the Floating Theatre in 1938 were standard rep comedy-dramas: *Shanghai Goldie, The G Man,* and *The Folks of Valley Center.* But the other three were inexpensive royalty comedies: *Love in a Hurry, Misplaced Husband,* and *Young Love,* plays more familiar to New York actors.

At the beginning of the season the leading lady was Joan Thayer from Boston. Seymoure advertised that she had been featured with the Marx Brothers. The comic was a blackface veteran of southern rep companies, Cotton Watts. One of the main features of the concert was exotic dancer Jacqueline Rey, "of the French Casino in London."[52] Roberts, in addition to his Dance of Gold, performed "A Tisket a Tasket" as a black woman.[53] The orchestra leader was Roy Steadman, who had handled that responsibility in 1936. Pop Neel, of course, was back. Others back from the 1937 season included the Corleys, the Spoffords, and the Lyles.

The Floating Theatre opened its season in St. Michaels on April 22. It played two days there and two days just south of St. Michaels at Tilghman for the only time in its history (unless it played there in 1914). It then went to the mouth of the Chesapeake and started north from Deep Creek, which, in the middle and late 1930s had become the theatre's alternative to Norfolk. It played at Hopewell, Gloucester Point, and Cricket Hill before reaching Irvington, Virginia, for the week of June 6.

The Show Boat Players started the season in the south and reached Virginia after the Floating Theatre had been there. Charlie and Jack's business was not as good as it had been the previous year when they were first in for the harvest.[54]

An interesting addition to the Show Boat Players' roster in 1938 was the third party from the 1935 "suicide triangle" in Swansboro, the handsome leading man and singer, Rudolph Paul. Rachel Seymoure is of the opinion that Jack could refuse Gladys nothing.[55] Maisie Comardo believes that hiring Paul was evidence that the conflict between Jack and Rudy was more smoke than fire. "Rudy had a great voice and stage presence and would have been an asset to [the company], but it is unlikely that Charlie and Jack would have wanted him around if he was a Rudolph Valentino." Maisie believes that the Hunters and Pfeiffers were escaping from friction on the Floating Theatre and did not want to create more friction in their own company.[56]

Others with the company were Hi and Griff, a "brown and tan" act much traveled in the South and frequent performers on local radio shows; Art and Evelyn David, who were in their second year with Jack and Charlie; Framton and Lee, specialty dancers; and Jack and Marion Marsh Howe, novelty musicians.[57] Jack Pfeiffer's father, "Pop," manned the box office. Drotch Davids was in charge of the two canvassers.[58] There was no chorus line in the concert.

Charlie and Jack dug deeply into the past for their season: *The Sweetest Girl in Dixie* (1907), *Kentucky Sue* (1914), *George Washington, Jr.* (1906), *Wife in Name Only* (1903), *Trail of the Lonesome Pine* (1908), and *The Girl Who Ran Away* (1916). The only royalty play in the group was the comedy, *George Washington, Jr.*

183

The Floating Theatre and the Show Boat Players crisscrossed through Virginia for the last weeks in May and the first weeks in June. For the week of June 6, the Show Boat Players arrived in Kilmarnock, Virginia, while the Original Show Boat began a week's engagement in Irvington. (Kilmarnock and Irvington are five miles apart at the southeastern tip of the Northern Neck of Virginia, an area of relative isolation. Throughout the Floating Theatre's history, the two towns had been considered as one. Every year it had played at one or the other. From 1914 to 1916 it played at Irvington. From 1917 to 1931 it played at Kilmarnock. Every year from 1932 it played again at Irvington.)

The Rappahannock *Record* in Kilmarnock handled the situation with absolute impartiality. On the back page of the June 2 issue, the two ads and two news releases stood side by side, like mirror images of each other. Charlie and Jack bought the larger ad, but the two stories were identical in length, to the line.

After the "showdown in Lancaster County" both companies toured in the Chesapeake area for several months. The Show Boat Players continued north along the western shore, crossed the Bay at Annapolis to Centreville, went north to Chesapeake City, and then south along the Eastern Shore to Exmore, Virginia.

The Floating Theatre continued in the Rappahannock River area, playing once more at Urbanna, which it had avoided the previous year because of the new taxes. I have found no licensing records at Urbanna, and I don't know who backed down, Seymoure or the town council.

About that time the boat's leading lady quit. It was predictable. In April a reporter had written:

> Roberts is enthusiastic about [Joan Thayer] and only hopes he can persuade her to stay long enough to get a real taste of showboat life.
>
> She . . . isn't at all sure she's going to like it.
>
> She misses the convenience of hotels, for one thing. For another, she dreads having to walk the narrow plank that stretches from ship to shore.
>
> She's afraid she'll fall in.
>
> Roberts has sought to convince her that this is the worst part of the experience.
>
> When the weather turns warm and the plays are in shape and there are long, lazy days to fish, and swim and bask in a deck chair, he argues, she'll love it.[59]

We probably can assume that she wasn't the fishing, swimming, basking kind of person, or maybe she fell off the gangplank one too many times. She was replaced in Tappahannock by Muriel Gallock.[60]

On July 25, Seymoure and company reached Leonardtown, a week after the Show Boat Players performed on Abell's lot, practically next to St. Aloysius church. Seymoure found his entrance to the city still barred. The Floating Theatre played at Hazel's Wharf at Compton, five miles by road or water from Leonardtown. In an attempt, no doubt, at reconciliation, the showboat performed a special benefit for St. Francis Xavier's Church, a local Catholic chapel.

Sometime in the summer, Cotton Watts quit the Floating Theatre and was replaced by an old favorite of the showboat audiences, Seabee Hayworth. Marion came with him. There were other changes as well. Roy Steadman quit, and was replaced as orchestra director first by Red Corley,[61] then Art Reiss,[62] and finally Don Phillips.[63] A new leading man, Darl Hulit,[64] joined the boat; and the most recent leading lady, Muriel Gallock, did not last much more than a month. She was replaced by Pauline Osborne.[65]

The first of October the boat was in Charlestown, Maryland, playing a private performance at the Wellwood Country and Yacht Club.[66] The Wellwood Club was a private club connected, unofficially, with the Republican Club of Philadelphia. It was a gunning and sports club, but it was also a place where men could go and let themselves be more "free" than at home. The performance the Floating Theatre put on at Wellwood was more risqué than the ones they usually performed.[67] It was a balance, at least, to Father Knight's Leonardtown.

The Floating Theatre finished its tour of the Chesapeake in October and headed south. It played at Elizabeth City, Manteo, and Colerain. At Elizabeth City, Seymoure had new heating equipment installed in the boat for winter.[68] At Manteo, the company's juvenile quit. A local youth, Tom Fearing, was hired. The son of a local pharmacist, Tom had spent two seasons with the Lost Colony Show on Roanoke Island and had studied with the Carolina Playmakers at the University of North Carolina.[69]

After leaving Colerain on Sunday morning, November 6, the theatre sank again. The following is Thayer Roberts's and Tommy Fearing's account of the sinking:

> The Roanoke River disaster came around 7 o'clock in the morning while the show boat was in route from Colerain to Wiliamston, under tow of the tugs *Elk* and *Trouper,* and towing Captain Wally Smith's *Spray,* the engine of which had broken down. The tugs missed the snag which stabbed a hole in the show boat's port bow, and caused her to begin sinking rapidly. Fred Haddock, engineer of the *Elk,* awoke the members of the cast, and soon all were huddled on the roof, while under Capt. Milford Seymoure of the show boat and Capt. Cannon of the *Elk,* every effort was made to get her into shallow water.

The *Elk* and *Trouper* with their bows against the larger craft at stern and bow were pushing it toward shore, when the most tense moment of the whole episode occurred. Seeing that the *Trouper* was about to be caught under the overhang of the bow of the sinking boat, all hands gathered to pry her loose, leaving the *Elk* tenantless. It was then that the *Elk* slipped her mooring, starting out on her own with no one at the wheel. The *Trouper* had been freed, and Capt. Seymoure, Haddock and Roberts set out in hot pursuit of the runaway craft. Swinging around and out into the river, the *Elk* suddenly made a sharp turn, charging back directly at the show boat with a speed capable of making the wreck of the show boat complete. But at the last moment, she swerved and merely struck the floating theatre a hard glancing blow. As she passed, engineer J. D. Deans of the *Trouper* and Fearing jumped aboard and got the tug under control.

Mattresses had been lowered over the side in the hope that they might be sucked into the opening, but the hole was too big, and the show boat finally rested near the shore . . .

To Carl E. "Pop" Neel, who has ridden the show boat for more than 20 years, and who has been aboard at the two previous sinkings, the disaster was mere routine, and he remained in bed, in his cabin on the roof throughout the proceedings.

"I knew that the only thing to do was to go up on the roof," he says, "and I was already there."

"Pop," whose eightieth birthday falls within two weeks, has been a trouper for all but the first 12 of his years.

As soon as the floating theatre was firmly on the bottom, those aboard began to think about food, and Mr. Roberts dived repeatedly into the kitchen beneath the stage to open the icebox and bring up rations which were prepared aboard the *Spray*.

Most prepared of the passengers, says Mr. Roberts, was Rose, the 300 pound colored cook, who has been with the show boat for the past six years. It was learned for the first time that Rose, on the weekend trips from place to place, not only sleeps fully clothed and shod, but has all her belongings neatly done up in cardboard boxes. Her cabin was down under the stage, but she was among the first to reach top-side, though how she and her collections negotiated the narrow stairway, was inexplicable.[70]

The boat sank within fifteen minutes.[71] Seabee reported to *Billboard* that the actors saved most of "their street clothes and personal belongings, but all were heavy losers in stage wardrobe and show equipment." The new heating equipment installed two weeks earlier was lost.[72]

186

The Elizabeth City Iron Works was employed by Mrs. Howard to raise the boat. It took them about two weeks.[73]

The damage to the boat was almost as extensive as it had been when it sank in the Dismal Swamp Canal. Rachel Seymoure remembered that when the boat was pumped dry the plywood seats in the auditorium spread open like fans. Seymoure stated the cost of repairs as $10,000, with no insurance.[74]

1939

While the boat was on the ways in Elizabeth City, the actors had to seek other employment, and some did not return for the 1939 season. Notable among the missing were Seabee and Marion Hayworth, who set up a circle stock company for the winter out of High Point, North Carolina.[75] Darl Hulit went to High Point with Seabee, but returned to the Floating Theatre for the 1939 season.[76] Seabee's replacement on the showboat was Art Vernun, who was billed as a "comedian from the West making his first appearance in the East."[77] Art's wife, Ducky, accompanied him on the boat.[78] The new orchestra leader was Gus Schultz,[79] one of the members of Boob's company who hadn't come aboard in 1937. Schultz, however, was soon replaced by the showboat veteran Bob Fisher,[80] who stayed with the theatre until the end.

One employee of the showboat created some embarrassment for the management during the theatre's hiatus. Seventeen-year-old William Haddock, Jr., was brought into court in Elizabeth City, accused of destroying two brooder stoves. How or why he destroyed the stoves is not explained. When Judge Fentress Horner inquired as to why he had not replaced the stoves, Haddock explained that he worked on the Floating Theatre and had not been paid for eight weeks. "We understand that Mrs. Howard isn't able to pay us anything yet. And we aren't pressing her. The sinking of the boat put her behind with a lot of expensive repairs to be done. But we are sticking by the boat."[81]

Judge Horner was moved by the defense. "'All right,' he said, 'I believe I will continue prayer for judgment in this case.'"[82]

The story was too juicy for *Billboard* to ignore, and it ran a version of the events a month later. *Billboard* identified Haddock as an actor on the boat. "With a note of loyalty," Billy Boy reported, "worthy of True Blue Harold himself, [Haddock] added: 'We couldn't leave her now. We'll just have to depend on the crowds we draw at our stops on the way southward.'"[83]

Seymoure took exception to the *Billboard* story, and two weeks later Billy Boy published Milford's version. "There is no truth in the article whatsoever . . . Our reputation has always been that of paying off, and we have always had the respect of the people who worked for us . . . The boy who got into trouble was in it before he joined me, and he was not an actor, as your article stated, but one of our deckhands . . . Last season was a hectic one for us, as the sinking of the boat cost us many thousands of dollars, and after she sank everyone was paid off."[84]

The Floating Theatre resumed its season in Elizabeth City on January 9, and then moved south, playing two-night stands through North Carolina to make up for some of the time lost because of the sinking.[85] Seymoure still had it in his mind to reach Florida before turning north again.[86]

On the two-day jaunts through North Carolina, Roberts presented a comedy by Robert J. Sherman, *She Got What She Wanted*, and the old temperance melodrama, *Ten Nights in a Bar Room*.[87]

The theatre reached Wilmington on February 6. It slowed its pace and played there for two weeks. The visit was sponsored by the Lions Club.[88]

Continuing south after leaving Wilmington, the theatre played for the first and only time in Southport, North Carolina. The *Port State Pilot* of that town reported a sad occurrence on the boat:

> Mrs. H. C. Merritt of Tuckahoe, N. Y., died Thursday afternoon aboard the Floating Theatre a few hours after she had docked at Southport.
>
> The deceased, who was 50-years-of-age, was stricken with a heart ailment and died immediately. Coroner John G. Calson was called, but after viewing the body decided that death resulted from natural causes.
>
> Mrs. Merritt was the sister of Mrs. Nina Howard, owner of the Showboat, and was spending some time traveling about with her at the time of her death.
>
> The remains were shipped to New York state for burial.[89]

Mrs. Howard had been traveling with the showboat since the Hunters left. She occupied their old apartment on board.[90]

Early in March the theatre was scheduled to play at Conway, South Carolina, but heavy rain kept it away. "Due to high water in the Waccamaw River, the Original Floating Theatre will cancel its engagement at Conway March 6, and will play at Socastee from the 6th for one whole week."[91]

After Socastee, the theatre played a week at Georgetown, South Carolina, where Seymoure advertised: "To be presented during their stay here are such Broadway successes as *She Knew What She Wanted, Folks of Valley Center, Sally from Shanghai, Young Love, The Vampire,* and *Ten Nights in a Barroom.*" The advertisement, of course, was misleading. Half the plays advertised never saw the inside of a Broadway theatre. *Sally from Shanghai* was

Robert J. Sherman's *Shanghai Goldie; She Knew What She Wanted* sounded like Sidney Howard's 1925 hit, *They Knew What They Wanted*, but was actually Sherman's *She Got What She Wanted;* and *Folks of Valley Center* was a rep comedy-drama by E. L. Paul.

After Georgetown, the theatre went to Charleston for the first time in its career. It played two weeks and then closed for two weeks before heading back north.

When the theatre reopened, Toby comic Orville "Kirk" Kirkman replaced Art Vernun, who signed with a tent rep company in Illinois.[92] Kirkman came with his wife Helen Evans.[93] There is no record of Tom Fearing continuing with the cast.

On the way north, the showboat received several good reviews. This one is from a Wilmington paper:

> In a program that lasted almost four hours, Mr. Roberts, first in the drama, then in the traditional "Showboat" "concert," gave an audience that comfortably filled the colorful theatre, a repertoire that ran the gamut from the dramatically villainous "Landlord Slade" to comical blackface parts that all but "stopped the show." Those who didn't guess it last night may as well be told that the make-up of his own and the other characters was Roberts' own work. Few who saw the show will forget the face of the drunken sot—"Joe Morgan."
>
> And speaking of "Joe Morgan"—it was Darl Hulit, another versatile "Showboat" ace, who crowded Roberts for honors in the main piece [*Ten Nights in a Bar Room*] by giving a masterful interpretation of the part. He came through in the "concert" with several songs that evidently contributed much to the pleasure of the cash customers.
>
> "Kirk" Kirkman and Helen Evans handled the comic parts in the evening's performance and did a mighty good job of it.
>
> To the orchestra, headed by Bob Fisher, pianist and arranger, is due a lot of credit for the success of "showboat" attractions.[94]

And this review appeared in Beaufort, North Carolina:

> Never having seen any big time actors other than the Carolina Playmakers of Chapel Hill who have a pretty good reputation for histrionic ability, perhaps my judgment isn't worth much, but at the Tuesday and Wednesday performances of the Floating Theatre several members of the troupe impressed me with their ability as first class actors and actresses. Particularly was I impressed with the young hero part [Darl Hulit, most likely] in the Wednesday

night performance of "Young Love." His was the best acting I have ever seen, including on the screen in my opinion.[95]

The theatre spent six weeks working its way through North Carolina. In Washington, Seymoure reported that Harry Van, who was with the Adams Floating Theatre in its early years, was once again aboard. Seymoure also reported that Pop Neel, now "88," was soon to retire.[96] It must have been a difficult trip south for Pop. When the boat sank in the Roanoke River three months earlier he was only 80. Pop left the boat after it reached the Chesapeake. With his departure, the wisdom of the past was represented in publicity by Harry Van.

On the way to the Chesapeake, Roberts prepared a new repertory. He kept *She Knew What She Wanted* and *Ten Nights in a Bar Room*, and added three rep comedies, E. L. Paul's *Tropical Love*; Robert J. Sherman's *Husband Hunter*, expanded to include the women available from the chorus line and renamed *Husband Hunters*; and Wishert and Slout's *So This Is Alaska*. He also added a royalty farce, *Meet the Bride*.

On June 2, when the theatre was playing at Deep Creek on the Dismal Swamp Canal, the Texaco tanker *Rhode Island* ran into the Norfolk-Portsmouth toll bridge across the southern branch of the Elizabeth River. Two tenders on the bridge, C. L. Cunningham and Lee Zimmerman, were knocked from the elevator of the draw span and fell 150 feet into the water. They survived. Two unidentified women leaped from their falling car and ran to safety.[97] All traffic in the river was stopped for two weeks. The Floating Theater was trapped at Deep Creek.

By the second week, Seymoure was worried:

And who wouldn't be with a payroll of $110 a day to be met and business almost at a standstill as the good ship "Floating Theatre" cools her keel at Deep Creek awaiting the clearing in the channel . . . so she can get through to get to the "good business" that awaits at Gloucester Point and Urbanna and Tappahannock.[98]

By June 16, the War Department had removed enough of the bridge wreckage to allow vessels through at their own risk.[99] On Monday, June 19, the Floating Theatre opened, a week late, at Gloucester Point. They made up the week later by skipping Cricket Hill.[100]

Charlie Hunter and Jack Pfeiffer were late getting the Show Boat Players' 1939 season started. In May they went to Atlanta to hire a company.[101] They reached Elizabeth City with their company on the same day Seymoure finally opened in Gloucester Point. Charlie and Jack had their own problems that night. They lost the performance because of a power failure.[102]

Charlie and Jack again chose their season from old repertoire plays: *The Hoodlum* (1926) and *Dolly of the Follies,* by Ted and Virginia Maxwell; *Some Baby* (1929), by Charles F. Harrison; the mystery *Black Ghost* (1905); Ralph Kettering's comedy-drama, *Which Shall I Marry?* (1915); and Lem B. Parker's *Jesse James* (1927). Rudolph Paul was still with them, and their comic was Cotton Watts, who had had a brief tour with the Floating Theatre the year before.[103]

The side money was always important to the financial health of a rep company. Charlie kept an important source of income away from Seymoure. For many years, the Floating Theatre enjoyed an endorsement from the Phillips Foods people of Cambridge, Maryland. For a consideration, the theatre management praised Phillips Foods in the Phillips company's advertising newsletter, *P. D. Q.,* and advertised that the Floating Theatre used Phillips Foods exclusively. When Charlie left the Floating Theatre, he took the endorsement with him for the Show Boat Players.[104]

The Show Boat Players caught up with the Floating Theatre in the Rappahannock area, but the Players were moving faster and preceded the boat onto the Eastern Shore. Charlie and Jack closed their season early, at Church Hill, Maryland, on September 23.[105]

The week of July 10, the showboat was in Fredericksburg, Virginia.

Thayer Roberts had his room on the second tier of staterooms behind the stage. He had rigged a water barrel in his room for a shower to wash off the gold makeup from his Dance of Gold. It had been the custom on the Floating Theatre from its first year to hire boys in the port towns to carry water to the barrels in exchange for tickets to shows. In Fredericksburg, it was reported that Roberts was accused of being "overly friendly" with the boys who carried the water to his room. Mrs. Howard got him released by promising the magistrate that Roberts would not get off the boat while it was in the city.[106]

Still barred from Leonardtown, the theatre played at Abell's Wharf, two and a half miles by water and four and a half miles by land south of the city. The wharf was a big, barnlike building that provided slot machines, before they were legalized, for its sporty customers.[107]

The Washington, D. C., *Times-Herald* reporter Eugene Warner caught the Floating Theatre's act the following week at Solomons:

> I can honestly say it was not the best show I ever saw. All pretense of subtlety had been thrown overboard, yet it was hilarious. I laughed all the way through. The actors on stage seemed to know it was terrible, too, and laughed at themselves.
>
> The show boat was tied up to the dock, some of her lines looped around trees. A crowd of bronzed young fishermen stood around, waiting for the actresses to appear on the poop deck for a breath of

air. I went on in, not that I don't like actresses, but I couldn't wait
to see the inside.

It's like a little country theatre inside, seats sloping toward the stage,
an orchestra pit with four musicians in shirtsleeves, and signs of local
merchants alongside the proscenium. Here are a few of the signs:

DO YOUR SHOPPING AT SOLOMON'S VARIETY STORE
A Full Line of Ladies', Gents' and Children's
Wearing Apparel
Groceries and Meats

★ ★ ★ ★ ★

Lantern Grill
Rooms & Barber Shop

★ ★ ★ ★ ★

H. M. WOODBURN & CO.
Confectionery, Ice Cream
Cold Drinks & Fishing Boats

. . . The hero [Darl Hulit] turned out to be pink-cheeked with
thin, wavy blonde hair and a lovely golden mustache, a perpetual
juvenile, if you know the type.

The comedian had a red fright wig, a red nose, black freckles as
big as a dime, his pants kept falling down, and he carried a broom
[Kirk Kirkman as Toby].

The kids in the audience, the farmers' wives, and the fishermen
squealed, howled and shrieked at everything he did.

Here was one of his best gags: The hero was lying on a couch,
unconscious. Three women had been trying to marry him and the
unhappy hero had swooned.

The comedian tried to awaken him by: 1, shooting a gun; 2,
hammering his heels with a hammer; 3, ringing a cowbell; 4, hol-
lering at the top of his lungs. When all this failed, he got a length
of garden hose and put one end in the unconscious man's mouth.
Into a funnel at the other end he poured from a bottle labeled with
the letters "CASTOR OIL."

As far as I could see, that was about all there was to the first act.
Apparently there had been at one time a script but the actors had
just abandoned it and made up their own play as they went along,
ad-libbing their lines, much to their own amusement. It worked
out to the satisfaction of everybody.

Between the acts candy was sold by the "heavy," a villainous doctor in makeup [possibly Thayer Roberts]. He wore two pairs of glasses for comic effect, one on the tip of his nose, the other next to his eyes. "A prize with every package," he shouted, "blankets, shawls, kewpie dolls, pillows, and ladies underwear." The prizes were displayed down front.

The second act produced this gag: The comic began to sneeze. The doctor put up an umbrella to protect himself. The comic became insulted. The high point was reached when they stood kicking each other for about five minutes, after which they chased each other around the stage, over chairs, knocking down furniture and indulging in countless falls, the audience rocking the boat with its applause and howls of delight.

The big finale in Act Three: All three of the girls wanting to marry the hero must prove their identity by exhibiting a crescent-shaped scar just above the right knee. All three girls, two brunettes and a Mae West blonde are standing up front showing their knees to the audience.

After a scramble that convulsed the audience, the right girl got the hero, and everybody went home happy.

I don't know what all this goes to show. Probably that humor doesn't change. The same slapstick stuff wowed the colonial settlers and the Romans centuries before them. Ad-libbing, or faking one's lines, is distinctly pre-Elizabethan theatre. It was interesting to rediscover it in this oldest part of America.

Maybe the moral is that Eddie Cantor and Jack Benny with their high-priced gag writers are on the wrong track. They might do well to visit Solomons Island and learn that the public really likes corn—right off the cob.[108]

The play, most likely, was *Husband Hunters.*

The day after he attended the show, Warner interviewed Milford Seymoure:

"Do you like being a showboat captain?" I asked.

"Craziest business I ever was in!" he shouted. "I wish I'd never heard of the showboat! I hate 'em!"

"What would you like to do?"

"I'll tell you! I wanta go back to the Eastern Shore where I was born and lead a quiet life!"

"How'd you happen to get in it?"

"Aw, we met this thing driftn' around the bay and the first thing you know we had it . . . I'll tell you something more. Ma don't want me to, but I will. Business is rotton. We were tied up in some little old place in the woods, Abell, Md., last week, Rotten!"[109]

The Floating Theatre played St. Michaels the week of September 11, and then moved to the Chester River. It opened in Baltimore, for the first time in its history, on October 23.

Although he finished the tour of the Bay with the theater, Thayer Roberts did not play in Baltimore. It is a good guess that the incident in Fredericksburg was instrumental in his leaving.

According to Captain Cannon, the showboat had not played previously in Baltimore because the owners of the movie theaters argued that the Floating Theatre was a fire hazard. Cannon claimed to have negotiated the boat's first venture into the biggest market on the Chesapeake: "I finally arranged with a Baltimore church to sponsor us for 10 per cent. The Mayor was a member of that church and we opened on schedule."[110]

The showboat opened in Baltimore on October 23, and played through January 6, and possibly into the week of January 8. This eleven- or twelve-week stint was the longest single stand in the history of the Floating Theatre.

Performers continuing with the Floating Theatre from the 1939 season into early 1940 were Darl Hulit, who took over Roberts's role as director,[111] the Spoffords, the Corleys, the Kirkmans, Opal Lee, Ellen Douglas, and Rachel Seymoure. For the Baltimore engagement Rachel was elevated to star status.

> The leading woman of the company is Mrs. Milford Seymoure, who was Miss Rachel Fairbanks of St. Michaels. When she married Mr. Seymoure a few years ago, she had no idea of becoming an actress but looked after the box office. Now, says her husband:
> "She's the finest leading lady you could find anywhere, she works in the chorus and she does my bookkeeping. Quite a handy wife, don't you think?"[112]

Rachel is more modest in appraising her theatrical career. Because of her conservative upbringing she was most reluctant to go on stage. Whenever the boat was in St. Michaels she would not act before her hometown folks. She had to be persuaded to go on the stage at Easton, just up the Miles River from St. Michaels. It took extensive persuasion to get her to dance in the chorus.[113]

New cast members added at the beginning of the run in Baltimore included juvenile Harvey Koon from Portsmouth, Virginia,[114] comedian Earnest Candler, Bill Godby, Jack Irvin, and Felix Cole.[115]

Initially Seymoure presented two plays a week, each running three nights, but by the third week he realized he had hit a box office bonanza and scheduled each play for a week. He also began to play on Sundays.

The first play to run for a week was *Ten Nights in a Bar Room,* the feature play of the 1939 season under Thayer Roberts's direction. The play was restaged by Darl Hulit with "44 tunes of the Gay Nineties" specially arranged by Bob Fisher,[116] who was still working as the orchestra director.

During the theatre's stay in Baltimore, several veterans of the rep theatre joined the company. Peggy Lennox was a redheaded character actress who had once played in silent films. Her husband, Jim Burns, was a heavyset character actor who claimed to have once played opposite Pearl White.[117]

One of the most interesting people to play on the Floating Theatre also joined in November but stayed with the company only a few weeks. That was the comic, Slim Andrews. A Baltimore newspaper reported: "Slim, who hails from the Ozarks, has a collection of home-made instruments, including saw, bells, an electric amplifying guitar from which he extracts music calculated to please any ear."[118] Before coming with the Floating Theatre Andrews was with the Davis-Brunk players in Arkansas.[119] Shortly before his stint on the showboat, Andrews was "discovered" by Tex Ritter when Ritter was making a personal appearance tour in Arkansas. Tex Ritter, the father of actor John Ritter, was one of the first of the singing cowboys in Western movies in the 1930s. Ritter signed Andrews to a contract to be his comic sidekick in eight pictures a year and in personal appearances.[120] Andrews must have taken the Floating Theatre job to fill in until he started with Ritter.

Andrews played Toby roles in *Rooms for Tourists,*[121] *North Pole Honeymoon,*[122] and *Lure of the City,*[123] the weeks of November 12 and 19. On November 26, the showboat repeated *Ten Nights in a Bar Room.* The comic part of Sample Swichel was again played by Ernest Candler.[124] On December 3, the showboat opened another "old fashioned meller-drama," *Over the Hills to the Poor House.* Andrews played the comic role of Walt Mason.[125]

Mason was Andrews's last role on the Floating Theatre. For the next play, *Why Lindy Ran Away,* he was replaced by John "Ducky" Rhodes,[126] who came complete with actress wife Betty Lou Rhodes.[127]

The Times Theatre in Baltimore brought back the 1936 movie version of *Show Boat* while the Floating Theatre was in Baltimore, and the cast of the Floating Theatre attended a performance, in costume. They carried a sign with them advertising that the story "Was Written On Our Boat."[128]

In the final weeks in Baltimore, Darl Hulit and company presented *For Crying Out Loud, The G Man,* and *The Cohens and the Kellys.*

While in Baltimore, Seymoure made an interesting claim to newspaper reporter Carroll Dulaney, which I have been unable to confirm:

> Captain Seymoure says his boat was tied up in North Carolina waters when a man presented himself as a "Government Inspector," showed proper credentials and was made welcome. The man

made elaborate measurements of the showboat, thanked Captain Seymoure for his courtesy and left.

A month or so later, as Captain Seymoure's craft was pulled into Coinjock, N. C., the captain and his crew rubbed their eyes in amazement. There, tied up at the dock where the showboat usually lay, was another showboat, the exact duplicate of Captain Seymoure's craft.

As soon as he had recovered from his astonishment, Captain Seymoure made inquiries and learned that the new craft was a Federal Theatre Project showboat, built after his model to *compete for his business.*

As admission to the Federal Showboat was next to nothing, Captain Seymoure found this competition a serious thing. And everywhere he took his showboat he found the Government floating theatre had beat him to the stand.

This continued all summer, but finally the Government showboat closed its door and tied up permanently.[129]

Seymoure's story sounds like a typical complaint made by commercial theatres during the time of the Federal Theatre Project. Seymoure may have encountered a showboat sponsored by the Project, although I have not uncovered any in the areas the Floating Theatre visited. The details of Seymoure's story, however, were most likely invented.

During its stay in Baltimore, the showboat produced two old-fashioned melodramas. One of them, *Over the Hills to the Poor House,* was based on a poem by Will Carelton. It was produced as a play as early as 1889.[130] The other, *Ten Nights in a Bar Room,* was originally a novel by T. S. Arthur. It was first adapted as a play in 1847 by William Y. Pratt.[131] It was intended as a temperance play to persuade people not to drink, and was a mainstay of stock and repertoire theatres throughout the second half of the nineteenth century and the first two decades of the twentieth. It is the story of life in Simon Slade's bar in which poor, honest men are tricked by an evil gambler, and other honest men become hopelessly addicted to alcohol. Only with the death of his innocent daughter Mary—killed by accident in a barroom brawl—and the influence of her dead soul, is the hero, Joe Morgan, able to see the damage drink has done to him, and through him, to his family.

Melodramas such as *Ten Nights in a Bar Room* were not mainstays of the Floating Theatre's repertory under Adams and Hunter. Adams announced the play for 1914, but cancelled it. In 1937, Hunter produced it as part of the Show Boat Players' first season. I have no record of the Floating Theatre producing the play until Roberts presented it in 1938. For its last three seasons, however, the Original Floating Theatre had at least one old-fashioned melodrama as a part of every bill.

The production of *Ten Nights in a Bar Room* in Baltimore in 1939 was unlike productions in the nineteenth century and unlike Adams's production would have been in 1914, had he presented it then. Most likely it differed significantly from Hunter's production in 1937. Hulit integrated comic musical performances into the play, including a barbershop quartet. A reporter noted of the 1939 production, "Nowadays it is presented in a tongue-in-cheek fashion, intended to amuse rather than to uplift, with the florid phrases over-emphasized to provoke laughter rather than to point any moral lessons."[132]

When the Floating Theatre played the larger cities instead of the small towns that had supported it for most of its years, it found success in a comic view of nostalgia instead of the honest sentiment of the repertoire writers. Rachel Seymoure noted this when the theatre played at Tappahannock and the audience was divided between local residents and visitors from Richmond. Many of the visitors made fun of the plays and tried to engage in witty repartee with the actors during the performances. The locals objected to the behavior of the visitors. The locals came to enjoy the plays "honestly."[133]

It was not only the audiences that changed. The actors changed, too. The performers who replaced Charlie and Beulah were not committed to the sentiment of the repertoire plays. They shared the views of the more sophisticated city audiences. The theatre presented by the showboat no longer reflected the values of the players and of the audiences to which it was presented. The performers and the audiences found the old rep plays naive, sentimental, and ultimately ridiculous.

The problem was, comic nostalgia had limited appeal. A sophisticated audience might enjoy the plays of the showboat as an occasional diversion, but did not return to it year after year with the devotion that characterized a naive audience.

CHAPTER TWELVE

The Final Curtain

1940

From its successful run in Baltimore, the Floating Theatre sailed south. An actress on board indicated that the boat was headed for Florida, and she was concerned about the danger of being sunk on the way by a German U-boat. The Floating Theatre did not reach Florida, but not because of U-boats. It was delayed by nature.

After Baltimore, the theatre played Elizabeth City. Seymoure advertised that he was presenting the best plays from the theatre's "14 week engagement in Baltimore." By the most liberal count, he exaggerated by only two weeks, a modest effort for Seymoure.[1]

In Elizabeth City the theatre presented the melodrama *Over the Hills to the Poor House;* W. C. Herman's rep comedy-drama, *Why Lindy Ran Away;* and three royalty comedies, *Love Child, Rooms for Tourists,* and *For Crying Out Loud.* Hulit was still the producer and director.[2]

From Elizabeth City, the theatre went up the Roanoke River to play at Williamston, the port it was trying to make when it sank in 1938. It had no trouble reaching Williamston; this time the problem was getting away from Williamston. The Floating Theatre had left Baltimore and the Chesapeake Bay just ahead of a major cold spell. In Williamston, the weather caught up with it. The ship was frozen solid in its berth for two weeks.[3]

After the river thawed out, the theatre finally reached Plymouth, and then headed farther south, playing at Washington, Belhaven, Beaufort, and Wilmington, North Carolina, and Georgetown, South Carolina. It reached Charleston the first of April. Along the way Hulit added *Today's Children;* the *Abie's Irish Rose* clone *You Can't Beat the Irish;* two standard rep comedy-dramas, *Mountain Justice* and the *The Girl from Out Yonder;* and an old melodrama, *Song of the Sea,* to the repertory. He moved *Over The Hills to the Poor House* from Wednesday's teaser to Saturday's closer. The concert, also produced by Hulit,[4] was now the "Mermaid Review," featuring "GIRLS! GIRLS! GIRLS!"[5]

Bob Fisher continued as orchestra director. Others continuing in the cast were the Rhodes,[6] Harvey Koon, Peggy Lennox, and Jim Burns.[7]

Aycock Brown, columnist with the Beaufort, North Carolina, *News,* reported that the theatre played to about 60 percent capacity in Beaufort, which was what the theatre had been averaging since leaving Baltimore.[8] Jim Adams would have dropped a town that unproductive, but then Jim had had enough sense to sell the boat in 1933.

Brown also reported meeting Koon and Burns on board the Coast Guard vessel *Modoc* at Wilmington. They were there visiting Burns's son, who was the radio operator on the *Modoc.*[9]

The showboat played two weeks in Charleston, and then turned around and headed north again on April 14. In May it played at Greenville, North Carolina, for the first time since 1914. The theatre opened in Deep Creek on June 3.

During the winter of 1939–40, Hunter and Pfeiffer's tent was stored at the Massey racetrack, east of the town of Church Hill, Maryland, where they closed their season in 1939.

Massey's racetrack was built for training thoroughbreds but not for racing them. Instead, farmers in the area often brought their carriage horses to the track on Saturday afternoons and raced informally. Harry Massey was a good friend of Jim Adams and Jim kept racehorses at the track.[10] Charlie most likely stored his gear at the track for no cost.[11] On April 20, Harry Massey entertained Charlie and Beulah in honor of their twenty-fifth wedding anniversary.[12]

At the end of April, Charlie Hunter and Jack Pfeiffer reported to *Billboard* that they were dissolving their partnership of three years. "The outfit . . . will be divided and both boys will put out smaller shows, possibly in conjunction with motion pictures."[13] They reported that 1938 and 1939 had not been as successful as 1937,[14] the year they caught Seymoure by surprise and picked their way through the "clover patch of the Chesapeake"[15] before Seymoure, Brasfield, and company got moving.

One of the main causes of the breakup was the illness of the star. Beulah was hospitalized at Parrot Hospital in Kinston, North Carolina, in March, suffering from pernicious anemia. In April she was responding well to treatment but was still under her doctor's care. She decided to "hang up her wardrobe permanently."[16]

By the 1930s, acting had become easier for Charlie than it had for Beulah. Charlie was a character actor and, as the years went by, he grew into his roles. Beulah was an ingenue and, as the years went by, she grew out of her roles. All through her career, even as her face and voice grew older and her body heavier, she continued to play the only roles she knew—girls and young women. A resident of Oriental, North Carolina, who attended the Floating Theatre during its only visit to Vandemere, North Carolina

. . . was so enchanted with the darling little actress, Pollyanna, with the long blonde curls, that in adoration she took a gift to the boat for this beautiful child. What she saw was a shock she never forgot. The little "charmer" was not young, not pretty, and not a blonde with curly hair. Little Sally Laughinghouse learned about wigs and "show biz."[17]

At the time, Beulah was thirty-three years old. She continued playing ingenues for another thirteen years.

Charlie and Beulah stayed in their trailer at the Massey racetrack until late in May. Charlie rehearsed his new company there and began the season on May 27.[18] Charlie's new venture was "Charlie Hunter's Vaudefilm Show." He presented:

"Talking Pictures and Vaudeville"
Perfect Sound and Projection

DOUBLE FEATURES EVERY NIGHT ON THE SCREEN

Griff and Hi were still with him, and his star was Tommy Brink, the "Yodeling Cowboy."[19]

Charlie circled the Bay until October, and then he, too, called it quits, and went back to Michigan with Beulah.

Jack Pfeiffer toured "Jack Pfeiffer's Comedians." He presented:

TALKING PICTURES
AND
STAGE SHOW

★ ★ ★ ★ ★

Two Shows For the Price of One

On Monday nights he offered Bob Steele in the film *Alias John Law,* and on the stage, *The Country Boy.* In his company were Frank Williams, "Playing the Smallest Trombone in the world," Eleanor Franklin, Gladys Pennington, and, interestingly, Rudolph Paul, "The Georgia Singing Minstrel." The company starred Jack Pfeiffer, "That Black Face Boy From Alabama,"[20] and featured Griff and Hi, the "black and tan" act from the Show Boat Players.[21]

Jack played some of the Bay towns, but he went farther afield than Charlie, and they managed to stay out of each other's way.

Jack was still in the field in 1941, but by the middle of the year he had changed his format from plays and films to films and vaudeville.[22]

The Floating Theatre entered the Chesapeake in June 1940, and made the usual stops on the western shore.

During the season the company suffered a malady of modern times: an actress and a musician became addicted to cocaine.[23]

In July, Hulit advertised in *Billboard* for performers "in all lines."[24]

A week later, when the boat was in Irvington, Seymoure announced in the Rappahannock *Record* that this was the last tour the theatre would make.

> When the season is completed late in the fall at Baltimore, Milford Seymoure, of St. Michaels, Md., owner of the time-honored craft, will beach it at a small summer resort on the banks of the West River south of Annapolis, where it will be renovated for a motion picture house.[25]

It was an announcement he repeated at stops throughout the rest of the season.

The boat again played at Abell's Wharf instead of Leonardtown. It then continued north to Solomons, Galesville, and Annapolis. In Annapolis, the Washington *Post* reported the projected demise of the showboat, and the story was picked up by newspapers throughout the area, including *Billboard*[26] and the *News and Observer* of Raleigh, North Carolina. In that story Captain Cannon is quoted:

> Now that the steamboat traffic hereabouts is about gone, there aren't enough wharves to tie up to. It's hard to find a cast that will stay, too. It's a novelty and adventure, at first, to the young troupers, but they soon grow tired of acting and traveling all the time.[27]

While the boat was in Annapolis, reporter R. W. Kieffer of the Baltimore *Sunday Sun* interviewed Nina Howard. Kieffer reported that she had not definitely decided to moor the boat permanently in West River. She would decide after the theatre's run in Baltimore.[28]

Howard claimed that the theatre still played to full houses, but that the cost of operating the boat was between $700 and $800 a week. She also claimed that radio and moving pictures were not as serious problems for the boat as finding suitable docks for mooring.[29]

I cannot accept Howard's claims. Despite the loss of wharves, the showboat still played the towns that had sustained it during the 1920s.

Actress Felix Cole doing her laundry in her stateroom. Photograph by A. Aubrey Bodine, courtesy of the Mariners Museum, Newport News, Virginia.

An unidentified actor operating the lights and front curtain on the Floating Theatre. Photograph by A. Aubrey Bodine, courtesy of the Mariners Museum, Newport News, Virginia.

Dinner on the Floating Theatre. The actress on the left is Opal Lee Lyle; on the right, Felix Cole. The two men are unidentified. Photograph by A. Aubrey Bodine, courtesy of the Mariners Museum, Newport News, Virginia.

Howard reported the capacity of the house as 442 seats, reduced significantly from the original 800 by the changes made in the auditorium following the various sinkings of the boat. In 1940 the theatre charged twenty-five cents general admission and fifteen cents for the concert, a minimum of forty cents a seat per performance. If the theatre played to full houses, the boat would gross $178 a performance, or $1,060 a week, enough to cover expenses of $800 a week and turn a profit of $260, or almost twenty-five percent. On the other side, Howard's estimate of costs most likely did not include capital depreciation. To help with that, however, there was other income, such as fees for reserved seats and refreshments.

The truth is, the audiences were not there. Occasionally, as in Baltimore in 1939, the theatre stumbled onto a mother lode, but Aycock Brown's estimate that the theatre generally played to an average of sixty percent capacity was probably more accurate. Sixty percent attendance at the theatre would gross a minimum of only $638, not enough to cover Howard's estimated weekly costs.

Kieffer's 1940 article is the last contemporary feature article that I have found about the Floating Theatre. It is interesting in what it reveals about Nina Howard, about the current operations of the theatre, and about the physical changes in it. I have no evidence that the *Trouper* was built before 1913; but by 1940 the *Elk* may have been converted to diesel. (There is a contemporary reference in 1941 to the *Elk* being diesel powered.[30]) One notable fact is that the electric generators were once more located under the stage, a contributing cause to the boat's eventual destruction.

> Showboat audiences, [Howard] says, demand a special kind of diet. The people who live in the Chesapeake and Atlantic coast villages and see few Broadway hits like hilarious comedies without much subtlety. The city folk who do see current Broadway hits want the old-time thrillers, the melodramas that made their mothers weep, such as "Over the Hills to the Poor House," and "Ten Nights in a Barroom." This season Mrs. Howard's company revived "Song of the Breakers," a favorite that had them going in the old days, and its tear jerking lines are still working.
>
> Old jokes go over big, too, which probably proves that a joke that is really funny never grows stale. After every play the cast puts on what is advertised as a concert, but is in reality a vaudeville revue.
>
> Annapolis is not a typical waterside village. Even the people who don't run up to New York often to see a show consider themselves pretty cosmopolitan. The Annapolis audience that went to see "You Can't Beat the Irish" rocked the boat with their laughter; the plot was just as funny to them as when they first saw it in

"Abie's Irish Rose." The showboat actors gave it everything they had. In the vaudeville that followed the black-face comedian, Ernest Chandler, had them doubling in their seats. A boy in the balcony, sitting on the rail next to an open window, with his feet dangling over the heads of the audience, was in imminent danger of falling out into Spa Creek as he squirmed in uncontrollable mirth. The jokes were new to him and to the people who had heard them before they gave a sense of safety, a feeling that maybe the world hadn't changed so much after all . . .

Although Mrs. Howard doesn't act, she leads a busy life. Up at 5 in the morning, she buys the provisions for the thirty people on board, marketing at each community where they play, oversees the housekeeping affairs of the boat and at night sells tickets at the box office. A gray-haired, energetic woman, she never finds time hanging heavy on her hands. Looking out the open door of her cabin at the busy streets around the Annapolis harbor, she remarked with housewifely interest that now that they were near a 10-cent store she was going to refurbish her cabin. Mrs. Howard's cabin is above the box office, and is large enough for several easy chairs, a safe, a chest, a table and a dresser in addition to the bunk. Flowered cretonne curtains, pictures of ships and dogs and an antique glass goblet placed precariously on a shelf make the cabin cozy and homelike.

The theatre itself holds 442 people, including balcony seats. The interior finish is not lavish, but gilded organ pipes (mute) make an imposing decoration on each side of the stage; there are shaded bracket lights on the buff-colored walls between the double row of square windows, and a sky-blue ceiling gives an effect of even greater height to the auditorium. The two aisles have a strip of dark green painted down them, which looks at first glance like a strip of carpet. There are no box seats, but there is an orchestra pit where musicians in informal summertime attire, like most of the audience, play appropriate overtures and entr'actes.

Economy in the use of space is traditional for both boats and theatres; so it's double strength here. A set of steps, vases of flowers, chairs, a gilt easel made for "Ten Nights in a Barroom," are just some of the pieces of property flying from the stage ceiling. "Flying from the ceiling" is a theatrical term, not a nautical one. The combination of stage vernacular and sailor talk is a little confusing to anyone who doesn't know either language well.

In the middle of the stage floor is an open trapdoor, covered with wire screening. Through it you can look down into the galley where Rosa Teel, the colored cook, has bossed the baking of soda

Actor Darl Hulit applying makeup in his stateroom while the Floating Theatre was playing Washington, North Carolina. Photograph courtesy of Jacques Kelly.

Carl "Pop" Neel in August 1939, during his last year with the Floating Theatre. The picture was taken at Abell's Wharf near Leonardtown, Maryland, by George M. Knight. Photograph courtesy of Al Gough, Jr.

With the Floating Theatre in 1936, left to right, Roy Steadman, orchestra leader; Marshall Walker, director of the "Whiz-Bang Review"; and Carl "Pop" Neel, perennial member of the band. Photograph courtesy of the Mariners Museum, Newport News, Virginia.

biscuits and frying fish for ten years and grown fat—300 pounds and not trying to reduce, either—from eating them. Steps through the orchestra pit take you into the mess cabin where the assistant cooks were putting great platters of tomato salad on the three long tables being set for dinner.

In the mess cabin and the galley you have to watch your head, the beams being necessarily low because of the stage above, and you also have to watch your feet, because heavy beams that come above the level of the floor. Back of the galley are the theatre's two power plants which supply it with electricity; the boat uses as much power as a village with a population of 300.

To tow the 137x35 foot theatre is a 47-foot tug, the Elk, which is powered by a 150-horse-power Diesel engine. The tug is run by Capt. W. S. Cannon, who has been skipper of the outfit for fifteen years. Alongside the Elk stands an auxiliary tug, the Trouper, built forty years ago when gasoline engines were first being used, but still serviceable for running errands and helping out.[31]

Kieffer also reported that Rachel Seymoure was still the leading lady; that Darl Hulit was still aboard, as were some of the performers who joined in Baltimore in 1939 (Paul Brady, Peggy Lennox, and Jim Burns); and that musician and magician Bob Fisher, who came aboard the year before, after the boat sank in the Roanoke, was still conducting the orchestra. Because Ernest "Shorty" Candler was now the featured comedian, apparently Ducky Rhodes had left sometime during the summer.

On September 7, *Billboard* reported that the showboat was winding up its season with a week's engagement at the Wellwood Yacht and Country Club in Charlestown, Maryland.[32]

But the season didn't end then. The next week *Billboard* ran another want ad for the Floating Theatre.

WANTED

★ ★ ★ ★ ★

Tall Juvenile Man and Ingenue, fast Toby Comedian, all with specialties; Chorus Girls with specialties. Other useful Dramatic People, write quick, full particulars as to what you do, age, height, weight. Hap Ray and Bob Demorest, Jr., wire.

ORIGINAL FLOATING THEATRE
Cambridge, Md., week of Sept. 8;
St. Michaels, Md., week of Sept. 15.[33]

Throughout the rest of September and into October, the Floating Theatre moved without logical pattern up and down the Eastern Shore of the Chesapeake.

On October 5, the theatre was still advertising for performers.[34]

On October 28, it returned, as Howard had announced it would in August, to Baltimore. In the cast were leading lady Rachel Seymoure, Libby Mack, Wilma Candler, Ethel Candler, Rudy Hoff, Vern Spofford, and Paul Ruley.[35] Ernest Candler was still the chief comedian, but Darl Hulit was no longer with the company. The new leading man was Russ Cassidy.[36] Peggy Lennox was now the director.[37]

The showboat opened the Baltimore run with W. C. Herman's old comedy-drama, *Clouds and Sunshine,* about a schoolteacher who is about to be married to a minister when her first husband, an ex-convict she thought long dead, appears.[38] The second week the theatre presented Pauline Phelps and Marion Short's comedy-drama, *The Girl from Out Yonder,* the story of the lighthouse keeper's daughter who falls in love with a rich summer tourist. It is interesting to note that Lennox was going back to the ingenue plays of the Floating Theatre's earlier history, with Rachel Seymoure playing Beulah's roles.

Seymoure advertised the plays for a week's run each, apparently expecting another long stand in the city. But the audiences were not there the second time around. The theatre played for only two weeks in Baltimore in 1940, and perhaps part of the third.

I do not know what happened to the plans to beach the theatre in the West River, but by the middle of November the showboat was back in North Carolina.

1941

On its run south in the winter of 1940–1941, the Floating Theatre did not play at Elizabeth City. An Elizabeth City newspaper, however, noted that the theatre was in Coinjock for the week of November 18.[39]

The next place I could locate the theatre was in Georgetown, South Carolina, on Monday, January 6, where it opened a week's engagement with Robert J. Sherman's comedy-drama *Gossip,* starring Peggy Lennox.[40] Featured with the company were Bob Fisher's orchestra, "Marine Syncopation," Libby Mack in her "Dance of Temptation," and Ernest Candler, "The South's Greatest Black Face."[41]

The next week the boat was in Beaufort, South Carolina.[42] On this visit, the theatre was not able to play for the marines because of an outbreak of influenza on Parris Island.[43]

Two weeks later the theatre arrived at Thunderbolt, Georgia, near Savannah. It opened there on January 27 with *You Can't Beat the Irish.*[44]

Thunderbolt was the Floating Theatre's final stand. I do not know how long it played there before it closed. While in Thunderbolt it moored at a new dock built by Asa Candler of Atlanta.[45] Asa Candler apparently was not related to Ernest, Wilma, and Ethel Candler, performers on the showboat.[46]

In the middle of May, *Billboard* announced that the Original Floating Theatre had been sold to E. H. Brassell of Savannah.[47] The Savannah *Morning News* later reported that Brassell bought the theatre and both tugs at public auction for a reported price of $6,000.[48] However, the *Morning News* also reported that the auction was on June 26 (a date more than a month after *Billboard* reported the sale), and that the original cost of building the theatre was $65,000, an inflated figure even if the original costs of the two tugs were added. One thing is certain, however: Howard sold the boat at a loss, which is not surprising considering its age and condition when she sold it.

Brassell was in the commercial towing business, and with the increasing demands for shipping created by the escalating wars in Europe and Asia, he bought the whole rig for the tugs.[49]

Billboard reported that after Brassell bought the theatre, he towed it to Brunswick, Georgia.[50] The *Morning News* reported that the theatre remained at Thunderbolt. In either case, in November it was towed to the Savannah River and moored near Bernard Street in Savannah.[51]

On November 14, 1941, less than a month before Pearl Harbor, while the theatre was being towed across the river to "place it in the shallow water in the No. 2 slip at the Seaboard terminals," where Brassell planned to strip away the superstructure of the boat in order to use her as a cargo barge, the old showboat caught fire.[52]

> The cause of the blaze, which seemed to spread from stem to stern in a very short time, is unknown. Two small tugs, the Vida D. and the Elk, were towing the large boat to the Seaboard slip when the fire broke out. Three men were aboard the showboat at the time, two watchmen and T. B. Gamble, a member of the crew of the Elk.
>
> Mr. Gamble said he did not know which part of the boat caught fire first. Her bilges, he said, seemed to catch from stem to stern all at once, and the fire spread so rapidly that the three aboard of her had to hurry to reach the safety of the smaller tugs alongside . . .
>
> . . . [Later] the belief was expressed that oil and gasoline might have leaked from the generator motors into the boat's bilges, causing the flames to spread along the whole length.
>
> . . . At first the fire, which started about 4 o'clock, was confined to the inside and hull of the craft, causing smoke to billow from the many windows in the vessel's sides.

Attracted by the smoke, the Seaboard ferry Island Girl and the Atlantic Towing Company tug William F. McCauley, both equipped for fire fighting, hurried to the scene and began playing water on the boat. E. H. Brassell, the owner, arrived a few minutes later aboard the Diesel tug Gwendolyn, another of his boats. The blaze was very spectacular and many persons were attracted to the municipal wharf to see the fire.

Efforts to prevent the blaze from spreading were fruitless, and within a comparatively short time after the fire was discovered, flames and smoke were billowing from all openings in the top side of the boat. Dangerously near the Seaboard wharves, the tugs abandoned their fire fighting and devoted all efforts to shoving the burning boat into Seaboard No. 1 slip.

Last night when the tide dropped the vessel grounded in the mud in the slip while the flames ate lower and lower along her hull. She was burning in the mud flat when the tide left her entirely, and late last night only a few smouldering heavy timbers remained of the once palatial showboat.[53]

Some have expressed the opinion that Brassell wanted the tugs but that the theatre was of little value to him, and that the boat may have been burned for the insurance.[54] The *Morning News* reported that the loss was partially covered by insurance.

The equipment still on the boat, however, was in good condition.[55] That salvage and the use of the converted boat as a barge, even after the conversion costs, would have been worth more to Brassell than the insurance.

I think the *Playhouse* had no stomach for ending her years toting around whatever disagreeable cargo people wanted to throw into her, and she decided to chuck it all in a gesture befitting her station. She went out in a blaze that outshone all the dramatic pyrotechnics her actors had created in twenty-seven years.

CHAPTER THIRTEEN

Curtain Call

THE DEATH OF REPERTOIRE

*I*t is Rachel Seymoure's judgment that the fortunes of the Floating Theatre began to decline when Beulah and Charlie left the boat.[1] No doubt there is much to support her thesis. For two decades the Hunters had built supportive audiences in the tidewater towns. But even if the Hunters had stayed with the Floating Theatre, I doubt if its fortune would have been much different. Nina Howard and Milford Seymoure began their show business careers at a most inopportune time. They can hardly be faulted for failing in 1941. They lasted eight years longer than a prudent person in 1933 would have predicted.

Jim Adams sold his showboat under the pressure of the Great Depression. He was not alone in leaving the business. Frank Gillmore, who as secretary of Actors Equity helped organize the Tent and Repertoire Managers Protective Association, reported in 1933 that "there were between three and four hundred [tent shows] ten years ago. Today there may be about thirty, but I doubt if five are making a profit."[2] *Bruno's Bulletin*,[3] the Midwestern newsletter for rep companies, suspended publication between 1930 and 1934 because of the decline in rep business caused by the Depression.

By the late 1930s, economic conditions had improved. Pop Neel of the Floating Theatre remarked on the change. "A few years ago the farmers came with pennies and nickels to pay for their tickets. But this week I have a time keeping in change and dollar bills. Everyone comes up with a five or ten dollar bill to pay for their tickets and it keeps us chasing to the bank all day to keep enough change on hand."[4] But the good times did not bring back prosperity to the traveling theatres. Klassen observed, "The Depression had forced most veteran actors into 'outside' jobs during the winter months, and most were reluctant for financial reasons to resume show business . . . According to *Bruno's Bulletin*, in 1940 the number of shows in that year was less than half the number listed in 1929 [before the Great Depression]."[5]

There were a number of forces at work. Welby Choate of Choate's Comedians summarized the problems.

> When Japan attacked Pearl Harbor on December 7, 1941, a critical blow was dealt to the tent show industry. The most devastating effect of the war was that much of the young talent was swept away by the draft, creating a shortage of manpower and necessity for middle-aged performers to take over the juvenile and ingenue roles. This, of course, hurt the quality and credibility of the performances. There were also shortages of materials necessary to keep a show on the road. Gas was rationed and rubber was in short supply. Spare parts for trucks were almost impossible to find and factories were paying high wages for employees (higher than tent shows could pay).[6]

Choate could have added that there was a patriotic imperative for people to take the high-paying defense jobs. And those who still had their hearts set on show business found opportunities to perform in a patriotic setting with the USO. The wonder is not that rep companies closed, but that any survived the war.

Klassen lists fifteen rep companies, including two showboats—*Bryan's Showboat* and *The Goldenrod Showboat*—still playing during the war. Schaffner remembered that companies played only during the summer. By the the end of the war, "Winter house rep had become a thing of the past."[7]

Klassen lists only six companies still playing in 1953.[8] In 1989 there are only two repertoire companies maintaining the tradition of the 1920s, and both of them operate under "museum" conditions: the Rosier Players in Michigan, and the Schaffner Players in Iowa under the direction of Jimmie Davis, probably the last traditional Toby. Both companies are headed by veteran troupers who try to maintain the style and integrity of the old rep companies, but the supporting actors for both companies are college students and other amateurs.

Today there are no showboats touring the rivers of America. The few that are left are permanently moored and present typical summer theatre fare. The Driftwood Floating Theatre, in Kingston, New York, occasionally presents one of the old repertoire comedies.

WHATEVER BECAME OF . . . ?

In April 1928 Jim Adams purchased a tract of land in Chesapeake City, Maryland.[9] The tract was in an area known as Mt. Nebo. The year before Jim bought his land, the improvement of the Chesapeake and Delaware Canal was completed.[10] The canal was dredged deeper and wider and

Harry Van (Becker) sells tickets. Harry was with Adams in the early years and returned to the theatre in 1939. Photograph courtesy of Jacques Kelly.

Cook Rose Teal in the galley. Photograph courtesy of the Chesapeake Bay Maritime Museum, St. Michaels, Maryland.

The Floating Theatre sank in the Roanoke River in November 1938. Photograph courtesy of the photographer, Miller Warren.

the last of the locks, opened in 1829, was removed.[11] The land that Jim bought was east of the town and rose above the new anchoring basin. The location provided both a pleasant view and the convenience of docking his yacht in front of his house.

Later in 1928, Jim built the first of three houses on the tract. It was the smallest and was named "Done Rovin'."[12] In October 1930, Jim started construction of a new, larger house[13] he named "Linger Long."[14] When the second house was finished, Gertrude's widowed sister, Bertha Seeley, moved into the smaller house. For several years Mrs. Seeley had been a regular visitor with the Adamses in Chesapeake City. By 1932, Jim had built Mrs. Seeley a larger house on the tract, "The Shelter."[15] Eventually, the original house, Done Rovin', was occupied by Mrs. Seeley's daughter, Helen Matless. In 1950, Jim and Gertrude sold The Shelter to Bertha.[16]

After his third retirement, Jim kept his hand in business by running several Studebaker agencies. He also kept racehorses, but it is doubtful they added to his income.[17]

The Adamses and Mrs. Seeley enjoyed a brisk social life in Chesapeake City. They were well liked by their neighbors, who found Jim and Gertie to be pleasant but quiet. Bertha was more outgoing.[18] The Adamses and Mrs. Seeley entertained frequently, both local people and guests from out of town. They also joined local organizations. Gertrude and Bertha were members of Eastern Star[19] and the Sunshine Society.[20] At least one year Jim was chairman of the Chesapeake City Fire Company annual carnival.[21] With his experience and contacts, the carnivals must have been quite successful. In 1936, Gertie fell ill with pneumonia,[22] and she and Jim began to spend their winters in Florida.[23]

In the mid-1930s, Hilda Taylor was the English instructor and drama coach at the Chesapeake City High School. Jim Adams sometimes helped Miss Taylor with the direction of the plays and occasionally traveled with the troupe when it performed in neighboring towns. Hilda remembers that Jim helped in a quiet, supportive way, without the need for personal recognition.[24] In October 1934, while the Floating Theatre was touring the Eastern Shore of Maryland, Charlie and Beulah, while visiting Jim and Gertie, helped Hilda with her production of *The Sweetest Girl in Dixie*.[25]

Jim died in Chesapeake City on September 2, 1946. He was seventy-two. Gertrude died on September 9, 1952, at the age of seventy-seven. Bertha Seeley died in 1964 when she was eighty-four. Her daughter had preceded her in death in 1957. There are no relatives of the Adamses now living in Maryland.

When Jim died he left Gertrude his net worth of over $100,000, including two stores with dwelling units in Philadelphia, a vacant lot in Los Angeles, two homes and six garages in Chesapeake City, and a 1936 LaSalle sedan. There is no mention in his will of the watch the Jones-Adams com-

pany gave him in 1905 for his thirty-second birthday. There is listed a diamond pin valued at $600, which may have been made from the diamond
locket attached to the watch. The diamond ring McDougall observed in
1916 is listed, valued at $3,000.[26]

When Jim sold the Floating Theatre in 1933, Selba and Clara Adams
went home to Shepherd, Michigan, where they had wintered every year
they were on the showboat. Selba took over a local saloon and renamed it
the Show Boat Inn. The bar was located on Wright Avenue, the main drag
in Shepherd, a block or so from the railroad station. Oil had been discovered near Shepherd a few years before Selba opened his bar, and workers
from the oil fields found the Show Boat Inn a congenial place to relax. The
bar was a large room with a balcony around it for additional tables. Sometimes the crowd got raucous and people fell off the balcony. Hildegarde, the
wife of Selba's son Delmar, served as bouncer.[27]

Selba died in 1943.[28] Clara died in 1951. When Selba died, Hildegarde took over managing the bar because Delmar had had problems with
alcohol and could not have his name on the liquor license.[29]

After Charles Hunter closed his "vaudefilm" show in 1940, he and
Beulah joined Selba and Clara in Shepherd. Charlie worked as bartender
and pianist in the Show Boat Inn. People in Shepherd remember him as an
amiable fellow with a cigarette always dangling from his mouth. One anec-
dote still in circulation in Shepherd suggests that Charlie was still spinning
his yarns. In the story, Charlie came home and discovered an amorous
Swede in Beulah's bedroom. The Swede jumped through the window, leaving his shoes and socks behind.[30]

After Selba died, Charlie and Beulah moved to Saginaw and leased
a grocery store at 800 Mackinaw Street. They lived in the apartment above
the store.[31] In 1948, when a local theatre group produced *Show Boat*, Charlie
and Beulah were featured guests at the opening night.[32]

Charlie died of throat cancer in 1951.[33] Shortly afterward, Beulah
moved into a retirement apartment with her sister Susie. When Beulah died
in 1975,[34] she left her estate of $9,893.77, all in savings certificates,[35] to Susie,
who died in 1979.[36]

According to Rachel Seymoure, Nina Howard lost a great deal of
money operating the Floating Theatre. After its demise, she retired to Florida, where she died many years later. She is buried in Miami.

Milford Seymoure served on submarines in the Navy during World
War II. After the war, Milford and Nina Howard, and her new dog, Pepper,
circled the eastern part of the United States in her yacht, navigating through
the Intracoastal Waterway, the Hudson River, the Great Lakes, and the Mississippi River. Seymoure died in the winter of 1988–89 in Florida.

In 1942, Rachel Seymoure gave birth to a daughter, Rachel Jane
Seymoure. A few months later, she divorced Milford. A number of years

after her divorce, Rachel married Thomas Marsh. In 1991 she was living an active life in St. Michaels, Maryland.

After he left the showboat Pop Neel moved to the Elks' home in Bedford, Virginia.[37] He died on August 20, 1945. He would have been 87 on December 5 of that year.[38] Pop is buried in the Old Hollywood Cemetery in Elizabeth City, North Carolina. "Frank Jones, a fellow Elk and close friend, placed the inscribed marker at his grave."[39]

Daniel Webster Montague ended his years in the Saginaw-Shepherd area. In the 1930s he lived with Selba and his family. Danny ran around with a black man named Milton Sarden who, at six feet eight inches, was as tall as Danny was short. Sarden was known as "Eight Ball," and people suspected that he earned his living from the "rackets." He and Danny had a Henry J automobile plastered with political posters.[40]

Joe Gunn's "epitaph" was written by Al Gough:

> Joe crossed over the Jordan just in time for All Saints' Day 1952. His last years were spent on Gilbert Dorsey's farm, "Somerseat," in Oakville [St. Mary's County, Maryland] . . . Dr. Roy Guyther re-members receiving a call from Gilbert Dorsey: "Old Joe's down," said Gilbert, "look after him and see what you can do, Doc." Dr. Guyther visited him at St. Mary's hospital later that day. Shortly thereafter Joe received a visit from Father William C. Wehrle, S. J., who gave him the sacraments. The sweet chariot carried Joe to that "better land" he had sung of so many times later that evening. Dr. Guyther recounts receiving another call from Gilbert Dorsey the next day: "When I asked you to look after Joe that's not what I had in mind, Doc." Joe died on October 28th; prayers were held on the 31st, followed by his interment at St. John's Church Cemetery, Hollywood [Maryland]. That All Saints' day celebration must have been something. Joe would have started on his harmonica with "Old Black Joe;" the tempo must have picked up, and perhaps the heavens rumbled a little, when he was joined by his friends in "Old Man River."[41]

Marshall Walker set up a song-publishing company in Wichita, Kansas, in 1938,[42] but the next spring he was back into touring with a rep show.[43] Late in 1939, Walker became critically ill while playing in Oklahoma and died in January 1940. He was 53. Walker had experienced early eminence as one of the originators of the tab show. He had moderate success as a writer of songs, including "Somebody's Done Me Wrong," and "Thanks, Lord, for the Little Things," his last song, which he wrote for Al Jolson.[44] His career was at its height in the 1920s and early 1930s. By the time he played on the Floating Theatre, however, it was in decline.

Boob Brasfield suffered through a long illness in 1937 and 1938,[45] but survived to continue his career in show business. From 1942 until he retired in 1958 Boob played with Choate's Comedians in the Midwest.[46] Boob died in 1968 in Raymondville, Texas, at the age of 66.

Seabee Hayworth and Marion, after leaving the Floating Theatre, alternated between running a circle stock out of High Point, North Carolina, and working with various rep companies around the country. In March 1941, Seabee gave up the circle because of ill health brought on by overwork and toured his Pepper Box Revue as a vaudeville unit through Virginia and the Carolinas.[47] An old trouper, on reading of Seabee's illness, wrote to *Billboard* praising the show business veteran:

> Hayworth has forgotten more about tabloid and short-cast dramatic bills than a lot of us younger ones will ever know. I got a wonderful education in two seasons with his show. I have seen him take some meaningless bills and work them into a beautiful story . . . I have for many years watched "SeaBee" work and there was never a finer or funnier toby than he.[48]

Six months later, however, Seabee was back to his old habits of running back and forth between several shows at a time.[49]

L. D. Waldorf, who died in 1977, left the Floating Theatre after 1917 to get married. He lived the rest of his life in Elizabeth City at 708 Raleigh Street. His home was a party center for the showboat people when they were in town. After he left the showboat Waldorf worked as a tax collector, but he was always into music. He had a band; he played piano for the dining room of a local motel; and he gave private music lessons. Waldorf stuttered when he spoke, but not when he sang. While Jim Adams owned the Floating Theatre, Waldorf and his family had free passes to the shows. After Jim sold the boat, Waldorf found the new owners less friendly. After one of the sinkings of the boat, the original bathtub from the Adamses' apartment on board found its way into Waldorf's house.[50]

Thayer Roberts returned to Boob Brasfield's company after leaving the Floating Theatre.[51] Roberts eventually went to New York, where at one point he played with Helen Hayes. He also toured with Tyrone Power, Sr., in a Shakespeare play. Later in his career he moved to Hollywood, where he had roles in the films *Seventh Heaven* and *A Double Life*. He also performed in theatre in Hollywood, including the role of Buffalo Bill in *Annie Get Your Gun*. Roberts died in 1965. In an interview in 1953 he claimed to have "operated his own showboat on the Chesapeake."[52]

Pat Gallagher ran Pat's Showboat Grill in Easton, Maryland, until he suffered a stroke in December 1940. He died in January 1941. His wife, Mickie,

and daughter, Lana Lois, took his body home to Marshall, Illinois, for burial,[53] and Mickie continued operating the grill after Pat's death.

Tom Fearing joined the Navy Air Force and was killed during World War II.[54]

Lloyd "Arkansas Slim" Andrews made five films with Tex Ritter in 1940: *Arizona Frontier, Cowboy from Sundown, The Golden Trail, Pals of the Silver Sage*, and *Rainbow over the Range*. He made at least one more with Tex in 1941—*The Pioneers*—then their careers parted. Slim continued to make Westerns in 1941 and 1942, but his movie career fell into decline. His final films were *Kentucky Jubilee* in 1951, and *Tomahawk Territory* in 1952.

MORE FICTION

Edna Ferber is not the only fiction writer to draw inspiration from the James Adams Floating Theatre.

Hulbert Footner, in the early twenties, most likely 1921[55] (five years before Ferber published *Show Boat*), wrote a novel, *Country Love*, which was set on a fictional version of the Adams Floating Theatre.

Footner was a newspaperman from Canada who settled in Charles County, Maryland, before World War I. He wrote more than fifty books, primarily novels and books about the Chesapeake Bay. His most enduring work is *Rivers of the Eastern Shore* (Tidewater Publishers). Several of Footner's early novels were made into films, and he had one play produced in New York. He died in 1944.[56]

Footner is less faithful to the James Adams Floating Theatre in *Country Love* than Ferber is in *Show Boat*. Footner's story centers on a successful New York actress, Eve Allison, who is unhappy with the nature of her emotional involvement with a powerful New York producer. In reaction, she changes her name, joins the company of the showboat, and hides on the Chesapeake. There she meets and falls in love with Page Brookins, a gentleman from the "Absolom's Island" (Solomons Island) area of the Chesapeake, who helps her give up her big city needs and learn to be happy in the country.

Footner's showboat is the *Thespis*, better known to its patrons as Orlando Jolley's Floating Theatre. Mr. Jolley is a "round little man" who hires his actors in New York, something Adams never did.

Footner's description of the exterior of the showboat is more accurate than his description of the interior, although he has the Floating Theatre painted yellow (it never was), and Jolley up in the pilothouse steering. (This was years before the pilothouse appeared in *Show Boat*.)

One of the most curious descriptions in *Country Love* is the kitchen on the showboat. The kitchen is created, whenever it is needed, on stage, as a practical stage setting. The bedrooms are under the stage, where the galley was on the James Adams.

John Barth, a native of Cambridge, Maryland, published in 1956 his first novel, *The Floating Opera*. The floating opera to which the title refers is an imaginatively exaggerated image of the James Adams Floating Theatre: *"Adam's Original & Unparalleled Floating Opera,* Jacob R. Adam, owner and captain."[57]

In the preface for the 1988 edition of his novel, Barth wrote:

> I used to pore nostalgically over albums of Marylandia by the Balti-
> more photographer A. Aubrey Bodine. In one of them I found
> shots of Captain James Adams's Original Floating Theatre, a tug-
> towed showboat that I remembered having seen as a boy at the
> municipal wharf in my hometown . . . Its portentous name sug-
> gested allegory; I made notes toward a fiction in the form of . . .
> well, a philosophical blackface minstrel show. I had picked up
> from the postwar *Zeitgeist* some sense of the French Existentialist
> writers and had absorbed from my own experience a few routine
> disenchantments. I had imagined myself something of a nihilist—
> but by temperament a smiling nihilist, not the grim-faced kind. I
> would write some sort of nihilist minstrel show.
>
> It turned into a novel, *The Floating Opera,* because I found the
> minstrel-show conceit too artificial to sustain and because, while
> dreaming up a tidewater story of which the showboat might
> serve as climax, I discovered by happy accident the turn-of-the-
> century Brazilian novelist Joaquim Machado de Assis . . .
> Machado's tone and manner, as much as his narrative technics,
> showed me how I might get my disparate gods together on a
> tidewater showboat.[58]

At the climax of Barth's story, his "nihilistic" protagonist, Todd An-drews, a middle-aged lawyer who physically resembles Gregory Peck, de-cides to blow up the Floating Opera. He opens the gas jets in the galley area of the boat and hopes that the real explosion will correspond with the fake explosion at the conclusion of a simulated race on stage between the river steamboats the *Natchez* and the *Robert E. Lee.* For some reason unknown to the protagonist-narrator, the Floating Opera does not blow up. Later An-drews decides, "There is no reason for living (or for suicide),"[59] and con-cludes, "Possibly I would on some future occasion endeavor once again to blow up the Floating Opera, my good neighbors and associates, and/or my mere self; most possibly I would not."[60]

Barth makes no attempt to reproduce the historical Floating Theatre. He uses it as a metaphor and a plot device. The James Adams, of course, was neither lit nor heated by gas, and the entertainment Todd Andrews witnessed on the stage of Barth's Floating Opera—including a one-act com-

edy, recitations from Shakespeare, Barth's version of a minstrel show, and the great steamboat race—were never performed on the James Adams.[61]

Frederick Tilp, in 1978, published *This Was Potomac River*. Tilp presented the self-published book as a factual history. In the book is a Sea Scout's diary purportedly written in July 1931. Twice the diarist reports encountering the James Adams Floating Theatre, first at McGuires Wharf, Nomini Creek,[62] and later at Leonardtown.[63] On the dates cited, however, the Floating Theatre was on the other side of the Bay, at Centreville and St. Michaels.

I was troubled by the discrepancy when I discovered it, but Robert H. Burgess threw some light on the subject for me.

In 1971, Tilp wrote to Burgess complaining about a book, *Run to the Lee*, written by Kenneth F. Brooks. Tilp felt that the book was deceptive. Brooks apparently intended it to be a novel based on facts, but Tilp thought it had been presented as history. The success of the book bothered him, too. He wrote Burgess: "Hear that guy in Calvert County, Kenneth F. Brooks, is writing for Cornell another thriller-diller of a factual sail in old schooners of the Bay. If this guy makes money writing tidewater non-sense—then by damn—I start and really make a killing using every bit of imagination I have and/or can conjure up."[64]

Later, Tilp suggested to Burgess that they do a book together. Burgess would supply the facts, and Tilp would provide the imagination. Burgess rejected the offer.[65]

The Sea Scout diary in *This Was Potomac River*, as it relates to the Floating Theatre, is apparently an example of Tilp's historical fiction. As such, one passage in it is quite interesting: "Adams Floating Theatre is docked at McGuires Wharf (we have to forget the show, as it costs 35 cents each). Store keeper Mr. Pete Allen here is arguing with the Theatre owner to allow the bootleggers to unload their whiskey jugs off the ferry E. T. Somers from Leonardtown, which arrives daily at 10:00 AM, at the same dock."[66]

IN ÆTERNUM

For twenty-seven seasons the Floating Theatre—for nineteen years as the James Adams and for eight years as the Original—toured the cities and rivers of the mid-Atlantic and Southeast. Sometimes it fared well and sometimes it struggled financially, but it was always important culturally to the people it served, expecially those in the small towns of the Chesapeake Bay and Albemarle Sound.

The Floating Theatre followed in the long-established American tradition of itinerant actors, and especially of the uniquely American tradition of the showboat. The James Adams was an integral part of the American repertoire movement of the first half of the twentieth century, a movement that brought live theatre to the small towns and rural areas of the country. When that movement prospered, so did the James Adams. When that movement faltered, so did the James Adams. But the James Adams will always have an important part in the American theatre because of its unique relation to Edna Ferber, her novel *Show Boat*, and the musical and movies based on her book.

Today the James Adams could never be reproduced physically to sail the bays and rivers of the tidewater. It belonged to a simpler time. The changes in American life and the costs of building and operating such an enterprise in today's regulated society keep the Floating Theatre forever aground. But the old "opry barge" sails on in the memories of those who knew and loved it and knew and loved the show folks who sailed with it.

APPENDIX

Itinerary

The routes of the Floating Theatre have been compiled from the "Routes Ahead" section of *Billboard*, from advertisements and notices in local newspapers, from journals and letters, and in rare instances from interviews with local citizens.

A question mark in parentheses [(?)] indicates there is some question about the location or date or both. In a few cases I have projected the route of the Floating Theatre. Projected itinerary is marked by the word "projected" in parentheses.

1914—SEASON 1

JANUARY 1914
    27: Theatre launched, Washington, N.C.
MARCH 1914
    2–7: Washington, N.C.
    9–14: Greenville, N.C.
    16: Washington, N.C.
    17–18: Bath, N.C.
    19–21: Aurora, N.C.
    23–28: Belhaven, N.C.
    30–
APRIL 1914
    –4: Middletown, N. C. (?)
    6–11: Sky Cove, N. C. (?)
    13–18: Elizabeth City, N. C. (projected)
    20–22: South Mills, N. C. (projected)
    23–25: Deep Creek, Va. (projected)
    27–
MAY 1914
    –2: Hampton, Va. (projected)
    4–9: Smithfield, Va. (projected)
    11–16: Crittenden, Va. (projected) Mathews, Va. (?)
    18–23: Irvington, Va
    25–30: Urbanna, Va. (?) Tappahannock, Va. (?) Sharps, Va. (?)

JUNE 1914
    1–6: Reedville, Va.
    8–13: Tangier Island, Va. (?)
    15–20: Onancock , Va.
    22–27: Snow Hill, Md. (?)
    29–
JULY 1914
    –4: Pocomoke City, Md. (?) Saxis, Va. (?)
    6–11: Crisfield, Md.
    13–18: Deal Island, Md.
    20–25: Salisbury, Md.
    27–
AUGUST 1914
    –1: Vienna, Md. (projected)
    3–8: Sharptown, Md. (projected)
    10–15: Seaford, Del. (projected)
    17–22: Laurel, Del. (projected)
    24–29: Honga, Md. (projected)
    31–
SEPTEMBER 1914
    –5: Solomons, Md. (projected)
    7–12: Annapolis, Md.
    14–19: Port Deposit, Md.
    21–26: Elkton, Md.
    28–

OCTOBER 1914
  –3: Georgetown, Md. (projected)
  5–10: Chestertown, Md.
  12–17: Centreville, Md.
  19–24: Queenstown, Md.
  26–31: Rock Hall, Md.
NOVEMBER 1914
  2–7: St. Michaels, Md.
  9–14: Denton, Md.
  16–21: Hillsboro, Md. (?), Greensboro,
    Md. (?), Secretary, Md. (?), Cam-
    bridge, Md. (?)

1915—SEASON 2
Wintered in Elizabeth City, N.C.
JANUARY 1915
  18–23: Elizabeth City , N.C.
  25–30: Elizabeth City, N.C.
FEBRUARY 1915
  1–6: Elizabeth City, N.C.
  8–13: Elizabeth City, N.C.
  15–20: Rehearsing, Elizabeth City, N.C.
  22–26: Rehearsing, Elizabeth City, N.C.
  27: Elizabeth City, N.C.
MARCH 1915
  1–6: Hertford, N.C.
  8–13: Edenton, N.C.
  15–20: Plymouth, N.C.
  22–27: Columbia, N.C.
  29–
APRIL 1915
  –3: Elizabeth City, N.C.
  5–7: South Mills, N.C.
  8–10: Deep Creek, Va.
  12–17: Hampton, Va.
  19–24: Smithfield, Va.
  26–
MAY 1915
  –1: Crittenden, Va.
  3–8: Irvington, Va.
  10–15: Fredericksburg, Va.
  17–19: Port Royal, Va.
  20–22: Tappahannock, Va.
  24–25: Sharps, Va.
  26–29: Urbanna, Va.
  31–

JUNE 1915
  –5: Gwynn's Island, Va.
  7–12: Reedville, Va.
  14–19: Colonial Beach, Va.
  21–26: Kinsale, Va.
  28–
JULY 1915
  –3: Leonardtown, Md.
  5–10: Solomons, Md.
  12–17: Port Deposit, Md.
  19–24: North East, Md.
  26–31: Elkton, Md.
AUGUST 1915
  2–7: Chesapeake City, Md.
  9–14: Georgetown, Md.
  16–21: Chestertown, Md.
  23–28: Crumpton, Md.
  30–
SEPTEMBER 1915
  –4: Centreville, Md.
  6–11: Queenstown, Md.
  13–18: St. Michaels , Md.
  20–25: Stevensville, Md.
  27–
OCTOBER 1915
  –2: Denton, Md.
  4–9: Greensboro, Md.
  11–12: Cambridge, Md.
  13–16: Secretary, Md.
  18–23: Oxford, Md.
  25–27: Sharptown, Md.
  28–30: Vienna, Md.
NOVEMBER 1915
  1–6: Pocomoke City, Md.
  8–13: Onancock, Va.
  22–27: Tied up in Elizabeth City, N.C.
    End of season.

1916—SEASON 3
Wintered in Elizabeth City, N.C.
MARCH 1916
  –4: Elizabeth City, N.C.
  6–11: Hertford, N.C.
  13–18: Edenton, N.C.
  20–25: Columbia, N.C.
  27–

APRIL 1916
 –1: Elizabeth City, N.C.
 3–5: South Mills, N.C.
 6–8: Deep Creek, N.C.
 10–15: Crittenden, Va.
 17–22: Hampton, Va.
 24–29: Smithfield, Va.
MAY 1916
 1–6: West Point, Va.
 8–13: Gloucester Point, Va.
 15–20: Williams Wharf, Va.
 22–27: Urbanna, Va.
 29–
JUNE 1916
 –3: Sharps, Va.
 5–10: Port Royal, Va.
 12–17: Fredericksburg, Va.
 19–24: Tappahannock, Va.
 26–
JULY 1916
 –1: Irvington, Va.
 3–8: Reedville, Va.
 10–15: Nomini, Va.
 17–22: Leonardtown, Md.
 24–29: Port Deposit, Md.
 31–
AUGUST 1916
 –5: North East, Md.
 7–12: Chesapeake City, Md.
 14–19: Georgetown, Md.
 21–26: Betterton, Md.
 28–
SEPTEMBER 1916
 –2: Rock Hall, Md.
 4–9: Crumpton, Md.
 11–16: Centreville, Md.
 18–23: Queenstown, Md.
 25–30: Stevensville, Md.
OCTOBER 1916
 2–7: St. Michaels, Md.
 9–14: Denton, Md.
 16–21: Greensboro, Md.
 23–28: Hillsboro, Md.
 30–
NOVEMBER 1916
 –4: Secretary, Md.
 6–11: Oxford, Md.
 13–18: Onancock, Va.
 20–25: Harborton, Va.

DECEMBER 1916
 2: Tied up in Elizabeth City, N.C. End
 of season.

1917—SEASON 4
Wintered in Elizabeth City, N. C.
MARCH 1917
 9–10: Elizabeth City, N. C.
 11: Hertford, N. C.
 12–17: Hertford, N. C.
 19–24: Edenton, N. C.
 26–31: Columbia, N. C.
APRIL 1917
 2–4: South Mills, N. C.
 5–8: Deep Creek, Va.
 9–14: Smithfield, Va.
 16–21: Crittenden, Va.
 23–28: Gloucester Point, Va.
 30–
MAY 1917
 –5: Williams Wharf, Va.
 7–12: Urbanna, Va.
 14–19: Sharps, Va.
 21–26: Port Royal, Va.
 28–
JUNE 1917
 –2: Fredericksburg, Va.
 4–9: Tappahannock, Va.
 11–16: Kilmarnock, Va.
 18–23: Harborton, Va.
 25–30: Onancock, Va.
JULY 1917
 2–7: Reedville, Va.
 9–14: Lodge, Va.
 16–21: Mt. Holly, Va.
 23–28: Leonardtown, Md.
 30–
AUGUST 1917
 –4: Baltimore, Md. For repairs only. No
 performance.
 6–11: Port Deposit, Md.
 13–18: North East, Md.
 20–25: Elkton, Md.
 27–

SEPTEMBER 1917
–1: Chesapeake City, Md.
3–8: Georgetown, Md.
10–15: Rock Hall, Md.
17: Chestertown, for the night. No performance.
18–22: Crumpton, Md.
24–29: Chestertown, Md.
OCTOBER 1917
1–6: Centreville, Md.
8–13: Queenstown, Md.
15–20: Stevensville, Md.
22–27: St. Michaels, Md.
29–
NOVEMBER 1917
–3: Denton, Md.
5–10: Greensboro, Md.
12–17: Hillsboro, Md.
19–24: Oxford, Md.
DECEMBER 1917
3: Tied up in Elizabeth City, N.C. End of season.

1918—SEASON 5
Wintered in Elizabeth City, N.C.
MARCH 1918
8–9: Elizabeth City, N.C.
11–16: Hertford, N.C.
18–23: Edenton, N.C.
25–30: Columbia, N.C.
APRIL 1918
1–3: South Mills, N.C.
4–6: Deep Creek, Va.
8–13: Smithfield, Va.
15–20: Crittenden, Va.
22–27: Hampton, Va.
29–
MAY 1918
–4: Langley Army Air Force Base, Va.
6–11: Williams Wharf, Va.
13–18: Urbanna, Va.
20–25: Sharps, Va.
27–
JUNE 1918
–1: Port Royal, Va.
3–8: Fredericksburg, Va.
10–15: Tappahannock, Va.
17–22: Kilmarnock, Va.
24–29: Reedville, Va.

JULY 1918
1–6: Harborton, Va.
8–13: Onancock, Va.
15–20: Lodge, Va.
22–27: Leonardtown, Md.
29–
AUGUST 1918
–3: Port Deposit, Md.
5–10: Port Deposit, Md. The theatre stalled here, possibly for a cast change.
12–17: Port Deposit, Md.
19–24: North East, Md.
26–31: Elkton, Md.
SEPTEMBER 1918
2–7: Chesapeake City, Md. (?)
9–14: Georgetown, Md.
16–21: Rock Hall, Md. (?)
23–28: Crumpton, Md.
30–
OCTOBER 1918
–5: Chestertown, Md.
7–12: Queenstown, Md.
14–19: Stevensville, Md.
21–26: St. Michaels, Md.
28–
NOVEMBER 1918
–2: Baltimore, Md. For repairs only. No performance.

1919—SEASON 6
Wintered in Elkton, Md.
MARCH 1919
17–22: Elkton, Md.
24–29: Chesapeake City, Md.
31–
APRIL 1919
–5: North East, Md.
7–12: Port Deposit, Md.
14–19: Havre de Grace, Md.
21–26: Port Deposit, Md.
28–
MAY 1919
–3: Georgetown, Md.
6–10: Centreville, Md.
12–17: Crumpton, Md.
19–24: Chestertown, Md.
26–31: Queenstown, Md.

JUNE 1919
2–7: Stevensville, Md.
9–14: St. Michaels, Md.
16–21: Easton Point, Md.
23–28: Oxford, Md.
30–
JULY 1919
–5: Solomons, Md.
7–12: Leonardtown, Md.
14–19: Kinsale, Va.
21–26: Lodge, Va.
28–
AUGUST 1919
–2: Reedville, Va.
4–9: Onancock, Va. (?)
11–16: Harborton, Va.
18–23: Wardtown, Va.
25–30: Kilmarnock, Va.
SEPTEMBER 1919
1–6: Morattico, Va.
8–13: Scheduled visit to Totuskey
Bridge, Warsaw, Va., is cancelled.
Boat rerouted to Norfolk for dry
dock.
15–20: Norfolk, Va., for repairs. No performances.
29–
OCTOBER 1919
–4: Crittenden, Va.
6–11: Deep Creek, Va., Season ended
early because of death of Rose
Adams.
13–18: Crittenden, Va. Boat moored.
NOVEMBER 1919
24–29: Showboat towed to Elizabeth
City, N.C.

1920—SEASON 7
Wintered in Elizabeth City, N.C.
MARCH 1920
13: Elizabeth City, N.C.
15–20: Hertford, N.C.
22–27: Edenton, N.C.
29–
APRIL 1920
–3: Columbia, N.C.
5–10: Elizabeth City, N.C.
12–17: Deep Creek, Va.
19–24: Crittenden, Va.
26–

MAY 1920
–1: Smithfield, Va.
3–8: Hampton, Va.
10–15: Williams Wharf, Va.
17–22: Urbanna, Va.
24–29: Tappahannock, Va.
31–
JUNE 1920
–5: Weems, Va.
7–12: Kilmarnock, Va.
14–19: Wardtown, Va.
21–26: Harborton, Va.
28–
JULY 1920
–3: Onancock, Va.
5–10: Reedville, Va.
12–17: Mt. Holly (McGuire's Wharf),
Va.
19–24: Leonardtown, Md.
26–31: Lodge, Va.
AUGUST 1920
2–7: Wynne (Benedict Smiths), Md.
9–14: Solomons, Md.
16–21: Port Deposit, Md.
23–28: Havre de Grace, Md.
30–
SEPTEMBER 1920
–4: North East, Md.
6–11: Elkton, Md.
13–18: Chesapeake City, Md.
20–25: Georgetown, Md.
27–
OCTOBER 1920
–2: Centreville, Md.
4–9: Crumpton, Md. (?)
11–16: Chestertown, Md. (?)
18–23: Queenstown, Md. (?) Stevensville, Md. (?)
25–30: Rock Hall, Md. (?)
NOVEMBER 1920
1–6: St. Michaels, Md.
8–13: Easton Point, Md.
15–20: Denton, Md.
22–27: Greensboro, Md.
29: Oxford, Md.

1921—SEASON 8
Wintered in Oxford, Md.
MARCH 1921
  21–26: Oxford, Md. (?)
  28–30: Trappe, Md.
APRIL 1921
  1–2: Secretary, Md.
  4–9: Greensboro, Md.
  11–16: Denton, Md.
  18–23: Oxford, Md.
  25–30: St. Michaels, Md.
MAY 1921
  2–7: Stevensville, Md.
  9–14: Chestertown, Md.
  16–21: Crumpton, Md.
  23–28: Centreville, Md.
  30–
JUNE 1921
  –1: Rock Hall, Md. (?)
  2–4: Queenstown, Md.
  6–11: Port Deposit, Md.
  13–18: North East, Md.
  20–25: Elkton, Md.
  27–
JULY 1921
  –2: Chesapeake City, Md.
  4–9: Georgetown, Md.
  11–16: Solomons, Md.
  18–23: Leonardtown, Md.
  25–30: Mt. Holly, Va.
AUGUST 1921
  1–6: Lodge, Va.
  8–13: Reedville, Va.
  15–20: Harborton, Va. (?)
  22–27: Onancock, Va.
  29–
SEPTEMBER 1921
  –3: Wardtown, Va.
  5–10: Kilmarnock, Va.
  12–17: Warsaw (Totuskey Bridge), Va.
  19–24: Tappahannock, Va.
  26–
OCTOBER 1921
  –1: Port Royal, Va.
  3–8: Urbanna, Va.
  10–15: Mathews, Va.
  17–22: Gloucester, Va.
  24–29: Crittenden, Va.
  31–

NOVEMBER 1921
  –5: Smithfield, Va.
  7–12: Deep Creek, Va. (?) South Mills,
    N.C. (?)
  14–19: Elizabeth City, N. C.
  21–26: Manteo, N. C. (?) Hertford,
    N. C. (?)
  28–
DECEMBER 1921
  –3: Edenton, N. C. (?) Hertford, N. C.
    (?)
  5–10: Columbia, N. C. (?) Edenton,
    N.C. (?)
  12–17: Edenton, N. C. (?)

1922—SEASON 9
Wintered in Elizabeth City, N. C.
MARCH 1922
  19: Rehearsals start.
APRIL 1922
  3–8: Colerain, N. C.
  10–15: Murfreesboro, N. C.
  17–22: Winton, N. C.
  24–29: Gatesville, N. C. (?) Windsor,
    N. C. (?)
MAY 1922
  1–6: Plymouth, N. C.
  8–13: Edenton, N. C.
  15–20: Columbia, N. C.
  22–27: Elizabeth City, N. C.
  29–31: South Mills, N. C.
JUNE 1922
  1–3: Deep Creek, Va.
  5–10: Smithfield, Va.
  12–17: Smithfield, Va. (?)
  19–24: Lady, Va.
  26–
JULY 1922
  –1: Williams Wharf, Va.
  3–8: Urbanna, Va.
  10–15: Tappahannock, Va.
  17–22: Port Royal, Va.
  24–29: Sharps, Va.
  31–
AUGUST 1922
  –5: Kilmarnock, Va.
  7–12: Wardtown, Va.
  14–19: Harborton, Va.
  21–26: Onancock, Va.
  28–

SEPTEMBER 1922
 –2: Reedville, Va.
 4–9: Nomini (McGuire's Wharf), Va.
 11–16: Lodge, Va.
 18–23: Leonardtown (Foxwell's Point),
  Md.
 25–30: Solomons, Md.
OCTOBER 1922
 2–7: St. Michaels, Md.
 9–14: Stevensville, Md.
 16–21: Centreville, Md.
 23–28: Crumpton, Md.
 30–
NOVEMBER 1922
 –4: Chestertown, Md.
 6–11: Rock Hall, Md.
 13–18: Georgetown, Md.
 20–25: North East, Md.
 27–
DECEMBER 1922
 –2: Elkton, Md.

1923—SEASON 10
Wintered in Elkton, Md.
MARCH 1923
 26: Rehearsals begin.
APRIL 1923
 16–21: Chesapeake City, Md.
 23–28: Elkton, Md.
 30–
MAY 1923
 –5: North East, Md.
 7–12: Port Deposit, Md.
 14–19: Rock Hall, Md.
 21–26: Chestertown, Md.
 28–
JUNE 1923
 –2: Centreville , Md.
 4–9: Stevensville, Md.
 11–16: St. Michaels, Md.
 18–23: Oxford, Md.
 25–30: Solomons, Md.
JULY 1923
 2–7: Leonardtown (Foxwell's Point),
  Md.
 9–14: Mt. Holly, Va.
 16–21: Bundicks, Va.
 23–28: Reedville, Va.
 30–

AUGUST 1923
 –4: Onancock, Va.
 6–11: Harborton, Va.
 13–18: Kilmarnock, Va.
 20–25: Tappahannock, Va.
 27–
SEPTEMBER 1923
 –1: Urbanna, Va.
 3–8: Williams Wharf, Va.
 10–15: Glass, Va.
 17–22: Crittenden, Va.
 24–29: Smithfield, Va.
OCTOBER 1923
 1–6: Elizabeth City, N. C.
 8–13: Columbia, N. C.
 15–20: Plymouth, N. C.
 22–27: Williamston, N. C.
 29–
NOVEMBER 1923
 –3: Colerain, N. C.
 5–10: Murfreesboro, N. C.
 12–17: Winton, N. C.
 19–24: Edenton, N. C.
 26–
DECEMBER 1923
 –1: Hertford, N. C.

1924—SEASON 11
Wintered in Elizabeth City, N. C.
MARCH 1924
 17: Rehearsals begin.
APRIL 1924
 7–12: Plymouth, N. C.
 14–19: Winton, N. C.
 21–26: Murfreesboro, N. C.
 28–
MAY 1924
 –3: Tyner, N. C. (?) Franklin, Va. (?)
 5–10: Colerain, N. C.
 12–17: Hertford, N. C.
 19–24: Elizabeth City, N. C.
 26–28: South Mills, N. C.
 29–31: Deep Creek, Va.
JUNE 1924
 2–7: Smithfield, Va.
 9–14: Crittenden, Va.
 16–21: Glass, Va.
 23–28: Williams Wharf, Va.
 30–

JULY 1924
 –5: Urbanna, Va.
 7–12: Port Royal, Va.
 14–19: Tappahannock, Va.
 21–26: Kilmarnock, Va.
 28–
AUGUST 1924
 –2: Bundicks, Va.
 4–9: Mt. Holly, Va.
 11–16: Leonardtown, Md.
 18–23: Solomons, Md.
 25–30: Honga, Md. (?)
SEPTEMBER 1924
 1–6: Oxford, Md.
 8–13: St. Michaels, Md.
 15–20: Stevensville, Md. (?) Easton,
  Md. (?)
 22–27: Chestertown, Md.
 29–
OCTOBER 1924
 –4: Crumpton, Md.
 6–11: Queenstown, Md.
 13–18: Rock Hall, Md.
 20–25: Georgetown, Md.
 27–
NOVEMBER 1924
 –1: North East, Md.
 3–8: Port Deposit, Md.
 10–15: Chesapeake City, Md.
 17–22: Elkton, Md.

1925—SEASON 12
Wintered in Elizabeth City, N. C.
APRIL 1925
 –4: (4) Elizabeth City, N. C.
 6–11: Aurora, N. C. (?)
 16–18: Bath, N. C. (?)
 20–25: Belhaven, N. C.
 27–
MAY 1925
 –2: Washington, N. C.
 4–9: Oriental, N. C. (?)
 11–16: Vandemere, N. C.
 18–23: Swan Quarter, N. C.
 25–30: Columbia, N. C.
JUNE 1925
 8–13: Plymouth, N. C.
 15–20: Winton, N. C.
 22–27: Murfreesboro, N. C.
 29–

JULY 1925
 –4: Colerain, N. C.
 6–11: Edenton, N. C. (?)
 13–18: Hertford, N. C.
 20–25: Elizabeth City, N. C.
 27–29: South Mills, N. C.
 30–
AUGUST 1925
 –1: Deep Creek, Va, (?) South Mills,
  N. C. (?)
 3–8: Deep Creek , Va. (?) Smithfield,
  Va. (?)
 10–15: Glass, Va.
 17–22: Williams Wharf, Va.
 24–29: Urbanna, Va. (?) Cricket Hill,
  Va. (?)
 31–
SEPTEMBER 1925
 –5: Tappahannock, Va.
 7–12: Port Royal, Va.
 14–19: Kilmarnock, Va.
 21–26: Bundicks, Va.
 28–
OCTOBER 1925
 –3: Mt. Holly, Va.
 5–10: Leonardtown, Md.
 12–17: Solomons, Md.
 19–24: St. Michaels, Md.
 26–31: Chester, Md.
NOVEMBER 1925
 2–7: Chestertown, Md.
 9–14: Crumpton, Md.
 16–21: Centreville, Md.
 23–28: Oxford, Md.

1926—SEASON 13
Wintered in Crittenden, Va. Boat repaired.
MARCH 1926
 15: Rehearsals begin in Elizabeth City,
  N. C.
 22–27: Elizabeth City, N. C.
 29–
APRIL 1926
 –3: Coinjock, N. C.
 5–10: Columbia, N. C.
 12–17: Plymouth, N. C.
 20–24: Winton, N. C.
 26–

MAY 1926
- −1: Murfreesboro, N. C.
- 3–8: Colerain, N. C.
- 10–15: Edenton, N. C.
- 17–22: Hertford, N. C.
- 24–29: Elizabeth City, N. C.
- 31–

JUNE 1926
- −2: South Mills, N. C.
- 3–5: Deep Creek, Va.
- 7–12: Smithfield, Va.
- 14–19: Crittenden, Va.
- 21–26: Glass, Va.
- 28–

JULY 1926
- −3: Williams Wharf, Va.
- 5–10: Urbanna, Va.
- 12–17: Port Royal, Va.
- 19–24: Tappahannock, Va.
- 26–31: Kilmarnock, Va.

AUGUST 1926
- 2–7: Reedville, Va.
- 9–14: Bundicks, Va.
- 16–21: Mt. Holly, Va.
- 23–28: Leonardtown, Md.
- 30–

SEPTEMBER 1926
- −4: Solomons, Md.
- 7–11: Oxford, Md.
- 13–18: St. Michaels, Md.
- 20–25: Queenstown, Md.
- 27–

OCTOBER 1926
- −2: Crumpton, Md.
- 4–9: Chestertown, Md.
- 11–16: Centreville, Md.
- 18–23: Rock Hall, Md.
- 25–30: Georgetown, Md.

NOVEMBER 1926
- 1–6: Port Deposit, Md.
- 8–13: Chesapeake City, Md.
- 15–20: Elkton, Md. (?)

1927—SEASON 14
Wintered in Crittenden, Va.
MARCH 1927
- 21: Left Crittenden, Va., for Elizabeth City, N. C.

APRIL 1927
- 9: Elizabeth City, N. C.
- 11–16: Coinjock, N. C.
- 18–23: Columbia, N. C. (?)
- 25–30: Plymouth, N. C.

MAY 1927
- 2–7: Murfreesboro, N. C.
- 9–14: Winton, N. C.
- 16–21: Colerain, N. C.
- 23–28: Edenton, N. C.
- 30–

JUNE 1927
- −4: Hertford, N. C.
- 6–11: Elizabeth City, N. C.
- 13–18: Deep Creek, Va.
- 20–25: Glass, Va.
- 27–

JULY 1927
- −2: Williams Wharf, Va.
- 4–9: Urbanna, Va.
- 11–16: Port Royal, Va.
- 18–23: Fredericksburg, Va.
- 25–30: Tappahannock, Va.

AUGUST 1927
- 1–6: Kilmarnock, Va.
- 8–13: Reedville, Va.
- 16–21: Bundicks, Va.
- 22–27: Mt. Holly, Va.
- 29–

SEPTEMBER 1927
- −3: Leonardtown, Md.
- 5–10 Solomons, Md.
- 12–17: Oxford, Md.
- 19–24: Easton, Md.
- 26–

OCTOBER 1927
- −1: St. Michaels, Md.
- 3–8: Rock Hall, Md.
- 10–15: Centreville, Md.
- 17–22: Crumpton, Md.
- 24–29: Chestertown, Md.
- 31–

NOVEMBER 1927
- −5: Queenstown, Md. Season ends.
- 24–26: Showboat founders off Thimble Shoals, Va.
- 26: Towed to Norfolk, Va.

1928—SEASON 15
Wintered in Elizabeth City, N. C. Boat
   rebuilt.
APRIL 1928
   7: Elizabeth City, N. C.
   9–14: Elizabeth City, N. C.
   16–21: Hertford, N. C.
   23–28: Colerain, N. C.
   30–
MAY 1928
   –5: Murfreesboro, N. C.
   7–12: Winton, N. C.
   14–19: Plymouth, N. C.
   21–26: Edenton, N. C.
   28–
JUNE 1928
   –2: Columbia, N. C.
   4–9: Coinjock, N. C.
   11–16: Great Bridge, Va.
   18–23: Glass, Va.
   25–30: Williams Wharf, Va.
JULY 1928
   2–7: Urbanna, Va.
   9–14: Port Royal, Va.
   16–21: Fredericksburg, Va.
   23–28: Tappahannock, Va.
   30–
AUGUST 1928
   –4: Kilmarnock, Va.
   6–11: Reedville, Va.
   13–18: Bundicks, Va.
   20–25: Mt. Holly, Va.
   27–
SEPTEMBER 1928
   –1: Leonardtown, Md.
   3–8: Wynne, Md.
   10–15: Solomons, Md.
   17–22: Rock Hall, Md.
   24–29: Queenstown, Md.
OCTOBER 1928
   1–6: Chestertown, Md.
   8–13: Crumpton, Md.
   15–20: Centreville, Md.
   22–27: St. Michaels, Md.
   29–

NOVEMBER 1928
   –3: Easton, Md.
   5–10: Oxford, Md.
   12–17: Deal Island, Md. (?) Fishing
      Creek, Md. (?)
   19–24: Crisfield, Md.
   26–
DECEMBER 1928
   –1: Onancock, Va.
   3–8: Harborton, Va.

1929—SEASON 16
Wintered in Elizabeth City, N. C.
APRIL 1929
   1–6: Elizabeth City, N. C.
   8–13: Coinjock, N. C.
   15–20: Columbia, N. C.
   22–27: Plymouth, N. C.
   29–
MAY 1929
   –4: Windsor, N. C. (?) Williamston,
      N. C. (?)
   6–11: Murfreesboro, N. C.
   13–18: Winton, N. C.
   20–25: Edenton, N. C.
   27–
JUNE 1929
   –1: Hertford, N. C.
   3–8: Crittenden, Va.
   10–15: Glass, Va.
   17–22: Williams Wharf, Va.
   24–29: Urbanna, Va.
JULY 1929
   1–6: Port Royal, Va.
   8–13: Fredericksburg, Va.
   15–20: Tappahannock, Va.
   22–27: Kilmarnock, Va.
   29–
AUGUST 1929
   –3: Reedville, Va.
   5–10: Bundicks, Va.
   12–17: Mt. Holly, Va.
   19–24: Leonardtown, Md.
   26–31: Wynne, Md.
SEPTEMBER 1929
   2–7: Solomons , Md.
   9–14: Galesville, Md.
   16–21: St. Michaels, Md.
   23–28: Rock Hall, Md.
   30–

OCTOBER 1929
-5: Centreville, Md.
7–12: Crumpton, Md.
14–19: Chestertown, Md.
21–26: Queenstown, Md.
28–

NOVEMBER 1929
-2: Easton, Md.
4–9: Cambridge, Md. Season ends.
16: Showboat sinks in Dismal Swamp.
21: Towed to Elizabeth City, N. C.

1930—SEASON 17
Wintered in Elizabeth City, N. C. Boat
repaired.

MARCH 1930
24–29 Elizabeth City, N. C. Rehearsals
begin.
31–

APRIL 1930
-5: Elizabeth City, N. C.
7–12: Coinjock, N. C.
11–19: Manteo, N. C.
21–26: Columbia, N. C.
28–

MAY 1930
-3: Plymouth, N. C.
5–10: Murfreesboro, N. C.
12–17: Winton, N. C.
19–24: Edenton, N. C. (?) Franklin, Va.
(?)
26–31: Hertford, N. C. (?) Edenton,
N. C. (?)

JUNE 1930
2–4: South Mills, N. C.
5–7: Deep Creek, Va.
9–14: Glass, Va.
16–21: Williams Wharf, Va.
23–28: Urbanna, Va.
30–

JULY 1930
-5: Port Royal, Va.
7–12: Fredericksburg, Va.
14–19: Tappahannock, Va.
21–26: Bertrand, Va.
28–

AUGUST 1930
-2: Kilmarnock, Va.
4–9: Reedville, Va.
11–16: Bundicks, Va.
18–23: Mt. Holly, Va.
25–30: Leonardtown, Md.
31: Leonardtown, Md. Benefit for fire
department.

SEPTEMBER 1930
1–6: Wynne, Md.
8–13: Solomons, Md.
15–20: Galesville, Md.
22–27: Annapolis, Md.
29–

OCTOBER 1930
-4: Stevensville, Md.
6–11: Rock Hall, Md.
13–18: Centreville, Md.
20–25: Crumpton, Md.
27–

NOVEMBER 1930
-1: Chestertown, Md.
3–8: St. Michaels, Md.
10–15: Cambridge, Md.
21: Washington, D. C.
24–30: Alexandria, Va.

DECEMBER 1930
1–6: Alexandria, Va.
8–13: Alexandria, Va.
15–20: Alexandria, Va.

1931—SEASON 18
Wintered in Alexandria, Va.

APRIL 1931
20–25: Alexandria, Va. Rehearsals
begin.
27–

MAY 1931
-2: Leonardtown, Md.
4–9: Mt. Holly, Va.
11–16: Bundicks, Va.
18–23: Wynne, Md.
25–30: Solomons, Md.

JUNE 1931
1–6: Galesville, Md.
8–13: Annapolis, Md.
18–20: Chesapeake City, Md.
22–27: North East, Md.
29–

JULY 1931
  –4: Rock Hall, Md.
  6–11: Chestertown, Md.
  13–18: Centreville, Md.
  20–25: St. Michaels, Md.
  27–
AUGUST 1931
  –1: Mayo, Md.
  3–8: Solomons, Md.
  10–15: Leonardtown, Md.
  17–22: Kinsale, Va.
  24–29: Reedville, Va.
  31–
SEPTEMBER 1931
  –5: Kilmarnock, Va.
  7–12: Tappahannock, Va.
  15–19: Fredericksburg, Va.
  21–26: Port Royal, Va.
  28–
OCTOBER 1931
  –3: Urbanna, Va.
  5–10: Williams Wharf, Va.
  12–17: Glass, Va.
  19–24: Coinjock, N. C.
  26–31: Manteo, N. C.
NOVEMBER 1931
  2–7: Columbia, N. C., scheduled. Per-
    formances cancelled.
  2–7: Elizabeth City, N. C. Season ends.

1932—SEASON 19
Wintered in Elizabeth City, N. C.
MAY 1932
  12–14: Elizabeth City, N. C.
  16–18: South Mills, N. C.
  20–21: Deep Creek, Va.
  23–28: Norfolk, Va.
  30–
JUNE 1932
  –4: Norfolk, Va.
  6–11: Norfolk, Va.
  13–18: Norfolk , Va.
  20–25: Suffolk, Va.
  27–
JULY 1932
  –2: Gloucester Point, Va.
  4–9: Williams Wharf, Va.
  11–16: Urbanna, Va.
  18–23: Tappahannock, Va.
  25–30: Irvington, Va.

AUGUST 1932
  1–6: Reedville, Va.
  8–13: Mt. Holly, Va.
  15–20: Leonardtown, Md.
  22–27: Solomons, Md.
  29–
SEPTEMBER 1932
  –3: Galesville, Md.
  5–10: St. Michaels, Md.
  12–17: North East, Md.
  18: Chesapeake City, Md. Sacred con-
    cert.
  19–24: Chesapeake City, Md.
  26–
OCTOBER 1932
  –1: Delaware City, Del.
  3–8: Camden, N. J.
  10–15: Camden, N. J.
  17–22: Camden, N. J.
  24–29: Wilmington, Del.
  31–
NOVEMBER 1932
  –5: Wilmington, Del.
  7–12: Wilmington, Del.
  14–19: Wilmington, Del.

1933—SEASON 20
Wintered in Chesapeake City, Md.
MAY 1933
  15–20: Boat sold.
  24: Bohemia River, Md. Benton estate.
JUNE 1933
  6: Baltimore, Md. For repairs. No per-
    formances.
  12–17: Galesville, Md.
  19–24: St. Michaels, Md.
  26–
JULY 1933
  –1: Solomons, Md.
  3–8: Leonardtown, Md.
  10–15: Alliton's Wharf, Va.
  17–22: Kinsale, Va.
  24–29: Reedville, Va.
  31–
AUGUST 1933
  –5: Urbanna, Va.
  7–12: Tappahannock, Va.
  14–19: Irvington, Va.
  21–26: Cricket Hill, Va.
  22: Hurricane hit.
  28–

SEPTEMBER 1933
    –2: Cricket Hill, Va. Delayed by hurri-
        cane.
    4–9: Gloucester Point, Va.
    11–16: Smithfield, Va.
    18–23: Hopewell, Va.
    25–30: Hopewell, Va
OCTOBER 1933
    2–7: Portsmouth, Va.
    9–14: Coinjock, N. C.
    16–21: Elizabeth City, N. C.
    23–28: Manteo, N. C.
    30–
NOVEMBER 1933
    –4: Plymouth, N. C.
    6–11: Williamston, N. C.
    13–18: Columbia, N. C.
    20–25: Belhaven, N. C.
    27–
DECEMBER 1933
    –2: Washington, N. C. (?) Bath, N. C.
        (?)
    4–9: New Bern, N. C.
    11–16: Beaufort, N. C.
    18–23: Swansboro, N. C.
    25–31: Wilmington, N. C.

                1934—SEASON 21
JANUARY 1934
    1–27: Wilmington, N. C.
FEBRUARY 1934
    Wintered in Wilmington, N. C.
APRIL 1934
    2–7: Wilmington, N. C.
    9–14: Wilmington, N. C.
    16–21: Wilmington, N. C.
    23–28: Beaufort, N. C.
    30–
MAY 1934
    –5: Belhaven, N. C.
    7–12: Manteo, N. C.
    14–19: Elizabeth City, N. C.
    21–26: Smithfield, Va.
    28–
JUNE 1934
    –2: Hopewell, Va.
    4–9: Hopewell, Va.
    11–16: Gloucester Point, Va.
    18–23: Onancock, Va.
    25–30: Pocomoke City, Md.

JULY 1934
    2–7: Laurel, Del.
    9–14: Reedville, Va.
    16–21: Urbanna, Va.
    23–28: Tappahannock, Va.
    30–
AUGUST 1934
    –4: Port Royal, Va.
    6–11: Irvington, Va.
    13–18: Kinsale, Va.
    20–25: Leonardtown, Md.
    27–
SEPTEMBER 1934
    –1: Solomons, Md.
    3–8: Galesville, Md.
    10–15: Chesapeake City, Md.
    17–22: Crumpton, Md.
    24–29: Centreville, Md.
OCTOBER 1934
    1–6: St. Michaels, Md.
    8–13: Denton, Md.
    15–20: Secretary, Md.
    22–27: Easton, Md.
    30–
NOVEMBER 1934
    –3: Salisbury, Md.
    5–10: Harborton, Va.
    12–17: Cape Charles, Va.

                1935—SEASON 22
    Wintered in St. Michaels, Md.
APRIL 1935
    24: Baltimore, Md. (?) For repairs. No
        performances.
MAY 1935
    6–11: Onancock, Va.
    13–18: Cape Charles , Va.
    20–25: Smithfield, Va.
    27–
JUNE 1935
    –1: Gloucester Point, Va.
    3–8: Cricket Hill, Va.
    10–15: Urbanna, Va.
    17–22: Port Royal, Va.
    24–29: Fredericksburg, Va.
JULY 1935
    1–6: Tappahannock,Va.
    8–13: Irvington, Va.
    15–20: Reedville, Va.
    22–27: Leonardtown, Md.
    29–

AUGUST 1935
    –3: Kinsale, Va.
    5–10: Solomons, Md.
    12–17: Galesville, Md.
    19–24: North East, Md.
    26–31: Centreville, Md.
SEPTEMBER 1935
    2–7: Chesapeake City, Md.
    9–14: Crumpton, Md.
    16–21: St. Michaels, Md.
    23–28: Denton, Md.
    30–
OCTOBER 1935
    –5: Secretary, Md.
    7–12: Easton Point, Md.
    14–19: Cambridge, Md.
    21–26: Coinjock, N. C.
    28–
NOVEMBER 1935
    –2: Manteo, N. C.
    4–9: Elizabeth City, N. C.
    11–16: Colerain, N. C.
    18–23: Plymouth, N. C.
    25–30: Columbia, N. C.
DECEMBER 1935
    2–7: Belhaven, N. C.
    9–14: Washington, N. C.
    16–21: Engelhard, N. C.
    23–28: Swansboro, N. C.
    31–

1936—SEASON 23
JANUARY 1936
    –3: Wilmington, N. C.
    5–9: Wilmington, N. C.
    11: Wilmington, N.C.
FEBRUARY 1936
    Wintered in Wilmington, N. C.
MAY 1936
    4–9: Swansboro, N. C.
    11–16: Belhaven, N. C.
    18–23: Colerain, N. C.
    25–30: Elizabeth City, N. C.
JUNE 1936
    1–6: Smithfield, Va.
    8–13: Gloucester Point, Va.
    15–20: Cricket Hill, Va.
    22–27: Urbanna, Va.
    29–

JULY 1936
    –4: Tappahannock, Va.
    6–11: Fredericksburg, Va.
    13–18: Irvington, Va.
    20–25: Reedville, Va.
    27–
AUGUST 1936
    –1: Leonardtown, Md.
    3–8: Colonial Beach, Va.
    10–15: Kinsale, Va.
    17–22: Solomons, Md.
    24–29: Galesville, Md.
    31–
SEPTEMBER 1936
    –2: Baltimore, Md. For repairs. No per-
        formances.
    3–5: Green Haven, Md.
    7– 12: North East, Md.
    14–19: Chesapeake City, Md.
    21–26: Crumpton, Md.
    28–
OCTOBER 1936
    –3: Centreville, Md.
    5–10: St. Michaels, Md.
    12–17: Denton, Md.
    19–24: Easton Point, Md.
    26–31: Cambridge, Md.
NOVEMBER 1936
    2–7: Onancock, Va.
    9–14: Traveling through N. C.
    16–21: Little River, S. C.
    23–28: Conway, S. C.
    30–
DECEMBER 1936
    –5: Georgetown, S. C.
    7–12: Yonges Island, S. C.
    14–19: Beaufort, S. C.
    21–26: Savannah, Ga.
    28–

1937—SEASON 24
JANUARY 1937
    –2: Isle of Hope Resort, Ga.
    11–16: Merritt, Fla.
    18–23: St. Mary's, Ga.
    25–30: Brunswick, Ga. (?)

FEBRUARY 1937
1–3: Darien, Ga. End of season.
11: Charleston, S. C. Moored. No performances.
19: Elizabeth City, N. C. Boat arrives from South.
MARCH 1937
Wintered in Elizabeth City, N. C.
APRIL 1937
12–17: Rehearsals begin.
26–
MAY 1937
–1: Manteo, N. C.
3–8: Colerain, N. C.
10–15: Plymouth, N. C.
17–22: Windsor, N. C.
24–29: Elizabeth City, N. C.
31–
JUNE 1937
–5: Deep Creek, Va.
7–12: Suffolk, Va.
14–19: Smithfield, Va.
21–26: Hopewell, Va.
28–
JULY 1937
–3: Gloucester Point, Va.
5–11: Deltaville, Va.
12–17: Irvington, Va.
19–24: Tappahannock, Va.
26–31: Reedville, Va.
AUGUST 1937
2–7: Potomac Beach, Va.
9–14: Kinsale, Va.
16–21: Solomons, Md.
23–28: Galesville, Md.
SEPTEMBER 1937
30–4: Green Haven, Md.
6–11: North East, Md.
20–25: Centreville, Md.
27 –
OCTOBER 1937
–2: Havre de Grace, Md.
4–9: Crumpton, Md.
11–16: Grasonville, Md.
18–23: St. Michaels, Md.
25–30: Greensboro, Md.
NOVEMBER 1937
1–6: Easton, Md.
8–13: Cambridge, Md.

1938—SEASON 25
Wintered in St. Michaels, Md.
APRIL 1938
11–16: St. Michaels, Md. Rehearsing.
22–23: St. Michaels, Md.
25–26: Tilghman, Md.
MAY 1938
9–14: Deep Creek, Va.
16–21: Hopewell, Va.
23–28: Gloucester Point, Va.
30–
JUNE 1938
–4: Cricket Hill, Va.
6–11: Irvington, Va.
13–18: Fredericksburg, Va.
20–25: Urbanna, Va.
27–
JULY 1938
–2: Tappahannock, Va.
4–9: Reedville, Va.
11–16: Nomini, Va. (?) Colonial Beach, Va. (?) Potomac Beach, Va. (?)
18–23: Kinsale, Va.
25–30: Compton (Hazel's Wharf), Md.
AUGUST 1938
22–27: Centreville, Md.
29–
SEPTEMBER 1938
–3: Annapolis, Md.
5–10: St. Michaels, Md.
12–17: Crumpton, Md.
19–24: Rock Hall, Md.
26–30: North East, Md.
OCTOBER 1938
1: Charlestown, Md.
3–8: Cambridge, Md.
10–15: Crisfield, Md.
17–22: Elizabeth City, N. C.
24–29: Manteo, N. C.
31: Delayed at Manteo by wind.
NOVEMBER 1938
1–5: Colerain, N. C.
6: Boat strikes a log in Roanoke River and sinks.
7–12: Sunk.
14: Towed to Elizabeth City, N. C.
DECEMBER 1938
Elizabeth City. For repairs.

1939—SEASON 26

JANUARY 1939
2–7: Boat repaired in Elizabeth City, N. C.
9–10: Elizabeth City, N. C.
11–12: Hertford, N. C.
13–14: Edenton, N. C.
16–17: Williamston, N. C.
18–19: Plymouth, N. C.
30–

FEBRUARY 1939
–4: Swansboro, N. C. (?)
6–11: Wilmington, N. C.
13–18: Wilmington, N. C.
23–25: Southport, N. C.
27–

MARCH 1939
–4: Little River, S. C.
6–11: Socastee, S. C.
13–18: Georgetown, S. C.
20–25: Charleston, S. C.
27–

APRIL 1939
–1: Charleston, S. C.
3–8: Charleston, S. C. (?)
17–22: Oriental, N. C. (?)
24–29: New Bern, N. C. (?)

MAY 1939
1–6: Washington, N. C.
8–13: Columbia, N. C.
22–27: Windsor, N. C.
29–

JUNE 1939
–3: Manteo, N. C.
5–10: Deep Creek, Va.
12–17: Deep Creek, Va. Elizabeth River bridge out.
19–24: Gloucester Point, Va.
26 –

JULY 1939
–1: Tappahannock, Va.
3–8: Urbanna, Va.
10–15: Fredericksburg, Va.
17–22: Irvington, Va.
24–29: Kinsale, Va.

AUGUST 1939
7–12: Britton (Abell's Wharf), Md.
14–19: Solomons, Md.
21–26: Galesville, Md. (?)
28–

SEPTEMBER 1939
–2: Annapolis, Md. (?)
11–16: St. Michaels, Md.
25–30: Crumpton, Md.

OCTOBER 1939
2–7: Rock Hall, Md.
9–14: Centreville, Md.
16–21: Chestertown, Md.
23–28: Baltimore, Md.
30–

NOVEMBER 1939
–4: Baltimore, Md.
5–11: Baltimore, Md.
12–18: Baltimore, Md.
19–25: Baltimore, Md.
26–

DECEMBER 1939
–2: Baltimore, Md.
3–9: Baltimore, Md.
10–16: Baltimore, Md.
17–23: Baltimore, Md.
24–30: Baltimore, Md.

1940—SEASON 27
No stop for winter.

JANUARY 1940
1–6: Baltimore, Md. (?)
15–20: Elizabeth City, N. C.
22–27: Williamston, N. C.
29 –

FEBRUARY 1940
–3: Williamston, N. C. (?) Icebound.
5–10: Plymouth, N. C.
19–21: Belhaven, N. C.
26–

MARCH 1940
–2: Beaufort, N. C.
4–9: Jacksonville, N. C.
11–16: Wilmington, N. C.
25–30: Georgetown, S. C.

APRIL 1940
1–6: Charleston, S. C.
8–13: Charleston, S. C.
15–20: Little River, S. C.
22–27: New Bern, N. C.

MAY 1940
6–11: Greenville, N. C.
13–18: Washington, N. C.
27–

JUNE 1940
 –1: Manteo, N. C.
 3–8: Deep Creek, Va.
 10–15: Suffolk, Va.
 17–22: Gloucester Point, Va.
 24–29: Tappahannock, Va.
JULY 1940
 1–6: Urbanna, Va.
 8–13: Fredericksburg, Va.
 15–20: Irvington, Va.
 22–27: Colonial Beach, Va.
 29–
AUGUST 1940
 –3: Britton (Abell's Wharf), Md.
 5–10: Solomons, Md. (?)
 12–17: Galesville, Md. (?)
 19–24: Annapolis, Md.
 31: Charlestown, Md.
SEPTEMBER 1940
 9–14: Cambridge, Md.
 16–21: St. Michaels, Md.
 23–28: Easton Point, Md.
 30–

OCTOBER 1940
 –5: Crisfield, Md.
 7–12: Seaford, Del.
 14–19: Rock Hall, Md.
 28–
NOVEMBER 1940
 –2: Baltimore, Md.
 4–10: Baltimore, Md.
 11–16: Baltimore, Md. (?)
 18–23: Coinjock, N. C.

1941—SEASON 28
No stop for winter.
JANUARY 1941
 6–11: Georgetown, S. C
 13–18: Beaufort, S. C.
 27–
FEBRUARY 1941
 –1: Thunderbolt, Ga.
 3: Thunderbolt, Ga. (?)

Notes

CHAPTER 2   USS *PLAYHOUSE*

1 "Jones Shows to Spend the Winter Here," Washington, North Carolina, *Daily News.*

2 Wesley Stout, "Tonight at the River Landing," *The Saturday Evening Post*, p. 44.

3 Ibid.

4 Maude McDougall, "Dockstorming Versus Barnstorming," New York *Morning Telegraph.* Wesley Stout ("Tonight at the River Landing") wrote that Jim found the timbers for his boat "standing in the forests of South Carolina." I don't think Jim needed to go that far to find his lumber and I doubt that he would have used green timbers to build his boat.

5 McDougall ("Dockstorming") calls him "George," but the man she describes could only be Harry Van.

6 McDougall, "Dockstorming."

7 Stout, "Tonight at the River Landing."

8 Ibid.

9 "Floating Theatre Boat Estelle Successfully Launched Yesterday," Washington, North Carolina, *News.*

10 Leslie D. Waldorf, unpublished journal, 1917.

11 "Former Ocheyedan Man Buried Monday," Sibley, Iowa, *Gazette-Tribune.*

12 "Show Man Falls from the Estelle," Washington, North Carolina, *Daily News.*

13 "'Playhouse' First Floating Theatre Is Now Practically All Complete," Washington, North Carolina, *Daily News.*

14 *Merchant Vessels of the United States.*

15 W. J. Overman III, "The James Adams Floating Theatre, *Pasquotank Historical Society Year Book,* Vol. 3, p. 73.

16 "Floating Theatre Boat Estelle."

17 "'Playhouse' First Floating Theatre."

17 Advertisement, *Billboard*, February 14, 1914, p. 66.

19 Leslie D. Waldorf, "Old Showboat Provided Dramatic Entertainment for Tide Water for Years," Elizabeth City, North Carolina, *Independent Star,* 1954. Repeated by many other writers.

20 "Playhouse' First Floating Theatre."

21 Jack Griffith, "Adams' Floating Theatre as 'Jack' Griffith Sees It," *Billboard*, p. 18.

22 Maisie Comardo, interview.

23 Irvin Beauchamp, interview.

24 Comardo, interview.

25 Ibid.

26 R. W. Kieffer, "Show Boat: Showdown," Baltimore, Maryland, *Sunday Sun.*

27 Stout, "Tonight at the River Landing."

28 Comardo, interview.

29 Advertisement, Crisfield, Maryland, *Times,* July 4, 1914.

30 Examination of pictures of the theatre.

31 McDougall, "Dockstorming."

32 Ibid.

33 Ibid.

34 Griffith, "Adams Floating Theatre."

35 Larry S. Chowning, "Show Boat," *Chesapeake Bay Magazine*, p. 65.

36 Ibid.

37 Fragments of ads, 1915. Calvert Marine Museum.

38 Picture supplied by Marguerite Young.

39 McDougall, "Dockstorming."

40 "Local Briefs," Centreville, Maryland, *Record*, October 24, 1914.

41 Stout, "Tonight at the River Landing."

42 McDougall, "Dockstorming."

43 W. L. Moger, Sr., interview.

44 *Merchant Vessels*, 1918.

45 "First Show Playhouse Last Night," Washington, North Carolina, *Daily News*.

46 Oral Summer Coad, quoted in Alfred Bernheim, *The Business of Theatre*, p. 7.

47 Alfred L. Bernheim, *The Business of Theatre, an Economic History of the American Theatre 1750-1932*, p. 99.

48 Display in Museum of Repertoire Americana.

49 "Walter Sanford," *New York Times*, p. 19. Theatre historian Gerald Bordman pointed out to me the overlap between performers in rep and in the secondary theatres in New York and other large cities. He brought the case of Walter Sanford to my attention.

50 Philip Graham, *Showboats, the History of an American Institution*, p. 9.

51 "Playhouse' First Floating Theatre."

52 Ibid.

53 Clayton Hamilton, "Melodrama, Old and New," *The Bookman*, p. 310.

54 Ibid., p. 311.

55 Ibid., p. 312.

56 Ibid., p. 313.

57 Ibid., p. 311.

58 Ibid., p. 313.

59 Herbert Ross Brown, *The Sentimental Novel in America 1789-1860*, p. 361.

60 Both scripts are in the collection of the Museum of Repertoire Americana.

61 Constance Rourke, *American Humor*, p. 114.

62 "First Show Playhouse Last Night."

63 "Rep Tattles," *Billboard*, September 23, 1922, p. 28.

64 Masten and Neel with Adams," *Billboard*, p. 22.

65 McDougall, "Dockstorming."

CHAPTER 3   CIRCUS, CARNIVAL, AND VAUDEVILLE

1 "Obituary, Rose Adams," Saginaw, Michigan, *News-Currier-Herald*, p. 17.

2 A point made by James Adams's niece, Marguerite Young, and his grandniece, Vivian O'Leary.

3 Mr. and Mrs. Walter Cooling, who knew James and Gertrude Adams in Chesapeake City, MD.; George Grim and Don Bollman, who knew Selba Adams in Shepherd, Michigan; and Maisie Comardo, who knew Beulah in Elizabeth City, North Carolina, all emphasized the fun-loving nature of the Adamses.

4 Much of the Adams family information was provided by Vivian O'Leary from the family Bible.

5 Handbill provided by Marguerite Young.

6 Vivian O'Leary, interview.

7 Unidentified newspaper clipping provided by Marguerite Young.

8 *Shepherd Centennial: Salt River/Shepherd, 1857-1957*, p. 13.

9 Marriage license.

10 Archival material, Jack Tucker, Saginaw *News*.

11 Rose T. Marvin, "Shepherd Man's Show Boat Plot for Novel," Lansing, Michigan, *State Journal*.

12 "Show Boat Again on the Chesapeake," Baltimore, Maryland, *Sunday Sun*.

13 "Routes Ahead," *Billboard*, May 31, 1902, p. 8.

14 "Show Boat Again on the Chesapeake."

15 "Street Fair Notes," *Billboard*, January 3, 1903, p. 3.

16 Joe McKennon, *A Pictorial History of the American Carnival*, Vol. I, p. 11.

17 Ibid., p. 29.

18 Ibid., pp. 42-44.

19 Ibid., p. 51.

20 Ibid., p. 53.

21 "Street Fair Notes," *Billboard*, April 18, 1903, p. 8.

22 McKennon, *Pictorial History*, Vol. I, p. 61.

23 Advertisement, *Billboard*, May 1, 1900, p. 19.

24 "Street Fair Notes," *Billboard*, January 31, 1903, p. 15.

25 "Routes Ahead," *Billboard*, January 31, 1903.

26 "Street Fair Notes," *Billboard*, May 2, 1903, p. 8.

27 "Street Fair Notes," *Billboard*, November 14, 1903, p. 7.

28 "Street Fair Notes," *Billboard*, June 13, 1903, p. 10.

29 "Street Fair Notes," *Billboard*, September 26, 1903, p. 13.

30 Advertisement, *Billboard*, November 28, 1903, p. 24.

31 "Street Fair Notes," *Billboard*, September 26, 1903, p. 13.

32 "Street Fair Notes," *Billboard*, October 3, 1903, p. 14.

33 "Will Give Carnival," Washington, Indiana, *Gazette*, January 22, 1904.

34 "End of the Carnival," Washington, Indiana, *Herald*, May 9, 1904.

35 "Washington Will Have Spring Carnival," Washington, Indiana, *Herald*, April 5, 1904.

36 "Street Fair Notes," *Billboard*, July 23, 1904.

37 "Street Fair Notes," *Billboard*, March 19, 1904, p. 12.

38 Adams family Bible.

39 "Street Fair Notes," *Billboard*, July 23, 1904, p. 11.

40 "Street Fair Notes," February 27, 1904, p. 7.

41 "Street Fair Notes," July 23, 1904, p. 7.

42 "Hatch-Adams Show Quarantined," *Billboard*, November 12, 1904, p. 18.

43 "Street Fair Notes," *Billboard*, June 25, 1904, p. 6.

44 Advertisement, *Billboard*, October 1, 1904, p. 40.

45 "Hatch and Adams Dissolve Partnership," *Billboard*, December 3, 1904, p. 9.

46 "Street Fair Notes," *Billboard*, December 3, 1904.

47 McKennon, *Pictorial History*, Vol. II, pp. 22-24.

48 Ibid., p. 22.

49 "Street Fair Notes," *Billboard*, August 15, 1903, p. 11.

50 "Tent Shows," *Billboard*, March 11, 1905, p. 13.

51 McKennon, *Pictorial History*, Vol. II, p. 172.

52 "Street Fair Notes," *Billboard*, February 11, 1905, p. 11.

53 Adams mentioned to McDougall ("Dockstorming") that he had had experience with a medicine show.

54 "Tent Shows," *Billboard*, March 11, 1905, p. 13.

55 Advertisement, *Billboard*, March 11, 1905, p. 20.

56 "Street Fair Notes," *Billboard*, August 19, 1905, p. 20.

57 "Street Fair Notes," *Billboard*, September 16, 1905, p. 20.

58 "Tent Shows," *Billboard*, February 10, 1906, p. 20.

59 Advertisement, *Billboard*, May 12, 1906, p. 17.

60 Advertisement, *Billboard*, July 14, 1906, p. 30.

61 "Routes Ahead," *Billboard*, July 21, 1906, p. 34.

62 McKennon, *Pictorial History*, Vol. I, p. 68.

63 "Tent Shows," *Billboard*, September 8, 1906, p. 24.

64 Advertisement, *Billboard*, September 1, 1906, p. 10.

65 McKennon, *Pictorial History*, Vol. II, p. 24.

66 "Tent Shows," *Billboard*, September 8, 1906, p. 24.

67 McKennon, *Pictorial History,* Vol. I, p. 55.

68 "Circus Gossip," *Billboard,* October 13, 1906, p. 27.

69 "Tent Shows," *Billboard,* July 20, 1907, p. 23.

70 Stout, "Tonight at the River Landing," p. 44.

71 "Miscellaneous Routes," *Billboard,* March 14, 1908.

72 Picture supplied by Marguerite Young.

73 Picture postcard supplied by Marguerite Young.

74 "James Adams 10 Cent Shows," Gastonia, North Carolina, *Gazette,* May 6, 1910, p. 1.

75 "Last Show," Washington, North Carolina, *Daily News,* July 2, 1910, p. 1.

76 "The James Adams Show," Franklin, Virginia, *Tidewater News,* May 21, 1909, p. 1.

77 Stout, "Tonight at the River Landing."

78 McDougall, "Dockstorming."

79 Land deeds, Charlotte, North Carolina, book 377, page 535.

80 Ibid., book 426, page 101.

81 McDougall, "Dockstorming."

CHAPTER 4   THE FIRST TEN YEARS:
PLACES AND EVENTS

1 "First Show Playhouse Last Night."

2 Ibid.

3 "Good Show Given Again Last Night," Washington, North Carolina, *Daily News,* March 4, 1919.

4 "Playhouse Was Packed Last Night," Washington, North Carolina, *Daily News,* March 7, 1914.

5 Ibid.

6 Ronald B. Hartzer, *To Great and Useful Purpose, A History of the Wilmington District U.S. Army Corps of Engineers,* p. 58.

7 Mose Basnight, interview.

8 Mildred Gibbs, interview.

9 R. S. Spencer, interview.

10 "'Showboat' Comes to Dock in Baltimore, and an Earlier Patron Revisits It after 25 Years," Baltimore, Maryland, *Sunday Sun,* October 29, 1939.

11 "Floating Theatre," Fredericksburg, Virginia, *Free Lance-Star,* May 26, 1914.

12 "Reedville," Warsaw, Virginia, *Northern Neck News,* June 5, 1914.

13 "Floating Theatre."

14 "Local News Items,"Onancock, Virginia, *Accomack News,* June 20, 1914.

15 McDougall, "Dockstorming."

16 "Routes," *Billboard,* July 11, 1914.

17 "Routes," *Billboard,* June 27 and July 4, 1914.

18 "Additional Locals," Crisfield, Maryland, *Times,* July 11, 1914, p. 2.

19 "Week's News of Marion," Crisfield, Maryland, *Times,* July 18, 1914, p. 8.

20 "Floating Theatre in Salisbury for the Entire Week," Salisbury, Maryland, *Wicomico Times,* November 1, 1934, p. 1.

21 "Port Deposit," Elkton, Maryland, Cecil County *News,* September 16, 1914.

22 Advertisement, Elkton, Maryland, *Cecil Whig.*

23 "Local Briefs," Centreville, Maryland, *Record,* October 10, 1914.

24 Ibid.

25 "Local Briefs," Centreville, Maryland, *Record,* October 17, 1914.

26 "Local Briefs," Centreville, Maryland, *Record,* October 24, 1914.

27 "Saint Michaels," Easton, Maryland, *Star-Democrat,* October 31, 1914.

28 Advertisement, Denton, Maryland, *Journal,* November 7, 1914.

29 Advertisement, Elizabeth City, North Carolina, *Advance,* January 15, 1915.

30 Advertisement, Elizabeth City, North Carolina, *Advance,* January 19, 1915.

31 Advertisement, Elizabeth City, North Carolina, *Advance,* January 26, 1915.

32 Advertisement, Elizabeth City, North Carolina, *Advance,* January 29, 1915.

33 Advertisement, Elizabeth City, North Carolina, *Advance,* February 2, 1915.

34 Program, provided by Maisie Comardo.

35 Ibid.

36 Ibid.

37 Advertisement, Elizabeth City, North Carolina, *Advance,* February 23, 1915.

38 Advertisement, Elizabeth City, North Carolina, *Advance,* February 26, 1915.

39 Stout, "Tonight at the River Landing."

40 "Routes," *Billboard,* November 2, 1918.

41 Burgess, *This Was Chesapeake Bay,* p. 52.

42 Maisie Comardo, "Showboat People."

43 Leslie D. Waldorf, unpublished journals, 1917.

44 Burgess, *This Was Chesapeake Bay,* p. 52.

45 Advertisement, *Billboard,* February 8, 1919, p. 15.

46 "Routes," *Billboard,* November 27, 1920.

47 "Local News," Elkton, Maryland, *Cecil Democrat,* April 7, 1923.

48 "Floating Theatre to Winter in This City," Elizabeth City, North Carolina, *Independent,* September 28, 1923.

49 "Rep Tattles," *Billboard,* January 13, 1923, p. 28.

50 "Reminiscences of a Kent County Resident: James Adams Floating Theatre," *Kent Shoreman,* August 1973, p. 7.

51 Jayne Silliman, "The Story of Old Aurora," Washington, North Carolina, *Beauford County Magazine* 4, p. 9.

52 Mrs. Mason Lumpkin, interview.

53 Miriam Haynie, *Reedville 1874-1974,* (pages are not numbered).

54 McDougall, "Dockstorming."

55 Ibid.

56 Segar Cofer Dashiell, *Smithfield, a Pictorial History,* p. 131.

57 Segar Cofer Dashiell, interview.

58 Ann Wilmer, "'Hell Hole of Iniquity,' Showboating of Yore on the Rivers and the Bay," *Virginia Country,* Summer 1987, pp. 32-34.

59 Waldorf, journal, 1915.

60 "Leonardtown Is to Have a Novelty . . . ," Leonardtown, Maryland, *St. Mary's Enterprise,* July 31, 1915. All the materials on the Robert Emmett Floating Theatre were brought to my attention by Al Gough, Jr., of Leonardtown.

61 "Robert Emmett's Floating Theatre," Leonardtown, Maryland, *St. Mary's Enterprise,* August 14, 1915.

62 Al Gough, Jr., "It Don't Stop Here Anymore," Leonardtown, Maryland, *Chronicles of St. Mary's,* Summer 1989, p. 215.

63 Ibid.

64 "Robert Emmett's Floating Theatre."

65 Advertisement, *Billboard,* October 26, 1918.

66 Waldorf, journal, 1915.

67 Ibid., 1916.

68 "The Robert Emmett Floating Theatre . . . ," Leonardtown, Maryland, *St. Mary's Enterprise,* September 25, 1915.

69 Advertisement, Leonardtown, Maryland, *St. Mary's Enterprise,* July 15, 1916.

70 Ibid.

71 Gough, "It Don't Stop Here Anymore," p. 215.

72 Ibid.

73 Stout, "Tonight at the River Landing," p. 46.

74 Ibid.

75 "Repertoire Notes," *Billboard,* May 18, 1918, p. 22.

76 Stout, "Tonight at the River Landing," p. 46.

77 Advertisement, Warsaw, Virginia, *Northern Neck News,* September 5, 1919.

78 "Kilmarnock," Kilmarnock, Virginia, *Rappahannock Record,* August 27, 1919.

79 "Morattico," Kilmarnock, Virginia, *Rappahannock Record,* September 10, 1919.

80 Marvin, "Shepherd Man's Show Boat."

81 Advertisement, Mathews, Virginia, *Journal,* May 6, 1920.

82 "Routes," *Billboard*, October 4, 1919.

83 "Routes," *Billboard*, October 11, 1919.

84 "Adams Closes Show," *Billboard*, December 6, 1919, p. 14.

85 "Obituary, Rose Adams."

86 Ibid.

87 It is possible that the storm was in 1919 instead of 1920 and may have been the cause of the theatre going to Norfolk for repairs. I place it in 1920 because, in a 1926 story in the Minneapolis *Journal* ("Sea-Going Theatre Makes Fortune for Its Owner"), Hunter indicated that the theatre was coming from the Eastern Shore to Reedville, as it was in 1920. However, in a letter she wrote in the 1940s to Eunice Overman, Beulah indicated that the boat was going from Reedville to the Eastern Shore as it did in 1919. The situation is further complicated by the possibility that Beulah and Charlie were not on board at the time of the storm. (See chapter 5.)

88 "Sea-Going Theatre Makes Fortune For Its Owner," Minneapolis, Minnesota, *The Journal Magazine,* October 31, 1926, p. 7.

89 Marvin, "Shepherd Man's Show Boat."

90 "Sea-Going Theatre Makes Fortune."

91 Marvin, "Shepherd Man's Show Boat."

92 Stout, "Tonight at the River Landing," p. 44.

93 Marvin, "Shepherd Man's Show Boat."

94 Ibid.

95 Stout, "Tonight at the River Landing," p. 44.

96 Marvin, "Shepherd Man's Show Boat."

97 "Sea-Going Theatre Makes Fortune."

98 Advertisement, Elizabeth City, North Carolina, *Daily Advance*, November 16, 1921.

99 Adele Hersey, unpublished journal, November 17, 1921.

100 "Girl Falls Overboard Much Comedy Results," Elizabeth City, North Carolina, *Daily Advance*, November 19, 1921.

101 "Routes," *Billboard*, November 26 and December 3, 1921.

102 Hersey, journal, November 26, 1921.

CHAPTER 5   THE FIRST TEN YEARS: PERFORMERS

1 Most writers on the subject contend that there is no connection between the G-string character and the use of the G-string as a costume in burlesque. Billie Henderson Schuler, a repertoire trouper, argues that there is (interview with author) . The G-string character came before the costume. When the G-string character was evolving, the burlesque dancers wore panties. Billy thinks that the G-string costume was named because it was shaped like the beard of the G-string character. One might consider, also, the Freudian implications of the beard.

2 Donald Bogle, *Toms, Coons, Mulattoes, Mammies, & Bucks*, p. xx.

3 Neil Schaffner, in *The Fabulous Toby and Me*, relates his experiences as a Toby and presents convincing evidence that he was the originator of the character. Not all troupers agree with him. See Slout, *Theatre in a Tent*, p. 90 ff.

4 In *Billboard* on March 1, 1924, Robert J. Sherman advertised thirteen Toby shows, with "45 others to select from." Neil Shaffner wrote Toby shows almost exclusively.

5 Caroline Schaffner, interview.

6 Museum of Repertoire Americana, Mt. Pleasant, Iowa.

7 Waldorf, journal, 1915.

8 Comardo, "Showboat People."

9 Comardo, interview.

10 "Complete Change of Bill Is Presented on Show Boat," Norfolk, Virginia, *Ledger-Dispatch*, May 27, 1932.

11 Billie Henderson Schuller, interview.

12 Advertisement, *Billboard*, May 14, 1921, p. 17.

13 Neil Schaffner and Vance Johnson, *The Fabulous Toby and Me*, p. 14.

14 Neil Schaffner tells entertaining stories about how, as a young man, he talked his way into his first rep show. Schaffner and Johnson, *Toby and Me*, p. 23 ff.

15 "Actor's Child Barred," *Billboard,* November 19, 1910, p. 3.

16 Comardo, "Showboat People."

17 Griffith, "Adams's Floating Theatre."

18 McDougall, "Dockstorming."

19 Waldorf, "Old Showboat."

20 Graham, *Showboats*, pp. 133-134.

21 "The Folks Who Live in Boats on the City's Waterfront," Elizabeth City, North Carolina, *Independent*, July 8, 1932.

22 Comardo, interview.

23 Waldorf, journal, 1917.

24 Brief research in the deeds office in the Philadelphia City Hall revealed that Jim bought and sold perhaps a dozen lots and houses in the late 1910s and 1920s in the developing Kingsessing area of the city. I was not able to find a deed for the Rivoli Theatre, however.

25 "Adams' Floating Theatre," *Billboard*, June 18, 1918, p. 23.

26 After Jim and Gertie moved to Chesapeake City in 1928, their social activities were chronicled with some regularity in the "Chesapeake City" column in the *Cecil Democrat*, Elkton, Maryland.

27 "Chesapeake City," Elkton, Maryland, *Cecil Democrat*, December 12, 1931; May Irene Copinger, "Floating Theatre Makes Week Stands, Playing Popular Bills at Towns along the Shores of Bay," Baltimore, Maryland, *Sunday Sun*, November 22, 1925.

28 Stout, "Tonight at the River Landing"; Copinger, "Floating Theatre Makes Week Stands."

29 "Rep Tattles," *Billboard*, September 23, 1922, p. 28.

30 Dorothy Barlow, unpublished journal, 1926.

31 "No Play Tonight on Show Boat," Fredericksburg, Virginia, *Free Lance-Star,* July 16, 1928.

32 Advertisement, Fredericksburg, Virginia, *Free Lance-Star*, July 16, 1928.

33 Adams family Bible.

34 *Shepherd Centennial*, p. 5.

35 U.S. Census, Shepherd, Michigan, 1900 and 1910. Also, George Grim, interview.

36 Comardo, interview.

37 Ibid.

38 Griffith, "Adams Floating Theatre."

39 Comardo, letter.

40 "'Selb' Adams Adds Fiction to Radio Thriller," Shepherd, Michigan, *Isabella County Reporter,* March 23, 1933.

41 Robert Struble, interview.

42 Dr. James Adams, interview.

43 Harold Cline, interview.

44 Comardo, interview.

45 Beulah Adams, letter to Eunice Overman.

46 Edna Ferber, *A Peculiar Treasure*, p. 299.

47 Stout, "Tonight at the River Front," p. 44.

48 Waldorf, "Old Showboat."

49 Waldorf, journal, 1917.

50 "Adams Opens This Week," *Billboard*, March 13, 1920, p. 15.

51 "Howard Joins Adams," *Billboard,* July 17, 1920, p. 14.

52 Ibid.

53 Death certificate, Charles M. Hunter.

54 "Sam Hunter Died at an Early Hour Last Night," Ironton, Ohio, *Morning Irontonian*, March 10, 1923.

55 "Peter Hunter, Civil War Vet, Dies, Last Services Tuesday," Ironton, Ohio, *Sunday Tribune*, June 12, 1939.

56 Ironton, Ohio, *Business Directory*, 1907.

57 "Peter Hunter, Civil War Vet."

58 Comardo, interview.

59 Rachel Marsh, interview.

60 June Parker, interview.

61 Comardo, letter.

62 Waldorf, "Old Showboat."

63 Comardo, "Showboat People."

64 "Showboat Skipper Bemoans Passing of Floating Theatres," Baltimore, Maryland, *Sun,* April 25, 1935.

65 "Floating Theatre Here Next Week," Mathews, Virginia, *Journal,* June 11, 1936.

66 "Jones and Adams Dissolve Partnership," *Billboard,* September 8, 1906, p. 24.

67 Marriage license, Charles M. Hunter and Beulah Adams.

68 Picture provided by Marguerite Young.

69 "Howard Joins Adams." "Billy Boy" has their last name wrong, but from the article, there is no doubt but that the story is about Charlie and Beulah.

70 Ibid.

71 Advertisement, *Billboard,* October 18, 1919, p. 19.

72 Advertisement, *Billboard,* February 7, 1920, p. 22.

73 Advertisement, *Billboard,* February 28, 1920, p. 15.

74 Advertisement, *Billboard,* April 17, 1920, p. 14.

75 Advertisement, *Billboard,* May 8, 1920, p. 15.

76 Advertisement, *Billboard,* July 3, 1920, p. 15.

77 "Sea-Going Theatre Makes Fortune."

78 Comardo, interview.

79 Comardo, "Showboat People."

80 Marsh, interview.

81 Comardo, "Showboat People."

82 Comardo, interview.

CHAPTER 6   THE FIRST TEN YEARS: PERFORMANCES

1 Copinger, "Floating Theatre Makes Week Stands."

2 Schaffner and Johnson, *Toby and Me,* p. 60.

3 McDougall, "Dockstorming."

4 "Famous Novel, 'Lena Rivers,' to Be Acted in Montross August 6th," Warsaw, Virginia, *Northern Neck News,* July 30, 1937.

5 Gillian Lewis, interview.

6 Sherman family scrapbook.

7 Sherman copyrighted at least four plays as early as 1915: *A Daughter of Italy, The Perils of Geraldine, The Tramp's Redemption,* and *The Westerner.*

8 "Giving All His Time to Writing New Plays," *Billboard,* January 20, 1923, p. 29.

9 "Sherman Takes Over Additional Plays," *Billboard,* February 26, 1921, p. 16.

10 "Robert J. Sherman," *Billboard,* November 24, 1923, p. 28.

11 Advertisement, *Billboard,* March 28, 1925, p. 29.

12 Advertisement, *Billboard,* September 24, 1927, p. 31.

13 "Rep Tattles," *Billboard,* March 1, 1924, p. 28.

14 Schaffner and Johnson, *Toby and Me,* p. 108.

15 Advertisement, *Billboard,* January 26, 1924, p. 29.

16 "Original Floating Theatre," *Billboard,* June 10, 1937, p. 28.

17 Script made available by the Museum of Repertoire Americana, Mt. Pleasant, Iowa.

18 Stout, "Tonight at the River Landing," p. 44.

19 "The Methodist Church and Amusements," *Outlook* (2 March 1889): 9-10, quoted in Benjamin McArthur, *Actors and American Culture, 1880-1920, p. 130.*

20 McArthur, *Actors and American Culture,* p. 130.

21 Waldorf, journal, 1915A.

22 McDougall, "Dockstorming."

23 Gilman M. Ostrander, *American Civilization in the First Machine Age, 1820-1940,* p. 2.

24 Ibid., p. 11.

25 "Fairfields Notes," Warsaw, Virginia, *Northern Neck News,* July 13, 1917.

26 Allen Albert, "The Tents of the Conservative," *Scribner's Magazine,* July 1922, p. 55.

27 Joseph P. Watkins, "The James Adams Floating Theatre," *The World Magazine* July 1922, p. 8.

28 "Floating Theatre Still Touring Readers' Memories," Raleigh, North Carolina, *Independent*, February 28, 1980.

29 Advertisement, *Billboard*, March 7, 1925, p. 29.

30 MacArthur, *Actors and American Culture*, p. 65.

31 "Minor Locals," Elkton, Maryland, *Cecil County News*, August 4, 1915.

32 Graham, *Showboats*, p. 134.

33 "Fourth at Reedville," Warsaw, Virginia, *Northern Neck News*, July 7, 1916.

34 "The James Adams' Floating Theatre Has Been . . . ," Leonardtown, Maryland, *St. Mary's Enterprise*, July 28, 1917.

35 "Adams' Floating Theatre," *Billboard*, June 18, 1918.

36 Poster, Calvert Marine Museum.

37 Harley Sadler, "The Tent Repertoire Situation," *Billboard*, December 10, 1927, p. 48.

38 Miriam Haynie, "Called the Show Boat."

39 Norris Parks, interview.

40 John Beale, interview.

41 "Westmoreland," Warsaw, Virginia, *Northern Neck News*, June 25, 1920.

42 "Westmoreland," Warsaw, Virginia, *Northern Neck News*, July 16, 1920.

43 "Westmoreland," Warsaw, Virginia, *Northern Neck News*, October 2, 1925.

44 "Westmoreland," Warsaw, Virginia, *Northern Neck News*, August 20, 1926.

45 Comardo, interview.

46 "'Playhouse' First Floating Theatre Is Now Practically All Complete." Also, advertisement, Elkton, Maryland, *Cecil Whig*, September 19, 1914.

47 Stout, "Tonight at the River Landing," p. 44.

48 Harry Jackson, resident of Cecil County, Maryland, as reported to the author by Walter Cooling of Chesapeake City, Maryland.

49 Comardo, interview.

50 State Historical Society of Wisconsin, Ferber archives, box 4, folder 10.

51 Marsh, interview.

52 Advertisement, New Bern, North Carolina, *Times*, April 19, 1940; advertisement, Suffolk, Virginia, *News-Herald*, June 9, 1940.

53 Ed Newton, interview.

54 Barlow, journal, 1926.

55 Ibid.

56 Newton, interview.

57 McArthur, *Actors and American Culture*, p. 51.

58 Ibid.

59 Caroline Schaffner, interview.

60 Rourke, *American Humor*, p. 79.

61 Ibid., pp. 79-80.

62 Robert C. Toll, *Blacking Up, The Minstrel Show in Nineteenth-Century America*, p. 26.

63 Ibid., p. 28.

64 McArthur, *Actors and American Culture*, p. 51.

65 Toll, *Blacking Up*, p. 196.

66 Quoted in McArthur, *Actors and American Culture*, p. 52.

67 Bogle, *Toms*, p. 127.

CHAPTER 7   EDNA FERBER

1 Ferber, *A Peculiar Treasure*, p. 288.

2 Ibid.

3 Ibid., p. 289.

4 Thoda Cocroft, "The Floating Theatre Thrives," p. 396.

5 Rogers Dickinson, *Edna Ferber, Whose Novel "So Big" Was Awarded the Pulitzer Prize for the Best American Novel of 1924, A Biographical Sketch with a Bibliography*, p. 32.

6 Ferber, *A Peculiar Treasure*, pp. 289-291.

7 Hamilton Crockford, "Ship's Pilot, after 54 Years aboard Boats, Is Just Beginning to Learn about the Water," Richmond, Virginia, *Times-Dispatch*, January 21, 1951.

8 "Floating Theatre in Performance."

9 Marvin, "Shepherd Man's Show Boat."

10 Stout, "Tonight at the River Landing."

11 Ferber, *A Peculiar Treasure,* p. 291.

12 Marvin, "Shepherd Man's Show Boat."

13 Ferber, *A Peculiar Treasure,* p. 296.

14 Hartzer, *To Great and Useful Purpose,* p. 58.

15 Ferber, *A Peculiar Treasure,* pp. 295-296.

16 Michelle Francis, "The James Adams Floating Theatre: Edna Ferber's Showboat," *Carolina Comments,* p. 139.

17 Ibid., p. 138.

18 Ferber, *A Peculiar Treasure,* pp. 296-297.

19 Francis, "James Adams," pp. 139-140.

20 Ferber, *A Peculiar Treasure,* pp. 297-300.

21 Graham, *Showboats,* pp. 197-199.

22 Edited by Donald McDaniel, Worthington, Ohio.

23 Advertisement, Elizabeth City, North Carolina, *Independent,* April 3, 1925.

24 "Routes," *Billboard,* April 18, 1925.

25 Ibid., and April 25, 1925.

26 Ann Tyndall, "Show Boat Lives in Tidewater Memories," Washington, North Carolina, *Daily New,* February 1, 1974.

27 "Who's Who in This Issue," *Woman's Home Companion,* p. 118.

28 Ferber, *A Peculiar Treasure,* pp. 301-302.

29 Harriet F. Pilpel, interview.

30 Miles Kreuger, *Show Boat, the Story of a Classical American Musical,* p. 17.

31 Ferber, *A Peculiar Treasure,* p. 298.

32 Francis, "James Adams," p. 141; Ferber, *Show Boat,* p. 74.

33 Ferber, *A Peculiar Treasure,* pp. 298-299.

34 Ferber, *Show Boat,* pp. 68-69, 72-73.

35 Ferber, *A Peculiar Treasure,* p. 300.

36 Francis, "James Adams," p. 141.

37 Ibid.

38 Ferber, *Show Boat,* pp. 260-261.

39 Ibid., p. 374.

40 Francis, "James Adams," p. 141.

41 Ferber, *A Peculiar Treasure,* pp. 289-290.

42 Ferber, *Show Boat,* p. 394.

43 Ibid., pp. 142-143.

44 State Historical Society of Wisconsin, box 4, folder 10.

45 Ferber, *A Peculiar Treasure,* p. 298.

46 Ferber, *Show Boat,* p. 19.

47 Gough, "'It Don't Stop Here Anymore,'" p. 213.

48 Ibid.

49 Ibid.

50 Gough, interview with author.

51 Ferber, *Show Boat,* pp. 118-119.

52 "Shortage of Actors Reported by Feist," *Billboard,* March 14, 1925, p. 28.

53 State Historical Society of Wisconsin, box 4, folder 10.

54 Florence Haynie, interview with author.

55 "Famous Showboat Opens Here Monday," Camden, New Jersey, *Courier-Post,* September 30, 1932.

56 "Show Boat Coming," Mathews, Virginia, *Journal,* June 11, 1936. Ferber's description of the courting by the water barrel is on pp. 220-221 of *Show Boat.*

57 Adams family Bible.

58 Marriage license, Charles M. Hunter and Beulah Adams. Also see Francis, "James Adams," p. 138. If Francis had not reported the date and location of the wedding, I doubt that I would have found the license even after considerable searching.

59 "Real-life Showboat Captain," Saginaw, Michigan, *News,* November 21, 1948.

60 Ferber, letter to Bernard Sobel, January 25, 1928. State Historical Society of Wisconsin, box 1, folder 2.

61 Ferber, *Show Boat,* pp. 227-228.

CHAPTER 8   MORE ON *SHOW BOAT*

1 Kreger, *Showboat,* p. 76.

2 Ibid., p. 77.

3 Ibid.

4 Ibid., p. 76.

5 Ibid., p. 81.

6 Ibid., p. 84.

7 Saunders, "And So Hunter Stayed."

8 "Adamses and Hunters in Chicago," *Billboard*, March 5, 1927, p. 30.

9 Kreuger, *Show Boat*, p. 76.

10 Saunders, "And So Hunter Stayed."

11 Kreuger, *Show Boat*, p. 77.

12 "Reedville," September 4, 1931.

13 "'Showboat' to Be Filmed on Goldenrod," *Billboard*, March 12, 1927, p. 30.

14 Kreuger, *Show Boat*, p. 79.

15 Hugh Fordin, *Getting to Know Him, A Biography of Oscar Hammerstein II*, pp. 71-72. The quote was brought to my attention by Jacques Kelly of the Baltimore *Sun*.

16 Barlow, journal, 1926.

17 Fordin, *Getting to Know Him*, p. 88.

18 State Historical Society of Wisconsin, box 1, folder 2.

19 Ferber, *A Peculiar Treasure*, p. 302.

20 State Historical Society of Wisconsin, box 1, folder 2.

21 Ibid.

22 Ibid.

23 Ibid.

24 Julie Goldsmith Gilbert, *Ferber, A Biography*, pp. 365-366.

25 "Showboat Again Here Next Week," Onancock, Virginia, *Eastern Shore News*, November 22, 1928.

26 Kreuger, *Show Boat*, p. 84.

27 The Equity explanation was suggested to me by Billy Schuler.

28 Graham, *Showboats*, p. 121.

29 Ferber, *Show Boat*, p. 67.

30 Ibid., p. 80.

31 Still from film showing *Cotton Blossom* and towboat; Kreuger, *Show Boat*, p. 87.

32 Kreuger, *Show Boat*, illustration, p. 82.

33 Program for musical, *Show Boat*.

34 Gertrude S. Carraway, "To Write 'Showboat' Story: Ferber to Tell of Experience while in East Carolina," Greensboro, North Carolina, *Daily News*, February 10, 1929.

35 "Miss Ferber's Statement re the Setting of Her Novel," Elizabeth City, North Carolina, *Independent*, November 21, 1930.

36 "Mrs. Beulah Adams, 800 Mackinaw, Had More Than Passing Interest . . ." unidentified article, June 6, 1926.

37 Ferber, *A Peculiar Treasure*, p. 289.

38 Quoted in Dickenson, *Edna Ferber*, p. 16.

39 "Who's Who in This Issue," *Woman's Home Companion*, Copyright © Edna Ferber, 1926.

CHAPTER 9   TRIALS AND TRIBULATIONS

1 Frank Marlow, "The Play's the Thing," *Billboard*, September 8, 1928, p. 41.

2 "A Call to Action," *Billboard*, January 15, 1927, p. 5.

3 Bernheim, *Business of Theatre*, p. 100.

4 Script provided by the Museum of Repertoire Americana.

5 McKennon, *Pictorial History*, Vol. 1, p. 29.

6 Marlow, "The Play's the Thing."

7 Gough, "It Don't Stop Here Anymore," p. 220.

8 Ibid.

9 "The Best Show There Is Is 'Smiling Through,' says Captain Seymoure," unidentified clipping, June, 1939.

10 Public laws of North Carolina.

11 "Show Boat to Skip N. C. and Try the South," Elizabeth City, North Carolina, *Daily Independent*.

12 Fred Hollman, "Welcome to the T.R.M.P.A.," *Billboard*, p. 26.

13 Paul English, "T.R.M.P.A. Notes," *Billboard*, May 21, 1927, p. 26.

14 "Agreement Is Reached in Plan to Reduce Tent-Show Royalties," *Billboard*, July 2, 1927, p. 5.

15 "Fire and Theft Insurance for Actors' Equity Members," *Billboard*, September 3, 1927, p. 5.

16 "Public Getting Wise to 'Octopus' Tactics," *Billboard*, August 20, 1927, p. 5.

17 "Boycott of Alabama Cotton Planned by Showmen as Retaliation for Anti-Tent Show Legislation," *Billboard*, March 17, 1928, p. 5.

18 "Tent Shows Win Point in Alabama Controversy," *Billboard,* September 22, 1928, p. 32.

19 "Paul English, Who Has Been Managing . . . ," *Billboard,* April 29, 1933, p. 54.

20 Robert Klassen, *The Tent-Repertoire Theatre: A Rural American Institution,* unpublished Ph.D. dissertation, p. 2.

21 "Adams' Showboat Lauded," *Billboard,* October 29, 1927, p. 31.

22 "Performers Heavy Losers," *Billboard,* December 10, 1927, p. 48.

23 "Theatre Ship Sinking within Harbor Limits," Norfolk, Virginia, *Ledger-Dispatch,* November 25, 1927.

24 "James Adams Floating Theatre Sinks in Bay," Leonardtown, Maryland, *St. Mary's Beacon,* December 2, 1927.

25 Heralds, James Adams Floating Theatre, 1928 and 1929.

26 "Show Boat Again on the Chesapeake."

27 Ralph Pool, "Edna Ferber's Show Boat Being Rebuilt at Elizabeth City," Greensboro, North Carolina, *Daily News,* February 26, 1928.

28 "Adams Floating Theatre, Well Known in Carolina, Is Believed Total Loss," Elizabeth City, North Carolina, *Daily Advance,* November 26, 1927.

29 "Floating Theatre Sinks in Bay," *Billboard,* December 3, 1927, p. 30.

30 "Theatre Ship Sinking within Harbor Limits."

31 "Adams Floating Theatre, Well Known in Carolina, Is Believed Total Loss."

32 Heralds, *James Adams Floating Theatre,* 1928 and 1929.

33 "James Adams to Rebuild His Theatre Here," Elizabeth City, North Carolina, *Independent,* December 2, 1927.

34 "Cables and Gas Mains Broken by Show Boat Are Being Repaired," Norfolk, Virginia, *Ledger-Dispatch,* November 28, 1927.

35 "Floating Theatre Causes Havoc in Norfolk Harbor," Elizabeth City, North Carolina, *Daily Advance,* November 28, 1927.

36 Parks, interview.

37 "James Adams to Rebuild His Theatre Here."

38 Pool, "Edna Ferber's Show Boat."

39 "Floating Theatre Coming Next Week," Mathews, Virginia, *Journal,* June 12, 1930.

40 Schaffner and Johnson, *Toby and Me,* p. 29.

41 State Historical Society of Wisconsin, box 4, folder 10.

42 Francis, "James Adams," p. 140.

43 Wilmer, "Hell Hole," p. 33.

44 Advertisement, *Billboard,* March 3, 1928.

45 Program for the musical, *Show Boat.*

46 "To Start Program Wednesday Night," Fredericksburg, Virginia, *Free Lance-Star,* July 17, 1928.

47 Marvin, "Shepherd Man's Show Boat."

48 "Crowds Frolic at Floating Theatre," Mathews, Virginia, *Journal,* June 28, 1928.

49 "The Best Show There Is."

50 MGM made two movie versions of play, in 1932 with Norma Shearer, and in 1941 with Jeanette McDonald.

51 Comardo, interview.

52 "Best City's Show Boat Meets with Disaster in Dismal Swamp Canal; 'Pop' Neel Stands By His Craft," Elizabeth City, North Carolina, *Daily Advance,* November 16, 1929.

53 Ibid.

54 Ibid.

55 Ibid.

56 "Show Boat Is Safe in Ship Yard of City," Elizabeth City, North Carolina, *Daily Advance,* November 22, 1929.

57 "The Floating Theatre is Preparing For Tour," Elizabeth City, North Carolina, *Independent,* March 21, 1930.

58 Laurette Taylor also starred in the silent movie version made in 1923. MGM remade the movie as a talkie in 1933 with Marion Davies.

59 "Adams Boat Is Popular,"*Billboard,* July 26, 1930, p. 26.

60 "A Floating Theatre Which Stages Old Time Melodramas," Philadelphia, Pennsylvania, *Evening Bulletin.*

61 Ibid.

62 "James Adams in Stock Run," *Billboard,* December 13, 1930, p. 26.

63 "Chesapeake City," Elkton, Maryland, *Cecil Democrat,* November 8, 1930.

64 "Chesapeake City," Elkton, Maryland, *Cecil Democrat,* April 28, 1928.

65 "'Show Boat' Shifted Due to Fire Code," Washington, D. C., *Evening Star,* November 24, 1930, p. B1.

66 Advertisement, Washington, D. C., *Post,* November 24, 1930.

67 Eugene Warner, "Showboat Skipper Finds Its Glamour Mostly Fiction," Washington, D. C., *Times-Herald,* September 6, 1939.

68 Advertisement, Washington, D. C., *Post,* November 24, 1930.

69 "Front Row," Washington, D. C., *Evening Star,* November 25, 1930, p. B6.

70 Ibid.

71 "Routes," *Billboard,* December 20, 1930.

72 "Adams Cast in Rehearsal," *Billboard,* April 25, 1931, p. 24.

73 "James Adams in Stock Run."

74 Marguerite Young, letter to author.

75 Beulah Adams, letter to Overman.

76 "Kinsale," Warsaw, Virginia, *Northern Neck News,* August 14, 1931.

77 "Kinsale," Warsaw, Virginia, *Northern Neck News,* August 21, 1931.

78 "Social and Personal," Mathews, Virginia, *Journal,* October 8, 1931.

79 "Hottest July in Thirty Years," Mathews, Virginia, *Journal,* August 6, 1931.

80 "Former Ocheyedan Man Buried Monday."

81 "Social and Personal."

82 Ibid.

83 "Former Ocheyedan Man Buried Monday."

84 "Floating Theatre to Go to Colerain," Elizabeth City, North Carolina, *Daily Advance,* October 31, 1938.

85 "Floating Theatre to Be Here Next Week," Elizabeth City, North Carolina, *Independent,* October 30, 1931.

86 "There Was Pathos and Tearfulness on the Show Boat Sat. Nite," Elizabeth City, North Carolina, *Independent,* November 13, 1931.

87 "Deaths in the Profession," *Billboard,* January 6, 1923.

88 "Sam Hunter Died at an Early Hour Last Evening."

89 Death certificate, Samuel Hunter, March 9, 1923, Ironton Public Health Department.

90 "Deaths in the Profession," *Billboard,* January 23, 1926.

91 Program of *The Parson's Bride.*

92 "Deaths in the Profession," *Billboard,* February 16, 1929.

93 "Deaths in the Profession," *Billboard,* October 3, 1931.

94 "Extension of Tour of Show Boat Proposed," Elizabeth City, North Carolina, *Independent,* February 5, 1932.

95 Ibid.

96 Ibid.

97 "Tab Notes," *Billboard,* December 1, 1928.

98 "Hayworth Joins Med 'Opry,'" *Billboard,* May 27, 1933, p. 23.

99 "Extension of Tour of Show Boat Proposed."

100 Kreuger, *Show Boat,* p. 216.

101 The evidence is cumulative. Before Norfolk the theatre is advertised as "The James Adams Floating Theatre," and at Norfolk and after it is advertised as "The James Adams Show Boat." Also, there is a picture of the theatre in Chesapeake City in September, and the name painted on the side is "James Adams Show Boat." The idea, however, was not entirely new. When the theatre played in Alexandria in November and December 1930, Adams advertised in the papers as "The Famous and Original Show Boat," but for the 1931 season in his usual ports, the boat was the "James Adams Floating Theatre."

102 "'Show Boat' Here Monday," Norfolk, Virginia, *Ledger-Dispatch*, May 21, 1932.

103 Warner, "Showboat Skipper."

104 "James Adams Boat Scores in Norfolk," *Billboard*, June 4, 1932, p. 22.

105 Clinton J. Kraft, undated letter. He puts the year at 1932 or 1933. Rachel Seymoure was on the boat in 1933 and does not remember the incident.

106 "Minor Locals," Elkton, Maryland, *Cecil Democrat*, September 10, 1932.

107 "James Adams Does Well in Maryland," *Billboard*, October 1, 1932, p. 22.

108 "James Adams in Camden," *Billboard*, October 15, 1932, p. 22.

109 "Seagoing Showboat Is Being Built Here," Baltimore, Maryland, *News Post*, December 29, 1926.

110 Recorded in Dorothy Barlow's journal for October 1, 4, and 6, 1926.

111 "Seagoing Showboat Is Being Built Here."

112 *Dictionary of American Naval Fighting Ships*, p. 197.

113 "Seagoing Showboat Is Being Built Here."

114 Million Dollar Joy Boat Co., Inc., shareholders' report.

115 "Built as Sub Fighter, Ship to Be Showboat," Baltimore, Maryland, *News Post*, January 1, 1929.

116 "Show Boat Dream Ends," Camden, New Jersey, *Courier-Post*, October 13, 1932, p. 3.

117 Harry Hamilton, interview.

118 "Leyare's Joy Boat to Tour New Jersey," *Billboard*, May 14, 1932, p. 22.

119 "Showboat Pilot Freed," Camden, New Jersey, *Courier-Post*, October 15, 1932, p. 3.

120 "'Joy Ship' Aground after Order to Quit Burlington," Camden, New Jersey, *Courier-Post*, October 24, 1932.

121 "James Adams in Camden."

122 Shipley, "The Society Hour Glass," Wilmington, Delaware, *Delmarva Sunday Star*, October 23, 1932.

123 "Society Folk Volunteer Aid to 'Show Boat,'" Wilmington, Delaware, *Morning News*, October 22, 1932.

124 Shipley, "The Society Hour Glass," November 13, 1932.

125 "Many Reserve Seats for Show Boat Play," Wilmington, Delaware, *Morning News*, November 17, 1932.

126 "Airplanes to Stunt to Aid 'Show Boat,'" Wilmington, Delaware, *Morning News*, October 29, 1932.

127 Shipley, "The Society Hour Glass," November 20, 1932.

128 "James Adams Showboat Narrowly Escapes Gale," *Billboard*, November 26, 1932, p. 20.

129 Ibid.

CHAPTER 10 UNDER NEW MANAGEMENT

1 "Floating Theatre Sold," Easton, Maryland, *Star-Democrat*, May 19, 1933.

2 "Chesapeake City," Elkton, Maryland, *Cecil Democrat*, May 20, 1933.

3 "James Adams in New Hands," *Billboard*, May 27, 1933, p. 23.

4 Louis Azrael, "Louis Azrael Says," Baltimore, Maryland, *News Post*, September 6, 1936.

5 "Show Boat Is Now Owned by Nina B. Howard," Elizabeth City, North Carolina, *Independent*, October 27, 1933.

6 *Merchant Vessels of the United States*, 1933.

7 Clinton H. Johnson, "Show Boat's All Set to Puff Along," unidentified article.

8 "The Best Show There Is."

9 Azrael, "Louis Azrael Says," 1936.

10 Marsh, interview.

11 Ibid.

12 Comardo, letter to author.

13 Marsh, interview.

14 Ibid.

15 Ibid.

16 Miriam Haynie, "Called The Show Boat, 'Hell-Hole of Iniquity.'"

17 "Original Show Boat, Here for Repairs, Still Packs 'Em In on Its Old Circuit," unidentified article.

18 "Show Boat Is Now Owned by Nina B. Howard."

19 "Original Show Boat, Here for Repairs, Still Packs 'Em In."

20 Program for *The Broken Butterfly*.

21 "Original Show Boat, Here for Repairs, Still Packs 'Em In."

22 "Floating Theatre Sold."

23 "Original Showboat Here for Repairs, Rehearsals," Baltimore, Maryland, *News Post*, June 6, 1933.

24 "Routes," *Billboard*, June 10, 1933.

25 Shipley, "The Society Hour Glass," Wilmington, Delaware, *Sunday Star*, May 21, 1933.

26 Marsh, interview.

27 "County Swept by Destructive Northeast Storm," Mathews, Virginia, *Journal*, August 24, 1933.

28 Keiffer, "Show Boat: Showdown."

29 Marsh, interview.

30 "Hurricane Sweeps Gloucester," Gloucester, Virginia, *Gazette*, August 24, 1933.

31 John C. Wilson, *Virginia's Northern Neck, A Pictorial History*, p. 70.

32 Advertisement, Tappahannock, Virginia, *Rappahannock Times*, July 19, 1934.

33 "Adams' Showboat Opens on May 9."

34 Marsh, interview.

35 Hartzer, *To Great and Useful Purpose*, p. 58.

36 "Show Boat Plays to Large Crowds," Wilmington, North Carolina, *Morning Star*, December 27, 1933.

37 Advertisement, Wilmington, North Carolina, *Morning Star*, January 15, 1934.

38 Advertisement, Wilmington, North Carolina, *Morning Star*, January 18, 1934.

39 Advertisement, Wilmington, North Carolina, *Morning Star*, January 22, 1934.

40 Advertisement, Wilmington, North Carolina, *Morning Star*, January 26, 1934.

41 "Deaths in the Profession," *Billboard*, August 13, 1927.

42 "Charles F. Harrison, A Tribute by J. D. Colegrove," *Billboard*, November 24, 1928, p. 33.

43 "Remarkable Career Ends at Death of R. J. Sherman," Susquehanna, Pennsylvania, *Susquehanna Transcript*, p. 1.

44 "Show Boat Has Been Refurbished," Wilmington, North Carolina, *Morning Star*, March 31, 1934.

45 "Show Boat May Quit Carolina Taxes Too High," Elizabeth City, North Carolina, *Daily Advance*, May 18, 1934.

46 Advertisement, Wilmington, North Carolina, *Sunday Star News*, April 1, 1934.

47 Advertisement, Alexandria, Virginia, *Gazette*, December 7, 1930.

48 "Chesapeake City," Elkton, Maryland, *Cecil Democrat*, September 22, 1934.

49 "Floating Theatre in Salisbury for the Entire Week."

50 Marsh, interview.

51 "Showboat Skipper Bemoans Passing of Floating Theatres."

52 Marsh, interview.

53 Comardo, interview.

54 Arrington Littleton, interview. Marsh added details.

55 "Original Showboat on 23rd Annual Tour," unidentified clipping.

56 Ibid.

57 Marsh, interview. Carolyn Schaffner, interview.

58 "Marshall Walker Opens New Season October 29," *Billboard*, October 22, 1932, p. 24.

59 "Original Showboat on 23rd Annual Tour."

60 "Charlie Hunter Says N. C. Taxes Are Staggering," Elizabeth City, North Carolina, *Independent*, May 29, 1936.

61 "Showboat Captain Talks at Caro- lina," Elizabeth City, North Carolina, *Independent*, May 25, 1936.

62 "Tab Tattles," *Billboard*, May 30, 1936.

63 "Old Time Potomac River Show Boat Going Modern," Washington, D. C., *Sunday Star*, August 9, 1936.

64 "Show Boat Is in Port for Two-Week Stand," Charleston, South Carolina, March 1939, source unidentified.

65 John Blakely, photograph, Mariners' Museum.

66 "Original Showboat in Florida Wa- ters," *Billboard*, January 9, 1937, p. 26.

67 Eloise Bailey, "The Original Floating Theatre Came to Camden County," Woodbine, Georgia, *Camden County Tribune*, January 12, 1989.

68 "Show Boat Is Coming, but Not Hunters," Elizabeth City, North Caro- lina, *Daily Independent*, February 4, 1937.

69 Marsh, interview, and the banning of the Floating Theatre from Leonard- town, Maryland, in 1937.

70 Azrael, "Louis Azrael Says," Balti- more, Maryland, *News Post*, October 27, 1937.

CHAPTER 11   THE LAST HURRAH

1 "Show Boat Is Coming, but Not Hunters."

2 "The Floating Theatre Here for 2 Months," Elizabeth City, North Caro- lina, *Daily Independent*, February 22, 1937.

3 "Rehearsals on Show Boat Shortly," Elizabeth City, North Carolina, *Daily Independent*, April 10, 1937.

4 "The Floating Theatre Here for 2 Months."

5 Advertisement, Darien, Georgia, *Ga- zette*, January 29, 1937.

6 "Brasfield Show Takes to Water," *Bill- board*, April 17, 1937, p. 27.

7 Michael Kramme, "Showboat Casts as Reported in Bill Bruno's Bulletin," unpublished paper.

8 "Tent Showmen Learn Lesson," *Bill- board*, August 13, 1932, p. 22.

9 Advertisement, Portsmouth, Vir- ginia, *Star*, May 30, 1937.

10 Herald, *Original Floating Theatre*, 1937.

11 "Original Floating Theatre," *Bill- board*, June 5, 1937, p. 29.

12 Carolyn Schaffner, interview.

13 Boob Brasfield, vertical file.

14 Carolyn Schaffner, interview.

15 Thayer Roberts, vertical file.

16 Marsh, interview.

17 Museum of Repertoire Americana.

18 "Original Floating Theatre," *Bill- board*, May 29, 1937, p. 29.

19 "Actors Enact Real Drama; No Foolin!" Windsor, North Carolina, *Bertie Ledger-Advance*, May 21, 1937.

20 "Showboat Players Here—Now on Auto Trailers," Williamston, North Carolina, *Enterprise*, March 30, 1937.

21 Ibid., and herald for the Show Boat Players, 1937.

22 Herald for the Original Floating The- atre, 1937; advertisement, Kilmarn- ock, Virginia, *Rappahannock Record*, June 10, 1937.

23 Teacher's Courtesy Ticket, Show Boat Players, 1937.

24 "Tent," Smithfield, Virginia, *Times*, May 13, 1937.

25 "Show Boat Has Grand Opening," Smithfield, Virginia, *Times*, May 27, 1937.

26 Dashiell, interview.

27 Letter appeared in Smithfield *Times*, Gloucester *Gazette*, and other papers. Clippings in Calvert Marine Mu- seum.

28 "Original Floating Theatre," *Bill- board*, July 10, 1937, p. 28.

29 Ibid.

30 "Original Floating Theatre," *Bill- board*, June 19, 1937, p. 28.

31 "Coming Again," unidentified clip- ping.

32 "Rep Ripples," *Billboard*, October 30, 1937.

33 Rachel Seymoure, letter to Millard Fairbanks.

34 "Rep Ripples," *Billboard*, October 30, 1937.

35 Comardo, letter.

36 Gough, "It Don't Stop Here Any More," p. 222.

37 Ibid., p. 223

38 Charles E. Fenwick, "History of St. Aloysius Church," Leonardtown, Maryland, p. 61.

39 Minutes of the Commissioners of Leonardtown, July 7, 1937.

40 "Severe Electrical Storm Visits St. Mary's County," Leonardtown, Maryland, *St. Mary's Enterprise*, July 16, 1937.

41 Gough, "It Don't Stop Here Any More," p. 223.

42 Advertisement, Leonardtown, Maryland, *St. Mary's Enterprise*, August 13, 1937.

43 "Showboat Players Aided by Weather," *Billboard*, September 25, 1937, p. 27.

44 Advertisement, Easton, Maryland, *Star-Democrat*, October 15, 1937.

45 "Here Comes the Showboat, on Its Twenty-fourth Annual Tour," unidentified clipping, week of November 8, 1937.

46 Johnson, "Show Boat's All Set."

47 Warner, "Showboat Skipper."

48 Ibid.

49 "Rep Ripples," *Billboard*, April 23, 1938.

50 Johnson, "Show Boat's All Set."

51 Advertisement, Easton, Maryland, *Star Democrat*, April 22, 1938. The same wording was used all season and through most of 1939.

52 "Floating Theatre Coming Next Week," Gloucester, Virginia, *Gazette and Mathews Journal*, May 19, 1938.

53 Marsh, interview.

54 "Hunter-Pfeiffer End Partnership," *Billboard*, May 4, 1940, p. 28.

55 Marsh, interview.

56 Comardo, letter.

57 ". . . Where Virtue Triumphs . . . ," internally dated June 6, 1938, unidentified clipping.

58 Kramme, "Showboat Casts."

59 Johnson, "Show Boat's All Set."

60 "Floating Theatre Is Coming to Tapp'k 27th, for One Week," Tappahannock, Virginia, *Rappahannock Times*, June 16, 1938.

61 Advertisement, unidentified clipping, September 5, 1938.

62 "Original Showboat Finds Business Okeh," *Billboard*, September 24, 1938, p. 35.

63 Advertisement, Williamston, North Carolina, *Enterprise*, November 4, 1938.

64 "Original Showboat Finds Business Okeh."

65 ". . . Featuring Sea Bee Hayworth . . . ," unidentified clipping.

66 Handbill, *Original Floating Theatre*, October 1, 1938.

67 Nelson McCall, interview.

68 "'Original' Boat Hits Log, Sinks," *Billboard*, November 12, 1938, p. 28.

69 "Tom Fearing Joins Show Boat Troupe," Elizabeth City, North Carolina, *Daily Advance*, November 2, 1938.

70 "Third Trip to Bottom Inland Waters," unidentified clipping.

71 Marsh, interview.

72 "'Original' Boat Hits Log, Sinks."

73 "Showboat Riding the Waves Again," Williamston, North Carolina, *Enterprise*, November 15, 1938.

74 "The Best Show There Is."

75 "SeaBee Hayworth Adds Two Houses to Circle," *Billboard*, January 14, 1939, p. 27.

76 "Rep Ripples," *Billboard*, November 19, 1938.

77 Advertisement, Southport, North Carolina, *Port State Pilot*, February 22, 1939.

78 "Rep Ripples," *Billboard*, January 14, 1939.

79 Advertisement, Elizabeth City, North Carolina, *Daily Advance*, January 9, 1939.

80 "Roberts and Company Please Another Showboat Crowd," unidentified clipping.

81 "Judge Is Lenient to Showboat Worker," Elizabeth City, North Carolina, *Daily Advance*, January 11, 1939.

82 Ibid.

83 "Court Drama Reveals a Trouper's Loyalty," *Billboard*, February 4, 1939, p. 27.

84 "Yarn on Original Showboat All Wet, Says Cap Seymoure," *Billboard*, February 18, 1939, p. 27.

85 "Show Boat Players Get Prepared for Openings," Elizabeth City, North Carolina, *Daily Advance*, January 7, 1939.

86 "Show Boat Sinks in Roanoke River," Raleigh, North Carolina, *News and Observer*, November 8, 1938.

87 Advertisement, Elizabeth City, North Carolina, *Daily Advance*, January 9, 1939.

88 Advertisement, Wilmington, North Carolina, *Morning Star*, February 14, 1939.

89 "Showboat Lady Dies Suddenly," Southport, North Carolina, *Port State Pilot*, March 1, 1939.

90 Marsh, interview.

91 Advertisement, unidentified clipping, March 5, 1939.

92 "Rep Ripples," *Billboard*, May 6, 1939.

93 "Roberts and Company Please Another Showboat Crowd."

94 Ibid.

95 "I Overheard Jim Gray . . . ," unidentified clipping.

96 "First Floating Theatre Plays on Original Spot," Washington, North Carolina, *Daily News*, May 5, 1939.

97 "Toll Bridge Here Wrecked by Tanker," Norfolk, Virginia, *Ledger-Dispatch*, June 2, 1939, p. 1.

98 "Captain Milford Seymoure Is Worried," unidentified clipping.

99 "Boats Move in Channel," Norfolk, Virginia, *Ledger-Dispatch*, June 16, 1939.

100 Advertisement, Gloucester, Virginia, *Gazette and Mathews Journal*, June 15, 1939.

101 "Van Arnam's Funmakers," *Billboard*, May 13, 1939, p. 25.

102 "Crowd Waits Patiently for Show; Lights Fail; 'Some Baby' Tonight," Elizabeth City, North Carolina, *Daily Advance*, June 20, 1939.

103 Herald for Show Boat Players, 1939.

104 "America's Best-Known 'Show Boat' Veteran," *P. D. Q.-Phillips Delicious Quality*, October 1939.

105 "Rep Ripples," *Billboard*, October 7, 1939.

106 Marsh, interview.

107 Al Gough, Jr., interview.

108 Warner, "Showboat Skipper."

109 Ibid.

110 Crockford, "Ship's Pilot."

111 "Director," unidentified clipping.

112 Norman Clark, "Showboat Will Visit Us for First Time in Its History," Baltimore, Maryland, *News Post*, October 19, 1939.

113 Marsh, interview.

114 "Young Actor," Portsmouth, Virginia, *Star*, June 5, 1940.

115 "Showboat Pays First Visit to City," Baltimore, Maryland, *News Post*, October 23, 1939.

116 "Showboat Will Stay 3rd Week," Baltimore, Maryland, *News Post*, November 4, 1939.

117 Aycock Brown, "Covering the Waterfront," North Carolina, *News*, March 14, 1940.

118 "The Floating Theatre Now in Baltimore . . . ," unidentified clipping.

119 "Rep Ripples," *Billboard*, November 18, 1939.

120 "Rep Ripples," *Billboard*, August 10, 1940.

121 "Comedy Is Next Showboat Bill," Baltimore, Maryland, *News Post*, November 15, 1939.

122 "Showboat Still Drawing Crowds," Baltimore, Maryland, *News Post*, November 18, 1939.

123 "'Lure of City' Is Showboat's Bill," Baltimore, Maryland, *News Post*, November 23, 1939.

124 Program for *Ten Nights in a Bar Room*, Baltimore, November 26.

125 Program for *Over the Hills to the Poor House*, Baltimore, December 3.

126 "Melodrama on Showboat," Baltimore, Maryland, *News Post*, December 9, 1939.

127 "In Drama," Baltimore, Maryland, *News Post*, December 26, 1939.

128 "Show Boaters See 'Show Boat,'" Baltimore, Maryland, *News Post*, December 13, 1939.

129 Carroll Dulaney, "Day by Day," unidentified clipping.

130 Robert L. Sherman, *Drama Cyclopedia*, p. 416.

131 Ibid., p. 534.

132 "'Ten Nights in a Bar Room' Comes Back Again," Baltimore, Maryland, *Sunday American*, December 3, 1939.

133 Marsh, interview.

CHAPTER 12   THE FINAL CURTAIN

1 "Floating Theatre Giving Best Shows," Elizabeth City, North Carolina, *Daily Advance*, January 17, 1940.

2 Advertisement, February 29, 1940.

3 "Floating Theatre Is Icebound Here," Williamston, North Carolina, *Enterprise*, January 30, 1940.

4 Aycock Brown, "Showboat Sidelights," Beaufort, North Carolina, *News*, February 29, 1940.

5 Advertisement, Beaufort, North Carolina, *News*, February 22, 1940.

6 Brown, "Showboat Sidelights."

7 Brown, "Covering the Waterfront."

8 Ibid.

9 Ibid. A year later, May 24, 1941, while on a voyage to Greenland, the *Modoc* blundered into the middle of the British attack on the German battleship *Bismarck*, but managed to slip out of the way without damage. ("Geographica: A Mission, a Battle, and a Mystery Ship," *National Geographic*, March 1990.)

10 Struble, interview.

11 Leon Massey, interview.

12 "Hunter-Pfeiffer End Partnership."

13 Ibid.

14 Ibid.

15 Stout, "Tonight at the River Landing," p. 44.

16 "Hunter-Pfeiffer End Partnership."

17 Larry H. Prescott, *Pamlico County, 100 Years, 1872-1972*, p. 200.

18 "Rep Ripples," *Billboard*, May 25, 1940.

19 Advertisement, Leonardtown, Maryland, *St. Mary's Enterprise*, July 12, 1940.

20 Advertisement, Warsaw, Virginia, *Northern Neck News*, July 26, 1940.

21 Advertisement, Leonardtown, Maryland, *St. Mary's Enterprise*, July 12, 1940.

22 "Paul Brady Is Back in Baltimore . . . ," *Billboard*, July 26, 1941, p. 26.

23 Marsh, interview.

24 Advertisement, *Billboard*, July 13, 1940.

25 "Showboat Now on Final Tour," Kilmarnock, Virginia, *Rappahannock Record*, July 11, 1940.

26 "Original Showboat May Quit Cruising," *Billboard*, August 31, 1940, p. 38.

27 "Once Popular Showboat Closes Colorful Career," Raleigh, North Carolina, *News and Observer*, August 23, 1940.

28 Kieffer, "Show Boat."

29 Ibid.

30 "Flames Destroy Famed Showboat," Savannah, Georgia, *Morning News*, November 15, 1941.

31 Kieffer, "Show Boat."

32 "Original Showboat's Finale," *Billboard*, September 7, 1940, p. 24.

33 Advertisement, *Billboard*, September 14, 1940.

34 Advertisement, *Billboard*, October 5, 1940.

35 "Showboat to Return Monday," Baltimore, Maryland, *News Post*, October 22, 1940.

36 "Showboat Is at Long Dock," Baltimore, Maryland, *News Post*, October 29, 1940.

37 "Showboat to Open," unidentified clipping.

38 "Showboat to Return Monday."

39 "Original Show Boat to Dock in Coin-jock," Elizabeth City, North Carolina, *Daily Advance*, November 15, 1940.

40 "Floating Theatre Coming Next Week," Georgetown, South Carolina, *Times*, January 3, 1941

41 Advertisement, Georgetown, South Carolina, *Times*, January 3, 1941.

42 "Floating Theatre Coming Next Week," Beaufort, South Carolina, *Gazette*, January 9, 1941.

43 "Ban On at Parris Island to Prevent Flu Spread," Beaufort, South Carolina, *Gazette*, January 16, 1941.

44 Advertisement, Savannah, Georgia, *Morning News*, January 26, 1941.

45 "Colorful Phase of Theater Ends with River Blaze," Savannah, Georgia, *Morning News*, November 15, 1941.

46 Marsh, interview.

47 "Original Showboat Goes to New Owner," *Billboard*, May 14, 1941, p. 26.

48 "Colorful Phase of Theater Ends with River Blaze."

49 Ibid.

50 "Original Showboat Goes to New Owner."

51 Ibid.

52 "Flames Destroy Famed Showboat."

53 Ibid.

54 Marsh, interview.

55 "Flames Destroy Famed Showboat."

CHAPTER 13   CURTAIN CALL

1 Marsh, interview.

2 Larry Clark, *Toby Shows: A Form of American Popular Theatre*, unpublished Ph.D. dissertation, p. 126; Klassen, *Tent Repertoire Theatre*, p. 35.

3 Klassen, *Tent Repertoire Theatre*, p. 34.

4 George Knight, interview with Pop Neel, quoted in Gough, "It Don't Stop Here Any More," p. 218.

5 Klassen, *Tent Repertoire Theatre*, p. 36.

6 Welby C. Choate and Phillip D. Atteberry, *A History of Choate's Comedians*, p. 15.

7 Schaffner and Johnson, *Toby and Me*, p. 170; quoted in Klassen, *Tent Repertoire Theatre*, p. 37.

8 Klassen, *Tent Repertoire Theatre*, p. 37.

9 "Chesapeake City," Elkton, Maryland, *Cecil Democrat*, April 28, 1928.

10 Edward J. Ludwig, III, *The Chesapeake and Delaware Canal, Gateway to Paradise*, p. 29.

11 Ibid., p. 6.

12 John Watson, interview.

13 "Chesapeake City," Elkton, Maryland, *Cecil Democrat*, November 1, 1930.

14 Watson, interview.

15 "Chesapeake City," Elkton, Maryland, *Cecil Democrat*, August 13, 1932.

16 Deed, Cecil County land records.

17 Struble, interview.

18 Mr. and Mrs. Walter Cooling, interview.

19 "Chesapeake City," Elkton, Maryland, *Cecil Democrat*, February 6, 1932.

20 "Chesapeake City," Elkton, Maryland, *Cecil Democrat*, January 12, 1935.

21 "Chesapeake City," Elkton, Maryland, *Cecil Democrat*, June 13, 1936.

22 "Chesapeake City," Elkton, Maryland, *Cecil Democrat*, January 19, 1935.

23 "Chesapeake City," Elkton, Maryland, *Cecil Democrat*, November 7, 1936.

24 Cooling, interview.

25 "The Sweetest Girl in Dixie," Elkton, Maryland, *Cecil Democrat*, November 4, 1934.

26 Last Will and Testament, James Adams.

27 Cline, interview.

28 Death certificate, Selba Adams.

29 Don Bollman, interview.

30 George Grim, interview.

31 Dr. James Adams, interview.

32 "Real-Life Showboat Captain."

33 Dr. James Adams, interview.

34 Death certificate, Beulah Adams Hunter.

35 Last will and testament, Beulah Adams.

36 Death certificate, Susie Adams Frost.

37 Comardo, "Showboat People."

38 Burial records, Twilford's Funeral Home.

39 Overman, "James Adams Floating Theatre," p. 77.

40 Dr. James Adams, interview.

41 Gough, "It Don't Stop Here Any More," p. 225.

42 "Rep Ripples," *Billboard*, October 22, 1938, p. 26

43 "Rep Ripples," *Billboard*, May 27, 1939, p. 25.

44 "Final Curtain," *Billboard*, January 27, 1940, p. 29.

45 "Rep Ripples," *Billboard*, December 17, 1938, p. 27.

46 Choate and Atteberry, *Choate's Comedians*.

47 "Hayworth Gives Up Circle for Health; Continues with Unit," *Billboard*, March 1, 1941, p. 26.

48 "Monte Novarro Tosses Posey to Toby 'SeaBee' Hayworth," *Billboard*, March 8, 1941, p. 53.

49 "Hayworth Plans 2 Winter Units," *Billboard*, September 20, 1941, p. 27.

50 Comardo, interview.

51 "Rep Ripples," *Billboard*, November 16, 1940.

52 Thayer Roberts, Vertical file.

53 "Final Curtain," *Billboard*, January 4, 1941.

54 Fred Fearing, interview.

55 Paul Berry brought the book to my attention. The book is not dated, but Berry places it in 1921.

56 Paul Berry, interview.

57 John Barth, *The Floating Theatre*, p. 7.

58 Ibid., p. vi.

59 Ibid., p. 250.

60 Ibid., p. 251.

61 Ibid., 78-82.

62 Frederick Tilp, *This was Potomac River*, p. 259.

63 Ibid., p. 262.

64 Frederick Tilp, letter to Burgess.

65 Robert H. Burgess, letter to author.

66 Tilp, *This Was Potomac River*, p. 259.

Bibliography

BOOKS

Barth, John. *The Floating Opera* and *End of the Road*. New York: Doubleday, Anchor Press, 1988.

Bernheim, Alfred L. *The Business of the Theatre, an Economic History of the American Theatre 1750-1932*. New York: Benjamin Blom, Inc., 1932.

Bogle, Donald. *Toms, Coons, Mulattoes, Mammies, & Bucks*. New York: The Continuum Printing Company, rev., 1989.

Brown, Herbert Ross. *The Sentimental Novel in America 1789-1860*. Durham, North Carolina: Duke University Press, 1940.

Burgess, Robert H. *This Was Chesapeake Bay*. Centreville, Maryland: Tidewater Publishers, 1963.

Business Directory, Ironton, Ohio, 1907.

Choate, Welby C., and Atteberry, Phillip D. *A History of Choate's Comedians*. Manuscript, Museum of Repertoire Americana, no date.

City Directory. Charlotte, North Carolina. 1912, 1913, 1914, 1915.

Dashiell, Segar Cofer. *Smithfield, a Pictorial History*. Norfolk, Virginia: Donning Company, 1977.

Dickinson, Rogers. *Edna Ferber, Whose Novel "So Big" Was Awarded the Pulitzer Prize for the Best American Novel of 1924, A Biographical Sketch with a Bibliography*. Garden City, New York: Doubleday, Page & Co., 1925.

Dictionary of American Naval Fighting Ships. Vol. IV. Washington, D. C.: Navy Department, Naval History Division, 1969.

Ferber, Edna. *A Peculiar Treasure*. New York: Doubleday, Doran & Co., Inc., 1939.

——. *Show Boat*. Garden City, New York: Doubleday, Doran & Company, Inc., 1926.

Footner, Hulbert. *Country Love*. London: Hodder and Stoughton, Ltd., no date. (A copy is in the Calvert Marine Museum.)

Fordin, Hugh. *Getting to Know Him, A Biography of Oscar Hammerstein II*. New York: Random House, 1977.

Gilbert, Julie Goldsmith. *Ferber, A Biography*. Garden City, New York: Doubleday & Company, Inc., 1978.

Graham, Philip. *Showboats, the History of an American Institution*. Austin and London: University of Texas Press, 1951.

Hartzer, Ronald B. *To Great and Useful Purpose, A History of the Wilmington District U.S. Army Corps of Engineers*. Wilmington, N. C.: U.S. Army Corps of Engineers, 1984.

Haynie, Miriam. *Reedville 1874-1974*. Reedville, Virginia: The Bethany United Methodist Men, 1974.

Krueger, Miles. *Show Boat, the Story of a Classic American Musical*. New York: Oxford University Press, 1977.

Ludwig, Edward J. III. *The Chesapeake and Delaware Canal, Gateway to Paradise.* Elkton, Maryland: Cecil County Bicentennial Committee, 1979.

McArthur, Benjamin. *Actors and American Culture, 1880-1920.* Philadelphia, Pennsylvania: Temple University Press, 1984.

McKennon, Joe. *A Pictorial History of the American Carnival, Volumes I and II.* Sarasota, Florida: Carnival Publishers, 1972.

Merchant Vessels of the United States. Annual List. Washington, D. C.: GPO, annually.

Ostrander, Gilman M. *American Civilization in the First Machine Age: 1890-1940.* New York: Harper & Row, 1970.

Prescott, Larry H., ed. *Pamlico County, 100 Years, 1872-1972.* Pamlico County Historical Society, 1972.

Rourke, Constance. *American Humor.* New York: Harcourt, Brace and Company, 1931.

Schaffner, Neil with Johnson, Vance. *The Fabulous Toby and Me.* Englewood Cliffs, New Jersey: Prentice Hall, 1968.

Sherman, Robert L. *Actors and Authors with Composers and Managers Who Helped Make Them Famous, a Chronological Record and Brief Biography of Theatrical Celebrities from 1750 to 1950.* Chicago: Published by the author, no date.

———. *Drama Cyclopedia, a Bibliography of Plays and Players.* Chicago: Published by the author, 1944.

Shepherd Centennial: Salt River / Shepherd, 1857-1957. Shepherd, Michigan: Shepherd Area Historical Society, 1981.

Slout, William L. *Theatre in a Tent.* Bowling Green, Ohio: Bowling Green University Popular Press, 1972.

Tilp, Frederick. *This Was Potomac River.* Alexandria, Virginia: Published by the author, 1978.

Toll, Robert C. *Blacking Up, The Minstrel Show in Nineteenth-Century America.* New York: Oxford University Press, 1974.

Wilson, John C. *Virginia's Northern Neck, A Pictorial History.* Norfolk/Virginia Beach, Virginia: The Donning Company, 1984.

DISSERTATIONS

Birdwell, Christine Ruth. "Heroines of American Midwestern Repertoire Theatre Comedy-Dramas." Unpublished Ph.D dissertation, Michigan State University, 1984.

Clark, Larry. "Toby Shows: A Form of American Popular Theatre." Unpublished Ph.D. dissertation, University of Illinois, 1963.

Klassen, Robert. "The Tent-Repertoire Theatre: A Rural American Institution." Unpublished Ph.D. dissertation, Michigan State University, 1969.

Landis, Kelly Magnuson. "Circle Stock Repertoire Theatre in America." Unpublished Ph.D. dissertation, University of Illinois, 1988.

DOCUMENTS

Burial records. Twilford's Funeral Home, Elizabeth City, North Carolina.

Death certificate, Beulah Adams Hunter. Saginaw County, Michigan, Courthouse, May 1, 1975.

Death certificate, Samuel Hunter. Ironton, Ohio, Public Health Department, March 9, 1923.

Death certificate, Selba Adams. Isabella County, Michigan, Courthouse, July 13, 1943.

Death certificate, Susie Adams Frost. Saginaw County, Michigan, Courthouse, February 21, 1979.

Land deed, Cecil County, Elkton, Maryland. RRC 50, page 48.

Land deeds, Charlotte, North Carolina. Book 377, page 535. Book 426, page 101.

Last will and testament of Beulah Adams. Saginaw County, Michigan, Courthouse.

Last will and testament of James E. Adams. Cecil County Courthouse, Elkton, Maryland.

Marriage license, James E. Adams and Gertrude E. Powlson. Bay County Courthouse, Bay City, Michigan, July 5, 1895.

Marriage license, Charles M. Hunter and Beulah Adams. Wayne County Courthouse, Goldsboro, North Carolina, April 20, 1911.

Minutes of the Commissioners of Leonardtown, July 7, 1937. (Source: Al Gough, Jr.)

U. S. Census, Shepherd, Michigan, 1900 and 1910.

ARCHIVES

Calvert Marine Museum, Solomons, Maryland.

Chesapeake Bay Maritime Museum, St. Michaels, Maryland.

Isle of Wight Museum, Smithfield, Virginia.

Library for the Performing Arts, Lincoln Center, New York, New York.

Library of Congress, Copyright Division, Washington, D. C.

Mariners' Museum, Newport News, Virginia.

Maryland Room, Enoch Pratt Free Library, Baltimore, Maryland.

Maryland State Archives, Annapolis, Maryland.

McKeldin Library, Special Collections, University of Maryland, College Park, Maryland.

Museum of Repertoire Americana, Old Threshers, Mt. Pleasant, Iowa.

Museum of the Albemarle, Elizabeth City, North Carolina.

North Carolina Collection, University of North Carolina, Chapel Hill, North Carolina.

State Historical Society of Wisconsin, Madison, Wisconsin.

Virginia State Library and Archives, Richmond, Virginia.

ARCHIVAL MATERIAL

Adams, Beulah. Letter to Eunice Overman. Not dated, but written from 800 Mackinaw Street, Saginaw, Michigan (Source: Carlista Golden).

Adams family Bible (Source: Vivian O'Leary).

Adams Sisters vaudeville act, unidentified newspaper clipping (Source: Marguerite Young).

Advertisements, fragments from 1915 (Source: Calvert Marine Museum).

Barlow, Dorothy. Unpublished journals, 1925 and 1926 (Source: Mrs. George Davies).

Beard and Adams advertisement (Source: Marguerite Young).

Brasfield, Boob. Vertical file, Museum of Repertoire Americana.

Ferber, Edna. Archives, State Historical Society of Wisconsin.

Guest Book, St. Thomas Episcopal Church, Bath, North Carolina, 1925.

Handbill, Original Floating Theatre at Wellwood Country Club, North East, Maryland, October 1, 1938 (Source: Calvert Marine Museum).

Heralds: James Adams Floating Theatre, 1924, 1927 (Source: Marguerite Young); 1928, 1929, 1930, 1931 (Source: Curtis Showprint Company). Original Floating Theatre, 1937, 1939 (Source: Curtis Showprint Company). Show Boat Players, 1937 (Source: Chesapeake Bay Maritime Museum); 1938, 1939 (Source: Curtis Showprint Company).

Hersey, Adele (Mrs. Frederick). Journals, 1921–1933 (Source: Mariners Museum. The Hersey journals were brought to my attention by Robert H. Burgess.).

Kraft, Clinton J. Undated letter (Source: Calvert Marine Museum).

Photographs, Chesapeake Bay Maritime Museum.

Photographs, Mariners Museum.

Poster, Mathews County, Fourth of July, 1918 (Source: Calvert Marine Museum).

Poster, Seaford, Delaware, October 7–12, 1940 (Source: Chesapeake Bay Maritime Museum).

Program for *The Broken Butterfly* (Source: Calvert Marine Museum).

Program for *Over the Hills to the Poor House*, Baltimore, December 3–9, 1939 (Source: Chesapeake Bay Maritime Museum).

Program for musical, *Show Boat* (Source: Library for the Performing Arts).

Program for *Ten Nights in a Bar Room*, Baltimore, November 26–December 2, 1939 (Source: Chesapeake Bay Maritime Museum).

Roberts, Thayer. Vertical file, Library for the Performing Arts.

Seymoure, Milford. Newspaper clippings from scrapbook (Source: Calvert Marine Musuem).

Seymoure, Rachel. Letter to her brother, Millard Fairbanks, July 26, 1937 (Source: Chesapeake Bay Maritime Museum).

Shareholders' Report, Million Dollar Joy Boat, Inc. (Source: Chesapeake Bay Maritime Museum).

Sherman family scrapbook (Source: Nelson S. Sherman, Sr.).

Tilp, Frederick. Letter to Robert H. Burgess, February 9, 1971 (Source: Robert H. Burgess).

Tucker, Jack (writer for Saginaw, Michigan, *News*). Undated clipping from the Saginaw *News*.

Waldorf, Leslie D. Unpublished journals, 1915, 1915A, 1916, 1917 (Source: Maisie Comardo).

LETTERS AND INTERVIEWS

Adams, Dr. James. Midland, Michigan.

Basnight, Mose. Roanoke Island, North Carolina.

Beale, John. Hague, Virginia.

Beauchamp, Irvin. Warsaw, Virginia.

Berry, Paul. Solomons, Maryland.

Bollman, Don. Mecosta, Michigan.

Bordman, Gerald. Glen Roy, Pennsylvania.

Burgess, Robert H. Newport News, Virginia.

Cline, Harold. Shepherd, Michigan.

Cooling, Mr. and Mrs. Walter. Chesapeake City, Maryland.

Comardo, Maisie. Leicester, New York.

Dashiell, Segar Cofer. Smithfield, Virginia.

Fearing, Fred. Elizabeth City, North Carolina.

Footner, Geoffrey M. Hurlock, Maryland.

Gibbs, Mildred. Middletown, North Carolina.

Glazer, Irvin. Springfield, Pennsylvania.

Gough, Al, Jr. Leonardtown, Maryland.

Grim, George. Shepherd, Michigan.

Hamilton, Harry. Georgetown, Maryland.

Haynie, Florence. Richmond, Virginia.

Littleton, Arrington. Swansboro, North Carolina.

Lewis, Gillian. Kilmarnock, Virginia.

Loeschke, Maravene. Baltimore, Maryland.

Lumpkin, Mrs. Mason. Irvington, Virginia.

Marsh, Rachel. St. Michaels, Maryland.

Massey, Leon. Church Hill, Maryland.

McCall, Nelson. Charlestown, Maryland.

McDaniel, Donald. Worthington, Ohio.

Moger, W. L., Sr. Newport News, Virginia.

Newton, Ed. Hague, Virginia.

O'Leary, Vivian. Dearborn, Michigan.

Parker, June. Tappahannock, Virginia.

Parks, Norris. Newport News, Virginia.

Pilpel, Harriet F. New York, New York.

Schaffner, Caroline. Mt. Pleasant, Iowa.

Schuler, Billie Henderson. Marquette, Michigan.

Sherman, Nelson S. Halstead, Pennsylvania.

Spencer, R. S. Engelhard, North Carolina.

Stateler, Nyle. Continental, Ohio.

Struble, Robert. Deerfield Beach, Florida.

Watson, John. Chesapeake City, Maryland.

Young, Marguerite. Englewood, Florida.

ARTICLES (AUTHORS KNOWN)

Albert, Allen D. "The Tents of the Conservative." *Scribner's Magazine* July, 1922: 54-59.

Azrael, Louis. "Louis Azrael Says." Baltimore, Maryland, *News Post* September 6, 1937.

———. "Louis Azrael Says." Baltimore, Maryland, *News Post* October 27, 1936.

Bailey, Eloise. "The Original Floating Theatre Came to Camden County." Woodbine, Georgia *Camden County Tribune*, January 12, 1989.

Brown, Aycock. "Covering the Waterfront." Beaufort, North Carolina, *News* March 14, 1940.

———. "Showboat Sidelights." Beaufort, North Carolina, *News* February 29, 1940.

Burgess, Robert H. "A View of the Chesapeake That Has Disappeared." *Chesapeake Bay Magazine* January, 1982: 19-22.

Carraway, Gertrude S. "To Write 'Showboat' Story: Ferber to Tell of Experience While in East Carolina." Greensboro, North Carolina, *Daily News* February 10, 1929.

Chowning, Larry S. "Show Boat." *Chesapeake Bay Magazine* June, 1987: 62-65.

Clark, Norman. "Showboat Will Visit Us for First Time in Its History." Baltimore, Maryland, *News Post* October 19, 1939.

Cocroft, Thoda. "The Floating Theater Thrives." *The Bookman* December, 1927: 396-398.

Comardo, Maisie. "Showboat People." Unpublished (Source: Maisie Comardo).

Copinger, May Irene. "Floating Theatre Makes Week Stands, Playing Popular Bills at Towns along the Shores of Bay." Baltimore, Maryland, *Sunday Sun* November 22, 1925.

Crockford, Hamilton. "Ship's Pilot, after 54 Years aboard Boats, Is Just Beginning to Learn about the Water." Richmond, Virginia, *Times-Dispatch* January 21, 1951.

Dulaney, Carroll. "Day by Day." Unidentified newspaper clipping. (Source: Calvert Marine Museum.)

English, Paul. "T. R. M. P. A. Notes." *Billboard* May 21, 1927: 26.

Fenwick, Charles E. "History of St. Aloysius Church." Published upon the dedication of the new St. Aloysius Church, Leonardtown, Maryland, March 18, 1962 (Source: St. Aloysius Church archives).

Francis, Michelle. "The James Adams Floating Theatre: Edna Ferber's Showboat." *Carolina Comments*, vol. 28, no. 5, September, 1980: 135-142.

Gough, Al, Jr. "It Don't Stop Here Anymore." *Chronicles of St. Marys* Summer, 1989: 209-230.

Green, Joseph O. III. "Showboating in the Albemarle." *The State* February 15, 1972: 8 (Provided by Maisie Comardo).

Griffith, Jack. "Adams' Floating Theatre as 'Jack' Griffith Sees It." *Billboard* November 6, 1920: 18.

Hamilton, Clayton. "Melodrama, Old and New." *The Bookman* May, 1911: 309-314.

Haynie, Miriam. "Called the Show Boat 'Hell-Hole of Iniquity.'" Unidentified clipping internally dated 1934 (Source: Calvert Marine Museum).

Hollman, Fred. "Welcome to the T. R. M. P. A." *Billboard* March 27, 1926: 26.

Johnson, Clinton H. "Show Boat's All Set to Puff Along." Unidentified clipping from Baltimore, Maryland, paper (Source: Rare Books Department, University of Maryland Library).

Kieffer, R. W. "Show Boat: Showdown." Baltimore, Maryland, *Sunday Sun* September 15, 1940.

Kramme, Michael. "Showboat Casts as Reported in Bill Bruno's Bulletin." Unpublished paper (Source: Donald NcDaniel, *Showboat Centennials*).

Marlow, J. Frank. "The Play's the Thing." *Billboard* September 8, 1928: 41.

Marvin, Rose T. "Shepherd Man's Show Boat Plot for Novel." Lansing, Michigan, *State Journal* June 13, 1937.

McDougall, Maude. "Dockstorming Versus Barnstorming." New York *Morning Telegraph* October 29, 1916, section two: 1.

Overman, W. J. III. "The James Adams Floating Theatre." In Lou N. Overman & Edna M. Shannonhouse, eds., *1975 Year Book, Pasquotank Historical Society* 3: 70-79.

Pool, Ralph. "Edna Ferber's Show Boat Being Rebuilt at Elizabeth City." Greensboro, North Carolina, *Daily News* February 26, 1928.

Shipley, Ann. "The Society Hour Glass." Wilmington, Delaware, *Delmarva Sunday Star* October 23, 1932; November 13, 1932; November 20, 1932; May 21, 1933.

Silliman, Jayne. "The Story of Old Aurora." Washington, North Carolina, *Beauford County Magazine* 4: 7-11.

Sadler, Harley. "The Tent Repertoire Situation." *Billboard* December 10, 1927: 48.

Saunders, Elizabeth. "And So Hunter Stayed with the Show Boat." Elizabeth City, North Carolina, *Independent* April 6, 1928.

Stout, Wesley W. "Tonight at the River Landing." *The Saturday Evening Post* October 31, 1925: 44, 46.

Tyndall, Ann. "Show Boat Lives in Tidewater Memories." Washington, North Carolina, *Daily News* February 1, 1974.

Waldorf, Leslie D. "Old Showboat Provided Dramatic Entertainment for Tidewater for Years." Elizabeth City, North Carolina, *Independent Star* May 2, 1954.

Warner, Eugene. "Showboat Skipper Finds Its Glamour Mostly Fiction." Washington, D. C. *Times-Herald* September 6, 1939.

Watkins, Joseph P. "The James Adams Floating Theatre." *The World Magazine* September 11, 1927: 8.

Wilmer, Ann. "'Hell Hole of Iniquity,' Showboating of Yore on the Rivers and the Bay." *Virginia Country* Summer, 1987: 32-34.

ARTICLES (ANONYMOUS)

"Actor's Child Barred." *Billboard* November 19, 1910: 3.

"Actors Enact Real Drama; No Foolin!" Windsor, North Carolina, *Bertie Ledger-Advance* May 21, 1937.

"Adams Boat Is Popular." *Billboard* July 26, 1930: 26.

"Adams Cast in Rehearsal." *Billboard* April 25, 1931: 24.

"Adams Closes Show." *Billboard* December 6, 1919: 14.

"Adams' Floating Theatre." *Billboard* June 18, 1918: 23.

"Adams Floating Theatre . . . ," Tappahannock, Virginia, *Rappahannock Times* July 29, 1927.

"Adams Floating Theatre, Well Known in Carolina, Is Believed Total Loss." Elizabeth City, North Carolina, *Daily Advance* November 26, 1927.

"Adams Opens This Week." *Billboard* March 13, 1920: 15.

"Adams' Showboat Lauded." *Billboard* October 29, 1927: 31.

"Adams' Showboat Opens on May 9." *Billboard* April 23, 1932: 24.

"Adamses and Hunters in Chicago." *Billboard* March 5, 1927: 30.

"Additional Locals." Crisfield, Maryland, *Times* July 11, 1914: 2.

"Agreement Is Reached in Plan to Reduce Tent-Show Royalties." *Billboard* July 2, 1927: 5.

"Airplanes to Stunt to Aid 'Show Boat.'" Wilmington, Delaware, *Morning News* October 29, 1932.

"America's Best-Known 'Show Boat' Veteran." *P.D.Q.-Phillips Delicious Quality* October, 1939: 6.

"Ban On at Parris Island to Prevent Flu Spread." Beaufort, South Carolina, *Gazette* January 16, 1941.

"Bestcity's Show Boat Meets with Disaster in Dismal Swamp Canal; 'Pop' Neel Stands By His Craft." Elizabeth City, North Carolina, *Daily Advance* November 16, 1929.

"The Best Show There Is Is 'Smiling Through,' says Captain Seymoure." Unidentified clipping in the Calvert Marine Museum, June, 1939.

"Boats Move in Channel." Norfolk, Virginia, *Ledger-Dispatch* June 16, 1939.

"Boycott of Alabama Cotton Planned by Showmen as Retaliation for Anti-Tent Show Legislation." *Billboard* March 17, 1928: 5.

"Brasfield Show Takes to Water." *Billboard* April 17, 1937: 27.

"Built as Sub Fighter, Ship to Be Showboat." Baltimore, Maryland, *News Post* January 1, 1929.

"Cables and Gas Mains Broken by Show Boat Are Being Repaired." Norfolk, Virginia, *Ledger-Dispatch* November 28, 1927.

"A Call to Action." *Billboard* January 15, 1927: 50.

"Captain Milford Seymoure Is Worried." Unidentified newspaper clipping for week of June 1, 1939 (Source: Calvert Marine Museum).

"Charles F. Harrison, A Tribute by J. D. Colegrove." *Billboard* November 24, 1928: 33.

"Charlie Hunter Says N. C. Taxes Are Staggering." Elizabeth City, North Carolina, *Independent* May 29, 1936.

"Chesapeake City." Elkton, Maryland, *Cecil Democrat* April 28, 1928; November 1, 1930; November 8, 1930; December 12, 1931; February 6, 1932; August 13, 1932; May 20, 1933; September 22, 1934; January 12, 1935; January 19, 1935; June 13, 1936; November 7, 1936.

"Circus Gossip." *Billboard* October 13, 1906: 27.

"Colorful Phase of Theater Ends with River Blaze." Savannah, Georgia, *Morning News* November 15, 1941.

"Comedy Is Next Showboat Bill." Baltimore, Maryland, *News Post* November 15, 1939.

"Coming Again." Unidentified clipping for the week of July 5-11, 1937 (Source: Calvert Marine Museum).

"Complete Change of Bill Is Presented on Show Boat." Norfolk, Virginia, *Ledger-Dispatch* May 27, 1932.

"County Swept by Destructive Northeast Storm." Mathews, Virginia, *Journal* August 24, 1933.

"Court Drama Reveals a Trouper's Loyalty." *Billboard* February 4, 1939: 27.

"Crowd Waits Patiently for Show; Lights Fail; 'Some Baby' Tonight." Elizabeth City, North Carolina, *Daily Advance* June 20, 1939.

"Crowds Frolic at Floating Theatre." Mathews, Virginia, *Journal* June 28, 1928.

"Deaths in the Profession." *Billboard* January 6, 1923: 28; January 23, 1926: 90; August 13, 1927: 164; February 16, 1929: 88; October 3, 1931: 60.

"Director." Unidentified newspaper clipping from Baltimore paper, 1939 (Source: Chesapeake Bay Maritime Museum).

"End of the Carnival." Washington, Indiana, *Herald* May 9, 1904.

"Extension of Tour of Show Boat Proposed." Elizabeth City, North Carolina, *Independent* February 5, 1932.

"Fairfields Notes." Warsaw, Virginia, *Northern Neck News* July 13, 1917.

"Famous Novel, 'Lena Rivers,' to Be Acted in Montross August 6th." Warsaw, Virginia, *Northern Neck News* July 30, 1937.

"Famous Showboat Opens Here Monday." Camden, New Jersey, *Courier-Post* September 30, 1932.

". . . Featuring Sea Bee Hayworth . . ." Unidentified clipping from Crisfield, Maryland, October, 1938 (Source: Calvert Marine Museum).

"Final Curtain." *Billboard* August 19, 1939: 27; January 4, 1941: 30.

"Fire and Theft Insurance for Actors' Equity Members." *Billboard* September 3, 1927: 5.

"First Floating Theatre Plays on Original Spot." Washington, North Carolina, *Daily News* May 5, 1939.

"First Show Playhouse Last Night." Washington, North Carolina, *Daily News* March 3, 1914.

"Flames Destroy Famed Showboat." Savannah, Georgia, *Morning News* November 15, 1941.

"Floating Theatre." Fredericksburg, Virginia, *Free Lance-Star* May 26, 1914.

"Floating Theatre Boat Estelle Successfully Launched Yesterday." Washington, North Carolina, *Daily News* January 28, 1914.

"Floating Theatre Causes Havoc in Norfolk Harbor." Elizabeth City, North Carolina, *Daily Advance* November 28, 1927.

"Floating Theatre Coming Next Week." Mathews, Virginia, *Journal* June 12, 1930.

"Floating Theatre Coming Next Week." Gloucester, Virginia, *Gazette and Mathews Journal* May 19, 1938.

"Floating Theatre Coming Next Week." Georgetown, South Carolina, *Times* January 3, 1941.

"Floating Theatre Coming Next Week." Beaufort, South Carolina, *Gazette* January 9, 1941.

"Floating Theatre Giving Best Shows." Elizabeth City, North Carolina, *Daily Advance* January 17, 1940.

"The Floating Theatre Here for 2 Months." Elizabeth City, North Carolina, *Daily Independent* February 22, 1937.

"Floating Theatre Here Next Week." Mathews, Virginia, *Journal* June 11, 1936.

"Floating Theatre in Performance." Unidentified clipping, October 15, 1930 (Source: Marguerite Young).

"Floating Theatre in Salisbury for the Entire Week." Salisbury, Maryland, *Wicomico Times* November 1, 1934: 1.

"Floating Theatre Is Coming to Tapp'k 27th, for One Week." Tappahannock, Virginia, *Rappahannock Times* June 16, 1938.

"Floating Theatre Is Icebound Here." Williamston, North Carolina, *Enterprise* January 30, 1940.

"The Floating Theatre Is Preparing for Tour." Elizabeth City, North Carolina, *Independent* March 21, 1930.

"The Floating Theatre Now in Baltimore . . . " Unidentified newspaper clipping, Baltimore, 1939 (Source: Calvert Marine Museum).

"Floating Theatre Sinks in Bay." *Billboard* December 3, 1927: 30.

"Floating Theatre Sold." Easton, Maryland, *Star-Democrat* May 19, 1933.

"Floating Theatre Still Touring Readers' Memories." Raleigh, North Carolina, *News and Observer* February 28, 1980.

"Floating Theatre to Be Here Next Week." Elizabeth City, North Carolina, *Independent* October 30, 1931.

"Floating Theatre to Go to Colerain." Elizabeth City, North Carolina, *Daily Advance* October 31, 1938.

"Floating Theatre to Winter in This City." Elizabeth City, North Carolina, *Independent* September 28, 1923.

"A Floating Theatre Which Stages Old Time Melodramas." Philadelphia *Evening Bulletin*, 1932. Date uncertain. Year determined by theatre's repertoire (Source: Marguerite Young).

"The Folks Who Live in Boats on the City's Waterfront." Elizabeth City, North Carolina, *Independent* July 8, 1932.

"Former Ocheyedan Man Buried Monday." Sibley, Iowa, *Gazette-Tribune* October 22, 1931.

"Fourth at Reedville." Warsaw, Virginia, *Northern Neck News* July 7, 1916.

"Front Row." Washington, D. C., *Evening Star* November 25, 1930: B6.

"Girl Falls Overboard Much Comedy Results." Elizabeth City, North Carolina, *Daily Advance* November 19, 1921.

"Giving All His Time to Writing New Plays." *Billboard* January 20, 1923: 29.

"Good Show Given Again Last Night." Washington, North Carolina, *Daily News* March 4, 1914.

"Hatch-Adams Show Quarantined." *Billboard* November 12, 1904: 18.

"Hatch and Adams Dissolve Partnership." *Billboard* December 3, 1904: 9.

"Hayworth Gives Up Circle for Health; Continues with Unit." *Billboard* March 1, 1941: 26.

"Hayworth Joins Med 'Opry.'" *Billboard* May 27, 1933: 23.

"Hayworth Plans 2 Winter Units." *Billboard* September 20, 1941: 27.

"Here Comes the Showboat, on Its Twenty-fourth Annual Tour." Unidentified newspaper clipping, Cambridge, Maryland, for week of November 8, 1937 (Source: Calvert Marine Museum).

"Hottest July in Thirty Years." Mathews, Virginia, *Journal* August 6, 1931.

"Howard Joins Adams." *Billboard* July 17, 1920: 14.

"Hunter-Pfeiffer End Partnership." *Billboard* May 4, 1940: 28.

"Hurricane Sweeps Gloucester." Gloucester, Virginia, *Gazette* August 24, 1933.

"In Drama." Baltimore, Maryland, *News Post* December 26, 1939.

"I Overheard Jim Gray. . . ." Unidentified newspaper clipping, possibly column by Aycock Brown of Beaufort, North Carolina, *News* (Source: Calvert Marine Museum).

"James Adams Boat Scores in Norfolk." *Billboard* June 4, 1932: 22.

"James Adams Does Well in Maryland." *Billboard* October 1, 1932: 22.

"The James Adams' Floating Theatre Has Been . . ." Leonardtown, Maryland, *St. Mary's Enterprise* July 28, 1917.

"James Adams Floating Theatre Sinks in Bay." Leonardtown, Maryland, *St. Mary's Beacon* December 2, 1927 (Source: Al Gough, Jr.).

"James Adams in Camden." *Billboard* October 15, 1932: 22.

"James Adams in New Hands." *Billboard* May 27, 1933: 23.

"James Adams in Stock Run." *Billboard* December 13, 1930: 26.

"The James Adams Show." Franklin, Virginia, *Tidewater News* May 21, 1909: 1.

"James Adams Showboat Narrowly Escapes Gale." *Billboard* November 26, 1932: 20.

"James Adams 10 Cent Shows." Gastonia, North Carolina, *Gazette* May 6, 1910: 1.

"James Adams to Rebuild His Theatre Here." Elizabeth City, North Carolina, *Independent* December 2, 1927.

"The Jones-Adams Congress of Novelties." *Billboard* November 11, 1905: 20.

"Jones and Adams Dissolve Partnership." *Billboard* September 8, 1906: 24.

"Jones Shows to Spend the Winter Here."
Washington, North Carolina, *Daily
News* September 14, 1913.

"'Joy Ship' Aground after Order to Quit
Burlington." Camden, New Jersey,
Courier-Post October 24, 1932.

"Judge Is Lenient to Showboat Worker."
Elizabeth City, North Carolina, *Daily
Advance* January 11, 1939.

"Kilmarnock." Kilmarnock, Virginia, *Rappahannock Record* August 27, 1919.

"Kinsale." Warsaw, Virginia, *Northern
Neck News* August 14, 1931; August
21, 1931.

"Last Show." Washington, North Carolina, *Daily News* July 2, 1910: 1.

"Leonardtown Is to Have a Novelty . . ."
Leonardtown, Maryland, *St. Mary's
Enterprise* July 31, 1915.

"Leyare's Joy Boat to Tour New Jersey."
Billboard May 14, 1932: 22.

"Local Briefs." Centreville, Maryland, *Record* October 10, 1914; October 17,
1914; October 24, 1914.

"Local News." Elkton, Maryland, *Cecil
Democrat* April 7, 1923.

"Local News Items." Onancock, Virginia,
Accomack News June 20, 1914.

"'Lure of City' Is Showboat's Bill." Baltimore, Maryland, *News Post* November 23, 1939.

"Many Reserve Seats for Show Boat
Play." Wilmington, Delaware, *Morning News* November 17, 1932.

"Marshal Walker Opens New Season October 29." *Billboard* October 22, 1932:
24.

"Masten and Neel with Adams." *Billboard*
April 6, 1918: 22.

"Melodrama on Showboat." Baltimore,
Maryland, *News Post* December 9,
1939.

"Minor Locals." Elkton, Maryland, *Cecil
County News* August 4, 1915; September 10, 1932.

"Miscellaneous Routes." *Billboard* March
14, 1908.

"Miss Ferber's Statement Re The Setting
of Her Novel." Elizabeth City, North
Carolina, *Independent* November 21,
1930.

"Monte Novarro Tosses Posey to Toby
'SeaBee' Hayworth." *Billboard* March
8, 1941: 53.

"Morattico." Kilmarnock, Virginia, *Rappahannock Record* September 10, 1919: 3.

"Mrs. Beulah Adams, 800 Mackinaw,
Had More Than Passing Interest . . .
" Unidentified article, June 6, 1962
(Source: Beulah Adams Hunter).

"No Play Tonight on Show Boat." Fredericksburg, Virginia, *Free Lance-Star*
July 16, 1928.

"Obituary, Rose Adams." Saginaw, Michigan, *News Courier-Herald* October 18,
1919: 7.

"Old Time Potomac River Show Boat
Going Modern." Washington, D. C.,
Sunday Star August 9, 1936.

"Once Popular Showboat Closes Colorful
Career." Raleigh, North Carolina,
News and Observer August 23, 1940
(Source: North Carolina Collection).

"'Original' Boat Hits Log, Sinks." *Billboard* November 12, 1938: 28.

"Original Floating Theatre." *Billboard*
May 29, 1937: 29; June 5, 1937: 29;
June 19, 1937: 28; July 10, 1937: 28.

"Original Show Boat, Here for Repairs,
Still Packs 'Em In on Its Old Circuit."
Unidentified clipping from Baltimore, Maryland, paper, week of June
5, 1933 (Source: Calvert Marine Museum).

"Original Showboat Finds Business
Okeh." *Billboard* September 24, 1938:
35.

"Original Showboat Goes to New
Owner." *Billboard* May 14, 1941: 26.

"Original Showboat Here for Repairs, Rehearsals." Baltimore, Maryland,
News Post June 6, 1933.

"Original Showboat in Florida Waters."
Billboard January 9, 1937: 26.

"Original Showboat May Quit Cruising,"
Billboard August 31, 1940: 38.

"Original Showboat on 23rd Annual
Tour." Unidentified clipping, May
23, 1936 (Source: Mariners' Museum).

"Original Showboat's Finale." *Billboard*
September 7, 1940: 24.

"Original Show Boat to Dock in Coinjock," Elizabeth City, North Carolina, *Daily Advance* November 15, 1940.

"Paul Brady Is Back in Baltimore . . ." *Billboard* July 26, 1941: 26.

"Paul English, Who Has Been Managing . . ." *Billboard* April 29, 1933: 54.

"Performers Heavy Losers." *Billboard* December 10, 1927: 48.

"Peter Hunter, Civil War Vet, Dies, Last Services Tuesday." Ironton, Ohio, *Sunday Tribune* June 12, 1939.

"'Playhouse' First Floating Theatre Is Now Practically All Complete." Washington, North Carolina, *Daily News* February 25, 1914.

"Playhouse Was Packed Last Night." Washington, North Carolina, *Daily News* March 7, 1914.

"Port Deposit." Elkton, Maryland, *Cecil County News* September 16, 1914.

Program of *The Parson's Bride, Billboard* September 7, 1929: 82.

"Public Getting Wise to 'Octopus' Tactics." *Billboard* August 20, 1927: 5.

"Real-Life Showboat Captain." Saginaw, Michigan, *News* November 21, 1948.

"Reedville." Warsaw, Virginia, *Northern Neck News* June 5, 1914; September 4, 1931.

"Rehearsals on Show Boat Shortly." Elizabeth City, North Carolina, *Daily Independent* April 10, 1937.

"Remarkable Career Ends at Death of R. J. Sherman." Susquehanna, Pennsylvania, *Susquehanna Transcript* August 9, 1939: 1.

"Reminiscences of a Kent County Resident: James Adams Floating Theatre." *Kent Shoreman* August, 1973: 7.

"Repertoire Notes." *Billboard* May 18, 1918: 22.

"Rep Ripples." *Billboard* October 30, 1937: 28; April 23, 1938: 26; November 19, 1938: 28; January 14, 1939: 27; May 6, 1939: 25; July 18, 1939: 26; October 7, 1939: 25; November 18, 1939: 26; May 25, 1940: 26; August 10, 1940: 26; November 16, 1940: 53; March 29, 1941: 26; June 7, 1941: 26; September 13, 1941: 27; October 18, 1941: 27.

"Rep Tattles." *Billboard* September 23, 1922: 28; January 13, 1923: 29; March 1, 1924: 28.

"The Robert Emmett Floating Theatre . . ." Leonardtown, Maryland, *St. Mary's Enterprise* September 25, 1915.

"Robert Emmett's Floating Theatre." Leonardtown, Maryland, *St. Mary's Enterprise* August 14, 1915; September 11, 1915.

"Robert J. Sherman." *Billboard* November 24, 1923: 28.

"Roberts and Company Please Another Showboat Crowd." Unidentified clipping from Wilmington, North Carolina (Source: Calvert Marine Museum).

"Routes." *Billboard* July 11, 1914; June 27, 1914; July 4, 1914; November 2, 1918; October 4, 1919; November 27, 1920; October 11, 1919; November 26, 1921; December 3, 1921; November 22, 1924; April 18, 1925; April 25, 1925; December 20, 1930; June 10, 1933.

"Routes Ahead." *Billboard* May 31, 1902: 8; January 31, 1903; July 21, 1906: 34.

"Saint Michaels." Easton, Maryland, *Star Democrat* October 31, 1914.

"Sam Hunter Died at an Early Hour Last Night." Ironton, Ohio, *Morning Irontonian* March 10, 1923.

"SeaBee Hayworth Adds Two Houses to Circle." *Billboard* January 14, 1939: 27.

"Seagoing Showboat Is Being Built Here," Baltimore, Maryland, *News Post* December 29, 1926.

"Sea-Going Theatre Makes Fortune for Its Owner." Minneapolis, Minnesota, *The Journal Magazine* October 31, 1926: 7.

"'Selb' Adams Adds Fiction to Radio Thriller." Shepherd, Michigan, *Isabella County Reporter* March 23, 1933 (Source: Irene Hamlin).

"Severe Electrical Storm Visits St. Mary's County." Leonardtown, Maryland, *St. Mary's Enterprise* July 16, 1937.

"Sherman Takes Over Additional Plays." *Billboard* February 26, 1921: 16.

"Shortage of Actors Reported by Feist." *Billboard* March 14, 1925: 28.

"Show Boat Again Here Next Week." Onancock, Virginia, *Eastern Shore News* November 22, 1928.

"Show Boat Again on the Chesapeake." Baltimore, Maryland, *Sunday Sun* February 26, 1928.

"Showboat Captain Talks at Carolina." Elizabeth City, North Carolina, *Independent*, May 25, 1936.

"'The Showboat' Comes to Dock in Baltimore, and an Earlier Patron Revisits It after 25 Years." Baltimore, Maryland, *Sunday Sun* October 29, 1939.

"Show Boat Coming." Mathews, Virginia, *Journal* June 11, 1936.

"Show Boat Dream Ends." Camden, New Jersey, *Courier-Post* October 13, 1932: 3.

"Show Boaters See 'Show Boat.'" Baltimore, Maryland, *News Post* December 13, 1939.

"Show Boat Has Been Refurbished." Wilmington, North Carolina, *Morning Star* March 31, 1934.

"Show Boat Has Grand Opening." Smithfield, Virginia, *Times* May 27, 1937.

"'Show Boat' Here Monday." Norfolk, Virginia, *Ledger-Dispatch* May 21, 1932.

"Showboat Is at Long Dock." Baltimore, Maryland, *News Post* October 29, 1940.

"Show Boat Is Coming, but Not Hunters." Elizabeth City, North Carolina, *Daily Independent* February 4, 1937.

"Show Boat Is in Port for Two-Week Stand." Unidentified clipping, Charleston, South Carolina, March, 1939 (Source: Calvert Marine Museum).

"Show Boat Is Now Owned by Nina B. Howard." Elizabeth City, North Carolina, *Independent* October 27, 1933.

"Show Boat Is Safe in Ship Yard of City." Elizabeth City, North Carolina, *Daily Advance* November 22, 1929.

"Showboat Lady Dies Suddenly." Southport, North Carolina, *Port State Pilot* March 1, 1939.

"Show Boat May Quit Carolina Taxes Too High." Elizabeth City, North Carolina, *Independent* May 18, 1934.

"Showboat Now on Final Tour." Kilmarnock, Virginia, *Rappahannock Record* July 11, 1940.

"Showboat Pays First Visit to City." Baltimore, Maryland, *News Post* October 23, 1939.

"Showboat Pilot Freed." Camden, New Jersey, *Courier-Post* October 15, 1932: 3.

"Showboat Players Aided by Weather." *Billboard* September 25, 1937: 27.

"Show Boat Players Get Prepared for Openings." Elizabeth City, North Carolina *Daily Advance* January 7, 1939.

"Showboat Players Here—Now on Auto Trailers." Williamston, North Carolina, *Enterprise* March 30, 1937.

"Show Boat Plays to Large Crowds." Wilmington, North Carolina, *Morning Star* December 27, 1933.

"Showboat Riding the Waves Again." Williamston, North Carolina, *Enterprise* November 15, 1938.

"'Show Boat' Shifted Due to Fire Code." Washington, D. C., *Evening Star* November 24, 1930: B1.

"Show Boat Sinks in Roanoke River." Raleigh, North Carolina, *News and Observer* November 8, 1938.

"Showboat Skipper Bemoans Passing of Floating Theatres." Baltimore, Maryland, *Sun* April 25, 1935.

"Showboat Still Drawing Crowds." Baltimore, Maryland, *News Post* November 18, 1939.

"'Showboat' to Be Filmed on Goldenrod." *Billboard* March 12, 1927: 30.

"Showboat to Open." Unidentified newspaper clipping , Baltimore, Maryland, November, 1940 (Source: Calvert Marine Museum).

"Showboat to Return Monday." Baltimore, Maryland, *News Post* October 22, 1940.

"Show Boat to Skip N. C. and Try the South." Elizabeth City, North Carolina, *Daily Independent* November 9, 1936.

"Show Boat to Try Again Next Week." Plymouth, North Carolina, *Roanoke Beacon* February 1, 1940.

"Showboat Will Stay 3rd Week." Baltimore, Maryland, *News Post* November 4, 1939.

"Show Man Falls from the Estelle." Washington, North Carolina, *Daily News* January 31, 1914.

"Social and Personal." Mathews, Virginia, *Journal* October 8, 1931.

"Society Folk Volunteer Aid to 'Show Boat.'" Wilmington, Delaware, *Morning News* October 22, 1932.

"Street Fair Notes." *Billboard* January 3, 1903: 3; January 17, 1903: 5; January 31, 1903: 15; April 18, 1903: 8; June 13, 1903: 10; August 15, 1903: 11; November 14, 1903: 7; December 12, 1903: 12; February 27, 1904: 7; June 25, 1904: 6; March 19, 1904: 12; July 23, 1904: 11, 23; December 3, 1904; February 11, 1905: 11; August 19, 1905: 20; September 16, 1905: 20.

"The Sweetest Girl in Dixie." Elkton, Maryland, *Cecil Democrat* November 4, 1934.

"Tab Notes." *Billboard* December 1, 1928: 35.

"Tab Tattles." *Billboard* May 30, 1936.

"'Ten Nights in a Barroom' Comes Back Again." Baltimore, Maryland, *Sunday American* December 3, 1939.

"Tent." Smithfield, Virginia, *Times* May 13, 1937.

"Tent Showmen Learn Lesson." *Billboard* August 13, 1932: 22.

"Tent Shows." *Billboard* March 11, 1905: 13; February 10, 1906: 20; September 8, 1906: 24; July 20, 1907: 23.

"Tent Shows Win Point in Alabama Controversy." *Billboard* September 22, 1928: 32.

"Theatre Ship Sinking within Harbor Limits." Norfolk, Virginia, *Ledger-Dispatch* November 25, 1927.

"There Was Pathos and Tearfulness on the Show Boat Sat. Nite." Elizabeth City, North Carolina, *Independent* November 13, 1931.

"Third Trip to Bottom Inland Waters." Unidentified clipping (Source: Calvert Marine Museum).

"Toll Bridge Here Wrecked by Tanker." Norfolk, Virginia, *Ledger-Dispatch* June 2, 1939: 1.

"Tom Fearing Joins Show Boat Troupe." Elizabeth City, North Carolina, *Daily Advance* November 2, 1938.

"To Start Program Wednesday Night." Fredericksburg, Virginia, *Free Lance-Star* July 17, 1928.

"Van Arnam's Funmakers." *Billboard* May 13, 1939: 25.

"Walter Sanford." *New York Times* August 4, 1942: 19.

"Washington Will Have Spring Carnival." Washington, Indiana, *Herald* April 5, 1904.

"Week's News of Marion," Crisfield, Maryland, *Times,* July 18, 1914, p. 8.

"Westmoreland." Warsaw, Virginia, *Northern Neck News* June 25, 1920; July 16, 1920; October 2, 1925; August 20, 1926.

"... Where virtue triumphs ..." Unidentified clipping, internally dated June 6, 1938 (Source: Calvert Marine Museum).

"Who's Who in This Issue." *Woman's Home Companion* August, 1926: 118.

"Will Give Carnival." Washington, Indiana, *Gazette* January 22, 1904.

"Yarn on Original Showboat All Wet, Says Cap Seymoure." *Billboard* February 18, 1939: 27.

"Young Actor." Portsmouth, Virginia, *Star* June 5, 1940.

NEWSPAPER ADVERTISEMENTS (CHRONOLOGICALLY ARRANGED)

May 1, 1900, *Billboard:* 19.

January 17, 1903. *Billboard* advertisement supplement: 10.

November 28, 1903. *Billboard:* 24.

October 1, 1904. *Billboard:* 40.

May 12, 1906. *Billboard:* 17.

July 14, 1906. *Billboard:* 30.

September 1, 1906. *Billboard:* 10.

February 14, 1914. *Billboard:* 66.

July 4, 1914. Crisfield, Maryland, *Times:* 5.

July 16, 1914. Salisbury, Maryland, *Wicomico News:* 8.

September 19, 1914. Elkton, Maryland, *Cecil Whig.*

November 7, 1914. Denton, Maryland, *Journal.*

January 15, 1915. Elizabeth City, North Carolina, *Advance.*

January 19, 1915. Elizabeth City, North Carolina, *Advance.*

January 26, 1915. Elizabeth City, North Carolina, *Advance.*

January 29, 1915. Elizabeth City, North Carolina, *Advance.*

February 2, 1915. Elizabeth City, North Carolina, *Advance.*

February 23, 1915. Elizabeth City, North Carolina, *Advance.*

February 26, 1915. Elizabeth City, North Carolina, *Advance.*

July 15, 1916. Leonardtown, Maryland, *St. Mary's Enterprise.*

October 26, 1918. *Billboard:* 19.

February 8, 1919. *Billboard:* 23.

September 5, 1919. Warsaw, Virginia, *Northern Neck News.*

October 18, 1919. *Billboard:* 15.

February 7, 1920. *Billboard:* 22.

February 28, 1920. *Billboard:* 15.

April 17, 1920. *Billboard:* 14.

May 6, 1920. Mathews, Virginia, *Journal.*

May 8, 1920. *Billboard:* 15.

July 3, 1920. *Billboard:* 15.

May 14, 1921. *Billboard:* 17.

November 16, 1921. Elizabeth City, North Carolina, *Daily Advance.*

January 26, 1924. *Billboard:* 29.

March 1, 1924. *Billboard:* 29.

March 7, 1925. *Billboard:* 29.

April 3, 1925. Elizabeth City, North Carolina, *Independent.*

May 23, 1925. *Billboard:* 29.

September 24, 1927. *Billboard:* 31.

March 3, 1928. *Billboard:* 31.

July 16, 1928. Fredericksburg, Virginia, *Free Lance-Star.*

November 24, 1930. Washington, D. C., *Post:* 12.

December 7, 1930. Alexandria, Virginia, *Gazette:* 5.

January 15, 1934. Wilmington, North Carolina, *Morning Star.*

January 18, 1934. Wilmington, North Carolina, *Morning Star.*

January 22, 1934. Wilmington, North Carolina, *Morning Star.*

January 26, 1934. Wilmington, North Carolina, *Morning Star.*

April 1, 1934. Wilmington, North Carolina, *Sunday Star News,*

July 19, 1934. Tappahannock, Virginia, *Rappahannock Times.*

January 29, 1937. Darien, Georgia, *Gazette.*

May 30, 1937. Portsmouth, Virginia, *Star.*

June 10, 1937. Kilmarnock, Virginia, *Rappahannock Record.*

August 13, 1937. Leonardtown, Maryland, *St. Mary's Enterprise.*

October 15, 1937. Easton, Maryland, *Star-Democrat.*

April 22, 1938. Easton, Maryland, *Star-Democrat.*

For September 5, 1938. Unidentified newspaper (Source: Calvert Marine Museum).

November 4, 1938. Williamston, North Carolina, *Enterprise.*

January 9, 1939. Elizabeth City, North Carolina, *Daily Advance.*

February 14, 1939. Wilmington, North Carolina, *Morning Star.*

February 22, 1939. Southport, North Carolina, *Port State Pilot.*

For March 5, 1939. Unidentified newspaper (Source: Calvert Marine Museum).

June 15, 1939. Gloucester, Virginia, *Gazette and Mathews Journal.*

February 22, 1940. Beaufort, North Carolina, *News.*

February 29, 1940. Beaufort, North Carolina, *News.*

April 19, 1940. New Bern, North Carolina, *Times.*

June 9, 1940. Suffolk, Virginia, *News-Herald*.

July 12, 1940. Leonardtown, Maryland, *St. Mary's Enterprise*.

July 13, 1940. *Billboard:* 27.

July 26, 1940. Warsaw, Virginia, *Northern Neck News*.

September 14, 1940. *Billboard:* 26.

October 5, 1940. *Billboard:* 26.

October 5, 1940. Chestertown, Maryland, *Kent County News*.

January 3, 1941. Georgetown, South Carolina, *Times*.

January 26, 1941. Savannah, Georgia, *Morning News*.

Index

Page numbers in italic type indicate photographs.